Introduction
to
Cryptography

Brent W Knapp

Contents

Algorithms & Protocols

List of Major Definitions

Preface

Cryptography is of course a vast subject. This book is to be used as in introduction to develop and explain the notion of provable security and its usage for the design of secure protocols.

Numbering and Notation

Numbering

Our definitions, theorems, lemmas, etc. are numbered as $X.y$ where X is the page number on which the object has been defined and y is a counter. This method should help you cross-reference important mathematical statements in the book.

Notation

We use $\mathbb{N}$ to denote the set of natural numbers, $\mathbb{Z}$ to denote the set of integers, and $\mathbb{Z}_p$ to denote the set of integers modulo p. The notation $[1, k]$ denotes the set $\{1, \ldots, k\}$. We often use $a = b \bmod n$ to denote modular congruency, i.e. $a \equiv b \pmod{n}$.

Algorithms

Let A denote an algorithm. We write $A(\cdot)$ to denote an algorithm with one input and $A(\cdot, \cdot)$ for two inputs. The output of a (randomized) algorithm $A(\cdot)$ on input x is described by a probability distribution which we denote by $A(x)$. An algorithm is *deterministic* if the probability distribution is concentrated on a single element.

Experiments

We denote by $x \leftarrow S$ the experiment of sampling an element x from a probability distribution S. If F is a finite set, then $x \leftarrow F$ denotes the experiment of sampling *uniformly* from the set F. We use semicolon to describe the ordered sequences of event that make up an experiment, e.g.,

$$x \leftarrow S; \ (y,z) \leftarrow A(x)$$

Probabilities

If $p(.,.)$ denotes a predicate, then

$$\Pr[x \leftarrow S; \ (y,z) \leftarrow A(x) : p(y,z)]$$

is the probability that the predicate $p(y,z)$ is true after the ordered sequence of events $(x \leftarrow S; \ (y,z) \leftarrow A(x))$. The notation

$$\{x \leftarrow S; \ (y,z) \leftarrow A(x) : \ (y,z)\}$$

denotes the probability distribution over $\{y,z\}$ generated by the experiment $(x \leftarrow S; \ (y,z) \leftarrow A(x))$. Following standard notation,

$$\Pr[A \mid B]$$

denotes the probability of event A *conditioned on* the event B. When the $\Pr[B] = 0$, then the conditional probability is not defined. In this course, we slightly abuse notation in this case, and define

$$\Pr[A \mid B] = \Pr[A] \quad \text{when } \Pr[B] = 0.$$

Big-O Notation

We denote by $O(g(n))$ the set of functions

$$\{f(n) \ : \exists c > 0, n_0 \text{ such that } \forall n > n_0, 0 \leq f(n) \leq cg(n)\}.$$

Chapter 1

Introduction

The word cryptography stems from the two Greek words *kryptós* and *gráfein* meaning "hidden" and "to write" respectively. Indeed, the most basic cryptographic problem, which dates back millenia, considers the task of using "hidden writing" to secure, or conceal communication between two parties.

1.1 Classical Cryptography: Hidden Writing

Consider two parties, Alice and Bob. Alice wants to *privately* send messages (called *plaintexts*) to Bob over an *insecure channel*. By an insecure channel, we refer to an "open" and tappable channel; in particular, Alice and Bob would like their privacy to be maintained even in face of an *adversary* Eve (for eavesdropper) who listens to all messages sent on the channel. How can this be achieved?

A possible solution Before starting their communication, Alice and Bob agree on a "secret code" that they will later use to communicate. A secret code consists of a *key*, an algorithm Enc to *encrypt* (scramble) plaintext messages into *ciphertexts* and an algorithm Dec to *decrypt* (or descramble) ciphertexts into plaintext messages. Both the encryption and decryption algorithms require the key to perform their task.

Alice can now use the key to encrypt a message, and then send the ciphertext to Bob. Bob, upon receiving a ciphertext, uses the key to decrypt the ciphertext and retrieve the original message.

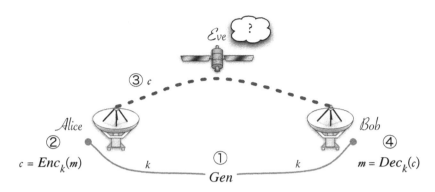

Figure 2.1: Illustration of the steps involved in private-key encryption. First, a key k must be generated by the Gen algorithm and privately given to Alice and Bob. In the picture, this is illustrated with a green "land-line." Later, Alice encodes the message m into a ciphertext c and sends it over the insecure channel—in this case, over the airwaves. Bob receives the encoded message and decodes it using the key k to recover the original message m. The eavesdropper Eve does not learn anything about m except perhaps its length.

1.1.1 Private-Key Encryption

To formalize the above task, we must consider an additional algorithm, Gen, called the *key-generation* algorithm; this algorithm is executed by Alice and Bob to generate the key k which they use to encrypt and decrypt messages.

A first question that needs to be addressed is what information needs to be "public"—i.e., known to everyone—and what needs to be "private"—i.e., kept secret. In historic approaches, i.e. *security by obscurity*, all three algorithms, $(\mathrm{Gen}, \mathrm{Enc}, \mathrm{Dec})$, and the generated key k were kept private; the idea was that the less information we give to the adversary, the harder it is to break the scheme. A design principle formulated by Kerchoff in 1884—known as *Kerchoff's principle*—instead stipulates that the only thing that one should assume to be private is the key k; everything else including (Gen, Enc, Dec) should be assumed to be public. Why should we do this? Designs of encryption algorithms are often eventually leaked, and when this happens the effects to privacy could be disastrous. Suddenly the scheme might be completely broken; this might even be the case if just a part of the algorithm's description is leaked. The more conservative approach advocated by Kerchoff instead guarantees that security is preserved even if everything but the key is known to the adversary. Furthermore, if a publicly known encryption scheme still has not been broken, this gives us more confidence in its "true" security (rather than if only the few people that designed it were unable to break it). As we will see later, Kerchoff's principle will be the first step to formally defining the security of encryption schemes.

Note that an immediate consequence of Kerchoff's principle is that all of the algorithms (Gen, Enc, Dec) can not be *deterministic*; if this were so, then Eve would be able to compute everything that Alice and Bob could compute and would thus be able to decrypt anything that Bob can decrypt. In particular, to prevent this we must require the key generation algorithm, Gen, to be randomized.

▷**Definition 3.2** (Private-key Encryption). The triplet of algorithms (Gen, Enc, Dec) is called a *private-key encryption scheme* over the message space $\mathcal{M}$ and the keyspace $\mathcal{K}$ if the following holds:

1. Gen (called the *key generation algorithm*) is a randomized algorithm that returns a key k such that $k \in \mathcal{K}$. We denote by $k \leftarrow$ Gen the process of generating a key k.

2. Enc (called the *encryption algorithm*) is a potentially randomized algorithm that on input a key $k \in \mathcal{K}$ and a message $m \in \mathcal{M}$, outputs a ciphertext c. We denote by $c \leftarrow \text{Enc}_k(m)$ the output of Enc on input key k and message m.

3. Dec (called the *decryption algorithm*) is a deterministic algorithm that on input a key k and a ciphertext c outputs a message $m \in \mathcal{M} \cup \perp$.

4. For all $m \in \mathcal{M}$,

$$\Pr[k \leftarrow \mathsf{Gen} : \mathsf{Dec}_k(\mathsf{Enc}_k(m)) = m] = 1$$

To simplify notation we also say that $(\mathcal{M}, \mathcal{K}, \mathsf{Gen}, \mathsf{Enc}, \mathsf{Dec})$ is a private-key encryption scheme if $(\mathsf{Gen}, \mathsf{Enc}, \mathsf{Dec})$ is a *private-key encryption scheme* over the messages space $\mathcal{M}$ and the keyspace $\mathcal{K}$. To simplify further, we sometimes say that $(\mathcal{M}, \mathsf{Gen}, \mathsf{Enc}, \mathsf{Dec})$ is a private-key encryption scheme if there exists some key space $\mathcal{K}$ such that $(\mathcal{M}, \mathcal{K}, \mathsf{Gen}, \mathsf{Enc}, \mathsf{Dec})$ is a private-key encryption scheme.

Note that the above definition of a private-key encryption scheme does not specify any secrecy (or privacy) properties; the only non-trivial requirement is that the decryption algorithm Dec uniquely recovers the messages encrypted using Enc (if these algorithms are run on input with the same key $k \in \mathcal{K}$). Later, we will return to the task of defining secrecy. However, first, let us provide some historical examples of private-key encryption schemes and colloquially discuss their "security" without any particular definition of secrecy in mind.

1.1.2   Some Historical Ciphers

The *Caesar Cipher* (named after Julius Ceasar who used it to communicate with his generals) is one of the simplest and well-known private-key encryption schemes. The encryption method consist of replacing each letter in the message with one that is a fixed number of places down the alphabet. More precisely,

▷**Definition 4.3** *The* Caesar Cipher *is defined as follows:*

$$
\begin{aligned}
\mathcal{M} &= \{A, B, \ldots, Z\}^* \\
\mathcal{K} &= \{0, 1, 2, \ldots, 25\} \\
\mathsf{Gen} &= k \text{ where } k \xleftarrow{r} \mathcal{K}. \\
\mathsf{Enc}_k m_1 m_2 \ldots m_n &= c_1 c_2 \ldots c_n \text{ where } c_i = m_i + k \bmod 26 \\
\mathsf{Dec}_k c_1 c_2 \ldots c_n &= m_1 m_2 \ldots m_n \text{ where } m_i = c_i - k \bmod 26
\end{aligned}
$$

In other words, encryption is a cyclic shift of k on each letter in the message and the decryption is a cyclic shift of $-k$. We leave it for the reader to verify the following proposition.

▷**Proposition 5.4** Caesar Cipher *is a private-key encryption scheme.*

At first glance, messages encrypted using the Ceasar Cipher look "scrambled" (unless k is known). However, to break the scheme we just need to try all 26 different values of k (which is easily done) and see if the resulting plaintext is "readable". If the message is relatively long, the scheme is easily broken. To prevent this simple *brute-force* attack, let us modify the scheme.

In the improved *Substitution Cipher* we replace letters in the message based on an arbitrary permutation over the alphabet (and not just cyclic shifts as in the Caesar Cipher).

▷**Definition 5.5** *The* Subsitution Cipher *is defined as follows:*

$$
\begin{aligned}
\mathcal{M} &= \{A, B, \ldots, Z\}^* \\
\mathcal{K} &= \text{the set of permutations of } \{A, B, \ldots, Z\} \\
\text{Gen} &= k \text{ where } k \xleftarrow{r} \mathcal{K}. \\
\text{Enc}_k(m_1 \ldots m_n) &= c_1 \ldots c_n \text{ where } c_i = k(m_i) \\
\text{Dec}_k(c_1 c_2 \ldots c_n) &= m_1 m_2 \ldots m_n \text{ where } m_i = k^{-1}(c_i)
\end{aligned}
$$

▷**Proposition 5.6** *The* Subsitution Cipher *is a private-key encryption scheme.*

To attack the substitution cipher we can no longer perform the brute-force attack because there are now 26! possible keys. However, if the encrypted message is sufficiently long, the key can still be recovered by performing a careful frequency analysis of the alphabet in the English language.

So what do we do next? Try to patch the scheme again? Indeed, cryptography historically progressed according to the following "crypto-cycle":

1. **A**, the "artist", invents an encryption scheme.

2. **A** claims (or even mathematically proves) that *known attacks* do not work.

3. The encryption scheme gets employed widely (often in critical situations).

4. The scheme eventually gets broken by improved attacks.

5. Restart, usually with a patch to prevent the previous attack.

Thus, historically, the main job of a cryptographer was *crypto-analysis*—namely, trying to break an encryption scheme. Cryptoanalysis is still an important field of research; however, the philosophy of modern theoretical cryptography is instead "if we can do the cryptography part right, there is no need for cryptanalysis".

1.2   Modern Cryptography: Provable Security

Modern Cryptography is the transition from cryptography as an *art* to cryptography as a principle-driven *science*. Instead of inventing ingenious ad-hoc schemes, modern cryptography relies on the following paradigms:

— Providing mathematical *definitions of security*.

— Providing *precise mathematical assumptions* (e.g. "factoring is hard", where *hard* is formally defined). These can be viewed as axioms.

— Providing *proofs of security*, i.e., proving that, if some particular scheme can be broken, then it contradicts an assumption (or axiom). In other words, if the assumptions were true, the scheme cannot be broken.

This is the approach that we develop in this course.

As we shall see, despite its conservative nature, we will succeed in obtaining solutions to paradoxical problems that reach far beyond the original problem of secure communication.

1.2.1   Beyond Secure Communication

In the original motivating problem of secure communication, we had two honest parties, Alice and Bob and a malicious eavesdropper Eve. Suppose, Alice and Bob in fact do not trust each other but wish to perform some joint computation. For instance, Alice and Bob each have a (private) list and wish to find the intersection of the two list without revealing anything else about the contents of their lists. Such a situation arises, for example, when two large financial institutions which to determine their "common risk exposure," but wish to do so without revealing anything else about their investments. One good solution would be to have a trusted center that does the computation and reveals only the answer to both parties. But, would either bank trust the "trusted" center with their sensitive information? Using techniques from modern cryptography, a solution can be provided without a trusted party. In fact, the above problem is a special case of what is known as *secure two-party computation*.

Secure two-party computation - informal definition: A secure two-party computation allows two parties A and B with private inputs a and b respectively, to compute a function $f(a, b)$ that operates on joint inputs a, b while guaranteeing the same *correctness* and *privacy* as if a trusted party had performed the computation for them, even if either A or B try to deviate from the proscribed computation in malicious ways.

Under certain number theoretic assumptions (such as "factoring is hard"), there exists a protocol for secure two-party computation.

The above problem can be generalized also to situations with multiple distrustful parties. For instance, consider the task of electronic elections: a set of n parties which to perform an election in which it is guaranteed that all votes are correctly counted, but each vote should at the same time remain private. Using a so called *multi-party computation* protocol, this task can be achieved.

A toy example: The match-making game

To illustrate the notion of secure-two party computation we provide a "toy-example" of a secure computation using physical cards. Alice and Bob want to find out if they are meant for each other. Each of them have two choices: either they love the other person or they do not. Now, they wish to perform some interaction that allows them to determine whether there is a match (i.e., if they both love each other) or not—and nothing more. For instance, if Bob loves Alice, but Alice does not love him back, Bob does not want to reveal to Alice that he loves her (revealing this could change his future chances of making Alice love him). Stating it formally, if LOVE and NO-LOVE were the inputs and MATCH and NO-MATCH were the outputs, the function they want to compute is:

$$f(\text{LOVE}, \text{LOVE}) = \text{MATCH}$$
$$f(\text{LOVE}, \text{NO-LOVE}) = \text{NO-MATCH}$$
$$f(\text{NO-LOVE}, \text{LOVE}) = \text{NO-MATCH}$$
$$f(\text{NO-LOVE}, \text{NO-LOVE}) = \text{NO-MATCH}$$

Note that the function f is simply an *and* gate.

The protocol: Assume that Alice and Bob have access to five cards, three identical hearts($\heartsuit$) and two identical clubs($\clubsuit$). Alice and Bob each get one heart and one club and the remaining heart is put on the table face-down.

   Next Alice and Bob also place their cards on the table, also turned over. Alice places her two cards on the left of the heart which is already on the table, and Bob places his two cards on the right of the heart. The order in which Alice and Bob place their two cards depends on their input as follows. If Alice *loves*, then Alice places her cards as $\clubsuit\heartsuit$; otherwise she places them as $\heartsuit\clubsuit$. Bob on the other hand places his card in the opposite order: if he *loves*, he places $\heartsuit\clubsuit$, and otherwise places $\clubsuit\heartsuit$. These orders are illustrated in Fig. 1.

   When all cards have been placed on the table, the cards are piled up. Alice and Bob then each take turns to privately cut the pile of cards once each so that the other person does not see how the cut is made. Finally, all cards are revealed. If there are three hearts in a row then there is a match and no-match otherwise.

Analyzing the protocol: We proceed to analyze the above protocol. Given inputs for Alice and Bob, the configuration of cards on the table before the cuts is described in Fig. 2. Only the first case—i.e., (LOVE, LOVE)—results in three hearts in a row. Furthermore this property is not changed by the cyclic shift induced by the cuts made by Alice and Bob. We conclude that the protocols correctly computes the desired function.

Figure 9.1: Illustration of the Match game with Cards

Figure 9.2: The possible outcomes of the Match Protocol. In case of a mismatch, all three outcomes are cyclic shifts of one-another.

In the remaining three cases (when the protocol outputs NO-MATCH), all the above configurations are cyclic shifts of one another. If one of Alice and Bob is honest—and indeed performs a random cut—the final card configuration is identically distributed no matter which of the three initial cases we started from. Thus, even if one of Alice and Bob tries to deviate in the protocol (by not performing a random cut), the privacy of the other party is still maintained.

Zero-knowledge proofs

Zero knowledge proofs is a special case of a secure computation. Informally, in a Zero Knowledge Proof there are two parties, Alice and Bob. Alice wants to convince Bob that some statement is true; for instance, Alice wants to convince Bob that a number N is a product of two primes p, q. A trivial solution would be for Alice to send p and q to Bob. Bob can then check that p and q are primes (we will see later in the course how this can be done) and next multiply the numbers to check if their product is N. But this solution reveals p and q. Is this necessary? It turns out that the answer is no. Using a zero-knowledge proof Alice can convince Bob of this statement without revealing the factors p and q.

1.3 Shannon's Treatment of Provable Secrecy

Modern (provable) cryptography started when Claude Shannon formalized the notion of private-key encryption. Thus, let us return to our original problem of securing communication between Alice and Bob.

1.3.1 Shannon Secrecy

As a first attempt, we might consider the following notion of security:

> The adversary cannot learn (all or part of) the key from the ciphertext.

The problem, however, is that such a notion does not make any guarantees about what the adversary can learn about the *plaintext* message. Another approach might be:

> The adversary cannot learn (all, part of, any letter of, any function of, or any partial information about) the plaintext.

This seems like quite a strong notion. In fact, it is too strong because the adversary may already possess some partial information about the plaintext that is acceptable to reveal. Informed by these attempts, we take as our intuitive definition of security:

> Given some *a priori* information, the adversary cannot learn any additional information about the plaintext by observing the ciphertext.

Such a notion of secrecy was formalized by Claude Shannon in 1949 [SHA49] in his seminal paper that started the modern study of cryptography.

▷**Definition 11.1** (Shannon secrecy). $(\mathcal{M}, \mathcal{K}, \mathsf{Gen}, \mathsf{Enc}, \mathsf{Dec})$ is said to be a private-key encryption scheme that is *Shannon-secret with respect to the distibution D* over the message space $\mathcal{M}$ if for all $m' \in \mathcal{M}$ and for all c,

$$\Pr\left[k \leftarrow \mathsf{Gen}; m \leftarrow D : m = m' \mid \mathsf{Enc}_k(m) = c\right]$$
$$= \Pr\left[m \leftarrow D : m = m'\right].$$

An encryption scheme is said to be *Shannon secret* if it is Shannon secret with respect to all distributions D over $\mathcal{M}$.

The probability is taken with respect to the random output of Gen, the choice of m and the random coins used by algorithm Enc. The quantity on the left represents the adversary's *a posteriori* distribution on plaintexts after observing a ciphertext; the quantity on the right, the *a priori* distribution. Since these distributions are required to be equal, this definition requires that the adversary does not gain any additional information by observing the ciphertext.

1.3.2 Perfect Secrecy

To gain confidence that our definition is the right one, we also provide an alternative approach to defining security of encryption schemes. The notion of *perfect secrecy* requires that the distribution of ciphertexts for any two messages are identical. This formalizes our intuition that the ciphertexts carry no information about the plaintext.

▷**Definition 11.2** (Perfect Secrecy). A tuple $(\mathcal{M}, \mathcal{K}, \mathsf{Gen}, \mathsf{Enc}, \mathsf{Dec})$ is said to be a private-key encryption scheme that is *perfectly secret* if for all m_1 and m_2 in $\mathcal{M}$, and for all c,

$$\Pr[k \leftarrow \mathsf{Gen} : \mathsf{Enc}_k(m_1) = c] = \Pr[k \leftarrow \mathsf{Gen} : \mathsf{Enc}_k(m_2) = c].$$

Notice that perfect secrecy seems like a simpler notion. There is no mention of "a-priori" information, and therefore no need to specify a distribution over the message space. Similarly, there is no conditioning on the ciphertext. The definition simply requires that for every pair of messages, the probabilities that either message maps to a given ciphertext c must be equal. Perfect security is syntactically simpler than Shannon security, and thus easier to work with. Fortunately, as the following theorem demonstrates, Shannon Secrecy and Perfect Secrecy are equivalent notions.

▷**Theorem 12.3** *A private-key encryption scheme is perfectly secret if and only if it is Shannon secret.*

Proof. We prove each implication separately. To simplify the notation, we introduce the following abbreviations. Let $\Pr_k [\cdots]$ denote $\Pr [k \leftarrow \text{Gen}; \cdots]$, $\Pr_m [\cdots]$ denote $\Pr [m \leftarrow D : \cdots]$, and $\Pr_{k,m} [\cdots]$ denote $\Pr [k \leftarrow \text{Gen}; m \leftarrow D : \cdots]$.

Perfect secrecy implies Shannon secrecy. The intuition is that if, for any two pairs of messages, the probability that either of messages encrypts to a given ciphertext must be equal, then it is also true for the pair m and m' in the definition of Shannon secrecy. Thus, the ciphertext does not "leak" any information, and the a-priori and a-posteriori information about the message must be equal.

Suppose the scheme $(\mathcal{M}, \mathcal{K}, \text{Gen}, \text{Enc}, \text{Dec})$ is perfectly secret. Consider any distribution D over $\mathcal{M}$, any message $m' \in \mathcal{M}$, and any ciphertext c. We show that

$$\Pr_{k,m} [m = m' \mid \text{Enc}_k(m) = c] = \Pr_m [m = m'].$$

By the definition of conditional probabilities, the left hand side of the above equation can be rewritten as

$$\frac{\Pr_{k,m} [m = m' \cap \text{Enc}_k(m) = c]}{\Pr_{k,m} [\text{Enc}_k(m) = c]}$$

which can be re-written as

$$\frac{\Pr_{k,m} [m = m' \cap \text{Enc}_k(m') = c]}{\Pr_{k,m} [\text{Enc}_k(m) = c]}$$

and expanded to

$$\frac{\Pr_m [m = m'] \Pr_k [\mathsf{Enc}_k(m') = c]}{\Pr_{k,m} [\mathsf{Enc}_k(m) = c]}$$

The central idea behind the proof is to show that

$$\Pr_{k,m} [\mathsf{Enc}_k(m) = c] = \Pr_k \left[\mathsf{Enc}_k(m') = c\right]$$

which establishes the result. To begin, rewrite the left-hand side:

$$\Pr_{k,m} [\mathsf{Enc}_k(m) = c] = \sum_{m'' \in \mathcal{M}} \Pr_m [m = m''] \Pr_k [\mathsf{Enc}_k(m'') = c]$$

By perfect secrecy, the last term can be replaced to get:

$$\sum_{m'' \in \mathcal{M}} \Pr_m [m = m''] \Pr_k [\mathsf{Enc}_k(m') = c]$$

This last term can now be moved out of the summation and simplified as:

$$\Pr_k \left[\mathsf{Enc}_k(m') = c\right] \sum_{m'' \in \mathcal{M}} \Pr_m [m = m''] = \Pr_k \left[\mathsf{Enc}_k(m') = c\right].$$

Shannon secrecy implies perfect secrecy. In this case, the intuition is Shannon secrecy holds for all distributions D; thus, it must also hold for the special cases when D only chooses between two given messages.

Suppose the scheme $(\mathcal{M}, \mathcal{K}, \mathsf{Gen}, \mathsf{Enc}, \mathsf{Dec})$ is Shannon-secret. Consider $m_1, m_2 \in \mathcal{M}$, and any ciphertext c. Let D be the uniform distribution over $\{m_1, m_2\}$. We show that

$$\Pr_k [\mathsf{Enc}_k(m_1) = c] = \Pr_k [\mathsf{Enc}_k(m_2) = c].$$

The definition of D implies that $\Pr_m [m = m_1] = \Pr_m [m = m_2] = \frac{1}{2}$. It therefore follows by Shannon secrecy that

$$\Pr_{k,m} [m = m_1 \mid \mathsf{Enc}_k(m) = c] = \Pr_{k,m} [m = m_2 \mid \mathsf{Enc}_k(m) = c]$$

By the definition of conditional probability,

$$\Pr_{k,m}\left[m = m_1 \mid \mathsf{Enc}_k(m) = c\right] = \frac{\Pr_{k,m}\left[m = m_1 \cap \mathsf{Enc}_k(m) = c\right]}{\Pr_{k,m}\left[\mathsf{Enc}_k(m) = c\right]}$$

$$= \frac{\Pr_m\left[m = m_1\right]\Pr_k\left[\mathsf{Enc}_k(m_1) = c\right]}{\Pr_{k,m}\left[\mathsf{Enc}_k(m) = c\right]}$$

$$= \frac{\frac{1}{2} \cdot \Pr_k\left[\mathsf{Enc}_k(m_1) = c\right]}{\Pr_{k,m}\left[\mathsf{Enc}_k(m) = c\right]}$$

Analogously,

$$\Pr_{k,m}\left[m = m_2 \mid \mathsf{Enc}_k(m) = c\right] = \frac{\frac{1}{2} \cdot \Pr_k\left[\mathsf{Enc}_k(m_2) = c\right]}{\Pr_{k,m}\left[\mathsf{Enc}_k(m) = c\right]}.$$

Cancelling and rearranging terms, we conclude that

$$\Pr_k\left[\mathsf{Enc}_k(m_1) = c\right] = \Pr_k\left[\mathsf{Enc}_k(m_2) = c\right].$$

$$\square$$

1.3.3   The One-Time Pad

Given our definition of security, we now consider whether perf-ectly-secure encryption schemes exist. Both of the encryption schemes we have analyzed so far (i.e., the Caesar and Substitution ciphers) are secure as long as we only consider messages of length 1. However, when considering messages of length 2 (or more) the schemes are no longer secure—in fact, it is easy to see that encryptions of the strings AA and AB have disjoint distributions, thus violating perfect secrecy (prove this).

Nevertheless, this suggests that we might obtain perfect secrecy by somehow adapting these schemes to operate on each element of a message independently. This is the intuition behind the *one-time pad* encryption scheme, invented by Gilbert Vernam in 1917 and Joseph Mauborgne in 1919.

▷**Definition 15.4** *The One-Time Pad encryption scheme is described by the following 5-tuple* $(\mathcal{M}, \mathcal{K}, \text{Gen}, \text{Enc}, \text{Dec})$:

$$
\begin{aligned}
\mathcal{M} &= \{0,1\}^n \\
\mathcal{K} &= \{0,1\}^n \\
\text{Gen} &= k = k_1 k_2 \ldots k_n \leftarrow \{0,1\}^n \\
\text{Enc}_k(m_1 m_2 \ldots m_n) &= c_1 c_2 \ldots c_n \text{ where } c_i = m_i \oplus k_i \\
\text{Dec}_k(c_1 c_2 \ldots c_n) &= m_1 m_2 \ldots m_n \text{ where } m_i = c_i \oplus k_i
\end{aligned}
$$

The $\oplus$ *operator represents the binary xor operation.*

▷**Proposition 15.5** *The One-Time Pad is a perfectly secure private-key encryption scheme.*

Proof. It is straight-forward to verify that the One Time Pad is a private-key encryption scheme. We turn to show that the One-Time Pad is perfectly secret and begin by showing the the following claims.

▷**Claim 15.6** *For any* $c, m \in \{0,1\}^n$,

$$
\Pr\left[k \leftarrow \{0,1\}^n : \text{Enc}_k(m) = c \right] = 2^{-k}
$$

▷**Claim 15.7** *For any* $c \notin \{0,1\}^n, m \in \{0,1\}^n$,

$$
\Pr\left[k \leftarrow \{0,1\}^n : \text{Enc}_k(m) = c \right] = 0
$$

Claim 15.6 follows from the fact that for any $m, c \in \{0,1\}^n$, there is only one k such that $\text{Enc}_k(m) = m \oplus k = c$, namely $k = m \oplus c$. Claim 15.7 follows from the fact that for every $k \in \{0,1\}^n$, $\text{Enc}_k(m) = m \oplus k \in \{0,1\}^n$.

From the claims we conclude that for any $m_1, m_2 \in \{0,1\}^n$ and every c, it holds that

$$
\Pr\left[k \leftarrow \{0,1\}^n : \text{Enc}_k(m_1) = c \right] = \Pr\left[k \leftarrow \{0,1\}^n : \text{Enc}_k(m_2) = c \right]
$$

which concludes the proof. □

So perfect secrecy is obtainable. But at what cost? When Alice and Bob meet to generate a key, they must generate one that is as long as all the messages they will send until the next time they meet. Unfortunately, this is not a consequence of the design of the One-Time Pad, but rather of perfect secrecy, as demonstrated by Shannon's famous theorem.

1.3.4   Shannon's Theorem

▷**Theorem 16.8 (Shannon)** *If scheme* $(\mathcal{M}, \mathcal{K}, \mathsf{Gen}, \mathsf{Enc}, \mathsf{Dec})$ *is a perfectly secret private-key encryption scheme, then* $|\mathcal{K}| \geq |\mathcal{M}|$.

Proof. Assume there exists a perfectly secret private-key encryption scheme $(\mathcal{M}, \mathcal{K}, \mathsf{Gen}, \mathsf{Enc}, \mathsf{Dec})$ such that $|\mathcal{K}| < |\mathcal{M}|$. Take any $m_1 \in \mathcal{M}$, $k \in \mathcal{K}$, and let $c \leftarrow \mathsf{Enc}_k(m_1)$. Let $\mathbf{Dec}(c)$ denote the set $\{m \mid \exists k \in \mathcal{K} \text{ such that } m = \mathsf{Dec}_k(c)\}$ of all possible decryptions of c under all possible keys. Since the algorithm Dec is deterministic, this set has size at most $|\mathcal{K}|$. But since $|\mathcal{M}| > |\mathcal{K}|$, there exists some message m_2 not in $\mathbf{Dec}(c)$. By the definition of a private encryption scheme it follows that

$$\Pr\left[k \leftarrow \mathcal{K} : \mathsf{Enc}_k(m_2) = c\right] = 0$$

But since

$$\Pr\left[k \leftarrow \mathcal{K} : \mathsf{Enc}_k(m_1) = c\right] > 0$$

we conclude that

$$\Pr\left[k \leftarrow \mathcal{K} : \mathsf{Enc}_k(m_1) = c\right] \neq \Pr\left[k \leftarrow \mathcal{K} : \mathsf{Enc}_k(m_2) = c\right]$$

which contradicts the hypothesis that $(\mathcal{M}, \mathcal{K}, \mathsf{Gen}, \mathsf{Enc}, \mathsf{Dec})$ is a perfectly secret private-key scheme.   □

Note that the proof of Shannon's theorem in fact describes an *attack* on every private-key encryption scheme for which $|\mathcal{M}| > |\mathcal{K}|$. It follows that for any such encryption scheme there exists $m_1, m_2 \in M$ and a constant $\epsilon > 0$ such that

$$\Pr\left[k \leftarrow \mathcal{K}; \mathsf{Enc}_k(m_1) = c : m_1 \in \mathbf{Dec}(c)\right] = 1$$

but

$$\Pr\left[k \leftarrow \mathcal{K}; \mathsf{Enc}_k(m_1) = c : m_2 \in \mathbf{Dec}(c)\right] \leq 1 - \epsilon$$

The first equation follows directly from the definition of private-key encryption, whereas the second equation follows from the fact that (by the proof of Shannon's theorem) there exists some key k for which $\mathsf{Enc}_k(m_1) = c$, but $m_2 \notin \mathbf{Dec}(c)$. Consider, now, a scenario where Alice uniformly picks a message m from $\{m_1, m_2\}$ and sends the encryption of m to Bob. We claim that Eve, having seen the encryption c of m can guess whether $m = m_1$ or $m = m_2$ with probability higher than $1/2$. Eve, upon receiving c simply checks if $m_2 \in \textbf{Dec}(c)$. If $m_2 \notin \textbf{Dec}(c)$, Eve guesses that $m = m_1$, otherwise she makes a random guess.

How well does this attack work? If Alice sent the message $m = m_2$ then $m_2 \in \textbf{Dec}(c)$ and Eve will guess correctly with probability $1/2$. If, on the other hand, Alice sent $m = m_1$, then with probability ϵ, $m_2 \notin \textbf{Dec}(c)$ and Eve will guess correctly with probability 1, whereas with probability $1 - \epsilon$ Eve will make a random guess, and thus will be correct with probability $1/2$. We conclude that Eve's success probability is

$$\Pr[m = m_2]\,(1/2) + \Pr[m = m_1]\,(\epsilon \cdot 1 + (1 - \epsilon) \cdot (1/2))$$
$$= \frac{1}{2} + \frac{\epsilon}{4}$$

Thus we have exhibited a *concise* attack for Eve which allows her to guess which message Alice sends with probability better than $1/2$.

A possible critique against this attack is that if ϵ is very small (e.g., 2^{-100}), then the effectiveness of this attack is limited. However, the following stonger version of Shannon's theorem shows that even if the key is only one bit shorter than the message, then $\epsilon = 1/2$ and so the attack succeeds with probability $5/8$.

▷**Theorem 17.9** *Let* $(\mathcal{M}, \mathcal{K}, \mathsf{Gen}, \mathsf{Enc}, \mathsf{Dec})$ *be a private-key encryption scheme where* $\mathcal{M} = \{0,1\}^n$ *and* $\mathcal{K} = \{0,1\}^{n-1}$. *Then, there exist messages* $m_0, m_1 \in \mathcal{M}$ *such that*

$$\Pr\left[k \leftarrow \mathcal{K}; \; \mathsf{Enc}_k(m_1) = c : m_2 \in \textbf{Dec}(c)\right] \leq \frac{1}{2}$$

Proof. Given $c \leftarrow \mathsf{Enc}_k(m)$ for some key $k \in \mathcal{K}$ and message $m \in \mathcal{M}$, consider the set $\textbf{Dec}(c)$. Since Dec is deterministic it follows that $|\textbf{Dec}(c)| \leq |\mathcal{K}| = 2^{n-1}$. Thus, for all $m_1 \in \mathcal{M}$ and $k \in \mathcal{K}$,

$$\Pr\left[m' \leftarrow \{0,1\}^n; \; c \leftarrow \mathsf{Enc}_k(m_1) : m' \in \textbf{Dec}(c)\right] \leq \frac{2^{n-1}}{2^n} = \frac{1}{2}$$

Since the above probability is bounded by $1/2$ for *every* key $k \in \mathcal{K}$, this must also hold for a random $k \leftarrow$ Gen.

$$\Pr\left[m' \leftarrow \{0,1\}^n;\ k \leftarrow \text{Gen};\ c \leftarrow \text{Enc}_k(m_1) : m' \in \textbf{Dec}(c)\right] \leq \frac{1}{2}$$
(17.2)

Additionally, since the bound holds for a random message m', there must exist some *particular* message m_2 that minimizes the probability. In other words, for every message $m_1 \in \mathcal{M}$, there exists some message $m_2 \in \mathcal{M}$ such that

$$\Pr\left[k \leftarrow \text{Gen};\ c \leftarrow \text{Enc}_k(m_1) : m_2 \in \textbf{Dec}(c)\right] \leq \frac{1}{2}$$

□

Thus, by Theorem 17.9, we conclude that if the key length is only one bit shorter than the message length, there exist messages m_1 and m_2 such that Eve's success probability is $1/2 + 1/8 = 5/8$.

▷**Remark 18.10** *Note that the theorem is stronger than stated. In fact, we showed that for every $m_1 \in \mathcal{M}$, there exists some string m_2 that satisfies the desired condition. We also mention that if we content ourselves with getting a bound of $\epsilon = 1/4$, the above proof actually shows that for every $m_1 \in \mathcal{M}$, it holds that for at least one fourth of the messages $m_2 \in \mathcal{M}$,*

$$\Pr\left[k \leftarrow \mathcal{K};\ \text{Enc}_k(m_1) = c : m_2 \in \textbf{Dec}(c)\right] \leq \frac{1}{4};$$

otherwise we would contradict equation (17.2).

This is clearly not acceptable in most applications of an encryption scheme. So, does this mean that to get any "reasonable" amount of security Alice and Bob must share a long key?

Note that although Eve's attack only takes a few lines of code to describe, its running-time is high. In fact, to perform her attack—which amounts to checking whether $m_2 \in \textbf{Dec}(c)$—Eve must try all possible keys $k \in \mathcal{K}$ to check whether c possibly could decrypt to m_2. If, for instance, $\mathcal{K} = \{0,1\}^n$, this requires her to perform 2^n (i.e., exponentially many) different decryptions. Thus, although the attack can be simply described, it is not "feasible" by any *efficient* computing device. This motivates us to consider only "feasible" adversaries—namely adversaries that are *computationally bounded*. Indeed, as we shall see later in Chapter 3.5, with respect to such adversaries, the implications of Shannon's Theorem can be overcome.

1.4 Overview of the Course

In this course we will focus on some of the key *concepts* and *techniques* in modern cryptography. The course will be structured around the following notions:

Computational Hardness and One-way Functions. As illustrated above, to circumvent Shannon's lower bound we have to restrict our attention to computationally-bounded adversaries. The first part of the course deals with notions of resource-bounded (and in particular *time-bounded*) computation, computational hardness, and the notion of one-way functions. One-way functions—i.e., functions that are "easy" to compute, but "hard" to invert by efficient algorithms—are at the heart of modern cryptographic protocols.

Indistinguishability. The notion of indistinguishability formalizes what it means for a computationally-bounded adversary to be unable to "tell apart" two distributions. This notion is central to modern definitions of security for encryption schemes, but also for formally defining notions such as pseudo-random generation, commitment schemes, zero-knowledge protocols, etc.

Knowledge. A central desideratum in the design of cryptographic protocols is to ensure that the protocol execution *does not leak more "knowledge" than what is necessary*. In this part of the course, we investigate "knowledge-based" (or rather *zero knowledge*-based) definitions of security.

Authentication. Notions such as *digital signatures* and *messages authentication codes* are digital analogues of traditional written signatures. We explore different notions of authentication and show how cryptographic techniques can be used to obtain new types of authentication mechanism not achievable by traditional written signatures.

Computing on Secret Inputs. Finally, we consider protocols which allow mutually distrustful parties to perform arbitrary computation on their respective (potentially secret) inputs. This includes *secret-sharing* protocols and *secure two-party (or multi-party) computation* protocols. We have described the later earlier in this chapter; secret-sharing protocols are methods which allow a set of n parties to receive "shares" of a secret with the property that any "small" subset of shares leaks no information about the secret, but once an appropriate number of shares are collected the whole secret can be recovered.

Composability. It turns out that cryptographic schemes that are secure when executed in isolation can be completely compromised if many instances of the scheme are simultaneously executed (as is unavoidable when executing cryptographic protocols in modern networks). The question of *composability* deals with issues of this type.

Chapter 2

Computational Hardness

2.1 Efficient Computation and Efficient Adversaries

We start by formalizing what it means for an algorithm to compute a function.

▷**Definition 21.1 (Algorithm)** *An* algorithm *is a deterministic Turing machine whose input and output are strings over alphabet* $\Sigma = \{0,1\}$.

▷**Definition 21.2 (Running-time)** *An algorithm* $\mathcal{A}$ *is said to run in time* $T(n)$ *if for all* $x \in \{0,1\}^*$, $\mathcal{A}(x)$ *halts within* $T(|x|)$ *steps.* $\mathcal{A}$ *runs in* polynomial time *if there exists a constant* c *such that* $\mathcal{A}$ *runs in time* $T(n) = n^c$.

▷**Definition 21.3 (Deterministic Computation)** *An algorithm* $\mathcal{A}$ *is said to* compute *a function* $f : \{0,1\}^* \to \{0,1\}^*$ *if for all* $x \in \{0,1\}^*$, $\mathcal{A}$, *on input* x, *outputs* $f(x)$.

We say that an algorithm is *efficient* if it runs in polynomial time. One may argue about the choice of polynomial-time as a cutoff for efficiency, and indeed if the polynomial involved is large, computation may not be efficient in practice. There are, however, strong arguments to use the polynomial-time definition of efficiency:

1. This definition is independent of the representation of the algorithm (whether it is given as a Turing machine, a C program, etc.) because converting from one representation to another only affects the running time by a polynomial factor.

2. This definition is also closed under composition which may simplify reasoning in certain proofs.

3. Our experience suggests that polynomial-time algorithms turn out to be efficient; i.e. polynomial almost always means "cubic time or better."

4. Our experience indicates that "natural" functions that are not known to be computable in polynomial-time require *much* more time to compute, so the separation we propose seems well-founded.

Note, our treatment of computation is an *asymptotic* one. In practice, concrete running time needs to be considered carefully, as do other hidden factors such as the size of the description of $\mathcal{A}$. Thus, when porting theory to practice, one needs to set parameters carefully.

2.1.1 Some computationally "hard" problems

Many commonly encountered functions are computable by efficient algorithms. However, there are also functions which are known or believed to be hard.

Halting: The famous Halting problem is an example of an *uncomputable* problem: Given a description of a Turing machine M, determine whether or not M halts when run on the empty input.

Time-hierarchy: The Time Hierarchy Theorem from Complexity theory states that there exist languages that are decideable in time $O(t(n))$ but cannot be decided in time $o(t(n) / \log t(n))$. A corollary of this theorem is that there are functions $f : \{0,1\}^* \rightarrow \{0,1\}$ that are computable in exponential time but not computable in polynomial time.

Satisfiability: The notorious **SAT** problem is to determine if a given Boolean formula has a satisfying assignment. **SAT** is *conjectured* not to be solvable in polynomial-time—this is the famous conjecture that **P** $\neq$ **NP**. See Appendix B for definitions of **P** and **NP**.

2.1.2 Randomized Computation

A natural extension of deterministic computation is to allow an algorithm to have access to a source of random coin tosses. Allowing this extra freedom is certainly plausible (as it is conceivable to generate such random coins in practice), and it is believed to enable more efficient algorithms for computing certain tasks. Moreover, it will be necessary for the security of the schemes that we present later. For example, as we discussed in chapter one, Kerckhoff's principle states that all algorithms in a scheme should be public. Thus, if the private key generation algorithm Gen did not use random coins in its computation, then Eve would be able to compute the same key that Alice and Bob compute. Thus, to allow for this extra resource, we extend the above definitions of computation as follows.

▷**Definition 23.4 (Randomized (PPT) Algorithm)** *A randomized algorithm, also called a probabilistic polynomial-time Turing machine and abbreviated as PPT, is a Turing machine equipped with an extra random tape. Each bit of the random tape is uniformly and independently chosen.*

Equivalently, a randomized algorithm is a Turing Machine that has access to a coin-tossing oracle that outputs a truly random bit on demand.

To define efficiency we must clarify the concept of *running time* for a randomized algorithm. A subtlety arises because the run time of a randomized algorithm may depend on the particular random tape chosen for an execution. We take a conservative approach and define the running time as the upper bound over all possible random sequences.

▷**Definition 23.5 (Running time)** *A randomized Turing machine $\mathcal{A}$ runs in time $T(n)$ if for all $x \in \{0,1\}^*$, and for every random tape,*

$A(x)$ *halts within* $T(|x|)$ *steps.* A *runs in* polynomial time *(or is an* efficient *randomized algorithm) if there exists a constant c such that* A *runs in time* $T(n) = n^c$.

Finally, we must also extend our notion of computation to randomized algorithms. In particular, once an algorithm has a random tape, its output becomes a distribution over some set. In the case of deterministic computation, the output is a singleton set, and this is what we require here as well.

▷**Definition 24.6** *A randomized algorithm* A *computes a function* $f : \{0,1\}^* \to \{0,1\}^*$ *if for all* $x \in \{0,1\}^*$, A *on input* x, *outputs* $f(x)$ *with probability* 1. *The probability is taken over the random tape of* A.

Notice that with randomized algorithms, we do not tolerate algorithms that on *rare* occasion make errors. Formally, this requirement may be too strong in practice because some of the algorithms that we use in practice (e.g., primality testing) do err with small negligible probability. In the rest of the book, however, we ignore this rare case and assume that a randomized algorithm always works correctly.

On a side note, it is worthwhile to note that a polynomial-time randomized algorithm A that computes a function with probability $\frac{1}{2} + \frac{1}{poly(n)}$ can be used to obtain another polynomial-time randomized machine A' that computes the function with probability $1 - 2^{-n}$. (A' simply takes multiple runs of A and finally outputs the most frequent output of A. The Chernoff bound (see Appendix A) can then be used to analyze the probability with which such a "majority" rule works.)

Polynomial-time randomized algorithms will be the principal model of efficient computation considered in this course. We will refer to this class of algorithms as *probabilistic polynomial-time Turing machine (p.p.t.)* or *efficient randomized algorithm* interchangeably.

Given the above notation we can define the notion of an efficient encryption scheme:

▷**Definition 24.7** (Efficient Private-key Encryption). A triplet of algorithms $(\mathsf{Gen}, \mathsf{Enc}, \mathsf{Dec})$ is called an *efficient private-key encryption scheme* if the following holds:

1. $k \leftarrow \mathsf{Gen}(1^n)$ is a p.p.t. such that for every $n \in \mathbb{N}$, it samples a key k.

2. $c \leftarrow \mathsf{Enc}_k(m)$ is a p.p.t. that given k and $m \in \{0,1\}^n$ produces a ciphertext c.

3. $m \leftarrow \mathsf{Dec}_k(c)$ is a p.p.t. that given a ciphertext c and key k produces a message $m \in \{0,1\}^n \cup \bot$.

4. For all $n \in \mathbb{N}$, $m \in \{0,1\}^n$,

$$\Pr\left[k \leftarrow \mathsf{Gen}(1^n) : \mathsf{Dec}_k(\mathsf{Enc}_k(m)) = m]\right] = 1$$

Notice that the Gen algorithm is given the special input 1^n—called the security parameter—which represents the string consisting of n copies of 1, e.g. $1^4 = 1111$. This security parameter is used to instantiate the "security" of the scheme; larger parameters correspond to more secure schemes. The security parameter also establishes the running time of Gen, and therefore the maximum size of k, and thus the running times of Enc and Dec as well. Stating that these three algorithms are "polynomial-time" is always with respect to the size of their respective inputs.

In the rest of this book, when discussing encryption schemes we always refer to efficient encryption schemes. As a departure from our notation in the first chapter, here we no longer refer to a message space $\mathcal{M}$ or a key space $\mathcal{K}$ because we assume that both are bit strings. In particular, on security parameter 1^n, our definition requires a scheme to handle n-bit messages. It is also possible, and perhaps simpler, to define an encryption scheme that only works on a single-bit message space $\mathcal{M} = \{0,1\}$ for every security parameter.

2.1.3 Efficient Adversaries

When modeling adversaries, we use a more relaxed notion of efficient computation. In particular, instead of requiring the adversary to be a machine with constant-sized description, we

allow the size of the adversary's program to increase (polyno-
mially) with the input length, i.e., we allow the adversary to
be *non-uniform*. As before, we still allow the adversary to use
random coins and require that the adversary's running time is
bounded by a polynomial. The primary motivation for using
non-uniformity to model the adversary is to simplify definitions
and proofs.

▷**Definition 26.8 (Non-Uniform PPT)** *A non-uniform probabilistic
polynomial-time machine (abbreviated n.u. p.p.t.) A is a sequence
of probabilistic machines $A = \{A_1, A_2, \ldots\}$ for which there exists a
polynomial d such that the description size of $|A_i| < d(i)$ and the
running time of A_i is also less than $d(i)$. We write $A(x)$ to denote the
distribution obtained by running $A_{|x|}(x)$.*

Alternatively, a non-uniform p.p.t. machine can also be defined as a *uniform* p.p.t. machine A that receives an advice string
for each input length. In the rest of this text, any adversarial
algorithm $\mathcal{A}$ will implicitly be a non-uniform PPT.

2.2   One-Way Functions

At a high level, there are two basic desiderata for any encryption
scheme:

— it must be feasible to generate c given m and k, but

— it must be hard to recover m and k given only c.

This suggests that we require functions that are easy to compute but hard to invert—*one-way functions*. Indeed, these functions turn out to be the most basic building block in cryptography.
There are several ways that the notion of one-wayness can be
defined formally. We start with a definition that formalizes our
intuition in the simplest way.

▷**Definition 26.1** (Worst-case One-way Function). A function $f :
\{0,1\}^* \to \{0,1\}^*$ is worst-case *one-way* if:

1. **Easy to compute.** There is a p.p.t. C that computes $f(x)$ on all inputs $x \in \{0,1\}^*$, and

2. **Hard to Invert** there is no adversary $\mathcal{A}$ such that

$$\forall x \ \Pr[\mathcal{A}(f(x)) \in f^{-1}(f(x))] = 1$$

It can be shown that assuming **NP** $\not\subseteq$ **BPP**, one-way functions according to the above definition must exist.[1] In fact, these two assumptions are equivalent (show this!). Note, however, that this definition allows for certain pathological functions to be considered as one-way—e.g., those where inverting the function for *most* x values is easy, but every machine fails to invert $f(x)$ for infinitely many x's. It is an open question whether such functions can still be used for good encryption schemes. This observation motivates us to refine our requirements. We want functions where for a randomly chosen x, the probability that we are able to invert the function is very small. With this new definition in mind, we begin by formalizing the notion of *very small*.

▷**Definition 27.2 (Negligible function)** *A function* $\varepsilon(n)$ *is* negligible *if for every c, there exists some n_0 such that for all $n > n_0$,* $\varepsilon(n) \leq \frac{1}{n^c}$.

Intuitively, a negligible function is asymptotically smaller than the inverse of any fixed polynomial. Examples of negligible functions include 2^{-n} and $n^{-\log \log n}$. We say that a function $t(n)$ is *non-negligible* if there exists some constant c such that for infinitely many points $\{n_0, n_1, \ldots\}$, $t(n_i) > n_i^c$. This notion becomes important in proofs that work by contradiction.

We can now present a more satisfactory definition of a one-way function.

▷**Definition 27.3 (Strong One-Way Function)** *A function mapping strings to strings* $f : \{0,1\}^* \to \{0,1\}^*$ *is a* strong one-way function *if it satisfies the following two conditions:*

1. *Easy to compute. (Same as per worst-case one-way functions)*

---

[1]See Appendix B for definitions of **NP** and **BPP**.

2. **Hard to invert.** *Any efficient attempt to invert f on random input succeeds with only negligible probability. Formally, for any adversary $\mathcal{A}$, there exists a negligible function ϵ such that for any input length $n \in \mathbb{N}$,*

$$\Pr\left[x \leftarrow \{0,1\}^n; y \leftarrow f(x) : f(\mathcal{A}(1^n, y)) = y\right] \leq \epsilon(n).$$

Notice the algorithm $\mathcal{A}$ receives the additional input of 1^n; this is to allow $\mathcal{A}$ to run for time polynomial in $|x|$, even if the function f should be substantially length-shrinking. In essence, we are ruling out pathological cases where functions might be considered one-way because writing down the output of the inversion algorithm violates its time bound.

As before, we must keep in mind that the above definition is *asymptotic*. To define one-way functions with concrete security, we would instead use explicit parameters that can be instantiated as desired. In such a treatment, we say that a function is (t, s, ϵ)-one-way if no $\mathcal{A}$ of size s with running time $\leq t$ will succeed with probability better than ϵ in inverting f on a randomly chosen input.

Unfortunately, many natural candidates for one-way functions will not meet the strong notion of a one-way function. In order to capture the property of one-wayness that these examples satisfy, we introduce the notion of a *weak one-way function* which relaxes the condition on inverting the function. This relaxed version only requires that all efficient attempts at inverting will fail with some non-negligible probability.

▷**Definition 28.4 (Weak One-Way Function)** *A function mapping strings to strings $f : \{0,1\}^* \rightarrow \{0,1\}^*$ is a* weak one-way *function if it satisfies the following two conditions.*

1. **Easy to compute.** *(Same as that for a strong one-way function.)*

2. **Hard to invert.** *There exists a polynomial function $q : \mathbb{N} \rightarrow \mathbb{N}$ such that for any adversary $\mathcal{A}$, for sufficiently large $n \in \mathbb{N}$,*

$$\Pr[x \leftarrow \{0,1\}^n; y \leftarrow f(x) : f(\mathcal{A}(1^n, y)) = y] \leq 1 - \frac{1}{q(n)}$$

Our eventual goal is to show that weak one-way functions can be used to construct strong one-way functions. Before showing this, let us consider some examples.

2.3   Multiplication, Primes, and Factoring

In this section, we consider examples of one-way functions. A first candidate is the function $f_{\text{mult}} : \mathbb{N}^2 \to \mathbb{N}$ defined by

$$f_{\text{mult}}(x,y) = \begin{cases} 1 & \text{if } x = 1 \lor y = 1 \\ x \cdot y & \text{otherwise} \end{cases}$$

Is this a one-way function? Clearly, by the multiplication algorithm, f_{mult} is easy to compute. But f_{mult} is not always hard to invert. If at least one of x and y is even, then their product will be even as well. This happens with probability $\frac{3}{4}$ if the input (x,y) is picked uniformly at random from $\mathbb{N}^2$. So the following attack A will succeed with probability $\frac{3}{4}$:

$$A(z) = \begin{cases} (2, \frac{z}{2}) & \text{if } z \text{ even} \\ (0,0) & \text{otherwise.} \end{cases}$$

Something is not quite right here, since f_{mult} is conjectured to be hard to invert on *some*, but not all, inputs[2]. The strong definition of a one-way function is too restrictive to capture this notion, so we now determine whether the function satisfies the weak notion of one-wayness. In order to do so, we must first introduce an assumption and some basic facts from number theory.

2.3.1   The Factoring Assumption

Denote the (finite) set of primes that are smaller than 2^n as

$$\Pi_n = \{q \mid q < 2^n \text{ and } q \text{ is prime}\}$$

Consider the following assumption, which we shall assume for the remainder of this course:

---
[2]Notice that by the way we have defined f_{mult}, $(1, xy)$ will never be a pre-image of xy. That is why some instances might be hard to invert.

▷**Assumption 30.1 (Factoring)** *For every adversary* $\mathcal{A}$, *there exists a negligible function* ϵ *such that*

$$\Pr[p \leftarrow \Pi_n; q \leftarrow \Pi_n; N \leftarrow pq : \mathcal{A}(N) \in \{p, q\}] < \epsilon(n)$$

The factoring assumption is a very important, well-studied conjecture. The best provable algorithm for factorization runs in time $2^{O((n \log n)^{1/2})}$, and the best heuristic algorithm runs in time $2^{O(n^{1/3} \log^{2/3} n)}$. Factoring composites that are a product of two primes is hard in a concrete way as well: In May 2005, the research team of F. Bahr, M. Boehm, J. Franke, and T. Kleinjung were able to factor a 663-bit challenge number (of the form described above). In particular, they started in 2003 and completed in May 2005 and estimate to have used the equivalent of 55 years of computing time of a single 2.2 GHz Opteron CPU. See [BBFK05] for details. In January 2010, Kleinjung and 12 colleagues [KAF+10] announced the factorization of the RSA-768 challenge modulus. They describe the amount of work required for this task as follows:

> We spent half a year on 80 processors on polynomial selection. This was about 3% of the main task, the *sieving*, which was done on many hundreds of machines and took almost two years. On a single core 2.2 GHz AMD Opteron processor with 2 GB RAM per core, sieving would have taken about fifteen hundred years.

They go on to mention that factoring a 1024-bit modulus "would be about a thousand times harder."

2.3.2   There are many primes

The problem of characterizing the set of prime numbers has been considered since antiquity. Euclid, in Book IX, Proposition 20, noted that there are an infinite number of primes. However, merely having an infinite number of them is not reassuring, since perhaps they are distributed in such a haphazard way as to make finding them extremely difficult. An empirical way to approach the problem is to define the function

$$\pi(x) = \text{number of primes} \leq x$$

and graph it for reasonable values of x as we have done in Fig. 2 below.

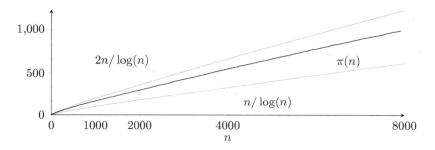

Figure 31.2: Graph of $\pi(n)$ for the first thousand primes

By inspecting this curve, at age 15, Gauss conjectured that $\pi(x) \approx x/\log x$. Since then, many people have answered the question with increasing precision; notable are Chebyshev's theorem (upon which our argument below is based), and the famous *Prime Number Theorem* which establishes that $\pi(N)$ approaches $\frac{N}{\ln N}$ as N grows to infinity. Here, we will prove a much simpler theorem which only lower-bounds $\pi(x)$:

▷**Theorem 31.3 (Chebyshev)** *For $x > 1$, $\pi(x) > \frac{x}{2\log x}$*

Proof. Consider the integer

$$X = \binom{2x}{x} = \frac{(2x)!}{(x!)^2} = \left(\frac{x+x}{x}\right)\left(\frac{x+(x-1)}{(x-1)}\right)\cdots\left(\frac{x+1}{1}\right)$$

Observe that $X > 2^x$ (since each term is greater than 2) and that the largest prime dividing X is at most $2x$ (since the largest numerator in the product is $2x$). By these facts and unique factorization, we can write

$$X = \prod_{p<2x} p^{v_p(X)} > 2^x$$

where the product is over primes p less than $2x$ and $v_p(X)$ denotes the integral power of p in the factorization of X. Taking logs on both sides, we have

$$\sum_{p<2x} v_p(X) \log p > x$$

We now employ the following claim proven below.

▷**Claim 32.4** $\frac{\log 2x}{\log p} > v_p(X)$

Substituting this claim, we have

$$\sum_{p<2x} \left(\frac{\log 2x}{\log p}\right) \log p = \log 2x \left(\sum_{p<2x} 1\right) > x$$

Notice that the second sum is precisely $\pi(2x)$; thus

$$\pi(2x) > \frac{x}{\log 2x} = \frac{1}{2} \cdot \frac{2x}{\log 2x}$$

which establishes the theorem for even values. For odd values, notice that

$$\pi(2x) = \pi(2x-1) > \frac{2x}{2\log 2x} > \frac{(2x-1)}{2\log(2x-1)}$$

since $x/\log x$ is an increasing function for $x \geq 3$.

Proof. [Proof Of Claim 32.4] Notice that

$$v_p(X) = \sum_{i>1} \left(\lfloor 2x/p^i \rfloor - 2\lfloor x/p^i \rfloor\right)$$
$$< \log 2x / \log p$$

The first equality follows because the product $(2x)! = (2x)(2x-1)\ldots(1)$ includes a multiple of p^i at most $\lfloor 2x/p^i \rfloor$ times in the numerator of X; similarly the product $x! \cdot x!$ in the denominator of X *removes* it exactly $2\lfloor x/p^i \rfloor$ times. The second line follows because each term in the summation is at most 1 and after $p^i > 2x$, all of the terms will be zero. □

□

An important corollary of Chebyshev's theorem is that at least a $1/2n$-fraction of n-bit numbers are prime. As we shall see in §2.6.5, primality testing can be done in polynomial time—i.e., we can efficiently check whether a number is prime or composite. With these facts, we can show that, under the factoring assumption, f_{mult} is a weak one-way function.

▷**Theorem 33.5** *If the factoring assumption is true, then f_{mult} is a weak one-way function.*

Proof. As already mentioned, $f_{mult}(x,y)$ is clearly computable in polynomial time; we just need to show that it is hard to invert.

Consider a certain input length $2n$ (i.e, $|x| = |y| = n$). Intuitively, by Chebyshev's theorem, with probability $1/4n^2$ a random input pair x, y will consists of two primes; in this case, by the factoring assumption, the function should be hard to invert (except with negligible probability).

We proceed to a formal proof. Let $q(n) = 8n^2$; we show that non-uniform p.p.t. cannot invert f_{mult} with probability greater than $1 - \frac{1}{q(n)}$ for sufficiently large input lengths. Assume, for contradiction, that there exists a non-uniform p.p.t. A that inverts f_{mult} with probability at least $1 - \frac{1}{q(n)}$ for infinitely many $n \in \mathbb{N}$. That is, the probability that A, when given input $z = xy$ for randomly chosen n-bit strings, x and y, produces either x or y is:

$$\Pr\left[x,y \leftarrow \{0,1\}^n, z = xy : A(1^{2n},z) \in \{x,y\}\right] \geq 1 - \frac{1}{8n^2} \quad (33.2)$$

We construct a non-uniform p.p.t machine A' which uses A to break the factoring assumption. The description of A' follows:

ALGORITHM 33.6: $A'(z)$: Breaking the factoring assumption

1: Sample $x, y \leftarrow \{0,1\}^n$
2: **if** x and y are both prime **then**
3: $\quad z' \leftarrow z$
4: **else**
5: $\quad z' \leftarrow xy$
6: **end if**
7: $w \leftarrow A(1^n, z')$
8: Return w if x and y are both prime.

Note that since primality testing can be done in polynomial time, and since A is a non-uniform p.p.t., A' is also a non-uniform p.p.t. Suppose we now feed A' the product of a pair of random n-bit primes, z. In order to give A a uniformly distributed input (i.e. the product of a pair of random n-bit numbers), A' samples a pair (x, y) uniformly, and replaces the product xy with the input z if both x and y are prime. By Chebychev's Theorem (31.3), A' fails to pass z to A with probability at most $1 - \frac{1}{4n^2}$. From Eq. (33.2), A fails to factor its input with probability at most $1/8n^2$. Using the union bound, we conclude that A' fails with probability at most

$$\left(1 - \frac{1}{4n^2}\right) + \frac{1}{8n^2} \leq 1 - \frac{1}{8n^2}$$

for large n. In other words, A' factors z with probability at least $\frac{1}{8n^2}$ for infinitely many n. In other words, there does not exist a negligible function that bounds the success probability of A', which contradicts the factoring assumption.   □

Note that in the above proof we relied on the fact that primality testing can be done in polynomial time. This was done only for ease of exposition, as it is unnecessary. Consider a machine A'' that proceeds just as A', but always lets $z = z'$ and always outputs w. Such a machine succeeds in factoring with at least the same if not greater probability. But A'' never needs to check if x and y are prime.

2.4 Hardness Amplification

We have shown that a natural function such as multiplication satisfies the notion of a *weak* one-way function if certain assumptions hold. In this section, we show an efficient way to transform any weak one-way function to a strong one. In this sense, the existence of weak one-way functions is equivalent to the existence of (strong) one-way functions. The main insight is that running a weak one-way function f on enough random inputs x_i produces a list of elements y_i which contains at least one member that is hard to invert.

▷**Theorem 35.1** *For any weak one-way function $f : \{0,1\}^* \to \{0,1\}^*$, there exists a polynomial $m(\cdot)$ such that function*

$$f'(x_1, x_2, \ldots, x_{m(n)}) = (f(x_1), f(x_2), \ldots, f(x_{m(n)})).$$

from $f' : (\{0,1\}^n)^{m(n)} \to (\{0,1\}^*)^{m(n)}$ is strongly one-way.

We prove this theorem by contradiction. We assume that f' is not strongly one-way and so there is an algorithm $\mathcal{A}'$ that inverts it with non-negligible probability. From this, we construct an algorithm $\mathcal{A}$ that inverts f with high probability. The pattern for such an argument is common in cryptographic proofs; we call it a *security reduction* because it essentially reduces the problem of "breaking" f (for example, the weak one-way function in the theorem above) into the problem of breaking f'. Therefore, if there is some way to attack f', then that same method can be used (via the reduction) to break the original primitive f that we assume to be secure.

The complete proof of Thm. 35.1 appears in §2.4.3 below. To introduce that proof, we first present two smaller examples. First, to gain familiarity with security reductions, we show a simple example of how to argue that if f is a strong one-way function, then $g(x,y) = (f(x), f(y))$ is also a strong one-way function. Next, we prove the hardness amplification theorem for the function f_{mult} because it is significantly simpler than the proof for the general case, and yet offers insight to the proof of Theorem 35.1.

2.4.1   A Simple Security Reduction

▷**Theorem 35.2** *If f is a strong one-way function, then $g(x,y) = (f(x), f(y))$ is a strong one-way function.*

Proof. Suppose for the sake of reaching contradiction that g is not a strong one-way function. Thus, there exists a non-uniform p.p.t. $\mathcal{A}'$ and a polynomial p such that for infinitely many n,

$$\Pr\left[(x,y) \leftarrow \{0,1\}^{2n}; z \leftarrow g(x,y) : \mathcal{A}'(1^{2n}, z) \in g^{-1}(z)\right] \geq \frac{1}{p(2n)}$$

We now construct another non-uniform p.p.t. $\mathcal{A}$ that uses $\mathcal{A}'$ in order to invert f on input u. In order to do this, $\mathcal{A}$ will choose a random y, compute $v \leftarrow f(y)$ and then submit the pair (u, v) to $\mathcal{A}'$. Notice that this pair (u, v) is identically distributed as the pair (x, y) in the equation above. Therefore, with probability $\frac{1}{p(2n)}$, the algorithm $\mathcal{A}'$ returns an inverse (a, b). Now the algorithm $\mathcal{A}$ can test whether $f(a) = u$, and if so, output a. Formally,

$$\Pr\left[x \leftarrow \{0,1\}^n;\ u \leftarrow f(x) : \mathcal{A}(1^n, u) \in f^{-1}(u)\right]$$
$$= \Pr\left[\begin{array}{l} x, y \leftarrow \{0,1\}^{2n}; \\ u \leftarrow f(x); v \leftarrow f(y) \end{array} : \mathcal{A}'(1^{2n}, (u,v)) \in g^{-1}(u,v)\right]$$
$$= \Pr\left[(x,y) \leftarrow \{0,1\}^{2n};\ z \leftarrow g(x,y) : \mathcal{A}'(1^{2n}, z) \in g^{-1}(z)\right]$$
$$\geq \frac{1}{p(2n)}$$

$\square$

2.4.2   Analyzing the function f_{mult}

▷**Theorem 36.3** *Assume the factoring assumption and let $m_n = 4n^3$. Then $f' : (\{0,1\}^{2n})^{m_n} \to (\{0,1\}^{2n})^{m_n}$ is strongly one-way:*

$$f'((x_1, y_1), \ldots, (x_{m_n}, y_{m_n})) = (f_{\text{mult}}(x_1, y_1), \ldots, f_{\text{mult}}(x_{m_n}, y_{m_n}))$$

Proof. Recall that by Chebyschev's Theorem, a pair of random n-bit numbers are both prime with probability at least $1/4n^2$. So, if we choose $m_n = 4n^3$ pairs, the probability that none of them is a prime pair is at most

$$\left(1 - \frac{1}{4n^2}\right)^{4n^3} = \left(1 - \frac{1}{4n^2}\right)^{4n^2 n} \leq e^{-n} \qquad (36.2)$$

Thus, intuitively, by the factoring assumption f' is strongly one-way. More formally, suppose that f' is not a strong one-way function. Let $n' = 2n \cdot m(n) = 8n^4$, and let the notation $(\vec{x}, \vec{y})$ represent $(x_1, y_2), \ldots, (x_{m(n)}, y_{m(n)})$. Thus, there exists a non-uniform p.p.t. machine A and a polynomial p such that for infinitely many n',

$$\Pr\left[(\vec{x},\vec{y}) \leftarrow \{0,1\}^{n'} : A(1^{n'}, f'(\vec{x},\vec{y})) \in f'^{-1}(\vec{x},\vec{y})\right] \geq \frac{1}{p(n')}$$
(36.3)

We construct a non-uniform p.p.t. A' which uses A to break the factoring assumption.

ALGORITHM 37.4: $A'(z_0)$: BREAKING THE FACTORING ASSUMPTION

1: Sample $\vec{x}, \vec{y} \leftarrow \{0,1\}^{n'}$
2: Compute $\vec{z} \leftarrow f'(\vec{x}, \vec{y})$
3: **if** some pair (x_i, y_i) are both prime **then**
4:     replace z_i with z_0 (only once even if there are many such pairs)
5:     Compute $(x'_1, y'_1), \ldots, (x'_{m(n)}, y'_{m(n)}) \leftarrow A(1^{n'}, \vec{z})$
6:     Output x'_i
7: **end if**
8: Else, fail.

Note that since primality testing can be done in polynomial time, and since A is a non-uniform p.p.t., A' is also a non-uniform p.p.t. Also note that $A'(z_0)$ feeds A the uniform input distribution by uniformly sampling $(\vec{x}, \vec{y})$ and replacing some product $x_i y_i$ with z_0 only if both x_i and y_i are prime. From (36.3), A' fails to factor its inputs with probability at most $1 - 1/p(n')$; from (36.2), A' fails to substitute in z_0 with probability at most e^{-n} By the union bound, we conclude that A' fails to factor z_0 with probability at most

$$1 - \frac{1}{p(n')} + e^{-n} \leq 1 - \frac{1}{2p(n')}$$

for large n. In other words, A' factors z_0 with probability at least $1/2p(n')$ for infinitely many n'. This contradicts the factoring assumption. $\qquad\square$

We note that just as in the proof of Theorem 33.5 the above proof can be modified to not make use of the fact that primality testing can be done in polynomial time. We leave this as an exercise to the reader.

2.4.3 *Proof of Theorem 35.1

Proof. Since f is weakly one-way, let $q : \mathbb{N} \to \mathbb{N}$ be a polynomial such that for any non-uniform p.p.t. algorithm $\mathcal{A}$ and any input length $n \in \mathbb{N}$,

$$\Pr\left[x \leftarrow \{0,1\}^n; y \leftarrow f(x) : f(\mathcal{A}(1^n, y)) = y\right] \leq 1 - \frac{1}{q(n)}.$$

We want to set m such that $\left(1 - \frac{1}{q(n)}\right)^m$ tends to 0 for large n. Since

$$\left(1 - \frac{1}{q(n)}\right)^{nq(n)} \approx \left(\frac{1}{e}\right)^n$$

we pick $m = 2nq(n)$. Let $\vec{x}$ represent $\vec{x} = (x_1, \ldots, x_m)$ where each $x_i \in \{0,1\}^n$.

Suppose that f' as defined in the theorem statement is not a strongly one-way function. Thus, there exists a non-uniform p.p.t. algorithm $\mathcal{A}'$ and $p' : \mathbb{N} \to \mathbb{N}$ be a polynomial such that for infinitely many input lengths $n \in \mathbb{N}$, $\mathcal{A}'$ inverts f' with probability $p'(nm)$:

$$\Pr\left[\vec{x} \leftarrow \{0,1\}^{nm}; \vec{y} = f'(\vec{x}) : f'(\mathcal{A}'(\vec{y})) = \vec{y}\right] > \frac{1}{p'(nm)}$$

Since m is polynomial in n, then the function $p(n) = p'(nm) = p'(2n^2 q(n))$ is also a polynomial. Rewriting the above probability, we have

$$\Pr\left[\vec{x} \leftarrow \{0,1\}^{nm}; \vec{y} = f'(\vec{x}) : f'(\mathcal{A}'(\vec{y})) = \vec{y}\right] > \frac{1}{p(n)} \quad (38.1)$$

A first idea for using A to invert f on the input y would be to feed A the input $(y, y, \ldots, y)$. But, it is possible that A always fails on inputs of such format (these strings form a very small fraction of all strings of length mn); so this plan will not work. A slightly better approach would be to feed A the string $(y, y_2, \ldots, y_m)$ where $y_{j \neq 1} = f(x_j)$ and $x_j \leftarrow \{0,1\}^n$. Again, this may not work since A could potentially invert only a small fraction of y_1's (but, say, all $y_2, \ldots y_m$'s). As we show below, letting $y_i = y$, where $i \leftarrow [m]$ is a random "position" will, however, work. More precisely, define the algorithm $\mathcal{A}_0$ which will attempt to use $\mathcal{A}'$ to invert f as per the figure below.

ALGORITHM 38.5: $\mathcal{A}_0(f, y)$ WHERE $y \in \{0,1\}^n$

1: Pick a random $i \leftarrow [1, m]$.
2: For all $j \neq i$, pick a random $x_j \leftarrow \{0,1\}^n$, and let $y_j = f(x_j)$.
3: Let $y_i \leftarrow y$.
4: Let $(z_1, z_2, \ldots, z_m) \leftarrow \mathcal{A}'(y_1, y_2, \ldots, y_m)$.
5: If $f(z_i) = y$, then output z_i; otherwise, fail and output $\perp$.

To improve our chances of inverting f, we will run $\mathcal{A}_0$ several times using independently chosen random coins. Define the algorithm $\mathcal{A} : \{0,1\}^n \rightarrow \{0,1\}^n \cup \perp$ to run $\mathcal{A}_0$ with its input $2nm^2p(n)$ times and output the first non-$\perp$ result it receives. If all runs of $\mathcal{A}_0$ result in $\perp$, then $\mathcal{A}$ also outputs $\perp$.

In order to analyze the success of $\mathcal{A}$, let us define a set of "good" elements G_n such that $x \in G_n$ if $\mathcal{A}_0$ can successfully invert $f(x)$ with non-negligible probability:

$$G_n = \left\{ x \in \{0,1\}^n \mid \Pr\left[\mathcal{A}_0(f(x)) \neq \perp\right] \geq \frac{1}{2m^2p(n)} \right\}$$

Otherwise, call x "bad." Note that the probability that $\mathcal{A}$ fails to invert $f(x)$ on a good x is small:

$$\Pr\left[\mathcal{A}(f(x)) \text{ fails} \mid x \in G_n\right] \leq \left(1 - \frac{1}{2m^2p(n)}\right)^{2m^2np(n)} \approx e^{-n}.$$

We claim that there are many good elements; there are enough for $\mathcal{A}$ to invert f with sufficient probability to contradict the weakly one-way assumption on f. In particular, we claim there are at least $2^n \left(1 - \frac{1}{2q(n)}\right)$ good elements in $\{0,1\}^n$. If this holds, then

$$\begin{aligned}
\Pr&\left[\mathcal{A}(f(x)) \text{ fails}\right] \\
&= \Pr\left[\mathcal{A}(f(x)) \text{ fails} \mid x \in G_n\right] \cdot \Pr\left[x \in G_n\right] \\
&\quad + \Pr\left[\mathcal{A}(f(x)) \text{ fails} \mid x \notin G_n\right] \cdot \Pr\left[x \notin G_n\right] \\
&\leq \Pr\left[\mathcal{A}(f(x)) \text{ fails} \mid x \in G_n\right] + \Pr\left[x \notin G_n\right] \\
&\leq \left(1 - \frac{1}{2m^2p(n)}\right)^{2m^2np(n)} + \frac{1}{2q(n)} \\
&\approx e^{-n} + \frac{1}{2q(n)} \\
&< \frac{1}{q(n)}.
\end{aligned}$$

This contradicts the assumption that f is $q(n)$-weak.

It remains to be shown that there are at least $2^n \left(1 - \frac{1}{2q(n)}\right)$ good elements in $\{0,1\}^n$. Suppose for the sake of reaching a contradiction, that $|G_n| < 2^n \left(\frac{1}{2q(n)}\right)$. We will contradict Eq.(38.1) which states that $\mathcal{A}'$ succeeds in inverting $f'(x)$ on a random input x with probability $\frac{1}{p(n)}$. To do so, we establish an upper bound on the probability by splitting it into two quantities:

$$
\Pr\left[x_i \leftarrow \{0,1\}^n; y_i = f'(x_i) : \mathcal{A}'(\vec{y}) \text{ succeeds}\right]
$$
$$
= \Pr\left[x_i \leftarrow \{0,1\}^n; y_i = f'(x_i) : \mathcal{A}'(\vec{y}) \neq \bot \wedge \text{some } x_i \notin G_n\right]
$$
$$
+ \Pr\left[x_i \leftarrow \{0,1\}^n; y_i = f'(x_i) : \mathcal{A}'(\vec{y}) \neq \bot \wedge \text{all } x_i \in G_n\right]
$$

For each $j \in [1, n]$, we have

$$
\Pr\left[x_i \leftarrow \{0,1\}^n; y_i = f'(x_i) : \mathcal{A}'(\vec{y}) \neq \bot \wedge x_j \notin G_n\right]
$$
$$
\leq \Pr\left[x_i \leftarrow \{0,1\}^n; y_i = f'(x_i) : \mathcal{A}'(\vec{y}) \text{ succeeds} \mid x_j \notin G_n\right]
$$
$$
\leq m \cdot \Pr\left[\mathcal{A}_0(f(x_j)) \text{ succeeds} \mid x_j \text{ is bad}\right]
$$
$$
\leq \frac{m}{2m^2 p(n)} = \frac{1}{2mp(n)}
$$

So taking a union bound, we have

$$
\Pr\left[x_i \leftarrow \{0,1\}^n; y_i = f'(x_i) : \mathcal{A}'(\vec{y}) \text{ succeeds} \wedge \text{ some } x_i \notin G_n\right]
$$
$$
\leq \sum_j \Pr\left[x_i \leftarrow \{0,1\}^n; y_i = f'(x_i) : \mathcal{A}'(\vec{y}) \text{ succeeds} \wedge x_j \notin G_n\right]
$$
$$
\leq \frac{m}{2mp(n)} = \frac{1}{2p(n)}.
$$

Also,

$$
\Pr\left[x_i \leftarrow \{0,1\}^n; y_i = f'(x_i) : \mathcal{A}'(\vec{y}) \text{ succeeds and all } x_i \in G_n\right]
$$
$$
\leq \Pr\left[x_i \leftarrow \{0,1\}^n : \text{all } x_i \in G_n\right]
$$
$$
< \left(1 - \frac{1}{2q(n)}\right)^m = \left(1 - \frac{1}{2q(n)}\right)^{2nq(n)} \approx e^{-n}
$$

Hence

$$\Pr\left[x_i \leftarrow \{0,1\}^n; y_i = f'(x_i) : \mathcal{A}'(\bar{y}) \text{ succeeds}\right] < \frac{1}{2p(n)} + e^{-n}$$

$$< \frac{1}{p(n)}$$

which contradicts (38.1).   □

2.5   Collections of One-Way Functions

In the last two sections, we have come to suitable definitions for strong and weak one-way functions. These two definitions are concise and elegant, and can nonetheless be used to construct generic schemes and protocols. However, the definitions are more suited for research in complexity-theoretic aspects of cryptography.

Practical considerations motivate us to introduce a more flexible definition that combines the practicality of a weak OWF with the security of a strong OWF. In particular, instead of requiring the function to be one-way on a randomly chosen string, we define a domain and a domain sampler for *hard-to-invert* instances. Because the inspiration behind this definition comes from "candidate one-way functions," we also introduce the concept of a *collection* of functions; one function per input size.

▷**Definition 41.1** (Collection of OWFs). A *collection of one-way functions* is a family $\mathcal{F} = \{f_i : \mathcal{D}_i \rightarrow \mathcal{R}_i\}_{i \in I}$ satisfying the following conditions:

1. It is easy to sample a function, i.e. there exists a p.p.t. *Gen* such that $Gen(1^n)$ outputs some $i \in I$.

2. It is easy to sample a given domain, i.e. there exists a p.p.t. that on input i returns a uniformly random element of $\mathcal{D}_i$

3. It is easy to evaluate, i.e. there exists a p.p.t. that on input $i, x \in \mathcal{D}_i$ computes $f_i(x)$.

4. It is hard to invert, i.e. for any p.p.t. $\mathcal{A}$ there exists a negligible function ϵ such that

$$\Pr\left[i \leftarrow Gen; x \leftarrow \mathcal{D}_i; y \leftarrow f_i(x) : f(\mathcal{A}(1^n, i, y)) = y\right] \le \epsilon(n)$$

Despite our various relaxations, the existence of a collection of one-way functions is equivalent to the existence of a strong one-way function.

▷**Theorem 42.2** *There exists a collection of one-way functions if and only if there exists a single strong one-way function.*

Proof idea: If we have a single one-way function f, then we can choose our index set ot be the singleton set $I = \{0\}$, choose $\mathcal{D}_0 = \mathbb{N}$, and $f_0 = f$.

The difficult direction is to construct a single one-way function given a collection $\mathcal{F}$. The trick is to define $g(r_1, r_2)$ to be $i, f_i(x)$ where i is generated using r_1 as the random bits and x is sampled from $\mathcal{D}_i$ using r_2 as the random bits. The fact that g is a strong one-way function is left as an excercise.   □

2.6 Basic Computational Number Theory

Before we can study candidate collections of one-way functions, it serves us to review some basic algorithms and concepts in number theory and group theory.

2.6.1 Modular Arithmetic

We state the following basic facts about modular arithmetic:

▷**Fact 42.1** *For $N > 0$ and $a, b \in \mathbb{Z}$,*

    1. $(a \bmod N) + (b \bmod N) \bmod N \equiv (a + b) \bmod N$

    2. $(a \bmod N)(b \bmod N) \bmod N \equiv ab \bmod N$

We often use $=$ instead of $\equiv$ to denote modular congruency.

2.6.2 Euclid's algorithm

Euclid's algorithm appears in text around 300B.C. Given two numbers a and b such that $a \geq b$, Euclid's algorithm computes the greatest common divisor of a and b, denoted $\gcd(a, b)$. It is not at all obvious how this value can be efficiently computed, without say, the factorization of both numbers. Euclid's insight was to notice that any divisor of a and b is also a divisor of b and $a - b$. The subtraction is easy to compute and the resulting pair $(b, a - b)$ is a smaller instance of original gcd problem. The algorithm has since been updated to use $a \bmod b$ in place of $a - b$ to improve efficiency. The version of the algorithm that we present here also computes values x, y such that $ax + by = \gcd(a, b)$.

ALGORITHM 43.2: EXTENDEDEUCLID(a, b) SUCH THAT $a > b > 0$

1: **if** $a \bmod b = 0$ **then**
2:     Return $(0, 1)$
3: **else**
4:     $(x, y) \leftarrow$ EXTENDEDEUCLID$(b, a \bmod b)$
5:     Return $(y, x - y(\lfloor a/b \rfloor))$
6: **end if**

Note: by polynomial time we always mean polynomial in the size of the input, that is $\text{poly}(\log a + \log b)$

Proof. On input $a > b \geq 0$, we aim to prove that Algorithm 43.2 returns (x, y) such that $ax + by = \gcd(a, b) = d$ via induction. First, let us argue that the procedure terminates in polynomial time. (See [KNU81] for a better analysis relating to the Fibonacci numbers; for us the following suffices since each recursive call involves only a constant number of divisions and subtraction operations.)

▷**Claim 43.3** *If* $a > b \geq 0$ *and* $a < 2^n$, *then* ExtendedEuclid(a, b) *makes at most* $2n$ *recursive calls.*

Proof. By inspection, if $n \leq 2$, the procedure returns after at most 2 recursive calls. Assume the hypothesis holds for $a < 2^n$. Now consider an instance with $a < 2^{n+1}$. We identify two cases.

1. If $b < 2^n$, then the next recursive call on $(b, a \bmod b)$ meets the inductive hypothesis and makes at most $2n$ recursive calls. Thus, the total number of recursive calls is less than $2n + 1 < 2(n + 1)$.

2. If $b > 2^n$, than the first argument of the next recursive call on $(b, a \bmod b)$ is upper-bounded by 2^{n+1} since $a > b$. Thus, the problem is no "smaller" on face. However, we

can show that the second argument will be small enough to satisfy the prior case:

$$a \bmod b = a - \lfloor a/b \rfloor \cdot b$$
$$< 2^{n+1} - b$$
$$< 2^{n+1} - 2^n = 2^n$$

Thus, after 2 recursive calls, the arguments satisfy the inductive hypothesis resulting in $2 + 2n = 2(n+1)$ recursive calls.

□

Now for correctness, suppose that b divided a evenly (i.e., $a \bmod b = 0$). Then we have $\gcd(a, b) = b$, and the algorithm returns $(0, 1)$ which is correct by inspection. By the inductive hypothesis, assume that the recursive call returns (x, y) such that

$$bx + (a \bmod b)y = \gcd(b, a \bmod b)$$

First, we claim that

▷**Claim 44.4** $\gcd(a, b) = \gcd(b, a \bmod b)$

Proof. Divide a by b and write the result as $a = qb + r$. Rearrange to get $r = a - qb$.

Observe that if d is a divisor of a and b (i.e. $a = a'd$ and $b = b'd$ for $a', b' \in \mathbb{Z}$) then d is also a divisor of r since $r = (a'd) - q(b'd) = d(a' - qb')$. Similarly, if d is a divisor of b and r, then d also divides a. Since this holds for all divisors of a and b and all divisors of b and r, it follows that $\gcd(a, b) = \gcd(b, r)$.

□

Thus, we can write

$$bx + (a \bmod b)y = d$$

and by adding 0 to the right, and regrouping, we get

$$d = bx - b(\lfloor a/b \rfloor)y + (a \bmod b)y + b(\lfloor a/b \rfloor)y$$
$$= b(x - (\lfloor a/b \rfloor)y) + ay$$

which shows that the return value $(y, x - (\lfloor a/b \rfloor)y)$ is correct. □
    The assumption that the inputs are such that $a > b$ is without loss of generality since otherwise the first recursive call swaps the order of the inputs.

2.6.3   Exponentiation modulo N

Given a, x, N, we now demonstrate how to efficiently compute $a^x \bmod N$. Recall that by *efficient*, we require the computation to take polynomial time in the size of the representation of a, x, N. Since inputs are given in binary notation, this requires our procedure to run in time $poly(\log(a), \log(x), \log(N))$.

The key idea is to rewrite x in binary as

$$x = 2^{\ell}x_{\ell} + 2^{\ell-1}x_{\ell-1} + \cdots + 2x_1 + x_0$$

where $x_i \in \{0, 1\}$ so that

$$a^x \bmod N = a^{2^{\ell}x_{\ell} + 2^{\ell-1}x_{\ell-1} + \cdots + 2^1 x_1 + x_0} \bmod N$$

This expression can be further simplified as

$$a^x \bmod N = \prod_{i=0}^{\ell} x_i a^{2^i} \bmod N$$

using the basic properties of modular arithmetic from Fact 42.1.

ALGORITHM 45.5: MODULAREXPONENTIATION(a, x, N)

1: $r \leftarrow 1$
2: **while** $x > 0$ **do**
3:     **if** x is odd **then**
4:         $r \leftarrow r \cdot a \bmod N$
5:     **end if**
6:     $x \leftarrow \lfloor x/2 \rfloor$
7:     $a \leftarrow a^2 \bmod N$
8: **end while**
9: **return** r

▷**Theorem 45.6** *On input (a, x, N) where $a \in [1, N]$, Algorithm 45.5 computes $a^x \bmod N$ in time $O(\log(x)\log^2(N))$.*

Proof. Rewrite $a^x \bmod N$ as $\prod_i x_i a^{2^i} \bmod N$. Since multiplying and squaring modulo N take time $\log^2(N)$, each iteration of the loop requires $O(\log^2(N))$ time. Because each iteration divides x by two, the loop runs at most $\log x$ times which establishes a running time of $O(\log(x)\log^2(N))$. □

Later, after we have introduced Euler's theorem, we present a similar algorithm for modular exponentiation which removes the restriction that $x < N$. In order to discuss this, we must introduce the notion of Groups.

2.6.4   Groups

▷**Definition 46.7** *A group G is a set of elements with a binary operator $\oplus : G \times G \to G$ that satisfies the following properties:*

1. *Closure: For all $a, b \in G$, $a \oplus b \in G$,*

2. *Identity: There is an element i in G such that for all $a \in G$, $i \oplus a = a \oplus i = a$. This element i is called the* identity *element.*

3. *Associativity: For all a, b and c in G, $(a \oplus b) \oplus c = a \oplus (b \oplus c)$.*

4. *Inverse: For all $a \in G$, there is an element $b \in G$ such that $a \oplus b = b \oplus a = i$ where i is the* identity.

Example: The Additive Group Mod N

We have already worked with the additive group modulo N, which is denoted as $(\mathbb{Z}_N, +)$ where $\mathbb{Z}_N = \{0, 1, \ldots, N-1\}$ and $+$ is addition modulo N. It is straightforward to verify the four properties for this set and operation.

Example: The Multiplicative Group Mod N

The multiplicative group modulo $N > 0$ is denoted $(\mathbb{Z}_N^*, \times)$, where $\mathbb{Z}_N^* = \{x \in [1, N-1] \mid \gcd(x, N) = 1\}$ and $\times$ is multiplication modulo N.

▷**Theorem 46.8** $(\mathbb{Z}_N^*, \times)$ *is a group*

Proof.   Observe that 1 is the identity in this group and that $(a * b) * c = a * (b * c)$ for $a, b, c \in \mathbb{Z}_N^*$. However, it remains to verify that the group is closed and that each element has an inverse. In order to do this, we must introduce the notion of a prime integer.

▷**Definition 46.9** *A prime is a positive integer $p > 1$ that is evenly divisible by only 1 and p.*

Closure Suppose, for the sake of reaching a contradiction, that there exist two elements $a, b \in \mathbb{Z}_N^*$ such that $ab \notin \mathbb{Z}_N^*$. This implies that $\gcd(a, N) = 1$, $\gcd(b, N) = 1$, but that $\gcd(ab, N) = d > 1$. The latter condition implies that d has a non-trivial prime factor that divides both ab and N. Thus, the prime factor must also divide either a or b (verify as an exercise), which contradicts the assumption that $\gcd(a, N) = 1$ and $\gcd(b, N) = 1$.

Inverse Consider an element $a \in \mathbb{Z}_N^*$. Since $\gcd(a, N) = 1$, we can use Euclid's algorithm on (a, N) to compute values (x, y) such that $ax + Ny = 1$. Notice, this directly produces a value x such that $ax = 1 \bmod N$. Thus, every element $a \in \mathbb{Z}_N^*$ has an inverse which can be efficiently computed. □

The groups $(\mathbb{Z}_N, +)$ and $(\mathbb{Z}_N^*, \times)$ are also *abelian* or commutative groups in which $a \oplus b = b \oplus a$.

The number of unique elements in $\mathbb{Z}_N^*$ (often referred to as the *order* of the group) is denoted by the the Euler Totient function $\Phi(N)$.

$$\begin{aligned} \Phi(p) &= p - 1 & &\text{if } p \text{ is prime} \\ \Phi(N) &= (p-1)(q-1) & &\text{if } N = pq \text{ and } p, q \text{ are primes} \end{aligned}$$

The first case follows because all elements less than p will be relatively prime to p. The second case requires some simple counting (show this by counting the number of multiples of p and q that are less than N).

The structure of these multiplicative groups offer some special properties which we exploit throughout this course. One of the first properties is the following identity first proven by Euler in 1758 and published in 1763 [EUL63].

▷**Theorem 47.10 (Euler)** $\forall a \in \mathbb{Z}_N^*, a^{\Phi(N)} = 1 \bmod N$

Proof. Consider the set $A = \{ax \mid x \in \mathbb{Z}_N^*\}$. Since $\mathbb{Z}_N^*$ is a group, every element ax of A must also be in $\mathbb{Z}_N^*$ and so it follows that $A \subseteq \mathbb{Z}_N^*$. Now suppose that $|A| < |\mathbb{Z}_N^*|$. By the pidgeonhole principle, this implies that there exist two group element $i, j \in \mathbb{Z}_N^*$ such that $i \neq j$ but $ai = aj$. Since $a \in \mathbb{Z}_N^*$, there exists an inverse a^{-1} such that $aa^{-1} = 1$. Multiplying on both sides we have $a^{-1}ai = a^{-1}aj \implies i = j$ which is a contradiction. Thus, $|A| = |\mathbb{Z}_N^*|$ which implies that $A = \mathbb{Z}_N^*$.

Because the group $\mathbb{Z}_N^*$ is abelian (i.e., commutative), we can take products and substitute the definition of A to get

$$\prod_{x\in\mathbb{Z}_N^*} x = \prod_{y\in A} y = \prod_{x\in\mathbb{Z}_N^*} ax$$

The product further simplifies as

$$\prod_{x\in\mathbb{Z}_N^*} x = a^{\Phi(N)} \prod_{x\in\mathbb{Z}_N^*} x$$

Finally, since the closure property guarantees that $\prod_{x\in\mathbb{Z}_N^*} x \in \mathbb{Z}_N^*$ and since the inverse property guarantees that this element has an inverse, we can multiply the inverse on both sides to obtain

$$1 = a^{\Phi(N)}.$$

$\square$

▷**Corollary 48.11 (Fermat's Little Thm.)** $\forall a \in \mathbb{Z}_p^*, a^{p-1} \equiv 1 \bmod p$.

▷**Corollary 48.12** $a^x \bmod N = a^{x \bmod \Phi(N)} \bmod N$.

Thus, given $\Phi(N)$, the operation $a^x \bmod N$ can be computed efficiently in $\mathbb{Z}_N^*$ for any x.

Example Compute $2^{6^{1241}} \bmod 21$ using only paper and pencil.

2.6.5 Primality Testing

An important task in generating the parameters of many cryptographic schemes will be the identification of a suitably large prime number. Eratosthenes (276–174BC), a librarian of Alexandria, is credited with devising an elementary sieving method to enumerate all primes. However, his method is not practical for choosing a large (i.e., 1000 digit) prime.

Instead, recall that Fermat's Little Theorem establishes that $a^{p-1} = 1 \bmod p$ for any $a \in \mathbb{Z}_p$ whenever p is prime. It turns

out that when p is not prime, then a^{p-1} is *usually not* equal to
1. The first fact and second phenomena form the basic idea
behind the a primality test: to test p, pick a random $a \in \mathbb{Z}_p$, and
check whether $a^{p-1} = 1 \bmod p$. Notice that efficient modular
exponentiation is critical for this test. Unfortunately, the second
phenomena is *on rare occasion* false. Despite there rarity (starting
with $561, 1105, 1729, \ldots$, there are only 255 such cases less than
10^8), there are an infinite number of counter examples collectively
known as the *Carmichael* numbers. Thus, for correctness, our
procedure must handle these rare cases. To do so, we add a
second check that verifies that none of the *intermediate* powers of a
encountered during the modular exponentiation computation of
a^{n-1} are non-trivial square-roots of 1. This suggest the following
approach known as the Miller-Rabin primality test presented by
Miller [MIL76] and Rabin [RAB80].

For positive N, write $N = u2^j$ where u is odd. Define the set

$$L_N = \left\{ \alpha \in \mathbb{Z}_N \mid \alpha^{N-1} = 1 \text{ and if } \alpha^{u2^{j+1}} = 1 \text{ then } \alpha^{u2^j} = 1 \right\}$$

ALGORITHM 49.13: MILLER-RABIN PRIMALITY TEST

1: Handle base case $N = 2$
2: **for** t times **do**
3:    Pick a random $\alpha \in \mathbb{Z}_N$
4:    **if** $\alpha \notin L_N$ **then**
5:       Output "composite"
6:    **end if**
7: **end for**
8: Output "prime"

Observe that testing whether $\alpha \in L_N$ can be done by using a
repeated-squaring algorithm to compute modular exponentiation,
and adding internal checks to make sure that no non-trivial roots
of unity are discovered.

▷**Theorem 49.14** *If N is composite, then the Miller-Rabin test outputs
"composite" with probability $1 - 2^{-t}$. If N is prime, then the test outputs
"prime."*

The proof of this theorem follows from the following lemma:

▷**Lemma 50.15** *If N is an odd prime, then $|L_N| = N - 1$. If $N > 2$ is composite, then $|L_N| < (N-1)/2$.*

We will not prove this lemma here. See [CLRS09] for a full proof. The proof idea is as follows. If N is prime, then by Fermat's Little Theorem, the first condition will always hold, and since 1 only has two square roots modulo N (namely, $1, -1$), the second condition holds as well. If N is composite, then either there will be some α for which α^{N-1} is not equal to 1 or the process of computing α^{N-1} reveals a square root of 1 which is different from 1 or -1. More formally, the proof works by first arguing that all of the $\alpha \notin L_N$ form a *proper* subgroup of $\mathbb{Z}_N^*$. Since the order of a subgroup must divide the order of the group, the size of a proper subgroup must therefore be less than $(N-1)/2$.

We mention that a more complicated (and less efficient) *deterministic* polynomial-time algorithm for primality testing was recently presented by Agrawal, Kayal, and Saxena [AKS04].

2.6.6 Selecting a Random Prime

Our algorithm for finding a random n-bit prime repeatedly samples an n-bit number and then checks whether it is prime.

ALGORITHM 50.16: SAMPLEPRIME(n)

1: **repeat**
2:    $x \xleftarrow{r} \{0,1\}^n$
3: **until** MILLER-RABIN(x) = "prime"
4: **return** x

Two mathematical facts allow this simple scheme to work. First, there are many primes: By Theorem 31.3, the probability that a uniformly sampled n-bit integer is prime exceeds $(2^n/n)/2^n = \frac{1}{n}$. Thus, the expected number of iterations of the loop in Algorithm 50.16 is polynomial in n.

Second, it is easy to determine whether a number is prime. Since the running time of the Miller-Rabin algorithm is also polynomial in n, the expected running time to sample a random prime using the simple guess-and-check approach is polynomial in n.

▷**Lemma 51.17** *Algorithm SamplePrime outputs a randomly selected n-bit prime number in time* $\mathrm{poly}(n)$.

2.7 Factoring-based Collection of OWF

Under the factoring assumption, we can prove the following result, which establishes our first realistic collection of one-way functions:

▷**Theorem 51.1** *Let* $\mathcal{F} = \{f_i : \mathcal{D}_i \to \mathcal{R}_i\}_{i \in I}$ *where*

$$I = \mathbb{N}$$

$$\mathcal{D}_i = \{(p,q) \mid p,q \text{ are prime and } |p| = |q| = \frac{i}{2}\}$$

$$f_i(p,q) = p \cdot q$$

If the Factoring Assumption holds, then $\mathcal{F}$ *is a collection of one-way functions.*

Proof. We can sample a random element of the index set $\mathbb{N}$. It is easy to evaluate f_i because multiplication is efficiently computable, and the factoring assumption states that inverting f_i is hard. Thus, all that remains is to present a method to efficiently sample two random prime numbers. This follows from Lemma 51.17 above. Thus all four conditions in the definition of a one-way collection are satisfied. ☐

2.8 Discrete Logarithm-based Collection

Another often used collection is based on the discrete logarithm problem in the group $\mathbb{Z}_p^*$ for a prime p.

2.8.1 Discrete logarithm modulo p

An instance (p,g,y) of the discrete logarithm problem consists of a prime p and two elements $g,y \in \mathbb{Z}_p^*$. The task is to find an x such that $g^x = y \bmod p$. In some special cases (e.g., $g = 1$ or when $p-1$ has many small prime factors), it is easy to either declare that no solution exists or solve the problem. However, when g is a *generator* of $\mathbb{Z}_p^*$, the problem is believed to be hard.

▷**Definition 52.1 (Generator of a Group)** *A element g of a multiplicative group G is a generator if the set $\{g, g^2, g^3, \ldots\} = G$. We denote the set of all generators of a group G by Gen_G.*

▷**Assumption 52.2 (Discrete Log)** *If G_q is a group of prime order q, then for every adversary $\mathcal{A}$, there exists a negligible function ϵ such that*

$$\Pr\left[q \leftarrow \Pi_n; g \leftarrow \mathrm{Gen}_{G_q}; x \leftarrow \mathbb{Z}_q : \mathcal{A}(g^x) = x\right] < \epsilon(n)$$

Recall that Π_n is the set of n-bit prime numbers. Note that it is important that G is a group of *prime*-order. Thus, for example, the normal multiplicative group $\mathbb{Z}_p^*$ has order $(p-1)$ and therefore does not satisfy the assumption.

Instead, one usually picks a prime of the form $p = 2q + 1$ (known as a Sophie Germain prime or a "safe prime") and then sets G to be the subgroup of squares in $\mathbb{Z}_p^*$. Notice that this subgroup has order q which is prime. The practical method for sampling safe primes is simple: first pick a prime q as usual, and then check whether $2q + 1$ is also prime. Unfortunately, even though this procedure always terminates in practice, its basic theoretical properties are unknown. It is unknown even (a) whether there are an infinite number of Sophie Germain primes, (b) and even so, whether this simple procedure for finding them continues to quickly succeed as the size of q increases. Another way to instantiate the assumption is to use the points on an elliptic curve for which these issues do not arise.

▷**Theorem 52.3** *Let* $\mathbf{DL} = \{f_i : \mathcal{D}_i \to \mathcal{R}_i\}_{i \in I}$ *where*

$$I = \{(q, g) \mid q \in \Pi_k, g \in \mathrm{Gen}_{G_q}\}$$
$$\mathcal{D}_i = \{x \mid x \in \mathbb{Z}_q\}$$
$$\mathcal{R}_i = G_p$$
$$f_{p,g}(x) = g^x$$

If the Discrete Log Assumption holds, then $\mathbf{DL}$ is a collection of one-way functions.

Proof. It is easy to sample the domain D_i and to evaluate the function $f_{p,g}(x)$. The discrete log assumption implies that $f_{p,g}$ is hard to invert. Thus, all that remains is to prove that I can be sampled efficiently. Unfortunately, given only a prime p, it is not known how to efficiently choose a generator $g \in Gen_p$. However, it is possible to sample both a prime *and* a generator g at the same time. One approach proposed by Bach and later adapted by Kalai is to sample a k-bit integer x in factored form (i.e., sample the integer and its factorization at the same time) such that $p = x + 1$ is prime. A special case of this approach is to pick safe primes of the form $p = 2q + 1$ as mentioned above. Given such a pair $p, (q_1, \ldots, q_k)$, one can use a central result from group theory to test whether an element is a generator. For example, in the case of safe primes, testing whether an element $g \in \mathbb{Z}_p^*$ is a generator consists of checking $g \neq \pm 1 \bmod p$ and $g^q \neq 1 \bmod p$. $\qquad\square$

As we will see later, the collection **DL** is also a special collection of one-way functions in which each function is a permutation.

2.9   RSA Collection

Another popular assumption is the RSA Assumption. The RSA Assumption implies the Factoring assumption; it is not known whether the converse is true.

▷**Assumption 53.1 (RSA Assumption)** *Given a triple (N, e, y) such that $N = pq$ where $p, q \in \Pi_n$, $\gcd(e, \Phi(N)) = 1$ and $y \in \mathbb{Z}_N^*$, the probability that any adversary $\mathcal{A}$ is able to produce x such that $x^e = y \bmod N$ is a negligible function $\epsilon(n)$.*

$$\Pr \left[\begin{array}{l} p, q \xleftarrow{r} \Pi_n; \ N \leftarrow pq; \ e \xleftarrow{r} \mathbb{Z}_{\Phi(N)}^*; \\ y \leftarrow \mathbb{Z}_N^*; \ x \leftarrow \mathcal{A}(N, e, y) \end{array} : x^e = y \bmod N \right] < \epsilon(n)$$

▷**Theorem 53.2 (RSA Collection)** *Let RSA $= \{f_i : \mathcal{D}_i \to \mathcal{R}_i\}_{i \in I}$ where*

$$I = \{(N, e) \mid N = p \cdot q \ s.t. \ p, q \in \Pi_n \ and \ e \in \mathbb{Z}_{\Phi(N)}^*\}$$
$$\mathcal{D}_i = \{x \mid x \in \mathbb{Z}_N^*\}$$
$$\mathcal{R}_i = \mathbb{Z}_N^*$$
$$f_{N,e}(x) = x^e \bmod N$$

Under the RSA Assumption, **RSA** *is a collection of one-way functions.*

Proof. The set I is easy to sample: generate two primes p, q, multiply then to generate N, and use the fact that $\Phi(N) = (p-1)(q-1)$ to sample a random element from $\mathbb{Z}^*_{\Phi(N)}$. Likewise, the set D_i is also easy to sample and the function $f_{N,e}$ requires only one modular exponentiation to evaluate. It only remains to show that $f_{N,e}$ is difficult to invert. Notice, however, that this does not *directly* follow from the our hardness assumption (as it did in previous examples). The RSA assumption states that it is difficult to compute the eth root of a *random* group element y. On the other hand, our collection first picks the root and then computes $y \leftarrow x^e \mod N$. One could imagine that picking an element that is *known* to have an eth root makes it easier to find such a root. We prove that this is not the case by showing that the function $f_{N,e}(x) = x^e \mod N$ is a permutation of the elements of $\mathbb{Z}^*_N$. Thus, the distributions $\{x, e \overset{r}{\leftarrow} \mathbb{Z}^*_N : (e, x^e \mod N)\}$ and $\{y, e \overset{r}{\leftarrow} \mathbb{Z}^*_N : (e, y)\}$ are identical, and so an algorithm that inverts $f_{N,e}$ would also succeed at breaking the RSA-assumption. $\square$

▷**Theorem 54.3** *The function $f_{N,e}(x) = x^e \mod N$ is a permutation of $\mathbb{Z}^*_N$ when $e \in \mathbb{Z}^*_{\Phi(N)}$.*

Proof. Since e is an element of the group $Z^*_{\Phi(N)}$, let d be its inverse (recall that every element in a group has an inverse), i.e. $ed = 1 \mod \Phi(N)$. Consider the inverse map $g_{N,e}(x) = x^d \mod N$. Now for any $x \in \mathbb{Z}^*_N$,

$$g_{N,e}(f_{N,e}(x)) = g_{N,e}(x^e \mod N) = (x^e \mod N)^d \mod N$$
$$= x^{ed} \mod N$$
$$= x^{c\Phi(N)+1} \mod N$$

for some constant c. Recall that Euler's theorem establishes that $x^{\Phi(N)} = 1 \mod N$. Thus, the above can be simplified as

$$x^{c\Phi(N)} \cdot x \mod N = x \mod N$$

Hence, RSA is a permutation. $\square$

This phenomena suggests that we formalize a new, stronger class of one-way functions.

2.10   One-way Permutations

▷**Definition 55.1** (One-way permutation). A collection $\mathcal{F} = \{f_i : \mathcal{D}_i \rightarrow R_i\}_{i \in I}$ is a collection of *one-way permutations* if $\mathcal{F}$ is a collection of one-way functions and for all $i \in I$, we have that f_i is a permutation.

A natural question is whether this extra property comes at a price—that is, how does the RSA-assumption that we must make compare to a natural assumption such as factoring. Here, we can immediately show that RSA is at least as strong an assumption as Factoring.

▷**Theorem 55.2** *The RSA assumption implies the Factoring assumption.*

Proof. We prove by contrapositive: if factoring is possible in polynomial time, then we can break the RSA assumption in polynomial time. Formally, assume there an algorithm A and polynomial function $p(n)$ so that A can factor $N = pq$ with probability $1/p(n)$, where p and q are random n-bits primes. Then there exists an algorithm A', which can invert $f_{N,e}$ with probability $1/p(n)$, where $N = pq$, p, $q \leftarrow \{0,1\}^n$ primes, and $e \leftarrow \mathbb{Z}^*_{\Phi(N)}$.

ALGORITHM 55.3: ADVERSARY $A'(N, e, y)$

1: Run $(p, q) \leftarrow A(N)$ to recover prime factors of N
2: If $N \neq pq$ then abort
3: Compute $\Phi(N) \leftarrow (p-1)(q-1)$
4: Compute the inverse d of e in $\mathbb{Z}^*_{\Phi(N)}$ using Euclid
5: Output $y^d \bmod N$

The algorithm feeds the factoring algorithm A with exactly the same distribution of inputs as with the factoring assumption. Hence in the first step A will return the correct prime factors with probability $1/p(n)$. Provided that the factors are correct, then we can compute the inverse of y in the same way as we construct the inverse map of $f_{N,e}$. And this always succeeds with probability 1. Thus overall, A' succeeds in breaking the RSA-assumption with probability $1/p(n)$. Moreover, the running time of A' is essentially the running time of A plus $O(\log^3(n))$. Thus, if A succeeds in factoring in polynomial time, then A' succeeds in breaking the RSA-assumption in roughly the same time.   □

Unfortunately, as mentioned above, it is not known whether the converse it true—i.e., whether the factoring assumption also implies the RSA-assumption.

2.11   Trapdoor Permutations

The proof that RSA is a permutation actually suggests another special property of that collection: if the factorization of N is unknown, then inverting $f_{N,e}$ is considered infeasiable; however if the factorization of N is *known*, then it is no longer hard to invert. In this sense, the factorization of N is a *trapdoor* which enables $f_{N,e}$ to be inverted.

This spawns the idea of trapdoor permutations, first conceived by Diffie and Hellman.

▷**Definition 56.1** (Trapdoor Permutations). A *collection of trapdoor permutations* is a family $\mathcal{F} = \{f_i : \mathcal{D}_i \to \mathcal{R}_i\}_{i \in \mathcal{I}}$ satisfying the following properties:

1. $\forall i \in \mathcal{I}$, f_i is a permutation,

2. *It is easy to sample a function:* ∃ p.p.t. Gen s.t. $(i,t) \leftarrow$ Gen(1^n), $i \in \mathcal{I}$ (t is trapdoor info),

3. *It is easy to sample the domain:* there exists a p.p.t. machine that given input $i \in \mathcal{I}$, samples uniformly in $\mathcal{D}_i$.

4. f_i *is easy to evaluate:* there exists a p.p.t. machine that given input $i \in \mathcal{I}, x \in \mathcal{D}_i$, computes $f_i(x)$.

5. f_i *is hard to invert:* for all p.p.t. $\mathcal{A}$, there exists a negligible function ϵ such that
$$\Pr\left[\begin{array}{l} (i,t) \leftarrow \text{Gen}(1^n); x \leftarrow \mathcal{D}_i; \\ y \leftarrow f(x); z \leftarrow A(1^n, i, y) \end{array} : f_i(z) = y \right] \leq \epsilon(k)$$

6. f_i *is easy to invert with trapdoor information:* there exists a p.p.t. machine that given input (i,t) from Gen and $y \in \mathcal{R}_i$, computes $f^{-1}(y)$.

Now by slightly modifying the definition of the family **RSA**, we can easily show that it is a collection of trapdoor permutations.

▷**Theorem 57.2** *Let **RSA** be defined as per Theorem 53.2 with the exception that*

$$[(N, e), d] \leftarrow \mathsf{Gen}(1^n)$$
$$f_{N,d}^{-1}(y) = y^d \bmod N$$

where $N = p \cdot q$, $e \in \mathbb{Z}^*_{\Phi(N)}$ and $e \cdot d = 1 \bmod \Phi(N)$. Assuming the RSA-assumption, the collection RSA is a collection of trapdoor permutations.

The proof is an exercise.

2.12   Rabin collection

The RSA assumption essentially claims that it is difficult to compute e^{th} roots modulo a composite N that is a product of two primes. A weaker assumption is that it is even hard to compute square roots modulo N (without knowing the factors of N). Note that computing square roots is not a special case of RSA since $\gcd(2, \phi(N)) \neq 1$. This assumption leads to the Rabin collection of trapdoor functions; interestingly, we will show that this assumption is equivalent to the Factoring assumption (whereas it is not known whether Factoring implies the RSA assumption). To develop these ideas, we first present a general theory of square roots modulo a prime p, and then extend it to square roots modulo a composite N.

Square roots modulo p

Taking square roots over the integers is a well-studied and efficient operation. As we now show, taking square roots *modulo* a prime number is also easy.

Define the set $\mathrm{QR}_p = \{x^2 \bmod p | x \in \mathbb{Z}^*_p\}$. These numbers are called the *quadratic residues* for p and they form a subgroup of $\mathbb{Z}^*_p$ that contains roughly half of its the elements.

▷**Lemma 57.1** *If $p > 2$ is prime, then QR_p is a group of size $\frac{p-1}{2}$.*

Proof. Since $1^2 = (-1)^2 = 1$, QR_p contains the identity. Since the product of squares is also a square, QR_p is closed. Associativity carries over from $\mathbb{Z}_p$. Finally, if $a = x^2 \in QR_p$, then $a^{-1} = (x^{-1})^2$ is also a square, and so QR_p contains inverses.

To analyze the size of QR_p, observe that if $x^2 = a$, then $(p - x)^2 = a$ and that because p is odd, $(p - x) \neq x$. On the other hand, if $x^2 = y^2$, then $(x + y)(x - y) = 0 \bmod p$. Because p is a prime, either $(x + y) = 0 \bmod p$ or $(x - y) = 0 \bmod p$. Thus, for every $a \in QR_p$ there are exactly two distinct values for $x \in \mathbb{Z}_p$ such that $x^2 = a$. It follows that $|QR_p| = (p - 1)/2$.   □

For every prime p, the square root operation can be performed efficiently. We show how to compute square roots for the special case of primes that are of the form $4k + 3$. The remaining cases are left as an exercise.

▷**Theorem 58.2** *If $p = 3 + 4k$ and $y \in QR_p$, then $(\pm y^{k+1})^2 = y$.*

Proof. Since $y \in QR_p$, let $y = a^2 \bmod p$. Thus,

$$(y^{k+1})^2 = a^{2(k+1)2} = a^{4k+4} = a^{p+1} = a^2 = y \bmod p$$

□

Exercise Show how to compute square roots if $p = 1 \bmod 4$.

Toward our goal of understanding square roots modulo a composite $N = p \cdot q$, we now introduce a new tool.

Chinese Remainder Theorem

Let $N = pq$ and suppose $y \in \mathbb{Z}_N$. Consider the numbers $a_1 \equiv y \bmod p$ and $a_2 \equiv y \bmod q$. The Chinese remainder theorem states that y can be uniquely recovered from the pair a_1, a_2 and vice versa.

▷**Theorem 58.3 (Chinese Remainder)** *Let $p_1, p_2, \ldots, p_k$ be pairwise relatively prime integers, i.e. $\gcd(p_i, p_j) = 1$ for $1 \leq i < j \leq k$ and $N = \prod_i^k p_i$. The map $C_N(y) : \mathbb{Z}_n \mapsto \mathbb{Z}_{p_1} \times \cdots \times \mathbb{Z}_{p_k}$ defined as*

$$C_N(y) \mapsto (y \bmod p_1, y \bmod p_2, \ldots, y \bmod p_k)$$

is one-to-one and onto.

Proof. For each i, set $n_i = N/p_i \in \mathbb{Z}$. By our hypothesis, for each $i \in [1,k]$, it follows that $\gcd(p_i, n_i) = 1$ and hence there exists $b_i \in \mathbb{Z}_{p_i}$ such that $n_i b_i = 1 \bmod p_i$. Let $c_i = b_i n_i$. Notice that $c_i = 1 \bmod p_i = 0 \bmod p_j$ for $j \neq i$. Set $y = \sum_i c_i a_i \bmod N$. Then $y = a_i \bmod p_i$ for each i.

Further, if $y' = a_i \bmod p_i$ for each i then $y' = y \bmod p_i$ for each i and since the p_is are pairwise relatively prime, it follows that $y \equiv y' \bmod N$, proving uniqueness. $\qquad\qquad\square$

Example Suppose $p = 7$ and $q = 11$. Since 7 and 11 are relatively prime, we have that

$$11 \cdot 2 \equiv 1 \bmod 7$$
$$7 \cdot 8 \equiv 1 \bmod 11$$

and therefore $b_1 = 2$ and $b_2 = 8$. Thus, we have

$$C(y) \mapsto (y \bmod 7, y \bmod 11)$$
$$C^{-1}(a_1, a_2) \mapsto a_1 \cdot 22 + a_2 \cdot 56 \bmod 77$$

Notice that computing the coefficients b_1 and b_2 requires two calls to Euclid's algorithm, and computing f^{-1} requires only two modular multiplications and an addition. Thus, computing the map in either direction can be done efficiently given the factors $p_1, \ldots, p_k$.

Square roots modulo N

We are now ready to study the problem of computing square roots in $\mathbb{Z}_N$ when $N = pq$. As before, we define the set $QR_N = \{x^2 \bmod n : x \in \mathbb{Z}_N^*\}$. Then we claim:

▷**Theorem 59.4** *Let $N = pq$ and for any $x \in \mathbb{Z}_N^*$, let $(y, z) \leftarrow C_N(x)$. Then $x \in QR_N \Leftrightarrow y \in QR_p$ and $z in QR_q$.*

Proof. $\Rightarrow$ Since $y \in QR_p$ and $z \in QR_q$, then there exists $a \in \mathbb{Z}_p^*$ such that $y \equiv a^2 \bmod p$ and $\exists b \in \mathbb{Z}_q^*$ such that $z \equiv b^2 \bmod q$. By the Chinese Remainder Theorem, there exists $s \leftarrow C_N^{-1}(a, b)$. We show that s is one square root of x in Z_n^*:

$$s^2 \bmod p \equiv a^2 \bmod p \equiv y \bmod p$$
$$s^2 \bmod q \equiv b^2 \bmod q \equiv z \bmod q$$

Therefore s^2 is congruent to x modulo N and hence s is x's square root, and $x \in QR_N$.

For the other direction of the proof, if $x \in QR_N$, then $\exists a \in \mathbb{Z}_N^*$ such that $x \equiv a^2 \bmod n$. Therefore

$$x \bmod p \equiv a^2 \bmod p \equiv (a \bmod p)^2 \bmod p \Rightarrow y \in QR_p$$
$$x \bmod q \equiv a^2 \bmod q \equiv (a \bmod q)^2 \bmod q \Rightarrow z \in QR_q$$

$\square$

Furthermore, we can characterize the size of the group QR_N.

▷**Theorem 60.5** *The mapping $x \to x^2 \bmod N$ is 4 to 1.*

Proof. From Thm. 59.4, if $x \in QR_N$, then $y \equiv x \bmod p \in QR_p$ and $z \equiv x \bmod q \in QR_q$.

Earlier, we proved that $|QR_p| = |\mathbb{Z}_p^*|/2$ and the mapping $x \to x^2$, $x \in \mathbb{Z}_p^*$ is 2 to 1. So we have unique square roots a_1, a_2 for y and b_1, b_2 for z. Take any two of them a_i, b_j, by Chinese remainder theorem $\exists s \in Z_N^*$, such that $s \equiv a_i \bmod p$ and $s \equiv b_j \bmod q$. And by the same argument in the proof of Thm. 59.4, s is a square root of x in $\mathbb{Z}_N^*$. There are in total 4 combinations of a_i and b_j, thus we have 4 such s that are x's square roots. $\square$

▷**Corollary 60.6** $|QR_N| = |\mathbb{Z}_N^*|/4$

Remark that given p and q, it is easy to compute the square roots for elements in Z_N^*. The proof above shows that the square root of $x \in \mathbb{Z}_N^*$ can be combined from square roots of $x \bmod p$ and $x \bmod q$ in Z_p^* and Z_q^* respectively. And from previous sections, we have shown that square root operation is efficient in Z_p^*. So given p and q, we can simply calculate the square roots of $x \bmod p$ and $x \bmod q$, and combine the result to get square roots of x. However, without p and q, it is not known whether square roots modulo N can be efficiently computed.

Example Continuing our example from above with $N = 7 \cdot 11 = 77$, consider $71 \in \mathbb{Z}_N^*$. Thus, we have $(1,5) \leftarrow C(42)$. Taking square roots mod 7 and 11, we have $(1,4)$, and now using C^{-1}, we arrive at $15 \leftarrow C^{-1}(0,3)$. Notice, however, that $(6,4)$, $(1,7)$, and $(6,7)$ are also roots. These pairs map to 48,29, and 62 respectively.

2.12.1 The Rabin Collection

▷**Theorem 61.7** *Let* $R = \{f_i : D_i \to R_i\}_{i \in I}$ *where*

$$I = \{N : N = p \cdot q, \text{ where } p, q \in \Pi_n\}$$
$$D_i = \mathbb{Z}_N^*$$
$$R_i = QR_N$$
$$f_N(x) = x^2 \bmod N$$

If the Factoring Assumption holds, then **R** *is a collection of one-way functions.*

Relationship for Factoring

The interesting fact is that the Rabin Collection relies only on the Factoring assumption, whereas the RSA collection requires a stronger assumption to the best of our knowledge. In other words, we can show:

▷**Theorem 61.8** *Rabin is a OWF iff factoring assumption holds.*

Proof. $\Rightarrow$ We first show that if factoring is hard then Rabin is a OWF. We prove this by contrapositive: if Rabin can be inverted then factoring can be done efficiently. Formally, if there exists an adversary $\mathcal{A}$ and polynomial function $p(n)$ such that $\mathcal{A}$ can invert f_N with probability $1/p(n)$ for sufficiently large n, that is if

$$\Pr\left[\begin{array}{l} p, q \leftarrow \Pi_n, N \leftarrow pq, x \leftarrow \mathbb{Z}_N^*, \\ y \leftarrow f_N(x), z \leftarrow \mathcal{A}(N, y) \end{array} : z^2 = y \bmod N\right] > 1/p(k)$$

then there exists $\mathcal{A}'$ that can factor the product of two random n-bits primes with probability $1/2p(n)$:

$$\Pr\left[p, q \leftarrow \Pi_n, N \leftarrow pq : \mathcal{A}'(N) \in \{p, q\}\right] > 1/2p(k)$$

We construct $A'(N)$ as follows:

ALGORITHM 62.9: FACTORING ADVERSARY $A'(N)$

1: Sample $x \leftarrow \mathbb{Z}_N^*$
2: Compute $y \leftarrow x^2 \bmod N$
3: Run $z \leftarrow A(y, N)$
4: If $z^2 \neq y \bmod N$ then abort.
5: Else output $\gcd(x - z, N)$.

First, because the input to A' is the product of two random k-bits primes and A' randomly samples x from Z_n^*, the inputs (y, N) to A in step 3 have exactly the same distribution as those from the Rabin collection. Thus algorithm A will return a correct square root of x with probability $1/p(k)$. And because A does not know x and it outputs one of the four square roots with equal probability, then with probability $1/2p(k)$, $z \not\equiv x$ and $z \not\equiv -x$. Since x and z are both square roots of y, we have

$$x^2 \equiv z^2 \bmod n \quad \Rightarrow \quad (x - z)(x + z) \equiv 0 \bmod n$$

When $z \not\equiv x$ and $z \not\equiv -x$, it can only be that they are congruent modulo p and q. Then the $\gcd(x - z, N)$ would be p or q with probability $1/2p(k)$. Thus adversary A' factors N.

Only if direction: We want to show if Rabin is hard then factoring is also hard. Similar to the proof of that RSA is OWP implies factoring is hard, we show by contrapositive, that is, if there exists an adversary A that factors $N = pq$ with probability $1/r(k)$ for some polynomial r, where p and q are random k-bits primes, then by using the Chinese Remainder Theorem, it is straightforward to compute square roots modulo N with $1/p(k)$.

The construction of $A'(N, y)$ is also similar to that in RSA case: first feed A with N, which returns p, q. Check whether $N = pq$, if not then abort, else compute square root of $y \bmod p$ and $y \bmod q$ in Z_p^* and Z_q^* respectively. Pick one pair of square roots a, b and compute $s = ac + bd$. Output s.

Since A receives N with the same distribution as in the factoring assumption, A will succeed in factoring with probability $1/r(k)$ and from the correct p, q we can compute the square root of u with probability 1. Overall A' succeeds with probability $1/r(k)$. $\qquad\qquad\qquad\qquad\qquad\qquad \square$

Rabin Collection of Trapdoor Permutations

Technically, Rabin is not a permutation, but by making some small adjustments, we can construct a collection of trapoor permutations as well:

▷**Theorem 63.10** *Let* $R = \{f_i : D_i \to R_i\}_{i \in I}$ *where*

$$I = \{N | N = pq, \text{ where } p, q \in \Pi_n, p = q = 3 \mod 4\}$$
$$D_i = QR_N$$
$$R_i = QR_N$$

$\text{Gen}(1^n) :$ *Samples a pair* $(N, (p, q))$ *s.t.* $N \in I$

$\quad f_N(x) = x^2 \mod N$

$\quad f_{p,q}^{-1}(y) = x$ *such that* $x^2 = y \mod N$ *and* $x \in QR_N$

If the Factoring Assumption holds, then **R** *is a collection of trapdoor permutations.*

As we'll show in future homeworks, each square in Q_N has four square roots, but only one of the roots is also a square. This makes Rabin a (trapdoor) permutation.

2.13   A Universal One Way Function

As we have mentioned in previous sections, it is not known whether one-way functions exist. Although we have presented specific assumptions which have lead to specific constructions, a much weaker assumption is to assume only that *some* one-way function exists (without knowing exactly which one). The following theorem gives a single constructible function that is one-way if this weaker assumption is true.

▷**Theorem 63.1** *If there exists a one-way function, then the following polynomial-time computable function $f_{universal}$ is also a one-way function.*

Proof. We will construct function $f_{universal}$ and show that it is weakly one-way. We can then apply the hardness amplification construction from §2.3 to get a strong one-way function.

The idea behind the construction is that $f_{\text{universal}}$ incorporates the computation of all efficient functions in such a way that inverting $f_{\text{universal}}$ allows us to invert all other functions. This ambitious goal can be approached by intrepreting the input y to $f_{\text{universal}}$ as a machine-input pair $y = \langle M, x \rangle$, and then defining the output of $f_{\text{universal}}(y)$ to be $M(x)$. The problem with this approach is that $f_{\text{universal}}$ will not be computable in polynomial time, since M may not even terminate on input x. We can overcome this problem by only running $M(x)$ for a number of steps related to $|y|$.

ALGORITHM 64.2: A UNIVERSAL ONE-WAY FUNCTION $f_{\text{UNIVERSAL}}(y)$

Interpret y as $\langle M, x \rangle$ where $|M| = \log(|y|)$
Run M on input x for $|y|^3$ steps
if M terminates then
    Output $M(x)$
else
    Output $\perp$
end if

In words, this function interprets the first $\log |y|$ bits of the input y as a machine M, and the remaining bits are considered input x. We assume a standard way to encode Turing machines with appropriate padding. We claim that this function is weakly one-way. Clearly $f_{\text{universal}}$ is computable in time $O(|y|^3)$, and thus it satisfies the "easy" criterion for being one-way. To show that it satisfies the "hard" criterion, we must assume that there exists some function g that is strongly one-way. By the following lemma, we can assume that g runs in $O(|y|^2)$ time.

▷**Lemma 64.3** *If there exists a strongly one-way function g, then there exists a strongly one-way function g' that is computable in time $O(n^2)$.*

Proof. Suppose g runs in time at most n^c for some $c > 2$. (If not, then the lemma already holds.) Let $g'(\langle a, b \rangle) = \langle a, g(b) \rangle$, where $|a| = n^c - n$ and $|b| = n$. Then if we let $m = |\langle a, b \rangle| = n^c$, the function g' is computable in time

$$\underbrace{|a|}_{\text{copying } a} + \underbrace{|b|^c}_{\text{computing } g} + \underbrace{O(m^2)}_{\text{parsing}} < 2m + O(m^2) = O(m^2)$$

2.13. A Universal One Way Function

Moreover, g' is still one-way, since any adversary that inverts g' can easily be used to invert g. □

Now, if $f_{universal}$ is not weakly one-way, then there exists a machine A such that for every polynomial q and for infinitely many input lengths n,

$$\Pr\left[y \leftarrow \{0,1\}^n; A(f(y)) \in f^{-1}(f(y))\right] > 1 - 1/q(n)$$

In particular, this holds for $q(n) = n^3$. Denote the event that A inverts as Invert.

Let M_g be the smallest machine which computes function g. Since M_g is a uniform algorithm it has some constant description size $|M_g|$. Thus, on a random n-bit input $y = \langle M, x \rangle$, the probability that machine $M = M_g$ (with appropriate padding of 0) is $2^{-\log n} = 1/n$. In other words

$$\Pr\left[y \xleftarrow{r} \{0,1\}^n : y = \langle M_g, x \rangle\right] \geq \frac{1}{n}$$

Denote this event as event PickG. We can now combine the above two equations to conclude that A inverts an instance of g with noticeable probability. By the Union Bound, either A fails to invert or the instance fails to be g with probability at most

$$\Pr[!\text{Invert} \vee !\text{PickG}] \leq (1/n^3) + (1 - 1/n) < \frac{n^3 - 1}{n^3}$$

Therefore, A must invert a hard instance of g with probability

$$\Pr[\text{Invert and PickG}] \geq \frac{1}{n^3}$$

which contradicts the assumption that g is strongly one-way; therefore $f_{universal}$ must be weakly one-way. □

This theorem gives us a function that we can safely assume is one-way (because that assumption is equivalent to the assumption that one-way functions exist). However, it is extremely impractical to compute. First, it is difficult to compute because it involves interpreting random turing machines. Second, it will require very large key lengths before the hardness kicks in. A very open problem is to find a "nicer" universal one way function (e.g. it would be very nice if f_{mult} is universal).

Chapter 3

Indistinguishability & Pseudo-Randomness

Recall that one main drawback of the One-time pad encryption scheme—and its simple encryption operation $\text{Enc}_k(m) = m \oplus k$—is that the key k needs to be as long as the message m. A natural approach for making the scheme more efficient would be to start off with a short random key k and then try to use some *pseudo-random generator* g to expand it into a longer "random-looking" key $k' = g(k)$, and finally use k' as the key in the One-time pad.

Can this be done? We start by noting that there can not exist pseudo-random generators g that on input k generate a *perfectly random* string k', as this would contradict Shannon's theorem (show this). However, remember that Shannon's lower bound relied on the premise that the adversary Eve is computationally unbounded. Thus, if we restrict our attention to efficient adversaries, it might be possible to devise pseudo-random generators that output strings which are "sufficiently" random-looking for our encryption application.

To approach this problem, we must first understand what it means for a string to be "sufficiently random-looking" to a polynomial time adversary. Possible answers include:

— Roughly as many 0 as 1.

— Roughly as many 00 as 11

— Each particular bit is roughly unbiased.

— Each sequence of bits occurs with roughly the same probability.

— Given any prefix, it is hard to guess the next bit.

— Given any prefix, it is hard to guess the next sequence.

All of the above answers are examples of specific *statistical tests*—and many more such test exist in the literature. For specific simulations, it may be enough to use strings that pass some specific statistical tests. However, for cryptography, we require the use of strings that pass *all* (efficient) statistical tests. At first, it seems quite overwhelming to test a candidate pseudo-random generator against *all* efficient tests. To do so requires some more abstract concepts which we now introduce.

3.1   Computational Indistinguishability

We introduce the notion of *computational indistinguishability* to formalize what it means for two probability distributions to "appear" the same from the perspective of a computationally bounded test. This notion is one of the cornerstones of modern cryptography. To begin our discussion, we present two games that illustrate important ideas in the notion of indistinguishability.

Game 1   Flip the page and spend no more than two seconds looking at Fig. 1 that appears on the next page. Do the two boxes contain the same arrangement of circles?

Now suppose you repeat the experiment but spend 10 seconds instead of two. Imagine spending 10 minutes instead of 10 seconds. If you are only given a short amount of time, the two boxes appear indistinguishable from one another. As you take more and more time to analyze the images, you are able to tease apart subtle differences between the left and right. Generalizing, even if two probability distrubutions are completely disjoint, it may be that an observer who is only given limited processing time cannot distinguish between the two distributions.

Game 2   A second issue concerns the size of a problem instance. Consider the following sequence of games parameterized by the

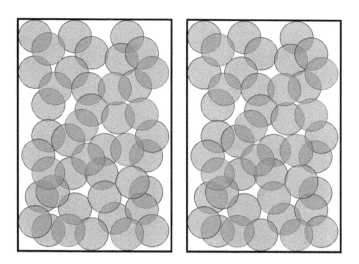

Figure 69.1: Are the two boxes the same or different?

value n in Fig. 2. The point of the game is to determine if the number of overlapping boxes is even or odd. An example of each case is given on the extreme left. The parameter n indicates the number of boxes in the puzzle. Notice that small instances of the puzzle are easy to solve, and thus "odd" instances are easily distinguishable from "even" ones. However, by considering a sequence of puzzles, as n increases, a human's ability to solve the puzzle correctly rapidly approaches $1/2$—i.e., no better than guessing.

As our treatment is asymptotic, the actual formalization of this notion considers sequences—called *ensembles*—of probability distributions (or growing output length).

▷**Definition 69.3 (Ensembles of Probability Distributions)** *A sequence $\{X_n\}_{n\in\mathbb{N}}$ is called an* ensemble *if for each $n \in \mathbb{N}$, X_n is a probability distribution over $\{0,1\}^*$.*

Normally, ensembles are indexed by the natural numbers $n \in \mathbb{N}$. Thus, for the rest of this book, unless otherwise specified, we use $\{X_n\}_n$ to represent such an ensemble.

▷**Definition 69.4 (Computational Indistinguishability).** Let $\{X_n\}_n$ and $\{Y_n\}_n$ be ensembles where X_n, Y_n are distributions over

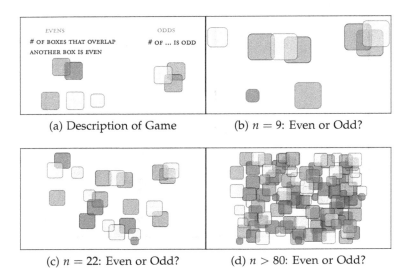

(a) Description of Game   (b) $n = 9$: Even or Odd?

(c) $n = 22$: Even or Odd?   (d) $n > 80$: Even or Odd?

Figure 70.2: A game parameterized by n

$\{0,1\}^{\ell(n)}$ for some polynomial $\ell(\cdot)$. We say that $\{X_n\}_n$ and $\{Y_n\}_n$ are *computationally indistinguishable* (abbr. $\{X_n\}_n \approx \{Y_n\}_n$) if for all non-uniform p.p.t. D (called the "distinguisher"), there exists a negligible function $\epsilon(\cdot)$ such that $\forall n \in \mathbb{N}$

$$\left| \Pr\left[t \leftarrow X_n, D(t) = 1\right] - \Pr\left[t \leftarrow Y_n, D(t) = 1\right] \right| < \epsilon(n).$$

In other words, two (ensembles of) probability distributions are computationally indistinguishable if no efficient distinguisher D can tell them apart better than with a negligible advantage.

To simplify notation, we say that D *distinguishes the distributions* X_n and Y_n with probability ϵ if

$$\left| \Pr\left[t \leftarrow X_n, D(t) = 1\right] - \Pr\left[t \leftarrow Y_n, D(t) = 1\right] \right| > \epsilon.$$

Additionally, we say D *distinguishes the ensembles* $\{X_n\}_n$ and $\{Y_n\}_n$ with probability $\mu(\cdot)$ if $\forall n \in \mathbb{N}$, D distinguishes X_n and Y_n with probability $\mu(n)$.

3.1.1 Properties of Computational Indistinguishability

We highlight some important (and natural) properties of the notion of indistinguishability. This properties will be used over and over again in the remainder of the course.

Closure Under Efficient Opertations

The first property formalizes the statement "If two distributions look the same, then they look the same no matter how you process them" (as long as the processing is efficient). More formally, if two distributions are indistinguishable, then they remain indistinguishable even after one applies a p.p.t. computable operation to them.

▷**Lemma 71.5 (Closure Under Efficient Operations)** *If the pair of ensembles* $\{X_n\}_n \approx \{Y_n\}_n$, *then for any n.u.p.p.t* M, $\{M(X_n)\}_n \approx \{M(Y_n)\}_n$.

Proof. Suppose there exists a non-uniform p.p.t. D and non-negligible function $\mu(n)$ such that D distinguishes $\{M(X_n)\}_n$ from $\{M(Y_n)\}_n$ with probability $\mu(n)$. That is,

$$|\Pr[t \leftarrow M(X_n) : D(t) = 1] - \Pr[t \leftarrow M(Y_n) : D(t) = 1]| > \mu(n)$$

It then follows that

$$|\Pr[t \leftarrow X_n : D(M(t)) = 1] - \Pr[t \leftarrow Y_n : D(M(t)) = 1]| > \mu(n).$$

In that case, the non-uniform p.p.t. machine $D'(\cdot) = D(M(\cdot))$ also distinguishes $\{X_n\}_n$, $\{Y_n\}_n$ with probability $\mu(n)$, which contradicts that the assumption that $\{X_n\}_n \approx \{Y_n\}_n$. $\quad\square$

Transitivity - The Hybrid Lemma

We next show that the notion of computational indistinguishability is transitive; namely, if $\{A_n\}_n \approx \{B_n\}_n$ and $\{B_n\}_n \approx \{C_n\}_n$, then $\{A_n\}_n \approx \{C_n\}_n$. In fact, we prove a generalization of this statement which considers $m = poly(n)$ distributions.

▷**Lemma 71.6 (Hybrid Lemma)** *Let* $X^1, X^2, \ldots, X^m$ *be a sequence of probability distributions. Assume that the machine D distinguishes X^1*

and X^m with probability ϵ. Then there exists some $i \in [1, \ldots, m-1]$ s.t. D distinguishes X^i and X^{i+1} with probability $\frac{\epsilon}{m}$.

Proof. Assume D distinguishes X^1, X^m with probability ϵ. That is,

$$\left| \Pr \left[t \leftarrow X^1 : D(t) = 1 \right] - \Pr \left[t \leftarrow X^m : D(t) = 1 \right] \right| > \epsilon$$

Let $g_i = \Pr \left[t \leftarrow X^i : D(t) = 1 \right]$. Thus, $|g_1 - g_m| > \epsilon$. This implies,

$$|g_1 - g_2| + |g_2 - g_3| + \cdots + |g_{m-1} - g_m|$$
$$\geq |g_1 - g_2 + g_2 - g_3 + \cdots + g_{m-1} - g_m|$$
$$= |g_1 - g_m| > \epsilon.$$

Therefore, there must exist i such that $|g_i - g_{i+1}| > \frac{\epsilon}{m}$.   □

▷**Remark 72.7 (A geometric interpretation)** *Note that the probability with which D outputs 1 induces a metric space over probability distributions over strings t. Given this view the hybrid lemma is just a restatement of the triangle inequality over this metric spaces; in other words, if the distance between two consecutive probability distributions is small, then the distance between the extremal distributions is also small.*

Note that because we lose a factor of m when we have a sequence of m distributions, the hybrid lemma can only be used to deduce transitivity when m is polynomially-related to the security parameter n. (In fact, it is easy to construct a "long" sequence of probability distributions in which each adjacent pair of distributions are indistinguishable, but where the extremal distributions are distinguishable.)

Example

Let $\{X_n\}_n$, $\{Y_n\}_n$ and $\{Z_n\}_n$ be pairwise *indistinguishable* probability ensembles, where X_n, Y_n, and Z_n are distributions over $\{0,1\}^n$. Assume further that we can efficiently sample from all three ensembles. Consider the n.u. p.p.t. machine $M(t)$ that samples $y \leftarrow Y_n$ where $n = |t|$ and outputs $t \oplus y$. Since

$\{X_n\}_n \approx_c \{Z_n\}_n$, closure under efficient operations directly implies that

$$\{x \leftarrow X_n; y \leftarrow Y_n : x \oplus y\}_n \approx_c \{y \leftarrow Y_n; z \leftarrow Z_n : z \oplus y\}_n$$

Distinguishing versus Predicting

The notion of computational indistinguishability requires that no efficient distinguisher can tell apart two distributions with more than a negligible advantage. As a consequence of this property, no efficient machine can *predict* which distribution a sample comes from with probability $\frac{1}{2} + \frac{1}{poly(n)}$; any such predictor would be a valid distinguisher (show this!). As the following useful lemma shows, the converse also holds: if it is not possible to predict which distribution a sample comes from with probability significantly better than $\frac{1}{2}$, then the distributions must be indistinguishable.

▷**Lemma 73.8 (The Prediction Lemma)** *Let $\{X_n^0\}_n$ and $\{X_n^1\}_n$ be two ensembles where X_n^0 and X_n^1 are probability distributions over $\{0,1\}^{\ell(n)}$ for some polynomial $\ell(\cdot)$, and let D be a n.u. p.p.t. machine that distinguishes between $\{X_n^0\}_n$ and $\{X_n^1\}_n$ with probability $\mu(\cdot)$ for infinitely many $n \in \mathbb{N}$. Then there exists a n.u. p.p.t. A such that*

$$\Pr\left[b \leftarrow \{0,1\}; t \leftarrow X_n^b : A(t) = b\right] \geq \frac{1}{2} + \frac{\mu(n)}{2}.$$

for infinitely many $n \in \mathbb{N}$.

Proof. Assume without loss of generality that D outputs 1 with higher probability when receiving a sample from X_n^1 than when receiving a sample from X_n^0, i.e.,

$$\Pr[t \leftarrow X_n^1 : D(t) = 1] - \Pr[t \leftarrow X_n^0 : D(t) = 1] > \mu(n) \quad (73.2)$$

This is without loss of generality since otherwise, D can be replaced with $D'(\cdot) = 1 - D(\cdot)$; one of these distinguishers works for infinitely many $n \in \mathbb{N}$. We show that D is also a "predictor":

$$\Pr\left[b \leftarrow \{0,1\}; t \leftarrow X_n^b : D(t) = b\right]$$

$$= \frac{1}{2}\left(\Pr\left[t \leftarrow X_n^1 : D(t) = 1\right] + \Pr\left[t \leftarrow X_n^0 : D(t) \neq 1\right]\right)$$

$$= \frac{1}{2}\left(\Pr\left[t \leftarrow X_n^1 : D(t) = 1\right] + 1 - \Pr\left[t \leftarrow X_n^0 : D(t) = 1\right]\right)$$

$$= \frac{1}{2} + \frac{1}{2}\left(\Pr\left[t \leftarrow X_n^1 : D(t) = 1\right] - \Pr\left[t \leftarrow X_n^0 : D(t) = 1\right]\right)$$

$$= > \frac{1}{2} + \frac{\mu(n)}{2}$$

$\square$

3.2   Pseudo-randomness

Using the notion of computational indistinguishability, we next turn to defining pseudo-random distributions.

3.2.1   Definition of Pseudo-random Distributions

Let U_n denote the uniform distribution over $\{0,1\}^n$, i.e, $U_n = \{t \leftarrow \{0,1\}^n : t\}$. We say that a distribution is pseudo-random if it is indistinguishable from the uniform distribution.

▷**Definition 74.1** (Pseudo-random Ensembles). The probability ensemble $\{X_n\}_n$, where X_n is a probability distribution over $\{0,1\}^{l(n)}$ for some polynomial $l(\cdot)$, is said to be *pseudorandom* if $\{X_n\}_n \approx \{U_{l(n)}\}_n$.

Note that this definition effectively says that a pseudorandom distribution needs to pass *all* efficiently computable statistical tests that the uniform distribution would have passesd; otherwise the statistical test would distinguish the distributions.

Thus, at first sight it might seem very hard to check or prove that a distribution is pseudorandom. As it turns out, there are *complete* statistical tests; such a test has the property that if a distribution passes only that test, it will also pass all other efficient tests. We proceed to present such a test.

3.2.2 A complete statistical test: The next-bit test

We say that a distribution passes the *next-bit test* if no efficient adversary can, given any prefix of a sequence sampled from the distribution, predict the next bit in the sequence with probability significantely better than $\frac{1}{2}$ (recall that this was one of the test originally suggested in the introduction of this chapter).

▷**Definition 75.2** *An ensemble* $\{X_n\}_n$ *where* X_n *is a probability distribution over* $\{0,1\}^{\ell(n)}$ *for some polynomial* $l(n)$ *is said to pass the Next-Bit Test if for every non-uniform p.p.t.* A, *there exists a negligible function* $\epsilon(n)$ *such that* $\forall n \in \mathbb{N}$ *and* $\forall i \in [0, \cdots, \ell(n)]$, *it holds that*

$$\Pr\left[t \leftarrow X_n : A(1^n, t_1 t_2 \ldots t_i) = t_{i+1}\right] < \frac{1}{2} + \epsilon(n).$$

Here, t_i *denotes the* i'*th bit of* t.

▷**Remark 75.3** *Note that we provide* A *with the additional input* 1^n. *This is simply allow* A *to have size and running-time that is polynomial in* n *and not simply in the (potentially) short prefix* $t_0 \ldots t_i$.

▷**Theorem 75.4 (Completeness of the Next-Bit Test)** *If a probability ensemble* $\{X_n\}_n$ *passes the next-bit test then* $\{X_n\}_n$ *is pseudorandom.*

Proof. Assume for the sake of contradiction that there exists a non-uniform p.p.t. distinguisher D, and a polynomial $p(\cdot)$ such that for infinitely many $n \in \mathbb{N}$, D distinguishes X_n and $U_{\ell(n)}$ with probability $\frac{1}{p(n)}$. We contruct a machine A that predicts the next bit of X_n for every such n. Define a sequence of *hybrid distributions* as follows.

$$H_n^i = \left\{x \leftarrow X_n : u \leftarrow U_{\ell(n)} : x_0 x_1 \ldots x_i u_{i+1} u_{i+2} \ldots u_{\ell(n)}\right\}$$

Note that $H_n^0 = U_{\ell(n)}$ and $H_n^{\ell(n)} = X_n$. Thus, D distinguishes between H_n^0 and $H_n^{\ell(n)}$ with probability $\frac{1}{p(n)}$. It follows from the hybrid lemma that there exists some $i \in [0, \ell(n)]$ such that D distinguishes between H_n^i and H_n^{i+1} with probability $\frac{1}{p(n)\ell(n)}$. Recall, that the only difference between H^{i+1} and H^i is that in

H^{i+1} the $(i+1)^{\text{th}}$ bit is x_{i+1}, whereas in H^i it is u_{i+1}. Thus, intuitively, D—given only the prefix $x_1 \ldots x_i$—can tell apart x_{i+1} from a uniformly chosen bit. This in turn means that D also can tell apart x_{i+1} from $\bar{x}_{i+1}$. More formally, consider the distribution $\tilde{H}_n^i$ defined as follows:

$$\tilde{H}_n^i = \left\{ x \leftarrow X_n \: : \: u \leftarrow U_{\ell(n)} \: : \: x_0 x_1 \ldots x_{i-1} \bar{x}_i u_{i+1} \ldots u_{l(m)} \right\}$$

Note that H_n^i can be sampled by drawing from H_n^{i+1} with probability $1/2$ and drawing from $\tilde{H}_n^{i+1}$ with probability $1/2$. Substituting this identity into the last of term

$$\left| \Pr\left[t \leftarrow H_n^{i+1} \: : \: D(t) = 1 \right] - \Pr\left[t \leftarrow H_n^i \: : \: D(t) = 1 \right] \right|$$

yields

$$\left| \begin{array}{l} \Pr\left[t \leftarrow H_n^{i+1} : D(t) = 1 \right] - \\ \left(\frac{1}{2}\Pr[t \leftarrow H_n^{i+1} : D(t) = 1] + \frac{1}{2}\Pr[t \leftarrow \tilde{H}_n^{i+1} : D(t) = 1] \right) \end{array} \right|$$

which simplifies to

$$\frac{1}{2} \left| \Pr\left[t \leftarrow H_n^{i+1} \: : \: D(t) = 1 \right] - \Pr\left[t \leftarrow \tilde{H}_n^{i+1} \: : \: D(t) = 1 \right] \right|$$

Combining this equation with the observation above that D distinguishes H_n^i and H_n^{i+1} with probability $\frac{1}{p(n)\ell(n)}$ implies that D distinguishes H_n^{i+1} and $\tilde{H}_n^{i+1}$ with probability $\frac{2}{p(n)\ell(n)}$. By the prediction lemma, there must therefore exist a machine A such that

$$\Pr\left[b \leftarrow \{0,1\}; t \leftarrow H_n^{i+1,b} \: : \: D(t) = b \right] > \frac{1}{2} + \frac{1}{p(n)\ell(n)}$$

where we let $H_n^{i+1,1}$ denote H_n^{i+1} and $H_n^{i+1,0}$ denote $\tilde{H}_n^{i+1}$. (i.e., A predicts whether a sample came from H_n^{i+1} or $\tilde{H}_n^{i+1}$.) We can now use A to construct a machine A' predicts x_{i+1} (i.e., the $(i+1)^{\text{th}}$ bit in the pseudorandom sequence):

ALGORITHM 76.5: $A'(1^n, t_1, \ldots, t_i)$: A NEXT-BIT PREDICTOR

Pick $\ell(n) - i$ random bits $u_{i+1} \ldots u_{\ell(n)} \leftarrow U^{\ell(n)-1}$
Run $g \leftarrow A(t_1 \ldots t_i u_{i+1} \ldots u_{\ell(n)})$

> **if** $g = 1$ **then**
>   Output u_{i+1}
> **else**
>   Output $\bar{u}_{i+1} = 1 - u_{i+1}$
> **end if**

Note that,

$$\Pr\left[t \leftarrow X_n : A'(1^n, t_1 \ldots t_i) = t_{i+1}\right]$$
$$= \Pr\left[b \leftarrow \{0,1\}; t \leftarrow H_n^{i+1,b} : A(t) = 1\right] > \frac{1}{2} + \frac{1}{p(n)\ell(n)}$$

which concludes the proof Theorem 75.4. □

3.3 Pseudo-random generators

We now turn to definitions and constructions of pseudo-random generators.

3.3.1 Definition of a Pseudo-random Generators

▷**Definition 77.1** (Pseudo-random Generator). A function $G : \{0,1\}^* \to \{0,1\}^*$ is a *Pseudo-random Generator (PRG)* if the following holds.

1. (efficiency): G can be computed in p.p.t.

2. (expansion): $|G(x)| > |x|$

3. The ensemble $\{x \leftarrow U_n : G(x)\}_n$ is pseudo-random.

3.3.2 An Initial Construction

To provide some intuition for our construction, we start by considering a simplified construction (originally suggested by Adi Shamir). The basic idea is to iterate a one-way permutation and then output, in reverse order, all the intermediary values. More precisely, let f be a one-way permutation, and define the generator $G(s) = f^n(s) \parallel f^{n-1}(s) \parallel \ldots \parallel f(s) \parallel s$. We use the $\parallel$ symbol here to represent string concatentation.

    The idea behind the scheme is that given some prefix of the output of the generator, computing the next block is equivalent

$$G(s) = \boxed{\;f^n(s)\;}\boxed{f^{n-1}(s)}\boxed{f^{n-2}(s)}\quad\cdots\quad\boxed{\;f(s)\;}\boxed{\;s\;}$$

Figure 78.2: Shamir's proposed PRG

to inverting the one-way permutation f. Indeed, this scheme results in a sequence of unpredictable *numbers*, but not necessarily unpredictable *bits*. In particular, a one-way permutation may never "change" the first two bits of its input, and thus those corresponding positions will always be predictable.

The reason we need f to be a permutation, and not a general one-way function, is two-fold. First, we need the domain and range to be the same number of bits. Second, and more importantly, we require that the output of $f^k(x)$ be uniformly distributed if x is uniformly distributed. This holds if f is a permutation, but may not hold for a general one-way function.

As we shall see, this construction can be modified to generate unpredictable bits as well. Doing so requires the new concept of a *hard-core bit*.

3.3.3   Hard-core bits

Intuitively, a predicate h is *hard-core* for a OWF f if $h(x)$ cannot be predicted significantly better than with probability $1/2$, even given $f(x)$. In other words, although a OWF might leak many bits of its inverse, it does not leak the hard-core bits—in fact, it essentially does not leak *anything* about the hard-core bits. Thus, hard-core bits are computationally unpredictable.

▷**Definition 78.3** (Hard-core Predicate). A predicate $h : \{0,1\}^* \to \{0,1\}$ is a hard-core predicate for $f(x)$ if h is efficiently computable given x, and for all nonuniform p.p.t. adversaries A, there exists a negligible ϵ so that $\forall k \in \mathbb{N}$

$$\Pr\left[x \leftarrow \{0,1\}^k : A(1^n, f(x)) = h(x)\right] \leq \frac{1}{2} + \epsilon(n)$$

Examples   The least significant bit of the RSA one-way function is known to be hardcore (under the RSA assumption). That is, given N, e, and $f_{RSA}(x) = x^e \bmod N$, there is no efficient algorithm that predicts $\mathrm{LSB}(x)$. A few other examples include:

- The function $\mathrm{half}_N(x)$ which is equal to 1 iff $0 \le x \le \frac{N}{2}$ is also hardcore for RSA, under the RSA assumption.

- The function $\mathrm{half}_{p-1}(x)$ is a hardcore predicate for exponentiation to the power $x \bmod p$ for a prime p under the DL assumption. (See §3.4.1 for this proof.)

We now show how hard-core predicates can be used to construct a PRG.

3.3.4 Constructions of a PRG

Our idea for constructing a pseudo-random generator builds on Shamir's construction above that outputs unpredictable numbers. Instead of outputting all intermediary numbers, however, we only output a "hard-core" bit of each of them. We start by providing a construction of a PRG that only expands the seed by one bit, and then give the full construction in Corollary 81.7.

▷**Theorem 79.4** *Let f be a one-way permutation, and h a hard-core predicate for f. Then $G(s) = f(s) \;\|\; h(s)$ is a PRG.*

Proof. Assume for contradiction that there exists a nonuniform p.p.t. adversary A and a polynomial $p(n)$ such that for infinitely many n, there exists an i such that A predicts the ith bit with probability $\frac{1}{p(n)}$. Since the first n bits of $G(s)$ are a permutation of a uniform distribution (and thus also uniformly distributed), A must predict bit $n + 1$ with advantage $\frac{1}{p(n)}$. Formally,

$$\Pr[A(f(s)) = h(s)] > \frac{1}{2} + \frac{1}{p(n)}$$

This contradicts the assumption that b is hard-core for f. We conclude that G is a PRG. $\qquad\square$

3.3.5   Expansion of a PRG

The construction above from Thm. 79.4 only extends an n-bit seed to $n + 1$ output bits. The following theorem shows how a PRG that extends the seed by only 1 bit can be used to create a PRG that extends an n-bit seed to $poly(n)$ output bits.

▷**Lemma 80.5** *Let* $G : \{0,1\}^n \to \{0,1\}^{n+1}$ *be a PRG. For any polynomial* ℓ, *define* $G' : \{0,1\}^n \to \{0,1\}^{\ell(n)}$ *as follows (see Fig. 6):*

$$G'(s) = b_1 \ldots b_{\ell(n)} \text{ where}$$
$$X_0 \leftarrow s$$
$$X_{i+1} \parallel b_{i+1} \leftarrow G(X_i)$$

Then G' *is a PRG.*

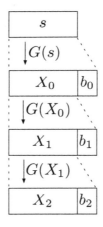

Figure 80.6: Illustration of the PRG G' that expands a seed of length n to $\ell(n)$. The function G is a PRG that expands by only 1 bit.

Proof.   Consider the following recursive definition of $G'(s) = G^m(s)$:

$$G^0(x) = \varepsilon$$
$$G^i(x) = b \parallel G^{i-1}(x') \text{ where } x' \parallel b \leftarrow G(x)$$

where ε denotes the empty string. Now, assume for contradiction that there exists a distinguisher D and a polynomial $p(\cdot)$ such that for infinitely many n, D distinguishes $\{U_{m(n)}\}_n$ and $\{G'(U_n)\}_n$ with probability $\frac{1}{p(n)}$.

Define the hybrid distributions $H_n^i = U_{m(n)-i}\|G^i(U_n)$, for $i = 1,\ldots,m(n)$. Note that $H_n^0 = U_{m(n)}$ and $H_n^{m(n)} = G^{m(n)}(U_n)$. Thus, D distinguishes H_n^0 and $H_n^{m(n)}$ with probability $\frac{1}{p(n)}$. By the Hybrid Lemma, for each n, there exist some i such that D distinguishes H_n^i and H_n^{i+1} with probability $\frac{1}{m(n)p(n)}$. Recall that,

$$H_n^i = U_{m-i}\|G^i(U_n)$$
$$= U_{m-i-1}\|U_1\|G^i(U_n)$$
$$H_n^{i+1} = U_{m-i-1}\|G^{i+1}(U_n)$$
$$= U_{m-i-1}\|b\|G^i(x) \text{ where } x\|b \leftarrow G(U_n)$$

Consider the n.u. p.p.t. $M(y)$ which outputs from the following experiment:

$$b_{prev} \leftarrow U_{m-i-1}$$
$$b \leftarrow y_1$$
$$b_{next} \leftarrow G^i(y_2\ldots y_{n+1})$$
$$\text{Output } b_{prev}\|b\|b_{next}$$

Algorithm $M(y)$ is non-uniform because for each input length n, it needs to know the appropriate i. Note that $M(U_{n+1}) = H_n^i$ and $M(G(U_n)) = H_n^{i+1}$. Since (by the PRG property of G) $\{U_{n+1}\}_n \approx \{G(U_n)\}_n$, it follows by closure under efficient operations that $\{H_n^i\}_n \approx \{H_n^{i+1}\}_n$, which is a contradiction. $\square$

By combining Theorem 79.4 and Lemma 80.5, we get the final construction of a PRG.

$\triangleright$**Corollary 81.7** *Let f be a OWP and h a hard core bit for f. Then*

$$G(x) = h(x) \| h(f(x)) \| h(f^{(2)}(x)) \| \ldots \| h(f^{\ell(n)}(x))$$

is a PRG.

Proof. Let $G'(x) = f(x) \| h(x)$. By Theorem 79.4 G' is a PRG. Applying Lemma 80.5 to G' shows that G also is a PRG. See Fig. 8. $\square$

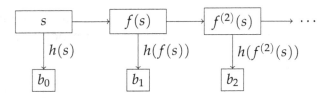

Figure 82.8: Illustration of a PRG based on a one-way permutation f and its hard-core bit h.

Note that the above PRG can be computed in an "on-line" fashion. Namely, we only need to remember x_i to compute the continuation of the output. This makes it possible to compute an *arbitrary* long pseudo-random sequence using only a short seed of a fixed length. (In other words, we do not need to know an upper-bound on the length of the output when starting to generate the pseudo-random sequence.)

Furthermore, note that the PRG construction can be easily adapted to work also with a collection of OWP, and not just a OWP. If $\{f_i\}$ is a collection of OWP, simply consider G defined as follows:

$$G(r_1, r_2) = h_i(f_i(x)) \parallel h_i(f_i^{(2)}(x)) \parallel \cdots$$

where r_1 is used to sample i and r_2 is used to sample x.

3.3.6 Concrete examples of PRGs

By using our concrete candidates of OWP (and their corresponding hard-core bits), we get the following concrete instantiations of PRGs.

Modular Exponentiation   (Blum-Micali PRG)

- Use the seed to generate p, g, x where p is a prime of the form $2q + 1$ and q is also prime, g is a generator for $\mathbb{Z}_p^*$, and $x \in \mathbb{Z}_p^*$.

- Output $half_{p-1}(x) \parallel half_{p-1}(g^x \bmod p) \parallel half_{p-1}(g^{g^x} \bmod p) \parallel \cdots$

RSA (RSA PRG)

- Use the seed to generate p, q, e where p, q are random n-bit primes p, q, and e is a random element in $\mathbb{Z}_N^*$ where $N = pq$.

- Output $LSB(x) \parallel LSB(x^e \bmod N) \parallel LSB((x^e)^e \bmod N) \parallel \cdots$ where $LSB(x)$ is the least significant bit of x.

Rabin (Blum-Blum-Schub)

- Use seed to generate random k-bit primes $p, q = 3 \bmod 4$ and $x \in QR_n$, where $n = pq$.

- Output $LSB(x) \parallel LSB(x^2 \bmod N) \parallel LSB((x^2)^2 \bmod N) \parallel \ldots$ where $LSB(x)$ is the least significant bit of x.

- This is efficient: given the state x_i, only one modular multiplication is needed to get the next bit. C.f. linear congruential generators $G(x_{i+1}) = ax_i + b$.

- We can efficiently compute the ith bit (i.e., $LSB(x^2)^i$) without needing to keep state $(x^2)^{i-1}$, provided that the primes p and q are known. This is because we can easily compute $\Phi(pq)$.

In all the above PRGs, we can in fact output $\log n$ bits at each iteration, while still remaining provably secure. Moreover, it is conjectured that it is possible to output $\frac{n}{2}$ bits at each iteration and still remain secure (but this has not been proven).

3.4 Hard-Core Bits from Any OWF

We have previously shown that if f is a one-way permutation and h is a hard-core predicate for f, then the function

$$G(s) = f(s) \parallel h(s)$$

is a pseudo-random generator. One issue, however, is how to find a hard-core predicate for a given one-way permutation. We have illustrated examples for some of the well-known permutations.

Here, we show that every one-way function (permutation resp.) can be transformed into another one-way function (permutation resp.) which has a hard-core bit. Combined with our previous results, this shows that a PRG can be constructed from any one-way permutation.

As a warm-up, we show that $half_{p-1}$ is a hardcore predicate for exponentiation mod p (assuming the DL assumption).

3.4.1   A Hard-core Bit from the Discrete Log problem

Recall that $half_n(x)$ is equal to 1 if and only iff $0 \leq x \leq \frac{n}{2}$.

▷**Lemma 84.1** *Under the DL assumption (52.2), the function $half_{p-1}$ is a hard-core predicate for the exponentiation function $f_{p,g}(x) = g^x$ mod p from the discrete-log collection DL.*

Proof.   First, note that it is easy to compute $half_{p-1}()$ given x. Suppose, for the sake of contradiction, that there exists a n.u. p.p.t. algorithm A and a polynomial $s(n)$ such that for infinitely many $n \in \mathbb{N}$

$$\Pr\left[f_{p,g} \leftarrow DL(n); x \leftarrow Z_p : A(1^n, f_{p,g}(x)) = half_{(p-1)}(x)\right]$$
$$> \frac{1}{2} + \frac{1}{s(n)}$$

We show how to use the algorithm A to construct a new algorithm B which solves the discrete logarithm problem for the same n and therefore violates the discrete log assumption. To illustrate the idea, let us first assume that A is always correct. Later we remove this assumption. The algorithm B works as follows:

ALGORITHM 84.2: DISCRETELOG(g, p, y) USING A

1: Set $y_k \leftarrow y$ and $k = |p|$
2: **while** $k > 0$ **do**
3:     **if** y_k is a square mod p **then**
4:         $x_k \leftarrow 0$
5:     **else**
6:         $x_k \leftarrow 1$
7:         $y_k \leftarrow y_k/g$ mod p to make a square
8:     **end if**

9:     Compute the square root $y_{k-1} \leftarrow \sqrt{y_k} \bmod p$
10:   Run $b \leftarrow A(y_{k-1})$
11:   IF $b = 0$ THen $y_{k-1} \leftarrow -y_{k-1}$
12:   Decrement k
13: **end while**
14: **return** x

Recall from Thm. 58.2 and the related exercises on that page, for every prime p, the modular square root operation can be performed efficiently.

Now if g is a generator, and y is square $y = g^{2x}$, notice that y has two square roots: g^x and $g^{x+p/2}$. (Recall that $g^{p/2} = -1 \bmod p$.) The first of these two roots has a smaller discrete log than y, and the other has a larger one. If it is possible to determine which of the two roots is the smaller root—say by using the adversary A to determine whether the exponent of the root is in the "top half" $[1, p/2]$ or not—then we can iteratively divide, take square-roots, and then choose the root with smaller discrete log until we eventually end up at 1. This is in fact the procedure given above.

Unfortunately, we are not guaranteed that A always outputs the correct answer, but only that A is correct noticeably more often than not. In particular, A is correct with probability $\frac{1}{2} + \epsilon$ where $\epsilon = s(n)$. To get around this problem, we can use self-reducibility in the group $\mathbb{Z}_p$. In particular, we can choose ℓ random values $r_1, \ldots, r_\ell$, and randomize the values that we feed to A in line 8 of Alg. 84.2. Since A must be noticeably more correct than incorrect, we can use a "majority vote" to get an answer that is correct with high probability.

To formalize this intuition, we first demonstrate that the procedure above can be used to solve the discrete log for instances in which the discrete log is in the range $[1, 2, \ldots, \epsilon/4 \cdot p]$. As we will show later, such an algorithm suffices to solve the discrete log problem, since we can guess and map any instance into this range. Consider the following alternative test in place of line 8 of Alg. 84.2.

   $lo \leftarrow 0$
   for $i = 1, 2, \ldots, \ell$ **do**
      $r_i \leftarrow \mathbb{Z}_p$

$z_i \leftarrow y_{k-1}g^{r_i}$
$b_i \leftarrow A(z_i)$
Increment lo if $(b_i = 0 \ \wedge \ r_i < p/2)$ or $(b_i = 1 \ \wedge \ r_i \geq p/2)$
end for
Set $b = 0$ if $lo > \ell/2$ and 1 otherwise

Suppose the discrete log of y_k is in the range $[1, 2, \ldots, s]$ where $s = \epsilon/4 \cdot p$. It follows that either the discrete log of y_{k-1} falls within the range $[1, 2, \ldots, s/2]$ or in the range $[p/2, \ldots p/2 + s/2]$. In other words, the square root will either be slightly greater than 0, or slightly greater than $p/2$. Let the event noinc represent the case when the counter lo is not incremented in line 13. By the Union Bound, we have that

$$\Pr\left[\text{noinc} \mid low(y_{k-1})\right] \leq \Pr[A(z_i) \text{ errs}]$$
$$+ \Pr[r_i \in [p/2 - s, p/2] \cup [p - s, p - 1]]$$

The last term on the right hand side arises from the error of re-randomizing. That is, when $r_i \in [p/2 - s, p/2]$, then the discrete log of z_i will be greater than $p/2$. Therefore, even if $\mathcal{A}$ answers correctly, the test on line 13 will not increment the counter lo. Although this error in unavoidable, since r_i is chosen randomly, we have that

$$\Pr[\text{noinc} \mid low(y_{k-1})] \leq \frac{1}{2} - \epsilon + 2(\epsilon/4) = \frac{1}{2} - \frac{\epsilon}{2}$$

Conversely, the probability that lo is incremented is therefore greater than $1/2 + \epsilon/2$. By setting the number of samples $\ell = (1/\epsilon)^2$, then by the corollary of the Chernoff bound given in Lemma 189.8, value b will be correct correct with probability very close to 1.

$\square$

In the above proof, we rely on specific properties of the OWP f. We proceed to show how the existence of OWPs implies the exitence of OWPs with a hard-core bit.

3.4.2 A General Hard-core Predicate from Any OWF

Let $\langle x, r \rangle$ denote the inner product of x and r, i.e., $\sum x_i r_i \bmod 2$. In other words, r decides which bits of x to take parity on.

▷**Theorem 87.3** *Let f be a OWF (OWP) and define function $g(x,r) = (f(x),r)$ where $|x| = |r|$. Then g is a OWF (OWP) and $h(x,r) = \langle x,r \rangle$ is a hardcore predicate for f.*

3.4.3 *Proof of Theorem 87.3

Proof. We show that if $\mathcal{A}$, given $g(x,r)$ can compute $h(x,r)$ with probability non-negligibly better than $1/2$, then there exists a p.p.t. adversary $\mathcal{B}$ that inverts f. More precisely, we use $\mathcal{A}$ to construct a machine $\mathcal{B}$ that on input $y = f(x)$ recovers x with non-negligible probability, which contradicts the one-wayness of f. The proof is fairly involved. To provide intuition, we first consider two simplified cases.

Oversimplified case: assume $\mathcal{A}$ always computes $h(x,r)$ correctly.   (Note that this is oversimplified as we only know that $\mathcal{A}$ computes $h(x,r)$ with probability non-negligibly better than $1/2$.) In this case the following simple procedure recovers x: $\mathcal{B}$ on input y lets $x_i = \mathcal{A}(y, e_i)$ where $e_i = 00..010..$ is an n bit string with the only 1 being in position i, and outputs $x_1, x_2, \ldots, x_n$. This clearly works, since by definition $\langle x, e_i \rangle = x_i$ and by our assumption $\mathcal{A}(f(x), r) = \langle x, r \rangle$.

Less simplified case: assume $\mathcal{A}$ computes $h(x,r)$ with probability $\frac{3}{4} + \epsilon(n)$ where $\epsilon(n) = \frac{1}{poly(n)}$.   In this case, the above algorithm of simply querying $\mathcal{A}$ with y, e_i no longer work for two reasons:

1. $\mathcal{A}$ might not work for all y's,

2. even if $\mathcal{A}$ predicts $h(x,r)$ with high probabiliy for a given y, but a random r, it might still fail on the particular $r = e_i$.

To get around the first problem, we show that for a reasonable fraction of x's, $\mathcal{A}$ does work with high probability. We first define the "good set" of instances

$$S = \left\{ x \mid \Pr\left[r \leftarrow \{0,1\}^n : \mathcal{A}(f(x),r) = h(x,r)\right] > \frac{3}{4} + \frac{\epsilon}{2} \right\}$$

Let us first argue that $\Pr[x \in S] \geq \frac{\epsilon}{2}$. Suppose, for the sake of contradiction, that it is not. Then we have

$$\Pr[x, r \leftarrow \{0,1\}^n : \mathcal{A}(f(x), r) = h(x, r)]$$
$$\leq (\Pr[x \in S] \cdot 1)$$
$$+ (\Pr[x \notin S] \cdot \Pr[\mathcal{A}(f(x), r) = h(x, r) | x \notin S])$$
$$< \left(\frac{\epsilon}{2}\right) + \left((1 - \epsilon/2) \cdot \left(\frac{3}{4} + \frac{\epsilon}{2}\right)\right)$$
$$< \frac{3}{4} + \epsilon$$

which contradicts our assumption. The second term on the third line of the derivation follows because by definition of S, when $x \notin S$, then A succeeds with probability less than $\frac{3}{4} + \epsilon/2$.

The second problem is more subtle. To get around it, we "obfuscate" the queries y, e_i and rely on the linearity of the inner product operation. The following simple fact is useful.

▷**Fact 88.4** $\langle a, b \oplus c \rangle = \langle a, b \rangle \oplus \langle a, c \rangle \mod 2$

Proof.

$$\langle a, b \oplus c \rangle = \Sigma a_i(b_i + c_i) = \Sigma a_i b_i + \Sigma a_i c_i$$
$$= \langle a, b \rangle + \langle a, c \rangle \mod 2$$

□

Now, rather than asking $\mathcal{A}$ to recover $\langle x, e_i \rangle$, we instead pick a random string r and ask $\mathcal{A}$ to recover $\langle x, r \rangle$ and $\langle x, r + e_1 \rangle$, and compute the XOR of the answers. If $\mathcal{A}$ correctly answers both queries, then the i'th bit of x can be recovered. More precisely, $\mathcal{B}(y)$ proceeds as follows:

ALGORITHM 88.5: $\mathcal{B}(y)$

$m \leftarrow \text{poly}(1/\epsilon)$
for $i = 1, 2, \ldots, n$ **do**
  for $j = 1, 2, \ldots, m$ **do**
    Pick random $r \leftarrow \{0,1\}^n$
    Set $r' \leftarrow e_i \oplus r$
    Compute a guess $g_{i,j}$ for x_i as $\mathcal{A}(y, r) \oplus \mathcal{A}(y, r')$
  end for

    $x_i \leftarrow \text{majority}(g_{i,1}, \ldots, g_{i,m})$
  end for
  Output $x_1, \ldots, x_n$.

Note that for a "good" x (i.e., $x \in S$) it holds that:

- with probability at most $\frac{1}{4} - \frac{\epsilon}{2}$, $A(y, r) \neq h(x, r)$

- with probability at most $\frac{1}{4} - \frac{\epsilon}{2}$, $A(y, r') \neq h(x, r)$

It follows by the union bound that with probability at least $\frac{1}{2} + \epsilon$ both answers of A are correct. Since $\langle y, r \rangle \oplus \langle y, r' \rangle = \langle y, r \oplus r' \rangle = \langle y, e_i \rangle$, each guess g_i is correct with probability $\frac{1}{2} + \epsilon$. Since algorithm B attempts $poly(1/\epsilon)$ independent guesses and finally take a majority vote, it follows using the Chernoff Bound that every bit is x_i computed by B is correct with high probability. Thus, for a non-negligible fraction of x's, B inverts f, which is a contradiction.

The general case. We proceed to the most general case. Here, we simply assume that A, given random $y = f(x)$ and random r computes $h(x, r)$ with probability $\frac{1}{2} + \epsilon$ (where $\epsilon = \frac{1}{poly(n)}$). As before, define the set of good cases as

$$S = \left\{ x \mid \Pr\left[A(f(x), r) = h(x, r)\right] > \frac{1}{2} + \frac{\epsilon}{2} \right\}$$

It again follows that $\Pr[x \in S] \geq \frac{\epsilon}{2}$. To construct B, let us first assume that B can call a subroutine C that on input $f(x)$, produces samples

$$(b_1 = \langle x, r_1 \rangle, r_1), \ldots, (b_m = \langle x, r_m \rangle, r_m)$$

where $r_1, \ldots, r_m$ are independent and random. Consider the following procedure $B(y)$:

ALGORITHM 89.6: $B(y)$ FOR THE GENERAL CASE

  $m \leftarrow poly(1/\epsilon)$
  for $i = 1, 2, \ldots, n$ **do**
    $(b_1, r_1), \ldots, (b_m, r_m) \leftarrow C(y)$
    for $j = 1, 2, \ldots, m$ **do**
      Let $r'_j = e_i \oplus r_j$

Compute $g_{i,j} = b_j \oplus \mathcal{A}(y, r')$
end for
Let $x_i \leftarrow majority(g_1, \ldots, g_m)$
end for
Output $x_1, \ldots, x_n$.

Given an $x \in S$, it follows that each guess $g_{i,j}$ is correct with probability $\frac{1}{2} + \frac{\epsilon}{2} = \frac{1}{2} + \epsilon'$. We can now again apply the the Chernoff bound to show that x_i is wrong with probability $\leq 2^{-\epsilon'^2 m}$. Thus, as long as $m >> \frac{1}{\epsilon'^2}$, we can recover all x_i. The only problem is that $\mathcal{B}$ uses the magical subroutine C.

Thus, it remains to show how C can be implemented. As an intermediate step, suppose that C were to produce samples $(b_1, r_1), \ldots, (b_n, r_n)$ that were only *pairwise independent* (instead of being completely independent). It follows by the Pairwise-Independent Sampling inequality that each x_i is wrong with probability at most $\frac{1 - 4\epsilon'^2}{4m\epsilon'^2} \leq \frac{1}{m\epsilon'^2}$. By union bound, any of the x_i is wrong with probability at most $n/m\epsilon'^2$ which is less than $1/2$ when $m \geq \frac{2n}{\epsilon'^2}$. Thus, if we could get $2n/\epsilon'^2$ pairwise independent samples, we would be done. So, where can we get them from? A simple approach to generating these samples would be to pick $r_1, \ldots, r_m$ at random and *guess* $b_1, \ldots, b_m$ randomly. However, b_i would be correct only with probability 2^{-m}. A better idea is to pick $\log(m)$ samples $s_1, \ldots, s_{\log(m)}$ and guess $b'_1, \ldots, b'_{\log(m)}$; here the guess is correct with probability $1/m$. Now, generate $r_1, r_2, \ldots, r_{m-1}$ as all possible sums (modulo 2) of subsets of $s_1, \ldots, s_{\log(m)}$, and $b_1, b_2, \ldots, b_m$ as the corresponding subsets of b'_i. That is,

$$r_i = \sum_{j \in I_i} s_j \quad j \in I \text{ iff } i_j = 1$$
$$b_i = \sum_{j \in I_i} b'_j$$

It is not hard to show that these r_i are pairwise independent samples (show this!). Yet with probability $1/m$, all guesses for $b'_1, \ldots, b'_{\log(m)}$ are correct, which means that $b_1, \ldots, b_{m-1}$ are also correct.

Thus, for a fraction of ϵ' of x' it holds that with probability $1/m$, the algorithm $\mathcal{B}$ inverts f with probability $1/2$. That is, $\mathcal{B}$

inverts f with probability

$$\frac{\epsilon'}{2m} = \frac{\epsilon'^3}{4n} = \frac{(\epsilon/2)^3}{4n}$$

when $m = \frac{2n}{\epsilon^2}$. This contradicts the one-wayness of f.

3.5   Secure Encryption

We next use the notion of indistinguishability to provide a computational definition of security of encryption schemes. As we shall see, the notion of a PRG will be instrumental in the construction of encryption schemes which permit the use of a *short key* to encrypt a long message.

The intuition behind the definition of secure encryption is simple: instead of requiring that encryptions of any two messages are identically distributed (as in the definition of perfect secrecy), the computational notion of secure encryption requires only that encryptions of any two messages are indistinguishable.

▷**Definition 91.1** (Secure Encryption).   The encryption scheme (Gen, Enc, Dec) is said to be *single-message secure* if $\forall$ non uniform p.p.t. D, there exists a negligible function $\epsilon(\cdot)$ such that for all $n \in \mathbb{N}, m_0, m_1 \in \{0,1\}^n$, D distinguishes between the the following distributions with probability at most $\epsilon(n)$:

- $\{k \leftarrow \text{Gen}(1^n) : \text{Enc}_k(m_0)\}$
- $\{k \leftarrow \text{Gen}(1^n) : \text{Enc}_k(m_1)\}$

The above definition is based on the indistinguishability of the distribution of ciphertexts created by encrypting two different messages. The above definition does not, however, explicitly capture any *a priori* information that an adversary might have. Later in the course, we will see a definition which explicitly captures any *a priori* information that the adversary might have and in fact show that the indistinguishability definition is equivalent to it.

3.6   An Encryption Scheme with Short Keys

Recall that *perfectly* secure encryption schemes require a key that is at least as long as the message to be encrypted. In this section we show how a short key can be used to construct a secure encryption scheme. The idea is to use a one-time pad encryption scheme in which the pad is the output of a pseudo-random generator (instead of being truly random). Since we know how to take a small seed and construct a long pseudorandom sequence using a PRG, we can encrypt long messages with a short key.

More precisely, consider the following encryption scheme. Let $G(s)$ be a length-doubling pseudo-random generator.

ALGORITHM 92.1: ENCRYPTION SCHEME FOR n-BIT MESSAGE

$\mathsf{Gen}(1^n)$: $k \leftarrow U_{n/2}$

$\mathsf{Enc}_k(m)$: Output $m \oplus G(k)$

$\mathsf{Dec}_k(c)$: Output $c \oplus G(k)$

▷**Theorem 92.2** *Scheme* $(\mathsf{Gen}, \mathsf{Enc}, \mathsf{Dec})$ *described in Algorithm 92.1 is single-message secure.*

Proof. Assume for contradiction that there exists a distinguisher D and a polynomial $p(n)$ such that for infinitely many n, there exist messages m_n^0, m_n^1 such that D distinguishes between the following two distributions

- $\{k \leftarrow \mathsf{Gen}(1^n) : \mathsf{Enc}_k(m_0)\}$

- $\{k \leftarrow \mathsf{Gen}(1^n) : \mathsf{Enc}_k(m_1)\}$

with probability $1/p(n)$. Consider the following hybrid distributions:

- H_n^1 (Encryption of m_n^0): $\{s \leftarrow \mathsf{Gen}(1^n) : m_n^0 \oplus G(s)\}$.

- H_n^2 (OTP with m_n^1): $\{r \leftarrow U_n : m_n^0 \oplus r\}$.

- H_n^3 (OTP with m_n^1): $\{r \leftarrow U_n : m_n^1 \oplus r\}$.

- H_n^4 (Encryption of m_n^1): $\{s \leftarrow \mathsf{Gen}(1^n) : m_n^1 \oplus G(s)\}$.

By construction D distringuishes H_n^1 and H_n^4 with probability $1/p(n)$ for infinitely many n. It follows by the hybrid lemma that D also distinguishes two consequetive hybrids with probability $1/4p(n)$ (for infinitely many n). We show that this is a contradiction.

- Consider the n.u. p.p.t. machine $M^i(x) = m^i_{|x|} \oplus x^1$ and the distribution $X_n = \{s \leftarrow U_{\frac{n}{2}} : G(s)\}$. By definition, $H_n^1 = M^0(X_n)$, $H_n^4 = M^1(X_n)$ and $H_n^2 = M^0(U_n)$, $H_n^3 = M^1(U_n)$. But since $\{X_n\}_n \approx \{U_n\}_n$ (by the PRG property of G) it follows by closure under efficient operations that $\{H_n^1\}_n \approx \{H_n^2\}_n$ and $\{H_n^3\}_n \approx \{H_n^4\}_n$.

- Additionally, by the perfect secrecy of the OTP, H_n^2 and H_n^3 are identically distributed.

Thus, all consequetive hybrid distributions are indistinguishable, which is a contradiction. □

3.7 Multi-message Secure Encryption

As suggested by the name, *single-message* secure encryption only considers the security of an encryption scheme that is used to encrypt a single message. In general, we encrypt many messages and still require that the adversary cannot learn anything about the messages.

The following definition extends single-message security to multi-message security. The definition is identical, with the only exception being that we require that the encryptions of any two *vectors* or messages are indistinguishable.

▷**Definition 93.1** (Multi-message Secure Encryption). An encryption scheme (Gen, Enc, Dec) is said to be *multi-message secure* if for all non uniform p.p.t. D, for all polynomials $q(n)$, there exists a negligible function $\epsilon(\cdot)$ such that for all $n \in \mathbb{N}$ and $m_0, m_1, \ldots, m_{q(n)}, m'_0, m'_1, \ldots, m'_{q(n)} \in \{0,1\}^n$, D distinguishes between the the following distributions with probability at most $\epsilon(n)$:

---

[1]Note that M^i is *non-uniform* as for each input lenght n, it has the message m^i_n hard-coded.

- $\{k \leftarrow \mathsf{Gen}(1^n) : \mathsf{Enc}_k(m_0), \mathsf{Enc}_k(m_1), \ldots \mathsf{Enc}_k(m_{q(n)})\}$
- $\{k \leftarrow \mathsf{Gen}(1^n) : \mathsf{Enc}_k(m'_0), \mathsf{Enc}_k(m'_1), \ldots \mathsf{Enc}_k(m'_{q(n)})\}$

It is easy to see that the single-message secure encryption scheme in Scheme 92.1 (i.e., $\mathsf{Enc}_k(m) = m \oplus G(s)$, where G is a PRG) is not multi-message secure. More generally,

▷**Theorem 94.2** *A multi-message secure encryption scheme cannot be deterministic and stateless.*

Proof. For any two messages m_0, m_1, consider the encryptions (c_0, c_1), (c'_0, c'_1) of the messages (m_0, m_0) and (m_0, m_1). If the encryption scheme is deterministic and stateless, $c_0 = c_1$, but $c'_0 \neq c_1$. □

Thus, any multi-message secure encryption scheme (that is stateless) must use randomness. One idea for such a scheme is to pick a random string r, then output $r||m \oplus f(r)$ for some function f. Ideally, we would like the output of f to be a random string as well. One way to get such an f might be to have a long pseudorandom sequence of length on the order of $n2^n$. Then f could use r as an index into this sequence and return the n bits at r. But no pseudorandom generator can produce an exponential number of bits; the construction in §3.2 only works for pseudorandom generators with polynomial expansion.

If we were to use a pseudorandom generator, then r could be at most $O(\log n)$ bits long, so even if r is chosen randomly, we would end up choosing two identical values of r with reasonable probability; this scheme would not be multi-message secure, though a stateful scheme that keeps track of the values of r used could be. What we need instead is a new type of "pseudo-random" function that allows us to index an exponentially long pseudo-random string.

3.8 Pseudorandom Functions

Before defining pseudorandom function, we first recall the definition of a random function.

3.8.1 Random Functions

The scheme $r||m \oplus f(r)$ would be multi-message secure if f were a random function. We can describe a random functions in two different ways: a combinatorial description—as a random function table—and compuational description—as a machine that randomly chooses outputs given inputs and keeps track of its previous answers. In the combinatorial description, the random function table can be view as a long array that stores the values of f. So, $f(x)$ returns the value at position nx.

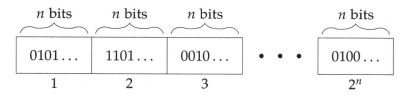

Note that the description length of a random function is $n2^n$, so there are 2^{n2^n} random functions from $\{0,1\}^n \to \{0,1\}^n$. Let RF_n be the distribution that picks a function mapping $\{0,1\}^n \to \{0,1\}^n$ uniformly at random.

A computational description of a random function is instead as follows: a random function is a machine that upon receiving input x proceeds as follows. If it has not seen x before, it chooses a value $y \leftarrow \{0,1\}^n$ and returns y; it then records that $f(x) = y$. If it has seen x before, then it looks up x, and outputs the same value as before.

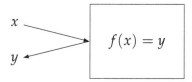

It can be seen that both of the above descriptions of a random functions give rise to identical distributions.

The problem with random functions is that (by definition) they have a long description length. So, we cannot employ a random function in our encryption scheme. We will next define a *pseudorandom* function, which mimics a random function, but has a short description.

3.8.2   Definition of Pseudorandom Functions

Intuitively, a pseudorandom function (PRF) "looks" like a random function to any n.u. p.p.t. adversary. In defining this notion, we consider an adversary that gets *oracle* access to either the PRF, or a truly random function, and is supposed to decide which one it is interacting with. More precisely, an oracle Turing machine M is a Turing machine that has been augmented with a component called an *oracle*: the oracle receives requests from M on a special tape and writes its responses to a tape in M. We now extend the notion of indistinguishability of distributions, to indistinguishability of distributions of oracles.

▷**Definition 96.1** (Oracle Indistinguishability). Let $\{O_n\}_{n\in\mathbb{N}}$ and $\{O'_n\}_n$ be ensembles where O_n, O'_n are probability distributions over functions $f : \{0,1\}^{\ell_1(n)} \to \{0,1\}^{\ell_2(n)}$ for some polynomials $\ell_1(\cdot), \ell_2(\cdot)$. We say that $\{O_n\}_n$ and $\{O'_n\}_n$ are *computationally indistinguishable* (denoted by $\{O'_n\}_n \approx \{O'_n\}_{n\in\mathbb{N}}$) if for all non-uniform p.p.t. oracles machines D, there exists a negligible function $\epsilon(\cdot)$ such that $\forall n \in \mathbb{N}$

$$\left| \begin{array}{l} \Pr\left[F \leftarrow O_n : D^{F(\cdot)}(1^n) = 1\right] \\ - \Pr\left[F \leftarrow O'_n : D^{F(\cdot)}(1^n) = 1\right] \end{array} \right| < \epsilon(n).$$

It is easy to verify that oracle indistinguishability satisfies "closure under efficient operations", the Hybrid Lemma, and the Prediction Lemma.

We turn to define pseudorandom functions.

▷**Definition 96.2** (Pseudo-random Function). A family of functions $\{f_s : \{0,1\}^{|s|} \to \{0,1\}^{|s|}\}_{s\in\{0,1\}^*}$ is *pseudo-random* if

- (Easy to compute): $f_s(x)$ can be computed by a p.p.t. algorithm that is given input s and x
- (Pseudorandom): $\{s \leftarrow \{0,1\}^n : f_s\}_n \approx \{F \leftarrow \mathsf{RF}_n : F\}_n$.

Note that in the definition of a PRF, it is critical that the seed s to the PRF is not revealed; otherwise it is easy to distinguish f_s from a random function: simply ask the oracle a random query x and check whether the oracle's reply equals $f_s(x)$.

Also note that the number of pseudorandom functions is much smaller than the number of random function (for the same input lenghts); indeed all pseudorandom functions have a short description, whereas random functions in general do not.

▷**Theorem 97.3** *If a pseudorandom generator exists, then pseudorandom functions exist.*

Proof. We have already shown that any pseudorandom generator g is sufficient to construct a pseudorandom generator g' that has polynomial expansion. So, without loss of generality, let g be a length-doubling pseudorandom generator.

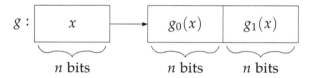

$$f_s(b_1 b_2 \ldots b_n) = g_{b_n}(g_{b_{n-1}}(\cdots (g_{b_1}(s)) \cdots))$$

f keeps only one side of the pseudorandom generator at each of n iterations. Thus, the possible outputs of f for a given input form a tree; the first three levels are shown in the following diagram. The leaves of the tree are the output of f.

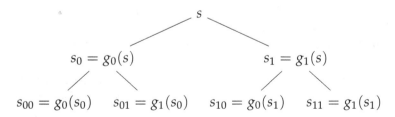

The intuition about why f is a pseudorandom function is that a tree of height n contains 2^n leaves, so exponentially many values can be indexed by a single function with n bits of input. Thus, each unique input to f takes a unique path through the tree. The output of f is the output of a pseudorandom generator on a random string, so it is also pseudo-random.

One approach to the proof is to look at the leaves of the tree. Build a sequence of hybrids by successively replacing each leaf with a random distribution. This approach, however, does not work because our hybrid lemma does not apply when there are exponentially many hybrids. Instead, we form hybrids by replacing successive levels of the tree: hybrid HF_n^i is formed by picking all levels through the ith uniformly at random, then applying the tree construction as before.

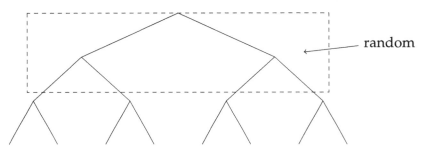

random

Note that $\mathsf{HF}_n^1 = \{s \leftarrow \{0,1\}^n : f_s(\cdot)\}$ (picking only the seed at random), which is the distribution defined originally. Further, $\mathsf{HF}_n^n = \mathsf{RF}_n$ (picking the leaves at random).

Thus, if $\mathcal{D}$ can distinguish $F \leftarrow \mathsf{RF}_n$ and f_s for a randomly chosen s, then $\mathcal{D}$ distinguishes $F_1 \leftarrow \mathsf{HF}_n^1$ and $F_n \leftarrow \mathsf{HF}_n^n$ with probability ϵ. By the hybrid lemma, there exists some i such that $\mathcal{D}$ distinguishes HF_n^i and HF_n^{i+1} with probability ϵ/n.

The difference between HF_n^i and HF_n^{i+1} is that level $i+1$ in HF_n^i is $g(U_n)$, whereas in HF_n^{i+1}, level $i+1$ is U_n. Afterwards, both distributions continue to use g to construct the tree.

To finish the proof, we will construct one more set of hybrid distributions. Recall that there is some polynomial $p(n)$ such that the number of queries made by $\mathcal{D}$ is bounded by $p(n)$. So, we can now apply the first hybrid idea suggested above: define hybrid HHF_n^j that picks F from HF_n^i, and answer the first j new queries using F, then answer the remaining queries using HF_n^{i+1}.

But now there are only $p(n)$ hybrids, so the hybrid lemma applies, and $\mathcal{D}$ can distinguish HHF_n^j and HHF_n^{j+1} for some j with probability $\epsilon/(np(n))$. But HHF_n^j and HHF_n^{j+1} differ only in that HHF_n^{j+1} answers its $j+1$st query with the output of a pseudorandom generator on a randomly chosen value, whereas

HHF_n^j answers its $j+1$st query with a randomly chosen value. As queries to HHF_n^j can be emulated in p.p.t. (we here rely on the equivalence between the combinatorial and the computational view of a random function; we omit the details), it follows by closure under efficient operations that D contradicts the pseudo-random property of g. □

3.9 Construction of Multi-message Secure Encryption

The idea behind our construction is to use a pseudorandom function in order to pick a separate random pad for every message. In order to make decryption possible, the ciphertext contains the input on which the pseudo-random function is evaluated.

ALGORITHM 99.1: MANY-MESSAGE ENCRYPTION SCHEME

Assume $m \in \{0,1\}^n$ and let $\{f_k\}$ be a PRF family.

$\text{Gen}(1^n) : k \leftarrow U_n$

$\text{Enc}_k(m)$: Pick $r \leftarrow U_n$. Output $(r, m \oplus f_k(r))$

$\text{Dec}_k((r,c))$: Output $c \oplus f_k(r)$

▷**Theorem 99.2** (Gen, Enc, Dec) *is a many-message secure encryption scheme.*

Proof. Assume for contradiction that there exists a n.u. p.p.t. distinguisher D, and a polynomial $p(\cdot)$ such that for infinitely many n, there exists messages $\bar{m} = \{m_0, m_1 \ldots, m_{q(n)}\}$ and $\bar{m}' = \{m_0', m_1' \ldots, m_{q(n)}'\}$ such that D distinguishes between encryptions of $\bar{m}$ and $\bar{m}'$ w.p. $\frac{1}{p(n)}$. (To simplify notation, here—and in subsequent proofs—we sometimes omit n from our notation and let m_i denote m_n^i, whenever n is clear from the context). Consider the following sequence of hybrid distributions: As above, it should be clear that H_i denotes H_n^i.

- H_1: real encryptions of $m_0, m_1 \ldots, m_{q(n)}$

$$s \leftarrow \{0,1\}^n$$
$$r_0, \ldots, r_{q(n)} \leftarrow \{0,1\}^n$$
$$(r_0, m_0 \oplus f_s(r_0)), \ldots, (r_{q(n)}, m_{q(n)} \oplus f_s(r_{q(n)}))$$

This is precisely what the adversary sees when receiving the encryptions of $m_0, \ldots, m_{q(n)}$.

- H_2: Replace f with a truly random function R:

$$R \leftarrow RF_n$$
$$r_0, \ldots, r_{q(n)} \leftarrow \{0,1\}^n$$
$$(r_0, m_0 \oplus R(r_0)), \ldots, (r_{q(n)}, m_{q(n)} \oplus R(r_{q(n)}))$$

- H_3 – using OTP on $m_0, m_1, \ldots, m_{q(n)}$

$$p_0 \ldots p_{q(n)} \leftarrow \{0,1\}^n$$
$$r_0, \ldots, r_{q(n)} \leftarrow \{0,1\}^n$$
$$(r_0, m_0 \oplus p_0, \ldots, m_{q(n)} \oplus p_{q(n)})$$

- H_4 – using OTP on $m'_0, m'_1, \ldots, m'_{q(n)}$

$$p_0 \ldots p_{q(n)} \leftarrow \{0,1\}^n$$
$$r_0, \ldots, r_{q(n)} \leftarrow \{0,1\}^n$$
$$(r_0, m'_0 \oplus p_0, \ldots m'_{q(n)} \oplus p_{q(n)})$$

- H_5 – Replace f with a truly random function R:

$$R \leftarrow \{\{0,1\}^n \to \{0,1\}^n\}$$
$$r_0, \ldots, r_{q(n)} \leftarrow \{0,1\}^n$$
$$(r_0, m'_0 \oplus R(r_0), \ldots (r_{q(n)}, m'_{q(n)} \oplus R(r_{q(n)}))\}$$

- H_6 – real encryptions of $m'_0, m'_1, \ldots, m'_{q(n)}$

$$s \leftarrow \{0,1\}^n$$
$$r_0, \ldots, r_{q(n)} \leftarrow \{0,1\}^n$$
$$(r_0, m'_0 \oplus f_s(r_0)), \ldots, (r_{q(n)}, m'_{q(n)} \oplus f_s(r_{q(n)}))\}$$

By the Hybrid Lemma, D distinguishes between to adjacent hybrid distributions with inverse polynomial probability (for infinitely many n). We show that this is a contradiction:

- First, note that D distinguish between H_1 and H_2 only with negligible probability; otherwise (by closure under efficient operations) we contradict the pseudorandomness property of $\{f_s\}_n$.

  The same argument applies for H_6 and H_5.

- H_2 and H_3 are "almost" identical except for the case when $\exists i, j$ such that $r_i = r_j$, but this happens only with probability

$$\binom{q(n)}{2} \cdot 2^{-n},$$

  which is negligible; thus, D can distinguishes between H_2 and H_3 only with negligible probability. The same argument applies for H_4 and H_5.

- Finally, H_3 and H_4 are identical by the perfect secrecy of the OTP.

This contradicts that D distinguishes two adjacent hybrids.   □

3.10   Public Key Encryption

So far, our model of communication allows the encryptor and decryptor to meet in advance and agree on a secret key which they later can use to send private messages. Ideally, we would like to drop this requirement of meeting in advance to agree on a secret key. At first, this seems impossible. Certainly the decryptor of a message needs to use a secret key; otherwise, nothing prevents the eavesdropper from running the same procedure as the decryptor to recover the message. It also seems like the encryptor needs to use a key because otherwise the key cannot help to decrypt the cyphertext.

   The flaw in this argument is that the encrypter and the decryptor need not share the *same* key, and in fact this is how public key cryptography works. We split the key into a secret decryption key sk and a public encryption key pk. The public key is published in a secure repository, where anyone can use it to encrypt messages. The private key is kept by the recipient so that only she can decrypt messages sent to her.

We define a public key encryption scheme as follows:

▷**Definition 102.1** (Public Key Encryption Scheme). A triple of algorithms $(\mathsf{Gen}, \mathsf{Enc}, \mathsf{Dec})$ is a public key encryption scheme if

1. $(pk, sk) \leftarrow \mathsf{Gen}(1^n)$ is a p.p.t. algorithm that produces a key pair (pk, sk)

2. $c \leftarrow \mathsf{Enc}_{pk}(m)$ is a p.p.t. algorithm that given pk and $m \in \{0,1\}^n$ produces a ciphertext c.

3. $m \leftarrow \mathsf{Dec}_{sk}(c)$ is a deterministic algorithm that given a ciphertext c and secret key sk produces a message $m \in \{0,1\}^n \cup \bot$.

4. There exists a polynomial-time algorithm M that on input $(1^n, i)$ outputs the ith n-bit message (if such a message exists) according to some order.

5. For all $n \in \mathbb{N}, m \in \{0,1\}^n$

$$\Pr\left[(pk, sk) \leftarrow \mathsf{Gen}(1^n) : \mathsf{Dec}_{sk}(\mathsf{Enc}_{pk}(m)) = m\right] = 1$$

We allow the decryption algorithm to produce a special symbol $\bot$ when the input ciphertext is "undecipherable." The security property for public-key encryption can be defined using an experiment similar to the ones used in the definition for secure private key encryption.

▷**Definition 102.2** (Secure Public Key Encryption). The public key encryption scheme $(\mathsf{Gen}, \mathsf{Enc}, \mathsf{Dec})$ is said to be *secure* if for all non uniform p.p.t. D, there exists a negligible function $\epsilon(\cdot)$ such that for all $n \in \mathbb{N}, m_0, m_1 \in \{0,1\}^n$, D distinguishes between the the following distributions with probability at most $\epsilon(n)$:

- $\{(pk, sk) \leftarrow \mathsf{Gen}(1^n) : (pk, \mathsf{Enc}_{pk}(m_0))\}_n$
- $\{(pk, sk) \leftarrow \mathsf{Gen}(1^n) : (pk, \mathsf{Enc}_{pk}(m_1))\}_n$

With this definitions, there are some immediate impossibility results:

Perfect secrecy Perfect secrecy is not possible (even for small message spaces) since an unbounded adversary could simply encrypt every message in $\{0,1\}^n$ with every random string and compare with the challenge ciphertext to learn the underlying message.

Deterministic encryption It is also impossible to have a deterministic encryption algorithm because otherwise an adversary could simply encrypt and compare the encryption of m_0 with the challenge ciphertext to distinguish the two experiments.

As with the case of private-key encryption, we can extend the definition to multi-message security. Fortunately, for the case of public-key encryption, multi-message security is equivalent to single-messages security. This follows by a simple application of the hybrid lemma, and closure under efficient operations; the key point here is that we can efficiently generate encryptions of any message, without knowing the secret key (this was not possible, in the case of private-key encryption). We leave it as an exercise to the reader to complete the proof.

We can consider a weaker notion of "single-bit" secure encryption in which we only require that encryptions of 0 and 1 are indistinguishable. Any single-bit secure encryption can be turned into a secure encryption scheme by simply encrypting each bit of the message using the single-bit secure encryption; the security of the new scheme follows directly from the multi-message security (which is equivalent to traditional security) of the single-bit secure encryption scheme.[2]

3.10.1 Constructing a Public Key Encryption Scheme

Trapdoor permutations seem to fit the requirements for a public key cryptosystem. We could let the public key be the index i of

---

[2]As we discuss in a later chapter, this same argument does not apply for stronger definitions of encryption such as chosen-ciphertext security. In fact, a more sophisticated argument is needed to show the same simple result.

the function to apply, and the private key be the trapdoor t. Then we might consider $Enc_i(m) = f_i(m)$, and $Dec_{i,t}(c) = f_i^{-1}(c)$. This makes it easy to encrypt, and easy to decrypt with the public key, and hard to decrypt without. Using the RSA function defined in Theorem 53.2, this construction yields the commonly used RSA cryptosystem.

However, according to our definition, this construction does not yield a secure encryption scheme. In particular, it is deterministic, so it is subject to comparison attacks. A better scheme (for single-bit messages) is to let $\mathsf{Enc}_i(x) = \{r \leftarrow \{0,1\}^n : \langle f_i(r), b(r) \oplus m \rangle\}$ where b is a hardcore bit for f. As we show, the scheme is secure, as distinguishing encryptions of 0 and 1 essentially requires predicting the hardcore bit of a one-way permutation.

ALGORITHM 104.3: 1-BIT SECURE PUBLIC KEY ENCRYPTION

$\mathsf{Gen}(1^n) : (f_i, f_i^{-1}) \leftarrow \mathsf{Gen}_T(1^n)$. Output $(pk, sk) \leftarrow ((f_i, b_i), f_i^{-1})$

$\mathsf{Enc}_{pk}(m)$: Pick $r \leftarrow \{0,1\}^n$. Output $(f_i(r), b_i(r) \oplus m)$.

$\mathsf{Dec}_{sk}(c_1, c_2)$: Compute $r \leftarrow f_i^{-1}(c_1)$. Output $b_i(r) \oplus c_2$.

Here, $(f_i, f^{-1})_{i \in I}$ is a family of one-way trapdoor permutations and b_i is the hard-core bit corresponding to f_i. Let Gen_T be the p.p.t. that samples a trapdoor permutation index from I.

▷**Theorem 104.4** *If trapdoor permutations exist, then scheme 104.3 is a secure single-bit public-key encryption system.*

Proof: As usual, assume for contradiction that there exists a n.u. p.p.t. D and a polynomial $p(\cdot)$, such that D distinguishes $\{(pk, sk) \leftarrow \mathsf{Gen}(1^n) : (pk, \mathsf{Enc}_{pk}(0))\}$ and $\{(pk, sk) \leftarrow \mathsf{Gen}(1^n) : (pk, \mathsf{Enc}_{pk}(1))\}$ w.p. $\frac{1}{p(n)}$ for infinitely many n. By the prediction lemma, there exist a machine A such that

$$\Pr\left[m \leftarrow \{0,1\}; (pk, sk) \leftarrow \mathsf{Gen}(1^n) : D(pk, \mathsf{Enc}_{pk}(m)) = m\right]$$
$$> \frac{1}{2} + \frac{1}{2p(n)}$$

We can now use A to construct a machine A' that predicts the hard-core predicate $b(\cdot)$:

- A' on input (pk, y) picks $c \leftarrow \{0,1\}$, $m \leftarrow A(pk, (y, c))$, and outputs $c \oplus m$.

Note that,

$$\Pr\left[(pk, sk) \leftarrow \mathsf{Gen}(1^n); r \leftarrow \{0,1\}^n : A'(pk, f_{pk}(r)) = b(r)\right]$$

$$= \Pr\left[\begin{array}{l} (pk, sk) \leftarrow \mathsf{Gen}(1^n); \\ r \leftarrow \{0,1\}^n; \\ c \leftarrow \{0,1\} \end{array} : A(pk, (f_{pk}(r), c)) \oplus c = b(r)\right]$$

$$= \Pr\left[\begin{array}{l} (pk, sk) \leftarrow \mathsf{Gen}(1^n); \\ r \leftarrow \{0,1\}^n; \\ m \leftarrow \{0,1\} \end{array} : A(pk, (f_{pk}(r), m \oplus b(r))) = m\right]$$

$$= \Pr\left[\begin{array}{l} m \leftarrow \{0,1\} \\ (pk, sk) \leftarrow \mathsf{Gen}(1^n) \end{array} : A(pk, \mathsf{Enc}_{pk}(m)) = m\right]$$

$$\geq \frac{1}{2} + \frac{1}{2p(n)}.$$

$\square$

3.11   El-Gamal Public Key Encryption scheme

The El-Gamal public key encryption scheme is a popular and simple public key encryption scheme that is far more efficient than the one just presented. However, this efficiency requires us to make a new complexity assumption called the Decisional Diffie-Hellman Assumption (DDH).

▷**Assumption 105.1 (Decisional Diffie-Hellman (DDH))** *The following ensembles are computationally indistinguishable*

$$\left\{ p \leftarrow \tilde{\Pi}_n, y \leftarrow \mathsf{Gen}_q, a, b \leftarrow \mathbb{Z}_q : p, y, y^a, y^b, y^{ab} \right\}_n \approx$$

$$\left\{ p \leftarrow \tilde{\Pi}_n, y \leftarrow \mathsf{Gen}_q, a, b, z \leftarrow \mathbb{Z}_q : p, y, y^a, y^b, y^z \right\}_n$$

Here the term $\tilde{\Pi}_n$ refers to the special subset of safe primes

$$\tilde{\Pi}_n = \{p \mid p \in \Pi_n \text{ and } p = 2q + 1, q \in \Pi_{n-1}\}$$

The corresponding q is called a *Sophie Germain prime*. We use such a multiplicative group $G = \mathbb{Z}_p$ because it has a special structure that is convenient to work with. First, G has a subgroup G_q of order q, and since q is prime, G_q will be a cyclic group. Thus, it is easy to pick a generator of the group G_q (since every element is a generator). When $p = 2q + 1$, then the subgroup G_q consists of all of the squares modulo p. Thus, choosing a generator involves simply picking a random element $a \in G$ and computing a^2. Note that all of the math is still done in the "big" group, and therefore modulo p.

It is crucial for the DDH assumption that the group within which we work is a *prime-order* group. In a prime order group, all elements except the identity have the same order. On the other hand, in groups like G, there are elements of order $2, q$ and $2q$, and it is easy to distinguish between these cases. For example, if one is given a tuple $T = (p, y, g, h, f)$ and one notices that both g, h are of order q but f is of order $2q$, then one can immediately determine that tuple T is not a DDH-tuple.

Notice that the DDH assumption implies the discrete-log assumption (Assumption 52.2) since after solving the discrete log twice on the first two components, it is easy to distinguish whether the third component is y^{ab} or not.

We now construct a Public Key Encryption scheme based on the DDH assumption.

ALGORITHM 106.2: EL-GAMAL SECURE PUBLIC KEY ENCRYPTION

Gen(1^n): Pick a safe prime $p = 2q + 1$ of length n. Choose a random element $g \in \mathbb{Z}_p$ and compute $h \leftarrow g^2 \mod p$. Choose $a \leftarrow \mathbb{Z}_q$. Output $pk \leftarrow (p, h, h^a \mod p)$ and sk as $sk \leftarrow (p, h, a)$.

Enc$_{pk}(m)$: Choose $b \leftarrow \mathbb{Z}_q$. Output $(h^b, h^{ab} \cdot m \mod p)$.

Dec$_{sk}(c = (c_1, c_2))$: Output $c_2 / c_1^a \mod p$.

Roughly speaking, this scheme is secure assuming the DDH assumption since h^{ab} is indistinguishable from a random element and hence, by closure under efficient operations, $h^{ab} \cdot m$ is indistinguishable from a random element too. We leave the formal proof as an exercise to the reader.

▷**Theorem 107.3** *If the DDH Assumption holds, then scheme 106.2 is secure.*

3.12   A Note on Complexity Assumptions

During these first two chapters, we have studied a hierarchy of constructions. At the bottom of this hierarchy are computationally difficult problems such as one-way functions, one-way permutations, and trapdoor permutations. Our efficient constructions of these objects were further based on specific number-theoretic assumptions, including factoring, RSA, discrete log, and decisional Diffie-Hellman.

Using these hard problems, we constructed several primitives: pseudorandom generators, pseudorandom functions, and private-key encryption schemes. Although our constructions were usually based on one-way permutations, it is possible to construct these same primitives using one-way functions. Further, one-way functions are a minimal assumption, because the existence of any of these primitives implies the existence of one-way functions.

Public-key encryption schemes are noticeably absent from the list of primitives above. Although we did construct two public key encryption schemes, it is unknown how to base such a construction on one-way functions. Moreover, it is known to be impossible to create a black-box construction from one-way functions.

Chapter 4

Knowledge

In this chapter, we investigate what it means for a conversation to "convey" knowledge.

4.1 When Does a Message Convey Knowledge

Our investigation is based on a behavioristic notion of knowledge which models knowledge as the ability to complete a task. A conversation therefore conveys knowledge when the conversation allows the recipient to complete a "new" task that the recipient could not complete before. To quantify the knowledge inherent in a message m, it is therefore sufficient to quantify how much easier it becomes to compute some new function given m.

To illustrate the idea, consider the simplest case of a conversation in when Alice sends a single message to Bob. As before, to describe such phenomena, we must consider a sequence of conversations of increasing size parameterized by n.

Imagine Alice always sends the same message 0^n to Bob. Alice's message is deterministic and it has a short description; Bob can easily produce the message 0^n himself. Thus, this message does not convey any knowledge to Bob.

Now suppose that f is a one-way function, and consider the case when Alice sends Bob the message consisting of "the preimage of the preimage ... (n times) of 0." Once again, the string that Alice sends is deterministic and has a short description.

However, in this case, it is not clear that Bob can produce the message himself because producing the message might require a lot of computation (or a very large circuit). This leads us to a first approximate notion of knowledge. The amount of knowledge conveyed in a message can be quantified by considering the running time and size of a Turing machine that generates the message. With this notion, we can say that any message which can be generated by a constant-sized Turing machine that runs in polynomial-time in n conveys no knowledge since Bob can generate that message himself. These choices can be further refined, but are reasonable for our current purposes.

So far the messages that Alice sends are deterministic; our theory of knowledge should also handle the case when Alice uses randomness to select her message. In this case, the message that Alice sends is drawn from a probability distribution. To quantify the amount of knowledge conveyed by such a message, we again consider the complexity of a Turing machine that can produce the same *distribution* of messages as Alice. In fact, instead of requiring the machine to produce the identical distribution, we may be content with a machine that samples messages from a computationally indistinguishable distribution. This leads to the following informal notion:

"Alice conveys zero knowledge to Bob if Bob can sample from a distribution of messages that is computationally indistinguishable from the distribution of messages that Alice would send."

Shannon's theory of information is certainly closely related to our current discussion; briefly, the difference between information and knowledge in this context is the latter's focus on the *computational* aspects, i.e. running time and circuit size. Thus, messages that convey zero information may actually convey knowledge.

4.2   A Knowledge-Based Notion of Secure Encryption

As a first case study of our behavioristic notion of knowledge, we can re-cast the theory of secure encryption in terms of knowledge. (In fact, this was historically the first approach taken by Goldwasser and Micali.) A good notion for encryption is to argue that an encrypted message conveys zero knowledge to an eavesdropper. In other words, we say that an encryption scheme is secure if the cipertext does not allow the eavesdropper to compute any new (efficiently computable) function about the plaintext message with respect to what she could have computed without the ciphertext message.

The following definition of zero-knowledge encryption[1] captures this very intuition. This definition requires that there exists a simulator algorithm S which produces a string that is indistinguishable from a ciphertext of any message m.

▷**Definition 111.1** (Zero-Knowledge Encryption). A private-key encryption scheme $(\text{Gen}, \text{Enc}, \text{Dec})$ is *zero-knowledge encryption scheme* if there exists a p.p.t. simulator algorithm S such that $\forall$ non uniform p.p.t. D, $\exists$ a negligible function $\epsilon(n)$, such that $\forall m \in \{0,1\}^n$ it holds that D distinguishes the following distributions with probability at most $\epsilon(n)$

- $\{k \leftarrow \text{Gen}(1^n) : \text{Enc}_k(m)\}$
- $\{S(1^n)\}$

Note that we can strengthen the definition to require that the above distributions are *identical*; we call the resulting notion *perfect zero-knowledge*.

A similar definition can be used for public-key encryption; here we instead that D cannot distinguish the following two distributions

- $\{pk, sk \leftarrow \text{Gen}(1^n) : pk, \text{Enc}_{pk}(m)\}$
- $\{pk, sk \leftarrow \text{Gen}(1^n) : pk, S(pk, 1^n)\}$

As we show below, for all "interesting" encryption schemes the notion of zero-knowledge encryption is equivalent to the indistinguishability-based notion of secure encryption. We show this for the case of private-key encryption, but it should be appreciated that the same equivalence (with essentially the same proof)

---

[1]This is a variant of the well-known notion of semanical security.

holds also for the case of public-key encryption. (Additionally, the same proof show that perfect zero-knowledge encryption is equivalent to the notion of perfect secrecy.)

▷**Theorem 112.2** *Let* $(\text{Gen}, \text{Enc}, \text{Dec})$ *be an encryption scheme such that* Gen, Enc *are both p.p.t, and there exists a polynomial-time machine* M *such that for every* n, $M(n)$ *outputs a messages in* $\{0, 1\}^n$. *Then* $(\text{Gen}, \text{Enc}, \text{Dec})$ *is secure if and only if it is zero-knowledge.*

Proof. We prove each direction separately.

Security implies ZK.   Intuitively, if it were possible to extract "knowledge" from the encrypted message, then there would be a way to distinguish between encryptions of two different messages. More formally, suppose that $(\text{Gen}, \text{Enc}, \text{Dec})$ is secure. Consider the following simulator $S(1^n)$:

1. Pick a message $m \in \{0, 1\}^n$ (recall that by our asumptions, this can be done in p.p.t.)

2. Pick $k \leftarrow \text{Gen}(1^n)$, $c \leftarrow \text{Enc}_k(m)$.

3. Output c.

It only remains to show that the output of S is indistinguishable from the encryption of any message. Assume for contradiction that there exist a n.u. p.p.t. distinguisher D and a polynomial $p(\cdot)$ such that for infinitely many n, there exist some message m'_n such that D distinguishes

- $\{k \leftarrow \text{Gen}(1^n) : \text{Enc}_k(m_n)\}$

- $\{S(1^n)\}$

with probability $p(n)$. Since $\{S(1^n)\} = \{k \leftarrow \text{Gen}(1^n); m'_n \leftarrow M(1^n) : \text{Enc}_k(m'_n)\}$, it follows that there exists messages m_n and m'_n such that their encryptions can be distinguished with inverse polynomial probability; this contradict the security of $(\text{Gen}, \text{Enc}, \text{Dec})$.

ZK implies Security. Suppose for the sake of reaching contradiction that $(\mathsf{Gen}, \mathsf{Enc}, \mathsf{Dec})$ is zero-knowledge, but there exists a n.u. p.p.t. distringuisher D and a polynomial $p(n)$, such that for infinitely many n there exist messages m_n^1 and m_n^2 such that D distinguishes

- $H_n^1 = \{k \leftarrow \mathsf{Gen}(1^n) : \mathsf{Enc}_k(m_n^1)\}$
- $H_n^2 = \{k \leftarrow \mathsf{Gen}(1^n) : \mathsf{Enc}_k(m_n^2)\}$

with probability $p(n)$. Let S denote the zero-knowledge simulator for $(\mathsf{Gen}, \mathsf{Enc}, \mathsf{Dec})$, and define the hybrid distribution H_3:

- $H_n^3 = \{S(1^n)\}$

By the hybrid lemma, D distinguishes between either H_n^1 and H_n^2 or between H_n^2 and H_n^3, with probability $\frac{1}{2p(n)}$ for infinitely many n; this is a contradiction. $\qquad \square$

4.3 Zero-Knowledge Interactions

So far, we have only worried about an honest Alice who wants to talk to an honest Bob, in the presence of a malicious Eve. We will now consider a situation in which neither Alice nor Bob trust each other.

Suppose Alice (the prover) would like to convince Bob (the verifier) that a particular string x is in a language L. Since Alice does not trust Bob, Alice wants to perform this proof in such a way that Bob learns nothing else except that $x \in L$. In particular, it should not be possible for Bob to later prove that $x \in L$ to someone else. For instance, it might be useful in a cryptographic protocol for Alice to show Bob that a number N is the product of exactly two primes, but without revealing anything about the two primes.

It seems almost paradoxical to prove a theorem in such a way that the theorem proven cannot be established subsequently. However, *zero-knowledge proofs* can be used to achieve exactly this property.

Consider the following toy example involving the popular "Where's Waldo?" children's books. Each page is a large complicated illustration, and somewhere in it there is a small picture of

Waldo, in his sweater and hat; the reader is invited to find him. Sometimes, you wonder if he is there at all.

The following protocol allows a prover to convince a verifier that Waldo is in the image without revealing any information about where he is in the image: Take a large sheet of newsprint, cut a Waldo-sized hole, and overlap it on the "Where's waldo" image, so that Waldo shows through the hole. This shows he is somewhere in the image, but there is no extra contextual information to show where.

A slightly more involved example follows. Suppose you want to prove that two pictures or other objects are distinct without revealing anything about the distinction. Have the verifier give the prover one of the two, selected at random. If the two really are distinct, then the prover can reliably say "this one is object 1", or "this is object 2". If they were identical, this would be impossible.

The key insight in both examples is that the verifier generates a puzzle related to the original theorem and asks the prover to solve it. Since the puzzle was generated by the verifier, the verifier already knows the answer—the only thing that the verifier does learn is that the puzzle *can* be solved by the prover, and therefore the theorem is true.

4.4   Interactive Protocols

To begin the study of zero-knowledge proofs, we must first formalize the notion of interaction. The first step is to consider an *Interactive Turing Machine*. Briefly, an interactive Turing machine (ITM) is a Turing machine with a read-only *input* tape, a read-only *auxiliary input* tape, a read-only *random* tape, a read/write *work-tape*, a read-only communication tape (for receiving messages) a write-only communication tape (for sending messages) and finally an *output* tape. The content of the input (respectively auxiliary input) tape of an ITM A is called *the input* (respectively *auxiliary input*) *of* A and the content of the output tape of A, upon halting, is called *the output of* A.

A protocol (A, B) is a pair of ITMs that share communication tapes so that the (write-only) send-tape of the first ITM is the (read-only) receive-tape of the second, and vice versa. The computation of such a pair consists of a sequence of rounds 1, 2, ... In each round only one ITM is active, and the other is idle. A round ends with the active machine either halting —in which case the protocol ends— or by it entering a special *idle* state. The string m written on the communication tape in a round is called the *message sent* by the active machine to the idle machine.

In this chapter, we consider protocols (A, B) where both A and B receive the *same* string as input (but not necessarily as auxiliary input); this input string is the *common input* of A and B. We make use of the following notation for protocol executions.

Executions, transcripts and views. Let M_A and M_B be vectors of strings $M_A = \{m_A^1, m_A^2, ...\}$, $M_B = \{m_B^1, m_B^2, ...\}$ and let $x, r_1, r_2, z_1, z_2 \in \{0,1\}^*$. We say that the pair

$$((x, z_1, r_1, M_A), (x, z_2, r_2, M_B))$$

is an execution of the protocol (A, B) if, running ITM A on common input x, auxiliary input z_1 and random tape r_1 with ITM B on x, z_2 and r_2, results in m_A^i being the ith message received by A and in m_B^i being the ith message received by B. We also denote such an execution by $A_{r_1}(x, z_1) \leftrightarrow B_{r_2}(x, z_2)$.

In an execution $((x, z_1, r_1, M_A), (x, z_2, r_2, M_B)) = (V_A, V_B)$ of the protocol (A, B), we call V_A the *view of A* (in the execution), and V_B the *view of B*. We let $\mathrm{view}_A[A_{r_1}(x, z_1) \leftrightarrow B_{r_2}(x, z_2)]$ denote A's view in the execution $A_{r_1}(x, z_1) \leftrightarrow B_{r_2}(x, z_2)$ and $\mathrm{view}_B[A_{r_1}(x, z_1) \leftrightarrow B_{r_2}(x, z_2)]$ B's view in the same execution. (We occasionally find it convenient referring to an execution of a protocol (A, B) as a *joint view* of (A, B).)

In an execution $((x, z_1, r_1, M_A), (x, z_2, r_2, M_B))$, the tuple (M_A, M_B) is called the transcript of the execution.

Outputs of executions and views. If e is an execution of a protocol (A, B) we denote by $\mathrm{out}_X(e)$ the output of X, where $X \in \{A, B\}$. Analogously, if v is the view of A, we denote by $\mathrm{out}(v)$ the output of A in v.

Random executions. We denote by $A(x, z_1) \leftrightarrow B(x, z_2)$, the probability distribution of the random variable obtained by selecting each bit of r_1 (respectively, each bit of r_2, and each bit of r_1 and r_2) randomly and independently, and then outputting $A_{r_1}(x, z_1) \leftrightarrow B_{r_2}(x, z_2)$. The corresponding probability distributions for view and out are analogously defined.

Time Complexity of ITMs. We say that an ITM A has time-complexity $t(n)$, if for every ITM B, every common input x, every auxiliary inputs z_a, z_b, it holds that $A(x, z_a)$ *always* halts within $t(|x|)$ steps in an interaction with $B(x, z_b)$, regardless of the content of A and B's random tapes). Note that time complexity is defined as an upperbound on the running time of A *independently* of the content of the messages it receives. In other words, the time complexity of A is the *worst-case* running time of A in *any* interaction.

4.5   Interactive Proofs

With this notation, we start by considering *interactive proofs* in which a prover wishes to convince a verifier that a statement is true (without consideration of the additional property of zero-knowledge). Roughly speaking, we require the following two properties from an interactive proof system: it should be possible for a prover to convince a verifier of a true statment, but it should not be possible for a malicious prover to convince a verifier of a false statement.

▷**Definition 116.1** (Interactive Proof). A pair of interactive machines (P, V) is an interactive proof system for a language L if V is a p.p.t. machine and the follwing properties hold.

1. (Completeness) For every $x \in L$, there exists a witness string $y \in \{0, 1\}^*$ such that for every auxiliary string z:

$$\Pr\left[\text{out}_V[P(x, y) \leftrightarrow V(x, z)] = 1\right] = 1$$

2. (Soundness) There exists some negligible function ϵ such that for all $x \notin L$ and for all prover algorithms P^*, and all

auxiliary strings $z \in \{0,1\}^*$,

$$\Pr\left[\mathsf{out}_V[P^*(x) \leftrightarrow V(x,z)] = 0\right] > 1 - \epsilon(|x|)$$

Note that the prover in the definition of an interactive proof need not be efficient. (Looking forward, we shall later consider a definition which requires the prover to be efficient.)

Note that we do not provide any auxilary input to the "malicious" prover strategy P^*; this is without loss of generality as we consider *any* prover strategy; in particular, this prover strategy could have the auxilary input hard-coded.

Note that we can relax the definition and replace the $1 - \epsilon(|x|)$ with some constant (e.g., $\frac{1}{2}$); more generally we say that an interactive proof has soundness error $s(n)$ if it satisfies the above definitiob, but with $1 - \epsilon(|x|)$ replaced by $1 - s(n)$.

The class of languages having an interactive proofs is denoted **IP**. It trivially holds that **NP** $\subset$ **IP**—the prover can simply provide the NP witness to the verifier, and the verifier checks if it is a valid witness. Perhaps surprisingly, there are languages that are not known to be in NP that also have interactive proofs: as shown by Shamir, every language in **PSPACE**—i.e., the set of languages that can be recognized in polynomial space—has an interactive proof; in fact, **IP** = **PSPACE**. Below we provide an example of an interactive proof for a language that is not known to be in **NP**. More precisely, we show an interactive proof for the Graph Non-isomorphism Language.

An Interactive Proof Graph Non-isomorphism

A graph $G = (V, E)$ consists of a set of vertices V and a set of edges E which consists of pairs of verticies. Typically, we use n to denote the number of verticies in a graph, and m to denote the number of edges. Recall that two graphs $G_1 = (V_1, E_1), G_2 = (V_2, E_2)$ are isomorphic if there exists a permutation σ over the vertices of V_1 such that $V_2 = \{\sigma(v_1) \mid v_1 \in V_1\}$ and $E_2 = \{(\sigma(v_1), \sigma(v_2)) \mid (v_1, v_2) \in E_1\}$. In other words, permuting the vertices of G_1 and maintaining the permuted edge relations results in the graph G_2. We will often write $\sigma(G_1) = G_2$ to indicate that graphs G_1 and G_2 are isomorphic via the permutation σ. Similarly, two graphs are non-isomorphic if there exists no permutation σ for which $\sigma(G_1) = G_2$. (See Fig. 2 for examples.)

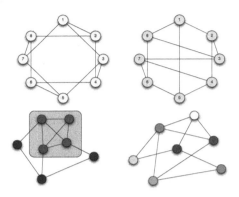

Figure 118.2: (a) Two graphs that are isomorphic, (b) Two graphs that are non-isomorphic. Notice that the highlighted 4-clique has no corresponding 4-clique in the extreme right graph.

Notice that the language of isomorphic graphs is in **NP** since the permutation serves as a witness. Let L_{niso} be the language of pairs of graphs (G_0, G_1) that have the same number of verticies but are not isomorphic. This language $L_{\text{niso}} \in$ **coNP** and is not known to be in **NP**. Consider the following protocol 118.3 which proves that two graphs are non-isomorphic.

PROTOCOL 118.3: PROTOCOL FOR GRAPH NON-ISOMORPHISM

Input:	$x = (G_0, G_1)$ where $|G_i| = n$
$V \xrightarrow{H} P$	The verifier, $V(x)$, chooses a random bit $b \in \{0, 1\}$, chooses a random permutation $\sigma \in S_n$, computes $H \leftarrow \sigma(G_b)$, and finally sends H to the prover.
$V \xleftarrow{b'} P$	The prover computes a b' such that H and $G_{b'}$ are isomorphic and sends b' to the verifier.
$V(x, H, b, b')$	The verifier accepts and outputs 1 if $b' = b$ and 0 otherwise.
	Repeat the procedure $|G_1|$ times.

▷**Proposition 118.4** *Protocol 118.3 is an interactive proof for L_{niso}.*

Proof. Completeness follows by inspection: If G_1 and G_2 are not isomorphic, then the Prover (who runs in exponential time in this protocol) will always succeed in finding b' such that $b' = b$. For soundness, the prover's chance of succeeding in one iteration of the basic protocol is $1/2$. This is because when G_1 and G_2 are isomorphic, then H is independent of the bit b. Since each iteration is independent of all prior iterations, the probability that a cheating prover succeeds is therefore upper-bounded by 2^{-n}. □

4.5.1 Interactive proofs with Efficient Provers

The Graph Non-isomorphism protocol required an exponential-time prover. Indeed, a polynomial time prover would imply that $L_{\text{niso}} \in \textbf{NP}$. In cryptographic applications, we require protocols in which the prover is efficient. To do so we are required to restrict our attention to languages in **NP**; the prover strategy should be efficient when given a **NP**-witness y to the statement x that it attempts to prove. See Appendix B for a formal definition of **NP** languages and witness relations.

▷**Definition 119.5** (Interactive Proof with Efficient Provers). An interactive proof system (P, V) is said to have an *efficient prover* with respect to the witness relation R_L if P is p.p.t. and the completeness condition holds for every $y \in R_L(x)$.

Note that although we require that the honest prover strategy P is efficient, the soundness condition still requires that not even an all powerful prover strategy P^* can cheat the verifier V. A more relaxed notion—called an *interactive argument* considers only P^*'s that are n.u. p.p.t.

Although we have already shown that the Graph Isomorphism Language has an Interactive Proof, we now present a new protocol which will be useful to us later. Since we want an efficient prover, we provide the prover the witness for the theorem $x \in L_{\text{iso}}$, i.e., we provide the permutation to the prover.

An Interactive Proof for Graph Isomorphism

PROTOCOL 120.6: PROTOCOL FOR GRAPH ISOMORPHISM

Input:	$x = (G_0, G_1)$ where $|G_i| = n$
P's **witness:**	σ such that $\sigma(G_0) = G_1$
$V \xleftarrow{H} P$	The prover chooses a random permutation π, computes $H \leftarrow \pi(G_0)$ and sends H.
$V \xrightarrow{b} P$	The verifier picks a random bit b and sends it.
$V \xleftarrow{\gamma} P$	If $b = 0$, the prover sends π. Otherwise, the prover sends $\gamma = \pi \cdot \sigma^{-1}$.
V	The verifier outputs 1 if and only if $\gamma(G_b) = H$.
P, V	Repeat the procedure $|G_1|$ times.

▷**Proposition 120.7** *Protocol 120.6 is an interactive proof for* L_{niso}.

Proof. If the two graphs G_1, G_2 are isomorphic, then the verifier always accepts because $\pi(H) = G_1$ and $\sigma(\pi(H)) = \sigma(G_1) = G_2$. If the graphs are not isomorphic, then no malicious prover can convince V with probability greater than $\frac{1}{2}$: if G_1 and G_2 are not isomorphic, then H can be isomorphic to at most one of them. Thus, since b is selected at random after H is fixed, then with probability $\frac{1}{2}$ it will be the case that H and G_i are not isomorphic. This protocol can be repeated many times (provided a fresh H is generated), to drive the probability of error as low as desired. □

As we shall see, the Graph-Isomorphism protocol is in fact also zero-knowledge.

4.6   Zero-Knowledge Proofs

In addition to being an interactive proof, the protocol 120.6 also has the property that the verifier "does not learn anything" beyond the fact that G_0 and G_1 are isomorphic. In particular, the verifier does not learn anything about the permutation σ. As discussed in the introduction, by "did not learn anything," we mean that the verifier is not able to perform any extra tasks after seeing a proof that $(G_0, G_1) \in L_{iso}$. As with zero-knowledge encryption, we can formalize this idea by requiring there to be a simulator algorithm that produces "interactive transcripts" that are identical to the transcripts that the verifier encounters during the actual execution of the interactive proof protocol.

▷**Definition 121.1 (Honest Verifier Zero-Knowledge)** *Let* (P, V) *be an efficient interactive proof for the language* $L \in NP$ *with witness relation* R_L. (P, V) *is said to be* honest verifier zero-knowledge *if there exists a p.p.t. simulator* S *such that for every n.u. p.p.t. distinguisher* D, *there exists a negligible function* $\epsilon(\cdot)$ *such that for every* $x \in L, y \in R_L(x), z \in \{0,1\}^*$, D *distinguishes the following distributions with probability at most* $\epsilon(n)$.

- $\{\text{view}_V[P(x,y) \leftrightarrow V(x,z)]\}$

- $\{S(x,z)\}$

Intuitively, the definition says whatever V "saw" in the interactive proof could have been generated by V himself by simply running the algorithm $S(x,z)$. The auxiliary input z to V denotes any a-priori information V has about x; as such the definition requires that V does not learn anything "new" (even considering this a-priori information).

This definition is, however, not entirely satisfactory. It ensures that when the verifier V follows the protocol, it gains no additional information. But what if the verifier is malicious and uses some other machine V^*. We would still like V to gain no additional information. To achieve this we modify the definition to require the existence of a simulator S for every, possibly malicious, efficient verifier strategy V^*. For technical reasons, we additionally slighty weaken the requirement on the simulator S and only require it to be an *expected p.p.t*—namely a machine whose *expected running-time* (where expectation is taken only over the internal randomness of the machine) is polynomial.[2]

▷**Definition 121.2 (Zero-knowledge)** *Let* (P, V) *be an efficient interactive proof for the language* $L \in NP$ *with witness relation* R_L. (P, V) *is said to be* zero-knowledge *if for every p.p.t. adversary* V^* *there exists an expected p.p.t. simulator* S *such that for every n.u. p.p.t.*

---

[2]In essence, this relaxation will greatly facilitate the construction of zero-knowledge protocols

distinguisher D, there exists a negligible function $\epsilon(\cdot)$ such that for every $x \in L, y \in R_L(x), z \in \{0,1\}^*$, D distinguishes the following distributions with probability at most $\epsilon(n)$.

- $\{\text{view}_{V^*}[P(x,y) \leftrightarrow V^*(x,z)]\}$

- $\{S(x,z)\}$

Note that here only consider p.p.t. adversaries V^* (as opposed to *non-uniform* p.p.t. adversaries). This only makes our definition stronger: V^* can anyway receive any non-uniform "advice" as its auxiliary input; in contrast, we can now require that the simulator S is only p.p.t. but is also given the auxiliary input of V^*. Thus, our definition says that even if V^* is non-uniform, the simulator only needs to get the same non-uniform advice to produce its transcript.

In the case of zero-knowledge encryption, we can strengthen the definition to require the above two distributions to be identically distributed; in this case the interactive proof is called perfect zero-knowledge.

An alternate formalization more directly considers what V^* "can do", instead of what V^* "sees". That is, we require that whatever V^* can do after the interactions, V^* could have already done it before it. This is formalized by simply exchanging view_{V^*} to out_{V^*} in the above definition. We leave it as an exercise to the reader to verify that the definitions are equivalent.

We can now show that the Graph-isomorphism protocol is zero-knowledge.

▷**Theorem 122.3** *Protocol 120.6 is a perfect zero-knowledge interactive proof for the Graph-isomorphism language (for some canonical witness relation).*

Proof. We have already demonstrated completeness and soundness in Proposition 120.7. We show how to construct an expected p.p.t. simulator for every p.p.t. verifier V^*. $S(x,z)$ makes use of V^* and proceeds as described in Algorithm 123.4. For simplicity, we here only provide a simulator for a single iteration of the Graph Isomorphism protocol; the same technique easily extends to the iterated version of the protocol as well. In fact, as we show in §7.2.1, this holds for every zero-knowledge protocol: namely, the sequential repetition of any zero-knowledge protocol is still zero-knowledge.

123.4: SIMULATOR FOR GRAPH ISOMORPHISM

1. Randomly pick $b' \leftarrow \{0,1\}$, $\pi \leftarrow S_n$
2. Compute $H \leftarrow \pi(G_{b'})$.
3. Emulate the execution of $V^*(x,z)$ by feeding it H and truly random bits as its random coins; let b denote the response of V^*.
4. If $b = b'$ then output the view of V^*—i.e., the messages H, π, and the random coins it was feed. Otherwise, restart the emulation of V^* and repeat the procedure.

We need to show the following properties:

- the expected running time of S is polynomial,

- the output distribution of S is correctly distributed.

Towards this goal, we start with the following lemma.

▷**Lemma 123.5** *In the execution of $S(x,z)$, H is identically distributed to $\pi(G_0)$, and $\Pr[b' = b] = \frac{1}{2}$.*

Proof. Since G_0 is an isomorphic copy of G_1, the distribution of $\pi(G_0)$ and $\pi(G_1)$ is the same for random π. Thus, the distribution of H is independent of b'. In particular, H has the same distribution as $\pi(G_0)$.

Furthermore, since V^* takes only H as input, its output, b, is also independent of b'. As b' is chosen at random from $\{0,1\}$, it follows that $\Pr[b' = b] = \frac{1}{2}$. □

From the lemma, we directly have that S has probability $\frac{1}{2}$ of succeeding in each trial. It follows that the expected number of trials before terminating is 2. Since each round takes polynomial time, S runs in expected polynomial time.

Also from the lemma, H has the same distribuion as $\pi(G_0)$. Thus, if we were always able to output the corresponding π, then the output distribution of S would be the same as in the actual protocol. However, we only output H if $b' = b$. Fortunetly, since H is independent from b', this does not change the output distribution. $\square$

4.7 Zero-knowledge proofs for NP

We now show that every language in **NP** has a zero-knowledge proof system assuming the existence of a one-way permutation. (In fact, using a more complicated proof, it can be shown that general one-way functions suffice.)

▷**Theorem 124.1** *If one-way permutations exist, then every language in* **NP** *has a zero-knowledge proof.*

Proof. Our proof proceeds in two steps:

Step 1: Show a ZK proof (P', V') (with efficient provers) for an NP-complete language; the particular language we will consider is *Graph 3 Coloring*—namely the language of all graphs whose vertices can be colored using only three colors $1, 2, 3$ such that no two connected vertices have the same color.

Step 2: To get a zero-knowledge proof (P, V) for any **NP** language, proceed as follows: Given a language L, instance x and witness y, both P and V reduce x into an instance of a Graph 3-coloring x'; this can be done using Cook's reduction (the reduction is deterministic which means that both P and V will reach the same instance x). Additionally, Cook's reduction can be applied to the witness y yielding a witness y' for the instance x'. The parties then execute protocol (P, V) on common input x', and the prover additionally uses y' as its auxiliary input.

It is easy to verify that the above protocol is a zero-knowledge proof if we assume that (P', V') is a zero-knowledge proof for Graph 3-coloring. Thus it remains to show a zero-knowledge proof for Graph 3-coloring.

To give some intuition, we start by proving a "physical" variant of the protocol. Given a graph $G = (V, E)$, where V is the set of verticies, and E is the set of edges, and a coloring C of the vertices V, the prover picks a random permutation π over the colors $\{1,2,3\}$ and physically colors the graph G with the permuted colors. It then covers each vertices with individual cups. The verifier is next asked to pick a random edge, and the prover is supposed to remove the two cups corresponding to the vertices of the edge, to show that the two vertices have different colors. If they don't the prover has been caught cheating, otherwise the interaction is repeated (each time letting the prover pick a new random permutation π.) As we shall see, if the procedure is repeated $O(n|E|)$, where $|E|$ is the number of edges, then the soundness error will be 2^{-n}. Additionally, in each round of the interaction, the verifier only learns something he knew before—two random (but different) colors. See Figure 2 for an illustration of the protocol.

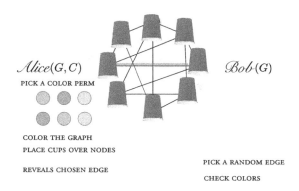

Figure 125.2: 3-Coloring

To be able to digitally implement the above protocol, we need to have a way to implement the "cups". Intuitively, we require two properties from the cups: a) the verifier should not be able to see what is under the cup—i.e., the cups should be *hiding*, b) the prover should not be able to change what is under a cup—i.e, the cups should be *binding*. The cryptographic notion that achieves both of these properties is a *commitment scheme*.

4.7.1   Commitment Schemes

Commitment schemes are usually referred to as the digital equivalent of a "physical" locked box. They consist of two phases:

Commit phase : Sender puts a value v in a locked box.

Reveal phase : Sender unlocks the box and reveals v.

We require that before the reveal phase the value v should remain hidden: this property is called *hiding*. Additionally, during the reveal phase, there should only exists a signle value that the commitment can be revealed to: this is called *binding*.

We provide a formalization of single-messages commitments where both the commit and the reveal phases only consist of a single message sent from the committer to the receiver.

▷**Definition 126.3** (Commitment). A polynomial-time machine Com is called a commitment scheme it there exists some polynomial $\ell(\cdot)$ such that the following two properties hold:

1. (Binding): For all $n \in \mathbb{N}$ and all $v_0, v_1 \in \{0,1\}^n$, $r_0, r_1 \in \{0,1\}^{l(n)}$ it holds that $\mathsf{Com}(v_0, r_0) \neq \mathsf{Com}(v_1, r_1)$.

2. (Hiding): For every n.u. p.p.t. distinguisher D, there exists a negligible function ϵ such that for every $n \in N$, $v_0, v_1 \in \{0,1\}^n$, D distinguishes the following distributions with probability at most $\epsilon(n)$.

   - $\{r \leftarrow \{0,1\}^{l(n)} : \mathsf{Com}(v_0, r)\}$
   - $\{r \leftarrow \{0,1\}^{l(n)} : \mathsf{Com}(v_1, r)\}$

Just as the definition of multi-message secure encryption, we can define a notion of "multi-value security" for commitments. It directly follows by a simple hybrid argument that any commitment scheme is multi-value secure.

▷**Theorem 126.4** *If one-way permutations exist, then commitment schemes* ▮ *exist.*

Proof. We construct a single-bit commitment scheme using a one-way permutation. A full-fledge commitment scheme to a value $v \in \{0,1\}^n$ can be obtained by individually committing to each bit of v; the security of the full-fledged construction follows as a simple application of the hybrid lemma (show this!).

Let f be a one-way permutation with a hard-core predicate h. Let $\mathrm{Com}(b,r) = f(r), b \oplus h(r)$. It directly follows from the construction that Com is binding. Hiding follows using identically the same proof as in the proof of Theorem 104.4. □

4.7.2 A Zero-knowledge Proof for Graph 3-Coloring

We can now replace the physical cups with commitments in the protocol for Graph 3-coloring described above. Consider the following protocol.

PROTOCOL 127.5: ZERO-KNOWLEDGE FOR GRAPH 3-COLORING

Common input: $G = (V, E)$ where $|V| = n$, $|E| = m$
Prover input: Witness $y = c_0, c_1, \ldots, c_m$

$P \to V$	Let π be a random permutation over $\{1, 2, 3\}$. For each $i \in [1, n]$, the prover sends a commitment to the color $\pi(c_i) = c'_i$.
$V \to P$	The verifier sends a randomly chosen edge $(i, j) \in E$
$P \to V$	The prover opens commitments c'_i and c'_j
V	V accepts the proof if and only if $c'_i \neq c'_j$
P, V	Repeat the procedure $n|E|$ times.

▷**Proposition 127.6** *Protocol 127.5 is a zero-knowledge protocol for the language of 3-colorable graphs.*

Proof. The completeness follows by inspection. If G is not 3 colorable, then for each coloring $c_1, \ldots, c_m$, there exists at least one edge which has the same colors on both endpoints. Thus, soundness follows by the binding property of the commitment scheme: In each iteration, a cheating prover is caught with probability $1/|E|$. Since the protocol is repeated $|E|^2$ times, the probability of successfully cheating in all rounds is

$$\left(1 - \frac{1}{|E|}\right)^{n|E|} \approx e^{-n}$$

For the zero-knowledge property, the prover only "reveals" 2 random colors in each iteration. The hiding property of the commitment scheme intuitively guarantees that "everything else" is hidden.

To prove this formally requires more care. We construct the simulator in a similar fashion to the graph isomorphism simulator. Again, for simplicity, we here only provide a simulator for a single iteration of the Graph 3-Coloring protocol. As previously mentioned, this is without loss of generality (see §7.2.1).

128.7: SIMULATOR FOR GRAPH 3-COLORING

---

1. Pick a random edge $(i', j') \in E$ and pick random colors $c'_i, c'_j \in \{1, 2, 3\}, c'_i \neq c'_j$. Let $c'_k = 1$ for all other $k \in [m] \setminus \{i', j'\}$
2. Just as the honest prover, commit to c'_i for all i and feed the commitments to $V^*(x, z)$ (while also providing it truly random bits as its random coins).
3. Let (i, j) denote the answer from V^*.
4. If $(i, j) = (i', j')$ reveal the two colors, and output the view of V^*. Otherwise, restart the process from the first step, but at most $n|E|$ times.
5. If, after $n|E|$ repetitions the simulation has not been sucessful, output fail.

By construction it directly follows that S is a p.p.t. We proceed to show that the simulator's output distribution is correctly distributed.

▷**Proposition 128.8** *For every n.u. p.p.t. distinguisher D, there exists a negligible function $\epsilon(\cdot)$ such that for every $x \in L, y \in R_L(x), z \in \{0, 1\}^*$, D distinguishes the following distributions with probability at most $\epsilon(n)$.*

— $\{\text{view}_{V^*}[P(x, y) \leftrightarrow V^*(x, z)]\}$

— $\{S(x, z)\}$

Assume for contradiction that there exists some n.u. distinguisher D and a polynomial $p(\cdot)$, such that for infinitely many $x \in L, y \in R_L(x), z \in \{0, 1\}^*$, D distinguishes

- $\{view_{V^*}[P(x,y) \leftrightarrow V^*(x,z)]\}$

- $\{S(x,z)\}$

with probability $p(|x|)$. First consider the following hybrid simulator S' that receives the real witness $y = c_1, \ldots, c_n$ (just like the Prover): S' proceeds exactly as S, except that instead of picking the colors c_i' and c_j' at random, it picks π at random and lets $c_i' = \pi(c_i)$ and $c_j' = \pi(c_j)$ (just as the prover). It directly follows that $\{S(x,z)\}$ and $\{S'(x,z,y)\}$ are identically distributed.

Next, consider the following hybrid simulator S'': S'' proceeds just as S, but just as the real prover commits to a random permutation of the coloring given in the witness y; except for that it does everything just like S—i.e., it picks i',j' at random and restarts if $(i,j) \neq (i',j')$. If we assume that S' never outputs `fail`, then clearly the following distributions are identical.

- $\{view_{V^*}[P(x,y) \leftrightarrow V^*(x,z)]\}$

- $\{S''(x,z,y)\}$

However, as i,j and i',j' are independently chosen, S' fails with probability

$$\left(1 - \frac{1}{|E|}\right)^{n|E|} \approx e^{-n}$$

It follows that

- $\{view_{V^*}[P(x,y) \leftrightarrow V^*(x,z)]\}$

- $\{S''(x,z,y)\}$

can be distinguished with probability at most $O(e^{-n}) < \frac{1}{2p(n)}$. By the hybrid lemma, D thus distinguishes $\{S'(x,z,y)\}$ and $\{S''(x,z)\}$ with probability $\frac{1}{2p(n)}$.

Next consider a sequence $S_0, S_1, \ldots, S_{2n|E|}$ of hybrid simulators where S_k proceeds just as S' in the first k iterations, and like S'' in the remaining ones. Note that $\{S_0(x,z,y)\}$ is identically distributed to $\{S''(x,z,y)\}$ and $\{S_{2n|E|}(x,z,y)\}$ is identically distributed to $\{S'(x,z,y)\}$. By the hybrid lemma, there exist some k such that D distinguishes between

- $\{S_k(x,z,y)\}$

- $\{S_{k+1}(x,z,y)\}$

with probability $\frac{1}{2n|E|p(n)}$. (Recall that the only difference between S_k and S_{k+1} is that in the $k+1$th iteration, S_k commits to 1's, whereas S_{k+1} commits to the real witness.) Consider, next, another sequence of $6|E|$ hybrid simulators $\tilde{S}_0,\ldots,\tilde{S}_{6|E|}$ where $\tilde{S}_e$ proceeds just as S_k if in the $k+1$th iteration the index, of the edge (i',j') and permutation π, is smaller than e; otherwise, it proceeds just as S_{k+1}. Again, note that $\{\tilde{S}_0(x,z,y)\}$ is identically distributed to $\{S_{k+1}(x,z,y)\}$ and $\{\tilde{S}_{6|E|}(x,z,y)\}$ is identically distributed to $\{S_k(x,z,y)\}$. By the hybrid lemma there exists some $e = (\tilde{i},\tilde{j},\tilde{\pi})$ such that D distinguishes

- $\{\tilde{S}_e(x,z,y)\}$

- $\{\tilde{S}_{e+1}(x,z,y)\}$

with probability $\frac{1}{12n|E|^2p(n)}$. Note that the only difference between $\{\tilde{S}_e(x,z,y)\}$ and $\{\tilde{S}_{e+1}(x,z,y)\}$ is that in $\{\tilde{S}_{e+1}(x,z,y)\}$, if in the kth iteration $(i,j,\pi) = (\tilde{i},\tilde{j},\tilde{\pi})$, then V^* is feed commitments to $\pi(c_k)$ for all $k \notin \{i,j\}$, whereas in $\{\tilde{S}_{e+1}(x,z,y)\}$, it is feed commitments to 1. Since $\tilde{S}_e$ is computable in n.u. p.p.t, by closure under efficient operations, this contradicts the (multi-value) computational hiding property of the commitments.   □

4.8   Proof of knowledge

4.9   Applications of Zero-knowledge

One of the most basic applications of zero-knowledge protocols are for secure identification to a server. A typical approach to identification is for a server and a user to share a secret password; the user sends the password to the server to identify herself. This approach has one major drawback: an adversary who intercepts this message can impersonate the user by simply "replaying" the password to another login session.

It would be much better if the user could prove identity in such a way that a *passive adversary* cannot subsequently impersonate the user. A slightly better approach might be to use a signature. Consider the following protocol in which the User and Server share a signature verification key V to which the User knows the secret signing key S.

1. The User sends the Server the "login name."

2. The server sends the User the string σ="Server name, r" where r is a randomly chosen value.

3. The user responds by signing the message σ using the signing key S.

Proving Your Identity without Leaving a Trace

In the above protocol, the "User" is trying to prove to "Server" that she holds the private key S corresponding to a public key V; r is a nonce chosen at random from $\{0,1\}^n$. We are implicitly assuming that the signature scheme resists chosen-plaintext attacks. Constraining the text to be signed in some way (requiring it to start with "server") helps.

This protocol has a subtle consequence. The server can prove that the user with public key V logged in, since the server has, and can keep, the signed message $\sigma = \{$"Server name", $r\}$. This property is sometimes undesirable. Imagine that the user is accessing a politically sensitive website. With physical keys, there is no way to prove that a key has been used. Here we investigate how this property can be implemented with cryptography.

In fact, a zero-knowledge protocol can solve this problem. Imagine that instead of sending a signature of the message, the User simply proves in zero-knowledge that it knows the key S corresponding to V. Certainly such a statement is in an **NP** language, and therefore the prior protocols can work. Moreover, the server now has no reliable way of proving to another party that the user logged in. In particular, no one would believe a server who claimed as such because the server could have easily created the "proof transcript" by itself by running the Simulator algorithm. In this way, zero-knowledge protocols provide a tangibly new property that may not exist with simple "challenge-response" identity protocols.

Chapter 5

Authentication

5.1 Message Authentication

Suppose Bob receives a message addressed from Alice. How does Bob ensure that the message *received* is the same as the message *sent* by Alice? For example, if the message was actually sent by Alice, how does Bob ensure that the message was not tampered with by any malicious intermediary?

In day-to-day life, we use signatures or other physical methods to solve the forementioned problem. Historically, governments have used elaborate and hard-to-replicate seals, watermarks, special papers, holograms, etc. to address this problem. In particular, these techniques help ensure that only, say, the physical currency issued by the government is accepted as money. All of these techniques rely on the physical difficulty of "forging" an official "signature."

In this chapter, we will discuss digital methods which make it difficult to "forge" a "signature." Just as with encryption, there are two different approaches to the problem based on whether private keys are allowed: *message authentication codes* and *digital signatures*. Message Authentication Codes (MACs) are used in the private key setting. Only people who know the secret key can check if a message is valid. Digital Signatures extend this idea to the public key setting. Anyone who knows the public key of Alice can verify a signature issued by Alice, and only those who know the secret key can issue signatures.

5.2   Message Authentication Codes

▷**Definition 134.1 (MAC)** (Gen, Tag, Ver) *is a message authentica-*
tion code (MAC) over the message space $\{\mathcal{M}_n\}_n$ *if the following*
hold:

- Gen *is a p.p.t. algorithm that returns a key* $k \leftarrow Gen(1^n)$.

- Tag *is a p.p.t. algorithm that on input key* k *and message* m
  outputs a tag $\sigma \leftarrow Tag_k(m)$.

- Ver *is a deterministic polynomial-time algorithm that on input* k,
  m *and* σ *outputs* "accept" *or* "reject".

- *For all* $n \in \mathbb{N}$, *for all* $m \in \mathcal{M}_n$,

$$\Pr[k \leftarrow Gen(1^n) : Ver_k(m, Tag_k(m)) = \text{"accept"}] = 1$$

The above definition requires that verification algorithms always
correctly "accepts" a valid signature.

The goal of an adversary is to forge a MAC. In this case,
the adversary is said to forge a MAC if it is able to construct
a tag σ' such that it is a valid signature for some message. We
could consider many different adversaries with varying powers
depending on whether the adversary has access to signed messages; whether the adversary has access to a signing oracle; and
whether the adversary can pick the message to be forged. The
strongest adversary is the one who has oracle access to Tag and
is allowed to forge any chosen message.

▷**Definition 134.2 (Security of a MAC)** *A MAC* (Gen, Tag, Ver) *is*
secure *if for all non-uniform p.p.t. adversaries A, there exists a negligi-*
ble function $\epsilon(n)$ *such that for all* n,

$$\Pr[k \leftarrow Gen(1^n); m, \sigma \leftarrow A^{Tag_k(\cdot)}(1^n) :$$
$$A \text{ did not query } m \ \wedge \text{Ver}_k(m, \sigma) = \text{"accept"}] \leq \epsilon(n)$$

We now show a construction of a MAC using pseudorandom
functions.

PROTOCOL 134.3: MAC SCHEME

Let $F = \{f_s\}$ be a family of pseudorandom functions such
that $f_s : \{0,1\}^{|s|} \to \{0,1\}^{|s|}$.

$\text{Gen}(1^n)$: $k \leftarrow \{0,1\}^n$

$\text{Tag}_k(m)$: Output $f_k(m)$

$\text{Ver}_k(m, \sigma)$: Ouptut "accept" if and only if $f_k(m) = \sigma$.

▷**Theorem 135.4** *If there exists a pseudorandom function, then the above scheme is a Message Authentication Code over the message space* $\{0,1\}_n$.

Proof. (Sketch) Consider the above scheme when a random function RF is used instead of the pseudorandom function F. In this case, A succeeds with a probability at most 2^{-n}, since A only wins if A is able to guess the n bit random string which is the output of $RF_k(m)$ for some new message m. From the security property of a pseudorandom function, there is no non uniform p.p.t. distinguisher which can distinguish the output of F and RF with a non negligible probability. Hence, we conclude that $(\text{Gen}, \text{Tag}, \text{Ver})$ is secure. □

5.3 Digital Signature Schemes

With message authentication codes, both the signer and verifier need to share a secret key. In contrast, digital signatures mirror real-life signatures in that anyone who knows Alice (but not necessarily her secrets) can verify a signature generated by Alice. Moreover, digital signatures possess the property of *non-repudiability*, i.e., if Alice signs a message and sends it to Bob, then Bob can prove to a third party (who also knows Alice) the validity of the signature. Hence, digital signatures can be used as certificates in a public key infrastructure.

▷**Definition 135.1 (Digital Signatures)** $(\text{Gen}, \text{Sign}, \text{Ver})$ *is a* digital signature scheme *over the message space* $\{M_n\}_n$ *if*

- $\text{Gen}(1^n)$ *is a p.p.t. which on input* n *outputs a public key* pk *and a secret key* sk: $pk, sk \leftarrow \text{Gen}(1^n)$.

- Sign *is a p.p.t. algorithm which on input a secret key* sk *and message* m *outputs a signature* σ: $\sigma \leftarrow \text{Sign}_{sk}(m)$.

- Ver *is a deterministic p.p.t. algorithm which on input a public key pk, a message m and a signature σ returns either* "accept" *or* "reject".

- *For all* $n \in \mathbb{N}$, *for all* $m \in \mathcal{M}_n$,

$$\Pr[pk, sk \leftarrow \mathsf{Gen}(1^n) : \mathsf{Ver}_{pk}(m, \mathsf{Sign}_{sk}(m)) = \text{"accept"}] = 1$$

The security of a digital signature can be defined in terms very similar to the security of a MAC. The adversary can make a polynomial number of queries to a signing oracle. It is not considerd a forgery if the adversary A produces a signature on a message m on which it has queried the signing oracle. Note that by definition of a public key infrastructure, the adversary has free oracle access to the verification algorithm Ver_{pk}.

▷**Definition 136.2** (Security of Digital Signatures). $(\mathsf{Gen}, \mathsf{Sign}, \mathsf{Ver})$ is secure if for all non-uniform p.p.t. adversaries A, there exists a negligible function $\epsilon(n)$ such that $\forall n \in \mathbb{N}$,

$$\Pr[pk, sk \leftarrow \mathsf{Gen}(1^n); m, \sigma \leftarrow A^{\mathsf{Sign}_{sk}(\cdot)}(1^n) :$$
$$A \text{ did not query } m \ \wedge \mathsf{Ver}_{pk}(m, \sigma) = \text{"accept"}] \leq \epsilon(n)$$

In contrast, a digital signature scheme is said to be *one-time secure* if Definition 136.2 is satisfied under the constraint that the adversary A is only allowed to query the signing oracle *once*. In general, however, we need a digital signature scheme to be many-message secure. The construction of the one-time secure scheme, however, gives insight into the more general construction.

5.4   A One-Time Signature Scheme for $\{0,1\}^n$

To produce a many-message secure digital signature scheme, we first describe a digital signature scheme and prove that it is one-time secure for n-bit messages. We then extend the scheme to handle arbitrarily long messages. Finally, we take that scheme and show how to make it many-message secure.

Our one-time secure digital signature scheme is a triple of algorithms $(\mathsf{Gen}, \mathsf{Sign}, \mathsf{Ver})$. Gen produces a secret key consisting of $2n$ random elements and a public key consisting of the image of the same $2n$ elements under a one-way function f.

PROTOCOL 137.1: ONE-TIME DIGITAL SIGNATURE SCHEME

$\mathsf{Gen}(1^n)$: For $i = 1$ to n, and $b = 0, 1$, pick $x_b^i \leftarrow U_n$. Output the keys:

$$\mathsf{sk} = \begin{pmatrix} x_0^1 & x_0^2 & & x_0^n \\ x_1^1 & x_1^2 & \cdots & x_1^n \end{pmatrix}$$

$$\mathsf{pk} = \begin{pmatrix} f(x_0^1) & f(x_0^2) & & f(x_0^n) \\ f(x_1^1) & f(x_1^2) & \cdots & f(x_1^n) \end{pmatrix}$$

$\mathsf{Sign}_{sk}(m)$: For $i = 1$ to n, $\sigma_i \leftarrow x_{m_i}^i$. Output $\sigma = (\sigma_1, \dots, \sigma_n)$.

$\mathsf{Ver}_{pk}(\sigma, m)$: Output accept if and only if $f(\sigma_i) = f(x_{m_i}^i)$ for all $i \in [1, n]$.

For example, to sign the message $m = 010$, $\mathsf{Sign}_{sk}(m)$ returns x_0^1, x_1^2, x_0^3. From these definitions, it is immediately clear that $(\mathsf{Gen}, \mathsf{Sign}, \mathsf{Ver})$ is a digital signature scheme. However, this signature scheme is not many-message secure because after two signature queries (on say, the message $0 \dots 0$ and $1 \dots 1$), it is possible to forge a signature on any message.

Nonetheless, the scheme is one-time secure. The intuition behind the proof is as follows. If after one signature query on message m, adversary A produces a pair m', σ' that satisfies $\mathsf{Ver}_{sk}(m', \sigma') = $ accept and $m \neq m'$, then A must be able to invert f on a new point. Thus A has broken the one-way function f.

▷**Theorem 137.2** *If f is a one-way function, then $(\mathsf{Gen}, \mathsf{Sign}, \mathsf{Ver})$ is one-time secure.*

Proof. By contradiction. Suppose f is a one-way function, and suppose we are given an adversary A that succeeds with probability $\epsilon(n)$ in breaking the one-time signature scheme. We construct a new adversary B that inverts f with probability $\frac{\epsilon(n)}{\text{poly}(n)}$.

B is required to invert a one-way function f, so it is given a string y and access to f, and needs to find $f^{-1}(y)$. The intuition behind the construction of B is that A on a given instance of

(Gen, Sign, Ver) will produce at least one value in its output that is the inverse of $f(x_j^i)$ for some x_j^i not known to A. Thus, if B creates an instance of (Gen, Sign, Ver) and replaces one of the $f(x_j^i)$ with y, then there is some non-negligible probability that A will succeed in inverting it, thereby inverting the one-way function.

Let m and m' be the two messages chosen by A (m is A's request to the signing oracle, and m' is in A's output). If m and m' were always going to differ in a given position, then it would be easy to decide where to put y. Instead, B generates an instance of (Gen, Sign, Ver) using f and replaces one of the values in pk with y. With some probability, A will choose a pair m, m' that differ in the position B chose for y. B proceeds as follows:

- Pick a random $i \in \{1, \ldots, n\}$ and $c \in \{0, 1\}$

- Generate pk, sk using f and replace $f(x_c^i)$ with y

- Internally run $m', \sigma' \leftarrow A(\text{pk}, 1^n)$

    - A may make a query m to the signing oracle. B answers this query if m_i is $1 - c$, and otherwise aborts (since B does not know the inverse of y)

- if $m_i' = c$, output σ_i', and otherwise output $\perp$

To find the probability that B is successful, first consider the probability that B aborts while running A internally; this can only occur if A's query m contains c in the ith bit, so the probability is $\frac{1}{2}$. This probability follows because B's choice of c is independent of A's choice of m (A cannot determine where B put y, since all the elements of pk, including y, are the result of applications of f to a random value). The probability that B chose a bit that differs between m and m' is greater than $\frac{1}{n}$ (since there must be at least one such bit), and A succeeds with probability ϵ.

Thus B returns $f^{-1}(y) = \sigma_i'$ and succeeds with probability greater than $\frac{\epsilon}{2n}$. The security of f implies that $\epsilon(n)$ must be negligible, which implies that (Gen, Sign, Ver) is one-time secure. $\square$

Now, we would like to sign longer messages with the same length key. To do so, we will need a new tool: collision-resistant hash functions.

5.5   Collision-Resistant Hash Functions

Intuitively, a hash function is a function $h(x) = y$ such that the representation of y is smaller than the representation of x, so h compresses x. The output of hash function h on a value x is often called the *hash* of x. Hash functions have a number of useful applications in data structures. For example, the Java programming language provides a built-in method that maps any string to a number in $[0, 2^{32})$. The following simple program computes the hash for a given string.

```
public class Hash {

    public void main(String args[]) {
        System.out.println( args[0].hashCode() );
    }
}
```

By inspeciting the Java library, one can see that when run on a string s, the hashCode function computes and returns the value

$$T = \sum_i s[i] \cdot 31^{n-i}$$

where n is the length of the string and $s[i]$ is the ith character of s. This function has a number of positive qualities: it is easy to compute, and it is n-wise independent on strings of length n. Thus, when used to store strings in a hash table, it performs very well.

For a hash function to be cryptographically useful, however, we require that it be hard to find two elements x and x' such that $h(x) = h(x')$. Such a pair is called a *collision*, and hash functions for which it is hard to find collisions are said to satisfy *collision resistance* or are said to be *collision-resistant*. Before we formalize collision resistance, we should note why it is useful: rather than signing a message m, we will sign the hash of m. Then even if an adversary A can find another signature σ on some bit string y, A will not be able to find any x such that $h(x) = y$, so A will not be able to find a message that has signature σ. Further, given the signature of some message m, A will not be able to find an m'

that has $h(m) = h(m')$ (if A could find such an m', then m and m' would have the same signature).

With this in mind, it is easy to see that the Java hash function does not work well as a cryptographic hash function. For example, it is very easy to change the last two digits of a string to make a collision. (This is because the contribution of the last two symbols to the output is $31 * s[n - 1] + s[n]$. One can easily find two pairs of symbols which contribute the same value here, and therefore when pre-pended with the same prefix, result in the same hash.)

5.5.1   A Family of Collision-Resistant Hash Functions

It is not possible to guarantee collision resistance against a non-uniform adversary for a single hash function h: since h compresses its input, there certainly exist two inputs x and x' that comprise a collision. Thus, a non-uniform adversary can have x and x' hard-wired into their circuits. To get around this issue, we must introduce a family of collision-resistant hash functions.

▷**Definition 140.1** *A set of functions* $H = \{h_i : D_i \to R_i\}_{i \in I}$ *is a family of collision-resistant hash functions (CRH) if:*

— *(ease of sampling)* Gen *runs in p.p.t:* $\text{Gen}(1^n) \in I$

— *(compression)* $|R_i| < |D_i|$

— *(ease of evaluation) Given* $x, i \in I$*, the computation of* $h_i(x)$ *can be done in p.p.t.*

— *(collision resistance) for all non-uniform p.p.t.* A*, there exists a negligible* ϵ *such that* $\forall n \in \mathbb{N}$*,*

$$\Pr[i \leftarrow \text{Gen}(1^n); x, x' \leftarrow A(1^n, i) : h_i(x) = h_i(x') \wedge x \neq x']$$

is less than $\epsilon(n)$*.*

Note that compression is a relatively weak property and does not even guarantee that the output is compressed by one bit. In practice, we often require that $|h(x)| < \frac{|x|}{2}$. Also note that if h is collision-resistant, then h is one-way.[1]

---

[1]The question of how to construct a CRH from a one-way permutation, however, is still open. There is a weaker kind of hash function: the universal

5.5.2 Attacks on CRHFs

Collision-resistance is a stronger property than one-wayness, so finding an attack on a collision-resistant hash functions is easier than finding an attack on a one-way function. We now consider some possible attacks.

Enumeration. If $|D_i| = 2^d$, $|R_i| = 2^n$, and x, x' are chosen at random, what is the probability of a collision between $h(x)$ and $h(x')$?

In order to analyze this situation, we must count the number of ways that a collision can occur. Let p_y be the probability that h maps a element from the domain into $y \in R_i$. The probability of a collision at y is therefore p_y^2. Since a collision can occur at either y_1 or y_2, etc., the probability of a collision can be written as

$$\Pr[collision] = \sum_{y \in R_i} p_y^2$$

Since $\sum_{y \in R_i} p_y = 1$, by the Cauchy-Schwarz Inequality 189.9, we have that

$$\sum_{y \in R_i} p_y^2 > \frac{1}{|R_i|}$$

The probability that x and x' are not identical is $\frac{1}{|D_i|}$. Combining these two shows that the total probability of a collision is greater than $\frac{1}{2^n} - \frac{1}{2^d}$. In other words, enumeration requires searching most of the range to find a collision.

Birthday attack. Instead of enumerating pairs of values, consider a set of random values $x_1, \ldots, x_t$. Evaluate h on each x_i and look for a collision between any pair x_i and $x_{i'}$. By the linearity of expectations, the expected number of collisions is the number of pairs multiplied by the probability that a random pair collides. This probability is

$$\binom{t}{2} \left(\frac{1}{|R_i|} \right) \approx \frac{t^2}{|R_i|}$$

one-way hash function (UOWF). A UOWF satisfies the property that it is hard to find a collision for a particular message; a UOWF can be constructed from a one-way permutation.

so $O(\sqrt{|R_i|}) = O(2^{n/2})$ samples are needed to find a collision with good probability. In other words, the birthday attack only requires the attacker to do computation on the order of the square root of the size of the output space.[2] This attack is much more efficient than the best known attacks on one-way functions, since those attacks require enumeration.

Now, we would like to show that, given some standard cryptographic assumptions, we can produce a CRH that compresses by one bit. Given such a CRH, we can then construct a CRH that compresses more.[3]

PROTOCOL 142.2: COLLISION RESISTANT HASH FUNCTION

Gen(1^n): Outputs a triple (g, p, y) such that p is an n-bit prime, g is a generator for $\mathbb{Z}_p^*$, and y is a random element in $\mathbb{Z}_p^*$.

$h_{p,g,y}(x, b)$: On input an n-bit string x and bit b, output

$$h_{p,g,y}(x, b) = y^b g^x \bmod p$$

▷**Theorem 142.3** *Under the Discrete Logarithm assumption, construction 142.2 is a collision-resistant hash function that compresses by 1 bit.*

Proof. Notice that both Gen and h are efficiently computable, and h compresses by one bit (since the input is in $\mathbb{Z}_p^* \times \{0,1\}$ and the output is in $\mathbb{Z}_p^*$). We need to prove that if we could find a collision, then we could also find the discrete logarithm of y.

To do so, suppose that A finds a collision with non-negligible probability ϵ. We construct a B that finds the discrete logarithm also with probability ϵ.

---

[2]This attack gets its name from the *birthday paradox*, which uses a similar analysis to show that with 23 randomly chosen people, the probability of two of them having the same birthday is greater than 50%.

[3]Suppose that h is a hash function that compresses by one bit. Note that the naïve algorithm that applies h k times to an $n + k$ bit string is not secure, although it compresses by more than 1 bit, because in this case m and $h(m)$ both hash to the same value.

Note first that if $h_i(x, b) = h_i(x', b)$, then it follows that

$$y^b g^x \bmod p = y^b g^{x'} \bmod p$$

which implies that $g^x \bmod p = g^{x'} \bmod p$ and $x = x'$.

Therefore, for a collision $h(x, b) = h(x', b')$ to occur, it holds that $b \neq b'$. Without loss of generality, assume that $b = 0$. Then,

$$g^x = y g^{x'} \bmod p$$

which implies that

$$y = g^{x-x'} \bmod p.$$

Therefore, $B(p, g, y)$ can compute the discrete logarithm of y by doing the following: call $A(p, g, y) \to (x, b), (x', b')$. If $b = 0$, then B returns $x - x'$, and otherwise it returns $x' - x$. $\square$

Thus we have constructed a CRH that compresses by one bit. Note further that this reduction is actually an algorithm for computing the discrete logarithm that is better than brute force: since the Birthday Attack on a CRH only requires searching $2^{k/2}$ keys rather than 2^k, the same attack works on the discrete logarithm by applying the above algorithm each time. Of course, there are much better (even deterministic) attacks on the discrete logarithm problem.[4]

5.5.3 Multiple-bit Compression

Given a CRHF function that compresses by one bit, it is possible to construct a CRHF function that compresses by polynomially-many bits. The idea is to apply the simple one-bit function repeatedly.

---

[4]Note that there is also a way to construct a CRH from the Factoring assumption:

$$h_{N,y}(x, b) = y^b x^2 \bmod N$$

Here, however, there is a trivial collision if we do not restrict the domain : x and $-x$ map to the same value. For instance, we might take only the first half of the values in $\mathbb{Z}_p^*$.

5.6 A One-Time Digital Signature Scheme for $\{0,1\}^*$

We now use a family of CRHFs to construct a one-time signature scheme for messages in $\{0,1\}^*$. Digital signature schemes that operate on the hash of a message are said to be in the *hash-and-sign* paradigm.

▷**Theorem 144.1** *If there exists a CRH from* $\{0,1\}^* \longrightarrow \{0,1\}^n$ *and there exists a one-way function (OWF), then there exists a one-time secure digital signature scheme for* $\{0,1\}^*$.

We define a new one-time secure digital signature scheme $(\text{Gen}', \text{Sign}', \text{Ver}')$ for $\{0,1\}^*$ by

---

PROTOCOL 144.2: ONE-TIME DIGITAL SIGNATURE FOR $\{0,1\}^*$

$\text{Gen}'(1^n)$: Run the generator $(pk, sk) \leftarrow \text{Gen}_{\text{Sig}}(1^n)$ and sampling function $i \leftarrow \text{Gen}_{\text{CRH}}(1^n)$. Output $\text{pk}' = (pk, i)$ and $\text{sk}' = (\text{sk}, i)$.

$\text{Sign}'_{sk}(m)$: Sign the hash of message m: ouptut $\text{Sign}_{sk}(h_i(m))$.

$\text{Ver}'_{pk}(\sigma, m)$: Verify σ on the hash of m: Output $\text{Ver}_{pk}(h_i(m), \sigma)$

Proof. We will only provide a sketch of the proof here.

Let $\{h_i\}_{i \in I}$ be a CRH with sampling function $\text{Gen}_{\text{CRH}}(1^n)$, and let $(\text{Gen}_{\text{Sig}}, \text{Sign}, \text{Ver})$ be a one-time secure digital signature scheme for $\{0,1\}^n$ (as constructed in the previous sections.)

Now suppose that there is a p.p.t. adversary A that breaks $(\text{Gen}', \text{Sign}', \text{Ver}')$ with non-negligible probability ϵ after only one oracle call m to Sign'. To break this digital signature scheme, A must output $m' \neq m$ and σ' such that $\text{Ver}'_{pk'}(m', \sigma') = \text{accept}$ (so $\text{Ver}_{pk}(h_i(m'), \sigma') = \text{accept}$). There are only two possible cases:

1. $h(m) = h(m')$.

   In this case, A found a collision (m, m') in h_i, which is known to be hard, since h_i is a member of a CRH.

2. *A never made any oracle calls, or $h(m) \neq h(m')$.*

   Either way, in this case, A obtained a signature σ' to a new message $h(m')$ using $(\mathsf{Gen}, \mathsf{Sign}, \mathsf{Ver})$. But obtaining such a signature violates the assumption that $(\mathsf{Gen}, \mathsf{Sign}, \mathsf{Ver})$ is a one-time secure digital signature scheme.

To make this argument more formal, we transform the two cases above into two adversaries B and C. Adversary B tries to invert a hash function from the CRH, and C tries to break the digital signature scheme.

$B(1^n, i)$ operates as follows to find a collision for h_i.

- Generate keys $\mathsf{pk}, \mathsf{sk} \leftarrow \mathsf{Gen}_{\mathsf{Sig}}(1^n)$

- Call A to get $m', \sigma' \leftarrow A^{\mathsf{Sign}_{\mathsf{sk}}(h_i(\cdot))}(1^n, (\mathsf{pk}, i))$.

- Output m, m' where m is the query made by A (if A made no query, then abort).

$C^{\mathsf{Sign}_{\mathsf{sk}}(\cdot)}(1^n, \mathsf{pk})$ operates as follows to break the one-time security of $(\mathsf{Gen}, \mathsf{Sign}, \mathsf{Ver})$.

- Generate index $i \leftarrow \mathsf{Gen}_{\mathsf{CRH}}(1^n)$

- Call A to get $m', \sigma' \leftarrow A(1^n, (\mathsf{pk}, i))$

  - When A make a call to $\mathsf{Sign}'_{(\mathsf{sk},i)}(m)$, query the signing oracle $\mathsf{Sign}_{\mathsf{sk}}(h_i(m))$

- Output $h_i(m'), \sigma'$.

So, if A succeeds with non-negligible probability, then either B or C must succeed with non-negligible probability. □

5.7 *Signing Many Messages

Now that we have extended one-time signatures on $\{0,1\}^n$ to operate on $\{0,1\}^*$, we turn to increasing the number of messages that can be signed. The main idea is to generate new keys for each new message to be signed. Then we can still use our one-time secure digital signature scheme $(\mathsf{Gen}, \mathsf{Sign}, \mathsf{Ver})$. The disadvantage is that the signer must keep state to know which key to use and what to include in a given signature.

We start with a pair $(pk_0, sk_0) \leftarrow \mathsf{Gen}(1^n)$. To sign the first message m_1, we perform the following steps:

- Generate a new key pair for the next message: $pk_1, sk_1 \leftarrow \mathsf{Gen}(1^n)$

- Create signature $\sigma_1 = \mathsf{Sign}_{sk_0}(m_1 \,||\, pk_1)$ on the concatenation of message m_1 and new public key pk_1.

- Output $\sigma'_1 = (1, \sigma_1, m_1, pk_1)$

Thus, each signature attests to the next public key. Similarly, to sign second message m_2, we generate $pk_2, sk_2 \leftarrow \mathsf{Gen}(1^n)$, set $\sigma_2 = \mathsf{Sign}_{sk_1}(m_2 \,||\, pk_2)$, and output $\sigma'_2 = (2, \sigma_2, \sigma'_1, m_2, pk_2)$. Notice that we need to include σ'_1 (the previous signature) to show that the previous public key is correct. These signatures satisfy many-message security, but the signer must keep state, and signature size grows linearly in the number of signatures ever performed by the signer. Proving that this digital signature scheme is many-message secure is left as an exercise. We now focus on how to improve this basic idea by keeping the size of the signature constant.

5.7.1   Improving the Construction

A simple way to improve this many-message secure digital signature scheme is to attest to two new key pairs instead of one at each step. This new construction builds a balanced binary tree of depth n of key pairs, where each node and leaf in the tree is associated with one public-private key pair pk, sk, and each non-leaf node public key is used to attest to its two child nodes. Each of the 2^n leaf nodes can be used to attest to a message. Such a digital signature algorithm can perform up to 2^n signatures with signature size n (the size follows because a signature using a particular key pair pk_i, sk_i must provide signatures attesting to each key pair on the path from $pk_i sk_i$ to the root). The tree looks as follows.

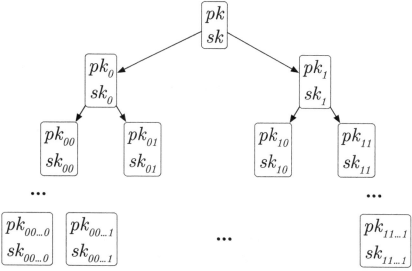

To sign the first message m, the signer generates and stores $pk_0, sk_0, pk_{00}, sk_{00}, \ldots, pk_{0^n}, sk_{0^n}$ along with all of their siblings in the tree. Then pk_0 and pk_1 are signed with sk, producing signature σ_0, pk_{00} and pk_{01} are signed with sk_0, producing signature σ_1, and so on. Finally, the signer returns the signature

$$\sigma = (pk, \sigma_0, pk_0, \sigma_1, pk_{00}, \ldots, \sigma_{n-1}, pk_{0^n}, \mathsf{Sign}_{sk_{0^n}}(m)$$

as a signature for m. The verification function Ver then uses pk to check that σ_0 attests for pk_0, uses pk_0 to check that σ_1 attests for pk_{00}, and so on up to pk_{0^n}, which is used to check that $\mathsf{Sign}_{sk_{0^n}}(m)$ is a correct signature for m.

For an arbitrary message, the next unused leaf node in the tree is chosen, and any needed signatures attesting to the path from that leaf to the root are generated (some of these signatures will have been generated previously). Then the leaf node key is used to sign the message in the same manner as above

Proving that this scheme is many-message secure is left as an exercise. The key idea is that fact that $(\mathsf{Gen}, \mathsf{Sign}, \mathsf{Ver})$ is one-time secure, and each signature is only used once. Thus, forging a signature in this scheme requires creating a second signature.

For all its theoretical value, however, this many-message secure digital signature scheme still requires the signer to keep a significant amount of state. The state kept by the signer is

- The number of messages signed

  To remove this requirement, we will assume that messages consist of at most n bits. Then, instead of using the leaf nodes as key pairs in increasing order, use the n-bit representation of m to decide which leaf to use. That is, use pk_m, sk_m to sign m.

- All previously generated keys

- All previously generated signatures (for the authentication paths to the root)

We can remove the requirement that the signer remembers the previous keys and previous signatures if we have a pseudo-random function to regenerate all of this information on demand. In particular, we generate a public key pk and secret key sk'. The secret key, in addition to containing the secret key sk corresponding to pk, also contains two seeds s_1 and s_2 for two pseudo-random functions f and g. We then generate pk_i and sk_i for node i by using $f_{s_1}(i)$ as the randomness in the generation algorithm $Gen(1^n)$. Similarly, we generate any needed randomness for the signing algorithm on message m with $g_{s_2}(m)$. Then we can regenerate any path through the tree on demand without maintaining any of the tree as state at the signer.

5.8   Constructing Efficient Digital Signature

Consider the following method for constructing a digital signature scheme from a trapdoor permutation:

- $Gen(1^n)$: $pk = i$ and $sk = t$, the trapdoor.

- $Sign_{sk}(m) = f^{-1}(m)$ using t.

- $Ver_{pk}(m, \sigma) = $ "accept" if $f_i(\sigma) = m$.

The above scheme is not secure if the adversary is allowed to choose the message to be forged. Picking $m = f_i(0)$ guarantees that 0 is the signature of m. If a specific trapdoor function like RSA is used, adversaries can forge a large class of messages. In the RSA scheme,

- $\text{Gen}(1^n)$: $pk = e, N$ and $sk = d, N$, such that $ed = 1 \bmod \Phi(N)$, and $N = pq$, p, q primes.

- $\text{Sign}_{sk}(m) = m^d \bmod N$.

- $\text{Ver}_{pk}(m, \sigma) = $ "accept" if $\sigma^e = m \bmod N$.

Given signatures on $\sigma_1 = m_1^d \bmod N$ and $\sigma_2 = m_2^d \bmod N$ an adversay can easily forge a signature on $m_1 m_2$ by multiplying the two signatures modulo N.

To avoid such attacks, in practice, the message is first hashed using some "random looking" function h to which the trapdoor signature scheme can applied. It is secure if h is a random function RF. (In particular, such a scheme can be proven secure in the Random Oracle Model.) We cannot, however, use a pseudorandom function, because to evaluate the PRF, the adversary would have to know the hashing function and hence the seed of the PRF. In this case, the PRF ceases to be computationally indistingiushable from a random function RF. Despite these theoretical problems, this hash-and-sign paradigm is used in practice using SHA1 or SHA256 as the hash algorithm.

5.9 Zero-knowledge Authentication

Chapter 6

Computing on Secret Inputs

6.1 Secret Sharing

Imagine the following situation: n professors sitting around a table wish to compute the *average* of their salaries. However, no professor wants to reveal their individual salary to the others; and this also includes revealing information that a coalition of $n - 2$ would be able to use to recover an individual salary. How can the professors achieve this task?

Here is one way:

1. If professor i's salary is s_i, then i chooses n random numbers $p_{i,1}, \ldots, p_{i,n}$ in a very large range $[-2^\ell, 2^\ell]$ such that $\sum_k p_{i,k} = s_i$.

2. For each professor $j = 1, \ldots, n$, professor i sends $p_{i,j}$ to professor j.

3. After receiving numbers $p_{j,1}, \ldots, p_{j,n}$, Professor j computes the value $t_j = \sum_k p_{j,k}$ and broadcasts it to the others.

4. Upon receiving numbers $t_1, \ldots, t_n$, each professor computes $S = \sum_k t_k$ and outputs S/n.

This protocol works when all of the players are honest because

$$\sum_{k=1}^{n} p_i = \sum_{k=1}^{n} t_i$$

Moreover, it also has the property that the protocol transcripts of any $n-2$ participants still remains informational theoretically independent of the other two professor salaries. This follows because each professor i is the only one who receives the secret value $p_{i,i}$.

Of course, there are a few odd properties of this protocol. For one, if the professors can only broadcast their secrets one-at-a-time, then the last one to broadcast "knows" the answer before everyone else. Thus, she may decide not to send a message, or decide to send a different message instead of t_n in order to get the other participants to compute the "wrong" answer. In other words, the protocol only works when all of the players honestly follow the protocol; and is secure even if the players curiously analyze their views of the protocol to learn information about the other players' inputs.

The principle behind this toy example is known as *secret sharing* and it is the simplest example of how players can collaborate to compute a function on privately held inputs. The simple idea illustrated here is called the XOR-sharing or sum-sharing. Each player distributes a value such that the XOR of all values results in the secret. We now consider a more general variant called threshold secret sharing in which k out of n shares are required in order to recover the secret value. This notion of secret sharing, due to Shamir, corresponds closely to Reed-Soloman error correcting codes.

6.1.1 k-out-of-n Secret Sharing

Let us formalize the notion of threshold secret sharing.

▷**Definition 152.1 ((k,n) Secret Sharing)** *A (k,n) Secret Sharing scheme consists of a pair of p.p.t. algorithms (Share, Recon) such that*

1. Share(x) *produces an n-tuple $(s_1, \ldots, s_n)$, and*

2. $\text{Recon}(s'_{i_1}, \ldots, s'_{i_k})$ is such that if $\{s'_{i_1}, \ldots, s'_{i_k}\} \subseteq \{s_1, \ldots, s_n\}$ then Recon outputs x.

3. For any two x and x', and for any subset of at most k indicies $S' \subset [1, n]$, $|S'| < k$, the following two distributions are statistically close:

$$\{(s_1, \ldots, s_n) \leftarrow \text{Share}(x) : (s_i \mid i \in S')\}$$

and

$$\{(s_1, \ldots, s_n) \leftarrow \text{Share}(x') : (s_i \mid i \in S')\}$$

6.1.2 Polynomial Interpolation

Before presenting a secret sharing scheme, we review a basic property of polynomials. Given any $n+1$ points on a polynomial $p(\cdot)$ of degree n, it is possible to fully recover the polynomial p, and therefore evaluate p at any other point.

▷**Lemma 153.2 (Lagrange)** *Given $n + 1$ points $(x_0, y_0), \ldots, (x_n, y_n)$ in which $x_0, \ldots, x_n$ are distinct, the unique degree-n polynomial that interpolates these points is*

$$P(x) = \sum_{i=0}^{n} y_i p_i(x)$$

where

$$p_i(x) = \prod_{j=0; j \neq i}^{n} \frac{x - x_j}{x_i - x_j}.$$

Proof. Notice that for the points $x_0, \ldots, x_n$, the value $p_i(x_j)$ is equal to 1 when $i = j$ and 0 for all other values of j. This follows because all $x_0, \ldots, x_n$ are distinct. Therefore, it is easy to see that $P(x_i) = y_i$ for all $i \in [0, n]$. Moreover, P is a polynomial of degree n.

To show that P is unique, suppose another polynomial P' of degree n also had the property that $P'(x_i) = y_i$. Notice that $Q(x) = (P - P')(x)$ is also a polynomial of degree at most n. Also, Q is zero on the $n + 1$ values $x_0, \ldots, x_n$. Therefore, by the fact below, Q must be the zero polynomial and $P = P'$. □

▷**Fact 153.3** *A non-zero polynomial of degree n can have at most n zeroes.*

6.1.3 Protocol

PROTOCOL 154.4: SHAMIR SECRET SHARING PROTOCOL

Share(x, k, n):

1. Let p be a prime such that $p > n$. Choose $n - 1$ random coefficients, $a_1, \ldots, a_{n-1}$ where $a_i \in \mathbb{Z}_p$.

2. Let $s(t) = x + a_1 t + a_2 t^2 + \cdots + a_n t^n$. Output the shares $s(1), \ldots, s(n)$.

Recon$((x_{i_1}, y_{i_1}), \ldots, (x_{i_k}, y_{i_k}))$: Interpolate the unique polynomial P that passes through all k points given as input using the Lagrange formula from Lemma 153.2. Output the value $P(0)$.

▷**Proposition 154.5** *The Shamir secret sharing scheme is a secure k-out-of-n secret sharing scheme.*

The proof is given as an exercise.

6.2 Yao Circuit Evaluation

In this section, we illustrate how two parties, A and B, who hold the secret inputs x and y respectively, can jointly compute any function $f(x, y)$ in a secure manner.

It is first important to understand exactly what we mean by "secure manner" in the above paragraph. For example, an obvious method to accomplish the task is to have A send x to B, and B to send y to A. Indeed, in some cases, this is a reasonable solution. However, imagine, for example, that the function $f(x, y)$ is the "millionaire's" function:

$$f(x, y) = \begin{cases} 1 & \text{if } x > y \\ 0 & \text{otherwise} \end{cases}$$

The problem with the obvious solution is that it reveals more information than just the value $f(x, y)$. In particular, Alice learns Bob's input (and vice versa), and such a revelation might change the future actions of Alice/Bob (recall the Match game from chapter 1).

A better protocol is one that reveals nothing more than the output to each of the parties. Obviously, for some functions, the output might allow one or both of the parties to reason about some properties of the other players' input. Nonetheless, it is the strongest property one can hope to achieve, and thus, it is important to formalize.

The theory of zero-knowledge offers a good way to capture this idea. Recall that zero-knowledge proofs are proofs that only reveal whether a statement is true. Similarly, we seek to design a protocol that reveals only the output to the parties. Using the *simulation paradigm*, one could formalize this notion by requiring that a protocol is secure when Alice's (or Bob's) *view* of the protocol can be generated by a simulator algorithm that is only given Alice (or Bob's) input and output value. As with zero-knowledge, this is a way of saying that the "protocol transcript" gives no more information to Alice (or Bob) than Alice's (or Bob's) input and output to $f(x,y)$.

To simplify the definition, we first consider a limited form of adversarial behavior that captures our concerns discussed above. An *honest-but-curious* adversary is a party who follows the instructions of the protocol, but will later analyze the protocol transcript to learn any extra information about the other player's input.

Let $f : \{0,1\}^n \times \{0,1\}^n \to \{0,1\}^n$ be a function and let $\pi = (A, B)$ be a two-party protocol for computing $f(x,y)$. As per §4.4, an execution of the protocol π will be represented by $A(x) \overset{\pi}{\leftrightarrow} B(y)$, and the random variable $\mathrm{view}_X[A(x) \overset{\pi}{\leftrightarrow} B(y)]$ represents party X's input, random tape, and the sequence of messages received by X from the other party. Similarly, $\mathrm{out}_X(e)$ represents the output of party X from execution e.

▷**Definition 155.1** (Two-party Honest-but-Curious Secure Protocol). A protocol π with security parameter 1^n securely computes a function $f(x,y)$ in the honest-but-curious model if there exists a pair of n.u. p.p.t. simulator algorithms S_A, S_B such that for all inputs $x, y \in \{0, 1\}^n$, it holds that both

$$\left\{ S_A(x, f(x, y)), f(x, y) \right\}_n$$
$$\approx_c \left\{ e \leftarrow [A(x) \overset{\pi}{\leftrightarrow} B(y)] : \mathsf{view}_A(e), \mathsf{out}_B(e) \right\}_n$$
$$\left\{ S_B(y, f(x, y)), f(x, y) \right\}_n$$
$$\approx_c \left\{ e \leftarrow [A(x) \overset{\pi}{\leftrightarrow} B(y)] : \mathsf{view}_B(e), \mathsf{out}_A(e) \right\}_n$$

Let us briefly remark about a subtle point of this definition. In the zero-knowledge definition, we only required the simulator to produce a view of the protocol transcript. This definition has the additional requirement that the output of the protocol execution be indistinguishable from the actual value $f(x, y)$. In general, this property ensures the "correctness" of the protocol. For the case of honest-but-curious adversaries, this requirement requires the protocol to actually compute $f(x, y)$. Were it not present, then a protocol that instructs both parties to output 0 would trivially be secure.

6.2.1 Circuit Representations

Our first step in constructing a secure two-party protocol is to write the function $f(x, y)$ as a circuit whose input wires correspond to the bits of x and the bits of y. For our purposes, each of the gates of the circuit can have unbounded fan-out, but a fan-in of two. We also assume that Alice and Bob have agreed upon a particular circuit that computes f. Let this circuit be named C. The future steps in the construction of the protocol involve manipulations of circuit C.

$$f(x, y)$$

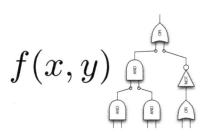

6.2.2 Garbled Wires

Let $(\mathsf{Gen}, \mathsf{Enc}, \mathsf{Dec})$ be a multi-message secure encryption scheme (see definition 93.1) with the following extra property: there exists a negligible function ϵ such that for every n and message $m \in \{0,1\}^n$, we have that

$$\Pr[k \leftarrow \mathsf{Gen}(1^n), k' \leftarrow \mathsf{Gen}(1^n), c \leftarrow \mathsf{Enc}_k(m) : \mathsf{Dec}_{k'}(c) = \perp]$$
$$> 1 - \epsilon(n)$$

In other words, the encryption scheme is such that when a ciphertext is decrypted with the incorrect key, then the output is almost always $\perp$. It is easy to modify construction 99.1 in order to build such an encryption scheme. All that is needed is a length-doubling pseudo-random function family (see definition 96.2) $\left\{ f_s : \{0,1\}^{|s|} \to \{0,1\}^{2|s|} \right\}$ and padding as illustrated in Algorithm 157.2.

ALGORITHM 157.2: A SPECIAL ENCRYPTION SCHEME

$\mathsf{Gen}(1^n) : k \leftarrow U_n.$
$\mathsf{Enc}_k(m) : r \leftarrow U_n.$ Output $(r, 0^n || x \oplus f_k(r)).$
$\mathsf{Dec}_k(c_1, c_2) :$ Compute $m_0 || m_1 \leftarrow c_2 \oplus f_k(c_1)$ where $|m_0| = n.$ If $m_0 = 0^n$, then output m_1. Otherwise, output $\perp$.

Given such an encryption scheme, associate to each wire w_i in the circuit C, a pair of randomly generated symmetric encryption keys k_0^i, k_1^i for a special encryption scheme described above. When this "garbled" version of the circuit is evaluated, the key k_b^i will represent the value b for wire i. An example is of this mapping of keys to wires is shown in the figure below.

6.2.3 Garbled Gates

In the previous step, we mapped the wires of circuit C to pairs of symmetric keys. In this step, we apply a similar mapping to each of the gates of C. The goal of these steps is to enable an evaluator of the circuit to compute, given the keys corresponding to the input wires of the gate, the key corresponding to the output wire of the gate.

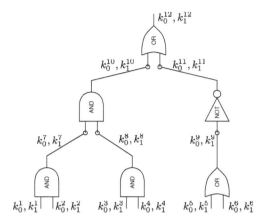

Thus, in order to preserve the semantics of each gate, a *garbled gate* must implement a mapping between a pair of keys corresponding to the inputs of the gate to a key corresponding to the output of the gate. For example, given keys k_0^1 and k_0^2 in the above circuit, the first garbled AND gate should map the pair to the key k_0^7. Additionally, in order to satisfy the security property, this mapping should not reveal any extra information about the key. For example, the mapping should not allow a party to learn whether the key corresponds to the wire value of 0 or 1.

Let us describe how to implement such a mapping for the AND gate. All logical gates will follow a similar construction. A logical gate consists of a truth table with four rows. Suppose the keys (k_0, k_1) corresponded to the first input, the keys (j_0, j_1) corresponded to the second input, and the keys (o_0, o_1) corresponded to the output keys. In the case of the AND gate, we thus need to compute the following association:

First Input	Second Input	Output
k_0	j_0	o_0
k_0	j_1	o_0
k_1	j_0	o_0
k_1	j_1	o_1

Since the evaluating player has the keys corresponding to one row of this table, a garbled gate can be implemented by doubly-encrypting each row of the table. In other words, we encrypt the output key o_i with the two input keys in each row. By using the special encryption scheme described in the previous section, a row that is decrypted with the wrong key will decrypt to the special $\perp$ symbol with high probability. Thus, the evaluating player can attempt to decrypt all four rows with the two keys that she knows. All but one row will evaluate to $\perp$. The one row that decrypts correctly results in the key associated to the output wire of this gate. There is one final detail: If the rows of the truth table occur in a canonical order, the evaluating player can then determine the associated input value—e.g., if the third row in the table above worked, the player could deduce that the inputs were $1, 0$. Therefore the rows of the doubly-encrypted truth table must be randomly shuffled.

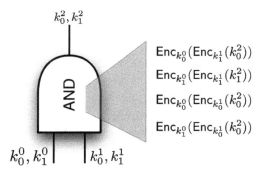

Figure 159.3: The implementation of a garbled AND gate. The gate contains four doubly-encrypted values of the key associated to the output wire of the gate. Each double-encryption corresponds to a row of the AND truth table; but the rows are permuted.

With these ideas in mind, we have the basis of a protocol. One of the parties can construct a garbled circuit for C, and the other party can evaluate it. During the evaluation, the evaluating party does not learn any intermediate value of the circuit. This follows because the value of each internal wire will be one of the two encryption keys associated with that wire, and only the player who constructed the circuit knows that association.

The one remaining problem is how to transfer the keys corresponding to the evaluator's input to the evaluating player.

6.2.4 Oblivious Transfer

The first player who constructs the garbled circuit knows for every wire (including the input wires) the association between the encryption key and the wire value 0 or 1. In order for the evaluating player to begin evaluating the circuit, the player must know the key corresponding to his input. If the evaluating player just asks the first player for the corresponding key, then the first player learns the second player's input. But if the second player sends over both keys, then the first player will be able to learn both $f(x,y)$ and also $f(x,\bar{y})$ which would violate the security definition. What is needed is a way for the second player to learn *exactly one* of the two messages known to the first player in such a way that the first player does not learn which message was requested.

At first, this proposed functionality seems impossible. However, in 1973, Wiener first proposed such a functionality based on the use of quantum communication channels. Later, Rabin (and then EGL) formalized a computational version of the functionality and coined it *oblivious transfer.*

A *1/k-oblivious transfer* protocol is a secure computation for party A to learn one of k secret bits held by party B, without B learning which secret A obtains. More concretely, in a $1/2$-oblivious transfer, A has bits a_1, a_2, and B has an integer $b \in [1,2]$. The function being computed is:

$$OT_{1/2}(a_1, a_2, b) = (\perp, a_b).$$

Here we make use of private outputs: A receives a constant output $\perp$, and B receives the requested bit.

Our construction of an $OT_{1/2}$ protocol in the honest-but-curious model requires a trapdoor permutation and an associate hardcore predicate. Alice selects a trapdoor permutation (i,t) and sends the permutation f_i to Bob. Bob then selects two random values y_1, y_2 in such a way that it knows the inverse $f_i^{-1}(y_b)$ and sends the pair to Alice. Finally, Alice uses y_i to encrypt the bit x_i using the standard hardcore-predicate encryption: $x_i \oplus h(y_i)$. It is straightforward to generalize this construction to handle n-bit values.

PROTOCOL 160.4: OBLIVIOUS TRANSFER PROTOCOL

Let $\{f_i\}_{i\in\mathcal{I}}$ be a family of trapdoor permutations, Gen sample a function from the family, and h be a hardcore predicate for any function from the family.

Sender input: Bits (a_1, a_2)

Receiver input: An index $b \in [1, 2]$

$A \to B$:] A runs $i, t \leftarrow \text{Gen}(1^n)$ and sends i to B.

$A \leftarrow B$: B computes the following. If $j \neq b$ then $y_j \leftarrow \{0,1\}^n$ else $x \leftarrow \{0,1\}^n$; $y_j \leftarrow f_i(x)$. B sends (y_1, y_2) to A.

$A \to B$: A computes the inverse of each value y_j and XORs the hard-core bit of the result with the input a_j:

$$z_j = h(f^{-1}(y_j)) \oplus a_j$$

A sends $(z_1, \ldots, z_4)$.

B outputs $h(x) \oplus z_b$

Intuitively, the protocol satisfies the privacy property: A learns nothing, because the y_j it receives are all uniformly distributed and independent of b, and B learns nothing beyond a_b, because if it did it would be able to predict the hardcore predicate.

▷**Proposition 161.5** *Construction 160.4 is an honest-but-curious one-out-of-2 Oblivious Transfer Protocol.*

Proof. To prove this proposition, we must exhibit two simulators, S_A and S_B which satisfy the honest-but-curious security definition for two-party computation (Def. 155.1). The simulator S_A is the easier case and works as follows:

1. $S_A((a_1, a_2), \bot)$: Complete the first instruction of the protocol and prints the corresponding message.

2. Randomly choose two string $y_1, y_2 \in \{0,1\}^n$ and print a message from Bob with these two values.

3. Follow the third step of the protocol using values y_1, y_2 and print a message with the computed values z_1, z_2.

4. Output $\perp$.

Observe that

$$\{S_A((a_1, a_2), \perp), OT_{1/2}((a_1, a_2), b)\}$$

and

$$\left\{ e \leftarrow [A(a_1, a_2) \overset{\pi}{\leftrightarrow} B(b)] : \mathsf{view}_A(e), \mathsf{out}_B(e) \right\}_n$$

are identically distributed. This follows because the only difference between S_A and the real protocol execution is step 2. However, since f is a permutation, the values y_1, y_2 are identically distributed.

The construction of S_B is left as an exercise. $\square$

Unfortunately, real adversaries are not necessarily honest, but it is sometimes possible to enforce honesty. For example, honesty might be enforced externally to the protocol by trusted hardware or software. Or, honesty might be enforced by the protocol itself through the use of coin-tossing protocols and zero-knowledge proofs of knowledge, which can allow parties to prove that they are following the protocol honestly. We discuss protocols in a more general setting in §??.

6.2.5   Honest-but-Curious Two-Party Secure Protocol

With all of these pieces, we can finally present an honest-but-curious protocol for evaluating any two-party function $f(x, y)$.

PROTOCOL 162.6: HONEST-BUT-CURIOUS SECURE COMPUTATION

A **input:** $x \in \{0, 1\}^n$

B **input:** $y \in \{0, 1\}^n$

$A \to B$: A generates a garbled circuit that computes a canonical circuit representation of f. A sends the circuit and the input keys corresponding to the bits of x to B.

$A \leftrightarrow B$: For each input bit $y_1, \ldots, y_n$ of y, A and B run a 1-out-of-2 Oblivious Transfer protocol in which A's inputs are the keys $(k_{i,0}, k_{i,1})$ corresponding to the input wire for y_i and B's input is the bit y_i.

$A \to B$: Using the keys for all input wires, B evaluates the circuit to compute the output $f(x, y)$. B sends the result to A. A and B output the result $f(x, y)$.

▷**Theorem 163.7** *Protocol 162.6 is an honest-but-curious two-party secure function evaluation protocol.*

Proof. To prove this result, we must exhibit two simulators S_A and S_B. The first simulator is the easiest one. Notice that the view of A consists of a random tape, a circuit, the transcript of n oblivious-transfer protocols, and the final output. The first two and the last component are easy to generate; the transcript from the oblivious transfer protocols can be generated using the simulator for the oblivious transfer protocol. Thus, the algorithm $S_A(x, f(x, y))$ proceeds as follows:

1. On input $x, f(x, y)$, select a random tape r, and run the first step of the protocol to generate a garbled circuit C'. Output C' as a message to Bob. Let $k_0^{y_i}, k_1^{y_i}$ be the key-pair for input wire y_i in circuit C'.

2. For $i \in [1, n]$, use the simulator $Sim'_A((k_0^{y_i}, k_1^{y_i}), \perp)$ for the $OT_{1/2}$ protocol to generate n transcripts of the oblivious transfer protocol for each of Bob's input wires.

3. Output a message from Bob to Alice containing the value $f(x, y)$.

The second simulator $S_B(y, f(x, y))$ works as follows:

1. On input $y, f(x, y)$, generate a random garbled circuit C' that always outputs the value $f(x, y)$ for all inputs. This can be done by creating an otherwise correct circuit, with the exception that all of the output wires correspond to

the bits of the output $f(x,y)$. As above, let $k_0^{y_i}, k_1^{y_i}$ be the key-pair for input wire y_i in circuit C'.

Generate a message from Alice consisting of the circuit C'.

2. For $i \in [1,n]$, use the simulator $Sim'_b(b, k_b^{y_i})$ to produce n transcripts of the $OT_{1/2}$ protocol.

3. Output a message from Bob to Alice containing the value $f(x,y)$.

Using a hybrid argument, we can show that the security of the encryption scheme implies that the circuit C' is computationally indistinguishable from a properly generated garbled circuit of C. The security of the simulator for the $OT_{1/2}$ protocol implies that the messages from the second step are identically distributed to the messages from a real execution of the protocol. Finally, the last step is also identically distributed.

□

6.3 Secure Computation

Let $P_1, \ldots, P_n$ be a set of parties, with private inputs $x_1, \ldots, x_n$, that want to compute a function $f(x_1, \ldots, x_n)$. Without loss of generality, suppose that the output of function f is a single public value. (If private outputs are instead desired, each party can supply a public key as part of its input, and the output can be a tuple with an encrypted element per party.) If a trusted external party T existed, all the parties could give their inputs to T, which would then compute f and publish the output; we call this the *ideal* model. In this model, T is trusted for both:

Correctness: The output is consistent with f and the inputs x_i, and

Privacy: Nothing about the private inputs is revealed beyond whatever information is contained in the public output.

In the absence of T, the (mutually distrusting) parties must instead engage in a protocol among themselves; we call this the *real* model. The challenge of secure computation is to emulate the ideal model in the real model, obtaining both correctness and privacy without a trusted external party, even when an adversary corrupts some of the parties.

▷**Definition 165.1** *A protocol securely computes a function f if for every p.p.t. adversary controlling a subset of parties in the real model, there exists a p.p.t. simulator controlling the same subset of parties in the ideal model, such that the output of all parties in the real model is computationally indistinguishable from their outputs in the ideal model.*

Goldreich, Micali, and Wigderson, building on a result of Yao, showed the feasibility of secure computation for any function. [Oded Goldreich, Silvio Micali, and Avi Wigderson. How to Play any Mental Game or A Completeness Theorem for Protocols with Honest Majority. In *19th ACM Symposium on Theory of Computing*, 1987, pages 218–229.]

▷**Theorem 165.2** *Let $f : (\{0,1\}^m)^n \to (\{0,1\}^m)^n$ be a poly-time computable function, and let t be less than $n/2$. Assume the existence of trapdoor permutations. Then there exists an efficient n-party protocol that securely computes f in the presence of up to t corrupted parties.*

The restriction on $n/2$ parties in this theorem is due to *fairness*: all parties must receive their outputs. A simple induction on the length of the protocol shows that fairness is impossible for $n = 2$. We can also define *secure computation without fairness*, in which the simulator is additionally allowed to decide which honest parties receive their outputs, to remove the $n/2$ restriction.

Chapter 7

Composability

7.1 Composition of Encryption Schemes

7.1.1 CCA-Secure Encryption

So far, we have assumed that the adversary only captures the ciphertext that Alice sends to Bob. In other words, the adversary's attack is a *ciphertext only* attack. One can imagine, however, stronger attack models. We list some of these models below:

Attack models:

- Known plaintext attack – The adversary may get to see pairs of form $(m_0, Enc_k(m_0)) \ldots$

- Chosen plain text (CPA) – The adversary gets access to an encryption oracle before and after selecting messages.

- Chosen ciphertext attack

  CCA1: ("Lunch-time attack") The adversary has access to an encryption oracle and to a decryption oracle before selecting the messages. (due to Naor and. Yung)

  CCA2: This is just like a CCA1 attack except that the adversary also has access to decryption oracle after selecting the messages. It is not allowed to decrypt the challenge ciphertext however. (introduced by Rackoff and Simon)

Fortunately, all of these attacks can be abstracted and captured by a simple definition which we present below. The different attacks can be captured by allowing the adversary to have *oracle*-access to a special function which allows it to mount either CPA, CCA1, or CCA2- attacks.

▷**Definition 168.1 (CPA/CCA-Secure Encryption)** *Let* $\Pi = (\text{Gen}, \text{Enc}, \text{Dec})$ *be an encryption scheme. Let the random variable* $\text{IND}_b^{O_1,O_2}(\Pi, A, n)$ *where* A *is a non-uniform p.p.t.,* $n \in \mathbb{N}$, $b \in \{0,1\}$ *denote the output of the following experiment:*

$$\text{IND}_b^{O_1,O_2}(\Pi, ma, n)$$
$$k \leftarrow \text{Gen}(1^n)$$
$$m_0, m_1, state \leftarrow A^{O_1(k)}(1^n)$$
$$c \leftarrow \text{Enc}_k(m_b)$$
$$\text{Output } A^{O_2(k)}(c, state)$$

Then we say π *is CPA/CCA1/CCA2 secure if* $\forall$ *non-uniform p.p.t.* A:

$$\left\{\text{IND}_0^{O_1,O_2}(\pi, A, n)\right\}_n \approx \left\{\text{IND}_1^{O_1,O_2}(\pi, A, n)\right\}_n$$

where O_1 *and* O_2 *are defined as:*

CPA	$[\text{Enc}_k; \text{Enc}_k]$
CCA1	$[\text{Enc}_k, \text{Dec}_k; \text{Enc}_k]$
CCA2	$[\text{Enc}_k, \text{Dec}_k; \text{Enc}_k, \text{Dec}_k]$

Additionally, in the case of CCA2 attacks, the decryption oracle returns $\perp$ *when queried on the challenge ciphertext c.*

7.1.2 A CCA1-Secure Encryption Scheme

We will now show that the encryption scheme presented in construction 99.1 satisfies a stronger property than claimed earlier. In particular, we show that it is CCA1 secure (which implies that it is also CPA-secure).

▷**Theorem 168.2** π *in construction 99.1 is CPA and CCA1 secure.*

Proof. Consider scheme $\pi^{RF} = (\text{Gen}^{RF}, \text{Enc}^{RF}, \text{Dec}^{RF})$, which is derived from π by replacing the PRF f_k in π by a truly random function. π^{RF} is CPA and CCA1 secure. Because the adversary only has access to the encryption oracle after chosing m_0 and m_1, the only chance adversary can differentiate $\text{Enc}_k(m_0) = r_0 \| m_0 \oplus f(r_0)$ and $\text{Enc}_k(m_1) = r_1 \| m_1 \oplus f(r_1)$ is that the encryption oracle happens to have sampled the same r_0 or r_1 in some previous query, or additionally, in a CCA1 attack, the attacker happens to have asked decryption oracle to decrypt ciphertext like $r_0 \| m$ or $r_1 \| m$. All cases have only negligible probabilities.

Given π^{RF} is CPA and CCA1 secure, then so is π. Otherwise, if there exists one distinguisher D that can differentiate the experiment results ($\text{IND}_0^{\text{Enc}_k;\text{Enc}_k}$ and $\text{IND}_1^{\text{Enc}_k;\text{Enc}_k}$ in case of CPA attack, while $\text{IND}_0^{\text{Enc}_k,\text{Dec}_k;\text{Enc}_k}$ and $\text{IND}_1^{\text{Enc}_k,\text{Dec}_k;\text{Enc}_k}$ in case of CCA1 attack) then we can construct another distinguisher which internally uses D to differentiate PRF from truly random function. $\square$

7.1.3   A CCA2-Secure Encryption Scheme

However, the encryption scheme π is not CCA2 secure. Consider the attack: in experiment $\text{IND}_b^{\text{Enc}_k,\text{Dec}_k;\text{Enc}_k,\text{Dec}_k}$, given ciphertext $r \| c \leftarrow \text{Enc}_k(m_b)$, the attacker can ask the decryption oracle to decrypt $r \| c + 1$. As this is not the challenge itself, this is allowed. Actually $r \| c + 1$ is the ciphertext for message $m_b + 1$, as

$$\begin{aligned}
\text{Enc}_k(m_b + 1) &= (r \| (m_b + 1)) \oplus f_k(r) \\
&= r \| m_b \oplus f_k(r) + 1 \\
&= r \| c + 1
\end{aligned}$$

Thus the decryption oracle would reply $m_b + 1$. The adversary can differentiate which message's encryption it is given.

We construct a new encryption scheme that is CCA2 secure. Let $\{f_s\}$ and $\{g_s\}$ be families of PRF on space $\{0,1\}^{|s|} \rightarrow \{0,1\}^{|s|}$.

ALGORITHM 169.3: π' : MANY-MESSAGE CCA2-SECURE ENCRYPTION

Assume $m \in \{0,1\}^n$ and let $\{f_k\}$ be a PRF family

$\text{Gen}'(1^n)$: $k_1, k_2 \leftarrow U_n$

$\text{Enc}'_{k_1,k_2}(m)$: Sample $r \leftarrow U_n$. Set $c_1 \leftarrow m \oplus f_{k_1}(r)$. Output the
ciphertext $(r, c_1, f_{k_2}(c))$

$\text{Dec}'_{k_1,k_2}((r, c_1, c_2))$: If $f_{k_2}(c_1) \neq c_2$, then output $\bot$. Otherwise
output $c_1 \oplus f_{k_1}(r)$

▷**Theorem 170.4** π' *is CCA2-secure.*

Proof. The main idea is to prove by contradiction. In specific, if
there is an CCA2 attack on π', then there is an CPA attack on π,
which would contradict with the fact that π is CPA secure.

A CCA2 attack on π' is a p.p.t. machine A', s.t. it can differen-
tiate $\left\{ \text{IND}_0^{\text{Enc}_k, \text{Dec}_k; \text{Enc}_k, \text{Dec}_k} \right\}$ and $\left\{ \text{IND}_1^{\text{Enc}_k, \text{Dec}_k; \text{Enc}_k, \text{Dec}_k} \right\}$. Visually,
it works as that in figure **??**. The attacker A' needs accesses to
the Enc'_k and Dec'_k oracles. To devise a CPA attack on π, we
want to construct another machine A as depicted in figure **??**.
To leverage the CCA2 attacker A', we simulate A as in figure **??**
which internally uses A'.

Formally, the simulator works as follows:

- Whenever A' asks for an encryption of message m, A asks
  its own encryption oracle Enc_{s_1} to compute $c_1 \leftarrow \text{Enc}_{s_1}(m)$.
  However A' expects an encryption of the form $c_1 \| c_2$ which
  requires the value s_2 to evaluate $g_{s_2}(c_1)$; A does not have
  access to s_2 and so instead computes $c_2 \leftarrow \{0,1\}^n$, and
  replies $c_1 \| c_2$.

- Whenever A' asks for a decryption $c_1 \| c_2$. If we previously
  gave A' $c_1 \| c_2$ to answer an encryption query of some mes-
  sage m, then reply m, otherwise reply $\bot$.

- Whenever A' outputs m_0, m_1, output m_0, m_1.

- Upon receiving c, feed $c \| r$, where $r \leftarrow \{0,1\}^n$ to A'.

- Finally, output A''s output.

Consider the encryption scheme $\pi'^{RF} = (\text{Gen}'^{RF}, \text{Enc}'^{RF}, \text{Dec}'^{RF})$
which is derived from π' by replacing every appearance of g_{s_2}
with a truly random function.

Note that the simulated Enc' is just Enc'^{RF}, and Dec' is very similar to Dec'^{RF}. Then A' inside the simulator is nearly conducting CCA2 attack on π'^{RF} with the only exception when A' asks an $c_1 || c_2$ to Dec' which is not returned by a previous encryption query and is a correct encryption, in which case Dec' falsely returns $\bot$. However, this only happens when $c_2 = f(c_1)$, where f is the truly random function. Without previous encryption query, the attacker can only guess the correct value of $f(c_1)$ w.p. $\frac{1}{2^n}$, which is negligible.

Thus we reach that: if A' breaks CCA2 security of π'^{RF}, then it can break CPA security of π. The premise is true as by assumption A' breaks CCA2 security of π', and that PRF is indistinguishable from a truly random function. $\qquad\square$

7.1.4 CCA-secure Public-Key Encryption

We can also extend the notion of CCA security to public-key encryption schemes. Note that, as the adversary already knows the the public key, there is no need to provide it with an encryption oracle.

▷**Definition 171.5 (CPA/CCA-Secure Public Key Encryption)** *If the triplet $\Pi = (\mathsf{Gen}, \mathsf{Enc}, \mathsf{Dec})$ is a public key encryption scheme, let the random variable $\mathsf{Ind}_b(\Pi, A, 1^n)$ where A is a non-uniform p.p.t. adversary, $n \in \mathbb{N}$, and $b \in \{0, 1\}$ denote the output of the following experiment:*

$$\mathsf{Ind}_b(\Pi, A, n)$$
$$(pk, sk) \leftarrow \mathsf{Gen}(1^n)$$
$$m_0, m_1, state \leftarrow A^{O_1(sk)}(1^n, pk)$$
$$c \leftarrow \mathsf{Enc}_{pk}(m_b)$$
$$Output\ A^{O_2(k)}(c, state)$$

We say that Π is CPA/CCA1/CCA2 secure if for all non-uniform p.p.t. A, the following two distributions are computationally indistinguishable:

$$\{\mathsf{Ind}_0(\Pi, A, n)\}_{n \in \mathbb{N}} \approx \{\mathsf{Ind}_1(\Pi, A, n)\}_{n \in \mathbb{N}}$$

The oracles O_1, O_2 are defined as follows:

$$CPA \quad [\cdot, \cdot]$$
$$CCA1 \quad [\text{Dec}, \cdot]$$
$$CCA2 \quad [\text{Dec}, \text{Dec}^*]$$

where Dec^* *answers all queries except for the challenge ciphertext c.*

It is not hard to see that the encryption scheme in Construction 104.3 is CPA secure. CCA2 secure public-key encryption schemes are, however, significantly hard to construct; such contructions are outside the scope of this chapter.

7.1.5 Non-Malleable Encryption

Until this point we have discussed encryptions that prevent a passive attacker from discovering any information about messages that are sent. In some situations, however, we may want to prevent an attacker from creating a new message from a given encryption.

Consider an auction for example. Suppose the Bidder Bob is trying to send a message containing his bid to the Auctioneer Alice. Private key encryption could prevent an attacker Eve from knowing what Bob bids, but if she could construct a message that contained one more than Bob's bid, then she could win the auction.

We say that an encryption scheme that prevents these kinds of attacks is *non-malleable*. In such a scheme, it is impossible for an adversary to output a ciphertext that corresponds to any function of a given encrypted message. Formally, we have the following definition:

▷**Definition 172.6 (Non-Malleable Encryption)** *Let the triple* (Gen,Enc,D *be a public key encryption scheme. Define the following experiment:*

$$\mathsf{NM}_b(\Pi, ma, n)$$
$$k \leftarrow \mathsf{Gen}(1^n)$$
$$m_0, m_1, state \leftarrow A^{O_1(k)}(1^n)$$
$$c \leftarrow \mathsf{Enc}_k(m_b)$$
$$c_1', c_2', c_3', \dots, c_\ell' \leftarrow A^{O_2(k)}(c, state)$$
$$m_i' \leftarrow \begin{cases} \bot & \text{if } c_i = c \\ \mathsf{Dec}_k(c_i') & \text{otherwise} \end{cases}$$
$$\text{Output } (m_1', m_2', \dots, m_\ell')$$

Then $(\mathsf{Gen}, \mathsf{Enc}, \mathsf{Dec})$ *is* non-malleable *if for every non-uniform p.p.t.* A, *and for every non-uniform p.p.t.* D, *there exists a negligible* ϵ *such that for all* $m_0, m_1 \in \{0, 1\}^n$,

$$\Pr\left[D(\mathsf{NM}_0(\Pi, A, n)) = 1\right] - \Pr\left[D(\mathsf{NM}_1(\Pi, A, n)) = 1\right] \le \epsilon(n)$$

One non-trivial aspect of this definition is the conversion to $\bot$ of queries that have already been made (step 4). Clearly without this, the definition would be trivially unsatisfiable, because the attacker could simply "forge" the encryptions that they have already seen by replaying them.

7.1.6 Relation-Based Non-Malleability

We chose this definition because it mirrors our definition of secrecy in a satisfying way. However, an earlier and arguably more natural definition can be given by formalizing the intuitive notion that the attacker cannot output an encryption of a message that is related to a given message. For example, we might consider the relation $R_{\text{next}}(x) = \{x + 1\}$, or the relation $R_{\text{within-one}}(x) = \{x - 1, x, x + 1\}$. We want to ensure that the encryption of x does not help the attacker encrypt an element of $R(x)$. Formally:

▷**Definition 173.7 (Relation-Based Non-Malleable Encryption)** *An encryption scheme* $(\mathsf{Gen}, \mathsf{Enc}, \mathsf{Dec})$ *is* relation-based non-malleable *if for every p.p.t. adversary* A *there exists a p.p.t. simulator* S *such that* *for all p.p.t.-recognizable relations R, there exists a negligible ϵ such that for all $m \in \mathcal{M}$ with $|m| = n$, and for all z, it holds that*

$$\left| \begin{array}{l} \Pr[NM(A(z), m) \in R(m)] \\ \quad - \Pr[k \leftarrow \mathrm{Gen}(1^n); c \leftarrow \mathcal{S}(1^n, z) : \mathrm{Dec}_k(c) \in R(m)] \end{array} \right| < \epsilon$$

where i ranges from 1 to a polynomial of n and NM is defined as above.

This definition is equivalent to the non-relational definition given above.

▷**Theorem 174.8** *Scheme* (Enc, Dec, Gen) *is a non-malleable encryption scheme if and only if it is a relation-based non-malleable encryption scheme.*

Proof. ($\Rightarrow$) Assume that the scheme is non-malleable by the first definition. For any given adversary $\mathcal{A}$, we need to produce a simulator $\mathcal{S}$ that hits any given relation R as often as $\mathcal{A}$ does. Let $\mathcal{S}$ be the machine that performs the first 3 steps of $NM(A(z), m')$ and outputs the sequence of cyphertexts, and let $\mathcal{D}$ be the distinguisher for the relation R. Then

$$\left| \begin{array}{l} \Pr[NM(\mathcal{A}(z), m) \in R(m)] - \\ \quad \Pr[k \leftarrow \mathrm{Gen}(1^n); c \leftarrow \mathcal{S}(1^n, z); m' = \mathrm{Dec}_k(c) : m' \in R(m)] \end{array} \right|$$
$$= |\Pr[\mathcal{D}(NM(\mathcal{A}(z), m))] - \Pr[\mathcal{D}(NM(\mathcal{A}(z), m'))]| \leq \epsilon$$

as required.

($\Leftarrow$) Assume that the scheme is relation-based non-malleable. Given an adversary $\mathcal{A}$, we know there exists a simulator $\mathcal{S}$ that outputs related encryptions as well as $\mathcal{A}$ does. The relation-based definition tells us that $NM(\mathcal{A}(z), m_0) \approx Dec(\mathcal{S}())$ and $Dec(\mathcal{S}()) \approx NM(\mathcal{A}(z), m_1)$. Thus, by the hybrid lemma, it follows that $NM(\mathcal{A}(z), m_0) \approx NM(\mathcal{A}(z), m_1)$ which is the first definition of non-malleability.   □

7.1.7 Non-Malleability and Secrecy

Note that non-malleability is a distinct concept from secrecy. For example, one-time pad is perfectly secret, yet is not non-malleable (since one can easily produce the encryption of $a \oplus b$ give then encryption of a, for example). However, if we consider security under CCA2 attacks, then the two definitions coincide.

▷**Theorem 175.9** *An encryption scheme* (Enc, Dec, Gen) *is CCA2 secret if and only if it is CCA2 non-malleable*

Proof. (Sketch) If the scheme is not CCA2 non-malleable, then a CCA2 attacker can break secrecy by changing the provided encryption into a related encryption, using the decryption oracle on the related message, and then distinguishing the unencrypted related messages. Similarly, if the scheme is not CCA2 secret, then a CCA2 attacker can break non-malleability by simply decrypting the cyphertext, applying a function, and then re-encrypting the modified message.   □

7.2   Composition of Zero-knowledge Proofs*

7.2.1   Sequential Composition

Whereas the definition of zero knowledge only talks about a *single* execution between a prover and a verifier, the definitions is in fact closed under sequential composition; that is, sequential repetitions of a ZK protocol results in a new protocol that still remains ZK.

▷**Theorem 175.1 (Sequential Composition)** *Let (P, V) be a perfect/computational zero-knowledge proof for the language L. Let $Q(n)$ be a polynomial, and let (P_Q, V_Q) be an interactive proof (argument) that on common input $x \in \{0,1\}^n$ proceeds in $Q(n)$ phases, each on them consisting of an execution of the interactive proof (P, V) on common input x (each time with independent random coins). Then (P_Q, V_Q) is an perfect/computational ZK interactive proof.*

Proof. (Sketch) Consider a malicious verifier V^{Q*}. Let

$$V^*(x, z, r, (\bar{m}_1, \ldots, \bar{m}_i))$$

denote the machine that runs $V^{Q*}(x, z)$ on input the random tape r and feeds it the messages $(\bar{m}_1, \ldots, \bar{m}_i)$ as part of the i first iterations of (P, V) and runs just as V^{Q*} during the $i + 1$ iteration, and then halts. Let S denote the zero-knowledge simulator for V^*. Let $p(\cdot)$ be a polynomial bounding the running-time of V^{Q*}. Condsider now the simulator S^{Q*} that proceeds as follows on input x, z

- Pick a length $p(|x|)$ random string r.

- Next proceed as follows for $Q(|x|)$ iterations:

  - In iteration i, run $S(x, z||r||(\bar{m}_1, \ldots, \bar{m}_i))$ and let $\bar{m}_{i+1}$ denote the messages in the view output.

The linearity of expectations, the expected running-time of S^Q is polynomial (since the expected running-time of S is). A standard hybrid argument can be used to show that the output of S^Q is correctly distributed.   □

7.2.2   Parallel/Concurrent Composition

Sequential composition is a very basic notion of compostion. An often more realistic scenario consider the execution of multiple protocols at the same time, with an arbitrary scheduling. As we show in this section, zero-knowledge is not closed under such "concurrent composition". In fact, it is not even closed under "parallel-composition" where all protocols executions start at the same time and are run in a lockstep fashion.

Consider the protocol (P, V) for proving $x \in L$, where P on input x, y and V on input x proceed as follows, and L is a language with a unique witness (for instance, L could be the language consisting of all elements in the range of a $1 - 1$ one-way function f, and the associated witness relation is $R_L(x) = \{y | f(y) = x\}$.

PROTOCOL 176.2: ZK PROTOCOL THAT IS NOT CONCURRENTLY SECURE

$P \to V$ P provides a zero-knowledge proof of knowledge of $x \in L$.

$P \leftarrow V$ V either "quits" or starts a zero-knowledge proof of knowledge $x \in L$.

$P \to V$ If V provides a convincing proof, P reveals the witness y.

It can be shown that the (P, V) is zero-knowledge; intuitively this follows from the fact that P only reveals y in case the verifier already knows the witness. Formally, this can be shown by "extracting" y from any verifier V^* that manages to convince P. More precisely, the simulator S first runs the simulator for the ZK proof in step 1; next, if V^* produces an accepting proof in step 2, S runs the extractor on V^* to extract a witness y' and finally feeds the witness to y'. Since by assumption L has a unique witness it follows that $y = y'$ and the simulation will be correctly distributed.

However, an adversary A that participates in two concurrent executions of (P, V), acting as a verifier in both executions, can easily get the witness y even if it did not know it before. A simply schedules the messages such that the zero-knowledge proof that the prover provides in the first execution is forwarded as the step 2 zero-knowledge proof (by the verifier) in the second execution; as such A convinces P in the second execution that it knows a witness y (although it is fact only is relaying messages from the the other prover, and in reality does not know y), and as a consequence P will reveal the witness to A.

The above protocol can be modified (by padding it with dummy messages) to also give an example of a zero-knowledge protocol that is not secure under even two parallel executions.

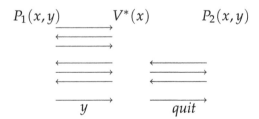

Figure 177.3: A Message Schedule which shows that protocol 176.2 does not concurrently compose. The Verifier feeds the prover messages from the second interaction with P_2 to the first interaction with prover P_1. It therefore convinces the first prover that it "knows" y, and therefore, P_1 sends y to V^*.

7.2.3 Witness Indistinguishability

- Definition

- WI closed under concurrent comp

- ZK implies WI

7.2.4 A Concurrent Identification Protocol

- y_1, y_2 is pk

- x_1, x_2 is sk

- WI POK that you know inverse of either y_1 or y_2.

7.3 Composition Beyond Zero-Knowledge Proofs

7.3.1 Non-malleable commitments

- Mention that standard commitment is malleable

- (could give construction based on adaptive OWP?)

Chapter 8

*More on Randomness and Pseudorandomness

8.1   A Negative Result for Learning

Consider a space $S \subseteq \{0,1\}^n$ and a family of concepts $\{C_i\}_{i \in I}$ such that $C_i \subseteq S$.

The Learning Question: For a random $i \in I$, given samples (x_j, b_j) such that $x_j \in S$ and $b_j = 1$ iff $x_j \in C_i$, determine for a bit string x if $x \in C_i$. The existence of PRFs shows that there are concepts that can not be learned.

$\triangleright$**Theorem 179.1** *There exists a p.p.t. decidable concept that cannot be learned.*

Proof sketch.

$$S = \{0,1\}^n$$
$$C_i = \{x \mid f_i(x)_{|1} = 1\} \qquad f_i(x)_{|1} \text{ is the first bit of } f_i(x)$$
$$I = \{0,1\}^n$$

No (n.u.) p.p.t. can predict whether a new sample x is in C_i better than $\frac{1}{2} + \epsilon$. $\qquad \square$

8.2   Derandomization

Traditional decision problems do not need randomness; a randomized machine can be replaced by a deterministic machine that tries all finite random tapes. In fact, we can do better if we make some cryptographic assumptions. For example:

▷**Theorem 180.1** *If pseudo-random generators (PRG) exist, then for every constant $\varepsilon > 0$, BPP $\subseteq$ DTIME(2^{n^ε}).*

Proof. where **DTIME**$(t(n))$ denotes the set of all languages that can be decided by deterministic machines with running-time bounded by $O(t(n))$.

Given a language $L \in$ **BPP**, let M be a p.p.t.Turing machine that decides L with probability at least $2/3$. Since the running time of M is bounded by n^c for some constant c, M uses at most n^c bits of the random tape. Note that we can trivially de-randomize M by deterministically trying out all 2^{n^c} possible random tapes, but such a deterministic machine will take more time than 2^{n^ε}.

Instead, given ε, let $g : \{0,1\}^{n^{\varepsilon/2}} \to \{0,1\}^{n^c}$ be a PRG (with polynomial expansion factor $n^{c-\varepsilon/2}$). Consider a p.p.t.machine M' that does the following given input x:

1. Read $\varepsilon/2$ bits from the random tape, and apply g to generate n^c pseudo-random bits.

2. Simulate and output the answer of M using these pseudo-random bits.

M' must also decide L with probability negligibly close to $2/3$; otherwise, M would be a p.p.t.distinguisher that can distinguish between uniform randomness and the output of g.

Since M' only uses $n^{\varepsilon/2}$ random bits, a deterministic machine that simulates M' on all possible random tapes will take time

$$2^{n^{\varepsilon/2}} \cdot \text{poly}(n) \in O(2^{n^\varepsilon})$$

$\square$

Remark: We can strengthen the definition of a PRG to require that the output of a PRG be indistinguishable from a uniformly random string, even when the distinguisher can run in sub-exponential time (that is, the distinguisher can run in time $t(n)$ where $t(n) \in O(2^{n^\varepsilon})$ for all $\varepsilon > 0$). With this stronger assumption, we can show that $\mathbf{BPP} \subseteq \mathbf{DTIME}(2^{\mathrm{poly}(\log n)})$, the class of languages that can be decided in *quasi-polynomial* time.

However, for cryptographic primitives, we have seen that randomness is actually required. For example, any deterministic public key encryption scheme must be insecure. But how do we get randomness in the real world? What if we only have access to "impure" randomness?

8.3 Imperfect Randomness and Extractors

In this section we discuss models of imperfect randomness, and how to extract truly random strings from imperfect random sources with *deterministic extractors*.

8.3.1 Extractors

Intuitively, an extractor should be an efficient and deterministic machine that produces truly random bits, given a sample from an imperfect source of randomness. In fact, sometimes we may be satisfied with just "almost random bits", which can be formalized with the notion of ε-closeness.

▷**Definition 181.1 (ε-closeness)** *Two distributions X and Y are ε-close, written $X \approx_\varepsilon Y$, if for every (deterministic) distinguisher D (with no time bound),*

$$\left| \Pr[x \leftarrow X : D(x) = 1] - \Pr[y \leftarrow Y : D(y) = 1] \right| \leq \varepsilon$$

▷**Definition 181.2 (ε-extractors)** *Let C be a set of distributions over $\{0,1\}^n$. An m-bit ε-extractor for C is a deterministic function $\mathrm{Ext} : \{0,1\}^n \rightarrow \{0,1\}^m$ that satisfies the following:*

$$\forall X \in C, \ \{x \leftarrow X : \mathrm{Ext}(x)\} \approx_\varepsilon U_m$$

where U_m is the uniform distribution over $\{0,1\}^m$.

8.3.2   Imperfect Randomness

An obvious example of imperfect randomness is to repeatedly toss a biased coin; every bit in the string would be biased in the same manner (i.e. the bits are independently and identically distributed). Van Neumann showed that the following algorithm is a 0-extractor (i.e. algorithm produces truly random bits): Toss the biased coin twice. Output 0 if the result was 01, output 1 if the result was 10, and repeat the experiment otherwise.

A more exotic example of imperfect randomness is to toss a sequence of different biased coins; every bit in the string would still be independent, but not biased the same way. We do not know any 0-extractor in this case. However, we can get a ε-extractor by tossing a sufficient large number of coins at once and outputting the XOR of the results.

More generally, one can consider distributions of bit strings where different bits are not even independent (e.g. bursty errors in nature). Given an imperfect source, we would like to have a measure of its "amount of randomness". We first turn to the notion of *entropy* in physics:

▷**Definition 182.3 (Entropy)** *Given a distribution X, the* entropy *of X, denoted by $H(x)$ is defined as follows:*

$$H(X) = \mathbb{E}\left[x \leftarrow X : \log\left(\frac{1}{\Pr[X = x]}\right)\right]$$
$$= \sum_x \Pr[X = x] \log\left(\frac{1}{\Pr[X = x]}\right)$$

When the base of the logarithm is 2, $H(x)$ is the Shannon entropy of X.

Intuitively, Shannon entropy measures how many truly random bits are "hidden" in X. For example, if X is the uniform distribution over $\{0,1\}^n$, X has Shannon entropy

$$H(X) = \sum_{x \in \{0,1\}^n} \Pr[X = x] \log_2\left(\frac{1}{\Pr[X = x]}\right) = 2^n(2^{-n} \cdot n) = n$$

As we will soon see, however, a source with high Shannon entropy can be horrible for extractors. For example, consider X

defined as follows:

$$X = \begin{cases} 0^n & \text{w.p. 0.99} \\ \text{uniformly random element in } \{0,1\}^n & \text{w.p. 0.01} \end{cases}$$

Then, $H(X) \approx 0.01n$. However, an extractor that samples an instance from X will see 0^n most of the time, and cannot hope to generate even just one random bit[1]. Therefore, we need a stronger notion of randomness.

▷**Definition 183.4 (Min Entropy)** *The* min entropy *of a probability distribution X, denoted by $H_\infty(x)$, is defined as follows:*

$$H_\infty(X) = \min_x \log_2 \left(\frac{1}{\Pr[X = x]} \right)$$

Equivalently,

$$H_\infty(X) \geq k \Leftrightarrow \forall x, \ \Pr[X = x] \leq 2^{-k}$$

▷**Definition 183.5 (k-source)** *A probability distribution X is called a k-source if $H_\infty(X) \geq k$. If additionally X is the uniform distribution on 2^k distinct elements, we say X is a k-flat source.*

Even with this stronger sense of entropy, however, extraction is not always possible.

▷**Theorem 183.6** *Let C be the set of all efficiently computable $(n-2)$-sources on $\{0,1\}^n$. Then, there are no 1-bit 1/4-extractors for C.*

Proof. Suppose the contrary that Ext is a 1/4-extractor for C. Consider the distribution X generated as follows:

1. Sample $x \leftarrow U_n$. If $\text{Ext}(x) = 1$, output x. Otherwise repeat.

2. After 10 iterations with no output, give up and output a random $x \leftarrow U_n$.

---

[1] A possible fix is to sample X many times. However, we restrict ourselves to one sample only motivated by the fact that some random sources in nature can not be independently sampled twice. E.g. the sky in the morning is not independent from the sky in the afternoon.

Since $U_n \in C$ and Ext is a $1/4$-extractor, we have

$$\Pr[x \leftarrow U_n : \text{Ext}(x) = 1] \geq 1/2 - 1/4 = 1/4$$

which implies that $|\{x \in \{0,1\}^n : \text{Ext}(x) = 1\}| \geq (1/4)2^n = 2^{n-2}$. We can then characterize X as follows:

$$X = \begin{cases} U_n \text{ w.p. } \leq \left(\frac{3}{4}\right)^{10} \\ \text{uniform sample from } \{x \in \{0,1\}^n, \text{Ext}(x) = 1\} \text{ o.w.} \end{cases}$$

Since $|\{x \in \{0,1\}^n, \text{Ext}(x) = 1\}| \geq 2^{n-2}$, both cases above are $(n-2)$-sources. This makes X a $(n-2)$-source. Moreover, X is computable in polynomial time since Ext is. This establishes $X \in C$.

On the other hand,

$$\Pr[x \in X : \text{Ext}(x) = 1] \geq 1 - \left(\frac{3}{4}\right)^{10} > 0.9$$

and so $\{x \in X : \text{Ext}(x)\}$ is definite not $1/4$-close to U_1, giving us the contradiction. □

8.3.3   Left-over hash lemma

Bibliography

[AKS04]   Manindra Agrawal, Neeraj Kayal, and Nitin Saxena. Primes is in p. *Annals of Mathematics*, 160(2):781–793, 2004.

[BBFK05]   Friedrich Bahr, Michael Böhm, Jens Franke, and Thorsten Kleinjung. Announcement of the factorization of rsa-200, May 2005. http://www.crypto-world.com/FactorAnnouncements.html.

[CLRS09]   Thomas H. Cormen, Charles E. Leiserson, Ronald L. Rivest, and Cliff Stein. *Introduction to Algorithms (3rd Edition)*. MIT Press, 2009.

[EUL63]   Leonhard Euler. Theoremata arithmetica nova methodo demonstrata. In *Novi Commentarii academiae scientiarum Petropolitanae 8*, pages 74–104. –, 1763.

[KAF$^+$10]   Thorsten Kleinjung, Kazumaro Aoki, Jens Franke, Arjen K. Lenstra, Emmanuel Thomé, Joppe W. Bos, Pierrick Gaudry, Alexander Kruppa, Peter L. Montgomery, Dag Arne Osvik, Herman te Riele, Andrey Timofeev, and Paul Zimmermann. Factorization of a 768-bit rsa modulus. eprint.iacr.org/2010/006.pdf, January 2010.

[KNU81]   Donald E. Knuth. *The Art of Computer Programming: Seminumerical algorithms*, volume 2. Addison-Wesley, 2nd edition edition, 1981.

[MIL76]   Gary Miller. Riemanns hypothesis and tests for primality. *J. Comput. System Sci*, 13(3):300–317, 1976.

[RAB80]   Michael Rabin. Probabilistic algorithm for testing
            primality. *J. Number Theory*, 12(1):128–138, 1980.

[SHA49]   Claude Shannon. Communication theory of secrecy
            systems. *Bell System Technical Journal*, 28(4):656–715,
            1949.

Appendix A

Background Concepts

Basic Probability

- Events A and B are said to be *independent* if

$$Pr[A \cap B] = Pr[A] \cdot Pr[B]$$

- The *conditional probability* of event A given event B, written as $\Pr[A \mid B]$ is defined as

$$\Pr[A \mid B] = \frac{\Pr[A \cap B]}{\Pr[B]}$$

- *Bayes theorem* relates the $\Pr[A \mid B]$ with $\Pr[B \mid A]$ as follows:

$$\Pr[A \mid B] = \frac{\Pr[B \mid A] \Pr[A]}{\Pr[B]}$$

- Events $A_1, A_2, \ldots, A_n$ are said to be *pairwise independent* if for every i and every $j \neq i$, A_i and A_j are independent.

- *Union Bound:* Let $A_1, A_2, \ldots, A_n$ be events. Then,

$$\Pr[A_1 \cup A_2 \cup \ldots \cup A_n] \leq \Pr[A_1] + \Pr[A_2] + \ldots + \Pr[A_n]$$

- Let X be a random variable with range Ω. The *expectation* of X is the value:

$$E[X] = \sum_{x \in \Omega} x \Pr[X = x]$$

The *variance* is given by,

$$Var[X] = E[X^2] - (E[X])^2$$

- Let $X_1, X_2, \ldots, X_n$ be random variables. Then,

$$E[X_1 + X_2 + \cdots + X_n] = E[X_1] + E[X_2] + \cdots + E[X_n]$$

- If X and Y are *independent random variables*, then

$$E[XY] = E[X] \cdot E[Y]$$
$$Var[X + Y] = Var[X] + Var[Y]$$

Markov's Inequality

If X is a positive random variable with expectation $E(X)$ and $a > 0$, then

$$Pr[X \geq a] \leq \frac{E(X)}{a}$$

Chebyshev's Inequality

Let X be a random variable with expectation $E(X)$ and variance σ^2, then for any $k > 0$,

$$Pr[|X - E(X)| \geq k] \leq \frac{\sigma^2}{k^2}$$

Chernoff's inequality

▷**Theorem 188.7** *Let $X_1, X_2, \ldots, X_n$ denote independent random variables, such that for all i, $E(X_i) = \mu$ and $|X_i| \leq 1$.*

$$Pr\left[\left|\sum X_i - \mu n\right| \geq \epsilon\right] \leq 2^{-\epsilon^2 n}$$

The constants in this statement have been specifically chosen for simplicity; they can be further optimized for tighter analysis.

A useful application of this inequality is the *Majority voting* lemma. Assume you can get independent and identically distributed, but *biased*, samples of a bit b; that is, these samples are correct only with probability $\frac{1}{2} + \frac{1}{\text{poly}(n)}$. Then, given $\text{poly}(n)$ samples, compute the most frequent value b' of the samples; it holds with high probability that $b = b'$.

▷**Lemma 189.8 (Majority vote)** *Let $b \in \{0,1\}$ be a bit and let $X_1, \ldots, X_\ell$ denote independent random variables such that $\Pr[X_i = b] \geq \frac{1}{2} + \frac{1}{p(n)}$ for some polynomial p. Then if $\ell > p(n)^2$,*

$$\Pr[\text{majority}(X_1, \ldots, X_\ell) = b] > 1 - 2^{??}$$

Proof. Without loss of generality, assume that $b = 1$. (Similar analysis will apply in the case $b = 0$.) In this case, $\mu = E[X_i] = \frac{1}{2} + \frac{1}{p(n)}$, and so $\mu\ell = \ell(\frac{1}{2} + \frac{1}{p(n)}) > \ell/2 + p(n)$. In order for the majority procedure to err, less than $\ell/2$ of the samples must agree with b; i.e. $\sum X_i < \ell/2$. Applying the Chernoff bound, we have that ...

□

Pairwise-independent sampling inequality

Let $X_1, X_2, \ldots, X_n$ denote pair-wise independent random variables, such that for all i, $E(X_i) = \mu$ and $|X_i| \leq 1$.

$$\Pr\left[\left| \frac{\sum X_i}{n} - \mu \right| \geq \epsilon \right] \leq \frac{1 - \mu^2}{n\epsilon^2}$$

Note that this is a Chernoff like bound when the random variables are only pairwise independent. The inequality follows as a corollary of Chebyshev's inequality.

Cauchy-Schwarz Inequality

In this course, we will only need Cauchy's version of this inequality from 1821 for the case of real numbers. This inequality states that

▷**Theorem 189.9 (Cauchy-Schwarz)** *For real numbers x_i and y_i,*

$$\left(\sum_i^n x_i y_i \right)^2 \leq \sum_i^n x_i^2 \cdot \sum_i^n y_i^2$$

Appendix B

Basic Complexity Classes

We recall the definitions of the basic complexity classes **DP, NP** and **BPP**.

The Complexity Class DP. We start by recalling the definition of the class **DP**, i.e., the class of languages that can be decided in (deterministic) polynomial-time.

▷**Definition 191.10 (Complexity Class DP)** *A language L is recognizable in (deterministic) polynomial-time if there exists a deterministic polynomial-time algorithm M such that $M(x) = 1$ if and only if $x \in L$. DP is the class of languages recognizable in polynomial time.*

The Complexity Class NP. We recall the class **NP**, i.e., the class of languages for which there exists a proof of membership that can be verified in polynomial-time.

▷**Definition 191.11 (Complexity Class NP)** *A language L is in NP if there exists a Boolean relation $R_L \subseteq \{0,1\}^* \times \{0,1\}^*$ and a polynomial $p(\cdot)$ such that R_L is recognizable in polynomial-time, and $x \in L$ if and only if there exists a string $y \in \{0,1\}^*$ such that $|y| \le p(|x|)$ and $(x,y) \in R_L$.*

The relation R_L is called a *witness relation* for L. We say that y is a witness for the membership $x \in L$ if $(x,y) \in R_L$. We will also let $R_L(x)$ denote the set of witnesses for the membership $x \in L$, i.e.,

$$R_L(x) = \{y : (x,y) \in L\}$$

We let co-**NP** denote the complement of the class **NP**, i.e., a language L is in co-**NP** if the complement to L is in **NP**.

The Complexity Class BPP. The class **BPP** contains the languages that can be decided in *probabilistic* polynomial-time (with two-sided error).

▷**Definition 192.12 (Complexity Class BPP)** *A language L is recognizable in probabilistic polynomial-time if there exists a probabilistic polynomial-time algorithm M such that*

- $\forall x \in L, \Pr[M(x) = 1] \geq 2/3$

- $\forall x \notin L, \Pr[M(x) = 0] \geq 2/3$

BPP is the class of languages recognizable in probabilistic polynomial time.

www.ingramcontent.com/pod-product-compliance
Lightning Source LLC
Chambersburg PA
CBHW071149050326
40689CB00011B/2033

Excel 2022 Basics

A Quick and Easy Guide to Boosting Your Productivity with Excel

Nathan George

Excel 2022 Basics: A Quick and Easy Guide to Boosting Your Productivity with Excel

Published 2022.

Published by GTech Publishing.

ISBN: 978-1-915476-06-7

https://www.excelbytes.com

Contents

Contents

Introduction

Excel 2022 Basics covers all you would need to successfully create workbooks that provide solutions for your data. Starting from the basics, you learn how to create, edit, format, and print your worksheets. You learn how to carry out different calculations with formulas and functions, work with Excel tables, summarize data from different perspectives with pivot tables, and visually analyze your data with different charts.

This book is concise and to the point, as you don't need to wade through a wall of text to learn how to quickly carry out a task in Excel. Hence you will not see the unnecessary verbosity and filler text you may find in some other Excel books in this book. The aim is to take even a complete beginner to someone skilled in Excel within a few short hours.

Who Is This Book For?

Excel 2022 Basics starts from the basics, so it is suitable for you if you're new to Excel or spreadsheets in general. This book is also for you if you have some Excel skills and want to expand on that by learning the new features in Excel.

The necessary topics have been covered to give you a solid foundation and the tools to create solutions for your data. However, the topics have been kept at a level to not be overwhelming if you're completely new to Excel and interested in a quick course without getting bogged down with the more advanced topics.

If you need something more advanced, like What-If Analysis, macros, advanced functions, in-depth pivot tables, etc., then this book is not for you. It might be a good idea to examine the table of contents to see if it covers your requirements.

This book is aimed at readers with Excel for Microsoft 365 or Excel 2021 (the current standalone version). However, many of the core Excel features remain the same for earlier versions of the software, like Excel 2019, 2016, and 2013. So, you would still find many lessons in this book relevant even if you have an earlier version of Excel.

As much as possible, I point out the features new in Excel when covered. Note, however, that if you're using an earlier version of Excel, some of the dialog boxes displayed in this book may differ from your version.

How to Use This Book

This book can be used as a step-by-step training guide or a reference manual that you come back to from time to time. You can read it cover to cover or skip to certain parts that cover topics you want to learn. Although the chapters have been organized logically, the book has been designed to enable you to read a chapter as a standalone tutorial to learn how to carry out a certain task.

There are many ways to perform the same task in Excel. So, for brevity, this book focuses on the most efficient way of carrying out a task. However, alternative ways to perform a task are also provided occasionally.

As much as possible, the menu items and commands mentioned are bolded to distinguish them from the other text. This book also includes many screenshots to illustrate the covered features and tasks.

Assumptions

When writing this book, the software assumptions are that you already have Excel for Microsoft 365 (or Excel 2021) installed on your computer and that you're working on the Windows 10 (or Windows 11) platform.

If you are using an older version of Excel, you can still use this book (as long as you're aware that some of the covered features may not be available in your version). Alternatively, you can get my *Excel 2019 Basics* book, the previous edition of this book.

If you are using Excel on a Mac, simply substitute any Windows keyboard commands mentioned in the book for the Mac equivalent. All the features within Excel remain the same for both platforms.

If you're using Excel on a tablet or touchscreen device, simply substitute any keyboard commands mentioned in the book with the equivalent on your touchscreen device.

Excel Versions

Excel for Microsoft 365 (2022 update) is the version of Excel that comes with a Microsoft 365 subscription while Excel 2021 is the latest standalone (perpetual license) version of Excel. In the last few years, Microsoft has adopted a release cycle where new features are released for Microsoft 365 products as they become available. Conversely, standalone versions get new features approximately every 2-3 years when a new version of Office is released.

This book covers the latest version of Excel for Microsoft 365 (2022 update) and Excel 2021.

Practice Files

Downloadable Excel files have been provided to save you time if you want to practice in Excel as you follow the examples in the book. All examples are fully detailed in the book, and these files have simply been provided to save you some typing, so they're optional.

You can practice by changing the data to view different results. Please note that practice files have only been included for chapters where the examples use a sizable amount of sample data. You can download the files with the following link:

https://www.excelbytes.com/excel-2022-basics-dl

Notes:

- Type the URL in your Internet browser's address bar, and press Enter to navigate to the download page. If you encounter an error, double-check that you have correctly entered all the URL characters.

- The files have been zipped into one download. Windows 10 (or Windows 11) has the functionality to unzip files. If your OS does not have this functionality, you'll need to get a piece of software like WinZip or WinRAR to unzip the file.

- The files are Excel files, so you will need to have Excel installed on your computer to open and use these files (preferably Excel 2013 and above).

- If you encounter any problems downloading these files, please contact me at **support@excelbytes.com**. Include the title of this book in your email, and the practice files will be emailed directly to you.

Chapter 1

Getting Started with Excel

To start Excel, click the Windows Start icon and enter "Excel" in the search bar. Windows displays the Excel app in the results below. Click Excel to start the application.

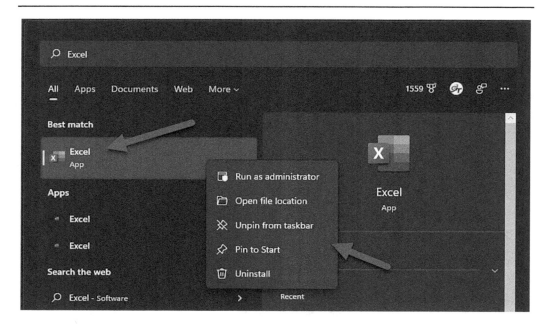

To access Excel faster next time, you can pin it to the **Start menu, taskbar**, or place a shortcut on your **desktop**.

Do the following to pin Excel to your **Start menu**:

1. Click the Windows **Start** icon.
2. On the Start menu, enter "Excel" in the search bar.
3. On the results list below, right-click **Excel** and select **Pin to Start**.

Do the following to pin Excel to your **taskbar:**

1. Click the Windows **Start** icon.
2. On the Start menu, enter "Excel" in the search bar.
3. Right-click **Excel** and select **Pin to taskbar**.

To place a copy of Excel's shortcut on your **desktop**, do the following:

1. Click the Windows **Start** icon.

2. On the Start menu, enter "Excel" in the search bar.

3. Right-click **Excel** and select **Open file location** on the shortcut menu.

    Windows will open the shortcut folder location of Excel in Windows Explorer.

4. In the folder, right-click **Excel**, and select **Copy** on the shortcut menu.

5. On your desktop, right-click any area and select **Paste**.

Creating a New Excel Workbook

Launch Excel from the Start menu or the shortcut you have created on your taskbar or desktop.

Excel will open and display the **Home** screen. The Excel start screen enables you to create a new blank workbook or open one of your recently opened workbooks. You also have a selection of predefined templates that you can use as the basis of your workbook.

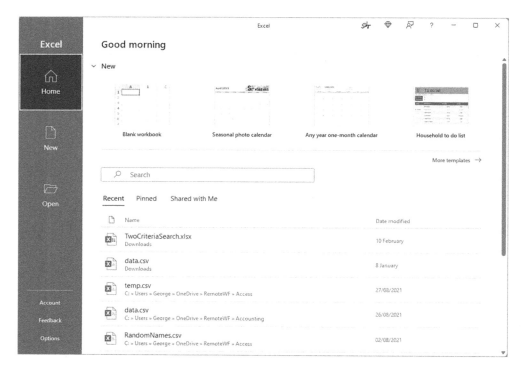

To create a new workbook, click **Blank workbook**. Excel creates a new workbook with a worksheet named **Sheet1**.

-Ω-**Tip** To quickly create a new workbook when you already have a workbook open, press **Ctrl + N** on your keyboard.

Creating A Workbook Based on A Template

To create a new workbook based on one of Excel's predefined templates, open Excel and click the **New** button on the left navigation pane to display the New screen. The categories of available templates are listed under the search bar next to **Suggested searches**.

You can narrow down the displayed templates by clicking one of the listed categories: Business, Personal, Planners and Trackers, Lists, Budgets, Charts, or Calendars.

Once you identify the template you want to use, double-click the thumbnail to create a new worksheet based on it.

Saving Your Excel Workbook

To save your workbook for the first time:

1. Click the **File** tab to go to the Backstage view.

2. In the Backstage view, click **Save As** (you'll see **Save a Copy** if your file has been previously saved to OneDrive).

3. On the next screen, click **OneDrive – Personal** (if you're using OneDrive) or **This PC** (if you're not saving it to OneDrive).

4. You get a text box to enter the file name on the right side of the window. Enter the name of your worksheet here.

5. To save the file to an existing folder, navigate to the folder using the list displayed below on the lower-right of the screen. Double-click a folder name to navigate to that folder.

    You can also create a new folder by clicking the **New Folder** button.

6. Click the **Save** button to save the workbook.

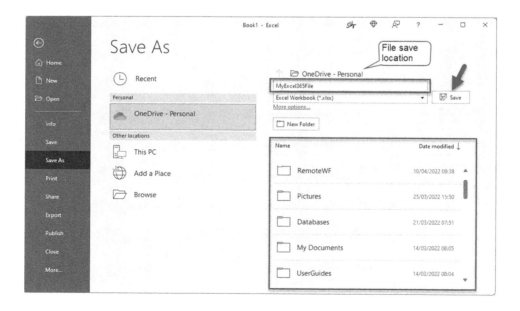

Excel returns you to the **Home** tab after it saves the file.

Note If your workbook has been previously saved to OneDrive or SharePoint, and **AutoSave** is set to on, you'll have **Save a Copy** in place of **Save As**. You can use Save a Copy to save your workbook as a different file.

When you save a file, you overwrite the previous version of the file. If you want to keep an old version of the file while working on it, you need to use **Save As** (or **Save a Copy**). Excel saves the workbook you're working on as a new file while the old version remains unchanged.

Tip To save your workbook quicker, you can use the **Ctrl+S** shortcut after the first save. For a list of the most frequently used shortcuts in Excel, see the Appendix in this book.

Opening an Existing Workbook

Click the **File** menu button to display the Backstage view, and then click **Open** or press **Ctrl+O**.

On the **Open** screen of the Backstage view, you'll see the following options:

- **Recent**: To open a recent workbook, select **Recent** and click the workbook you want to open on the right.

- **Shared with me**: Select this tab to see the files that others have shared with you. Files can be shared through outlook email attachments, a link in an email, a link in Teams, or other methods.

- **OneDrive - Personal**: To open a workbook saved on OneDrive, click OneDrive - Personal and select your file from the right.

> 📝 **Note** If you're not in the root folder of OneDrive, you can use the blue up-arrow to navigate to the folder that contains your workbook.

- **This PC**: To open a workbook from the Documents local folder on your PC, click **This PC** to display the Documents folder. Navigate to the folder containing your workbook. Click the file to open it.

- **Browse**: To browse for a file on your computer, click the **Browse** button and use the Open dialog box to locate the file you want to open. Then, select the file and click the **Open** button.

Closing a Workbook

Ensure you've saved the workbook (if you want to keep the changes).

Click **File** to display the Backstage view, and then click **Close**.

Or

Press the **Ctrl+W** shortcut keys to close the workbook.

The Excel User Interface

This section provides an overview of the Excel user interface to familiarize you with the names of various parts of the interface mentioned throughout the book.

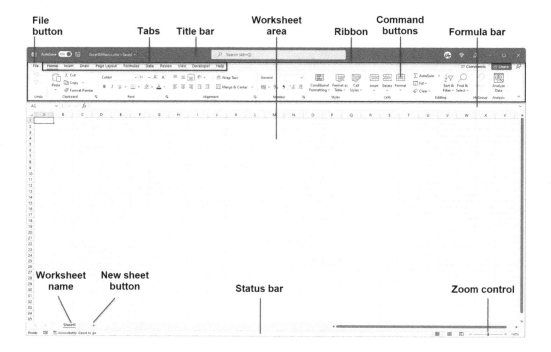

The **Ribbon** contains the bulk of the commands in Excel arranged into a series of tabs from Home to Help.

The **File** button/tab opens the Backstage view when clicked. The Backstage view has several menu options, including Home, New, Open, Info, Save, Save As, Print, Share, Export, Publish, and Close. You have the Account menu option at the bottom of the list to view your user information. You also have Options where you can change many of Excel's default settings.

Note that if your Excel workbook is saved on OneDrive and **AutoSave** is set to **On**, you'll not see the **Save As** menu option. Instead, you'll have **Save a Copy** in its place.

To exit the Backstage view, click the back button (the left-pointing arrow at the top-left of the page).

The **Home** tab provides the most used set of commands. The other tabs provide command buttons for specific tasks like inserting objects into your spreadsheet, formatting the page layout, working with formulas, working with datasets, reviewing your spreadsheet, etc.

The **Worksheet area** contains the cells that will hold your data. The row headings are numbered, while the column headings have letters. Each cell is identified by the combination of the column letter and row number. For example, the first cell on the sheet is A1, the second cell in the first row is B1, and the second cell in the first column is A2. You use these references to identify the cells on the worksheet.

A **workbook** is the Excel document itself. A **worksheet** is a sheet inside a workbook. Each workbook can have several worksheets. You can use the tabs at the bottom of the screen to name, move, copy, and delete worksheets. The plus (+) button next to the name tab enables you to add a new worksheet.

The **Formula bar** displays the contents of the active cell, including any formula.

The **Status bar** provides information on the current display mode. You can zoom in and out of your spreadsheet by clicking the plus (+) and minus (-) signs at the bottom-right of the status bar.

The **Dialog Box Launcher** is a button with a diagonal arrow in the lower-right corner of some groups. When clicked, Excel opens a dialog box containing additional command options related to that group. So, if you cannot see a command on the Ribbon for a task you want to perform, click the small dialog box launcher to display more options for that group.

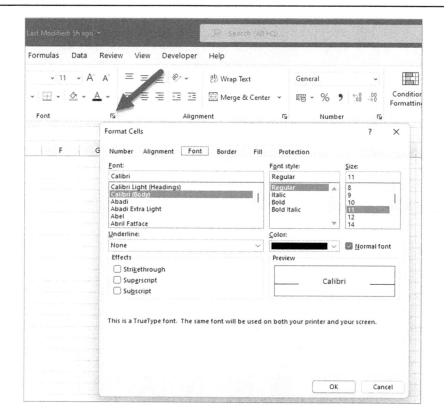

Using AutoSave

AutoSave is a feature on the top-left of the title bar that is enabled when a file is stored on OneDrive or SharePoint. It automatically saves your changes every few seconds as you are working. The main advantage of AutoSave is that if your PC were to crash for any reason, your changes right up to the point it crashed would have been saved to disk. So, you'll hardly lose any work.

With AutoSave on, the **Save As** menu option in the Backstage view is replaced by **Save a Copy**. If you're making changes to your workbook and you normally use **File** > **Save As** to avoid changing the original file, it is recommended that you use **File** > **Save a Copy** before making your changes. That way, AutoSave will not overwrite the original file with the changes but the copy.

If like me, you're in the habit of just closing a workbook without saving it, if you do not want to keep the changes, then AutoSave becomes an issue. In such a case, you can turn off AutoSave before you make any changes and then save your workbook manually if you want to keep the changes.

With **AutoSave** set to On, if you make a mistake that you want to undo, ensure you use the **Undo** button on the **Home** tab to undo the changes before closing the workbook.

Turning off AutoSave

Switching off AutoSave is not recommended. However, if you want to be able to just close Excel and discard all changes whenever you wish, you could turn off AutoSave for that particular file and manually save your workbook.

The default setting for AutoSave is On for files on the cloud (OneDrive or SharePoint). However, if you set AutoSave to Off for a particular workbook, Excel will remember the setting and keep it off every time you reopen it. If you switch it back to On, it will remember to keep it on for that workbook.

Restoring a Previous Version of your Workbook

You can also restore a previous version of your workbook from the Version History.

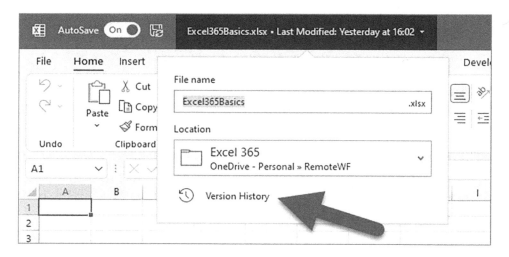

To restore an older version from the Version History list, do the following:

1. Click the file name on the title bar.

2. Click **Version History**.

   Excel displays the **Version History** pane on the right side of the window. The Version History pane shows you the different versions of your document, including the date and time they were saved. The versions are grouped under the date the file was saved. Look at the dates and times to find the version you want to restore.

3. Double click the version you want to restore, and Excel will open the workbook in a second window.

4. Click the **Restore** button displayed just under the Ribbon to revert to this version.

Renaming Your Workbook

You can rename a previously saved workbook from the pop-up menu displayed when you click the file name on the title bar. In the **File Name** box, you can enter a new name for the workbook and press Enter to rename the workbook.

Customizing the Ribbon

The area of the window containing the tabs and command buttons is called the **Ribbon**. You can customize the Ribbon to your liking by adding or removing tabs and command buttons.

To customize the Ribbon, right-click anywhere on the Ribbon, below the tabs, and select **Customize the Ribbon** from the pop-up menu.

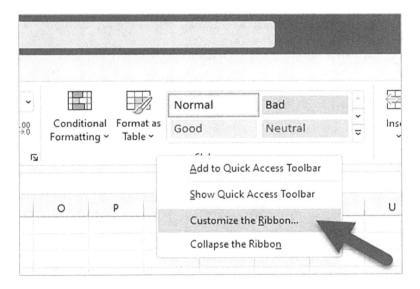

Excel opens the **Excel Options** window.

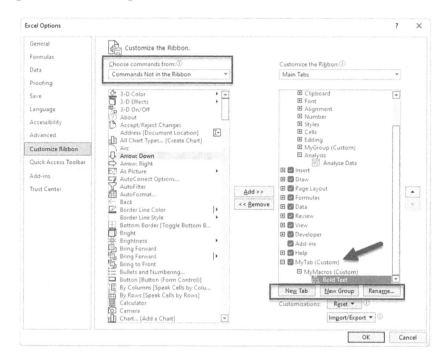

In the **Excel Options** window, the **Customize Ribbon** tab will be selected, and on that tab, you have two main boxes. On the right, you have the box that shows your current tabs - **Main Tabs**. On the left, you have the command buttons that you can add to the Ribbon.

To expand a group in the **Main Tabs** box, click the plus sign (+) to the left of an item. To collapse a group, click the minus sign (-).

To find commands not currently on your Ribbon, click the drop-down arrow on the left box (**Choose commands from**) and select **Commands Not in the Ribbon** from the drop-down list.

You will see a list of commands not on your Ribbon, which is useful as it filters out the commands already on your Ribbon.

Note You can't add or remove the default commands on the Ribbon, but you can uncheck them on the list to prevent them from being displayed. Also, you can't add command buttons to the default groups. You must create a new group (called a custom group) to add a new command button.

To create a new tab, do the following:

Click the **New Tab** button to create a new tab. Inside the tab, you must create at least one group before you can add a command button from the list of commands in the box on the left side of the Excel Options dialog box.

To create a custom group, do the following:

1. Select the tab in which you want to create the group. It could be one of the default tabs or the new one you've created.

2. Click the **New Group** button (located at the bottom of the dialog box, under the Main Tabs list). Excel will create a new group within the currently selected tab.

3. Select the new group and click **Rename** to give the group your preferred name.

You now have a custom group in which you can add commands.

To add commands to your custom group, do the following:

1. Select your custom group in the box on the right side of the screen.

2. Select the new command you want to add from the box on the left side of the screen and click the **Add** button to add it to your custom group.

   To remove a command from your custom group, select the command in the right box and click the **Remove** button.

3. Click **OK** to confirm the change.

When you view the customized tab on the Ribbon, you'll see your new group and your added command buttons.

The Quick Access Toolbar

The Quick Access Toolbar is no longer displayed by default in Microsoft 365 because the most used commands on it are now on the Ribbon by default. These commands are **Save**, **Undo**, and **Redo**.

You can skip this section if you seldom use the Quick Access Toolbar and don't need to display it.

To display the Quick Access Toolbar, right-click any blank area of the Ribbon and select **Show Quick Access Toolbar** from the pop-up menu.

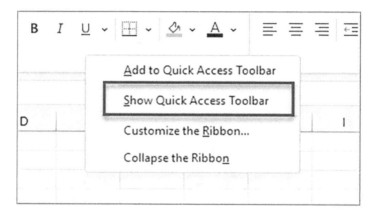

Excel will display the Quick Access Toolbar on a bar below the Ribbon by default. You can switch the toolbar to the title bar by right-clicking anywhere on the bar and selecting **Show Quick Access Toolbar Above the Ribbon**.

Note If you hide and redisplay the Quick Access Toolbar, Excel will remember where it was last positioned and display it there again.

The Quick Access Toolbar is a customizable toolbar with commands independent of the active tab on the Ribbon. The Quick Access Toolbar allows you to add commands you often use in Excel.

To customize the Quick Access Toolbar, click its drop-down arrow to display a drop-down menu.

Select items on the menu you want to add to the Quick Access Toolbar and deselect the items you want to remove.

To add commands to the Quick Access Toolbar that you can't find on the menu, do the following:

1. Click the **More Commands** menu option. Excel will open the Quick Access Toolbar pane in Excel Options.

2. In the drop-down list named **Choose commands from**, select **All Commands**.

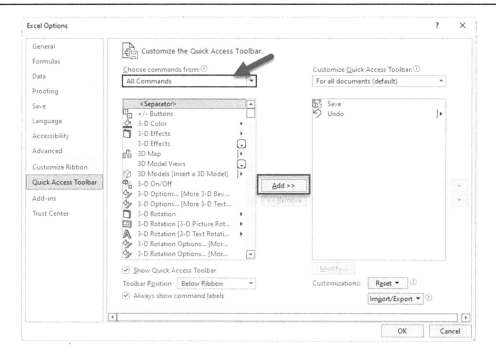

3. From the list of commands on the left, select a command you would like to add to the Quick Access Toolbar and click the **Add** button to add it to the list on the right. Do this for every command you want to add to the list.

4. To change the order of commands on the Quick Access Toolbar, select an item on the list on the right and use the up and down arrows to change its position.

5. Click **OK** when you are done.

Getting Help in Excel

To access help in Excel, click the Help tab and then the Help command button on the Ribbon. Excel displays the Help pane on the right side of the screen. You can use the search box in the Help pane to search for the topic for which you want help.

A quick way to access help is to press the **F1** key on your keyboard (while Excel is the active window) to display the Help pane on the right side of the screen.

Using Search

Another way to get help in Excel is to use the Search box on the title bar. Click the Search box or press **ALT+Q** to activate the search box.

Before you type anything, the search box will display a drop-down list of help topics related to your recent actions and other suggestions based on what you appear to be doing. If any of the suggestions is related to the topic for which you're seeking help, select it from the list. Otherwise, you can enter words or phrases regarding actions you want to perform or a topic for which you want further information.

Depending on the topic or how direct your question is, Excel will either list the steps needed to complete the task, take you to the appropriate dialog box, or display information related to the topic in the Help pane.

Chapter 2

Entering and Editing Data

This chapter will cover how to enter and edit data in your Excel worksheet, including using automated features like AutoFill and Flash Fill.

Entering and Editing Data Manually

Entering data:

Click a cell in the worksheet area, and a rectangular box will appear around the cell. This box is the **cell pointer** or the active cell. You can move the cell pointer with the left, right, up, or down arrow keys on your keyboard.

To enter data, simply type it directly into the cell, or you can click in the formula bar and type the data in there. To enter a formula, you need to prefix your entry with the equal sign (=). We will cover this later in the chapter on formulas.

Editing data:

When typing in the worksheet area, use the BACKSPACE key to go back and not the left arrow key if you want to make a correction. The arrow keys move the cell pointer from cell to cell. To use the arrow keys when editing data, select the cell, then click in the formula bar to edit the data there.

To overwrite data, click the cell to make it the active cell and just type in the new value. Your entry will overwrite the previous value.

If you only want to edit parts of the data in a cell, for example, a piece of text, then select the cell and click in the formula bar to edit the contents there.

Deleting data:

Select the data and hit the Delete key to delete data from your worksheet.

Default content alignment:

In Excel, numbers and formulas are right-aligned in the cell by default. Everything else is left-aligned by default. So, you can tell if Excel recognizes an entry as a number or text value.

Using AutoFill

The Autofill feature in Excel lets you fill cells with a series of sequential dates and numbers. It enables you to automate repetitive tasks as it is smart enough to figure out what data goes in a cell (based on another cell) when you drag the fill handle across cells.

Entering Dates with AutoFill

You may have a worksheet where you need to enter dates. You can enter *January* in one cell and use the AutoFill feature to automatically enter the rest of the months.

The **Fill Handle** is the small black square at the lower right of the cell pointer. When you hover over the lower right corner of the active cell, a black plus sign (+) appears. This change is an indication that when you drag the selection down (or to the right), Excel will either copy the contents of the first cell to the selected cells or use it as the first entry in a consecutive series.

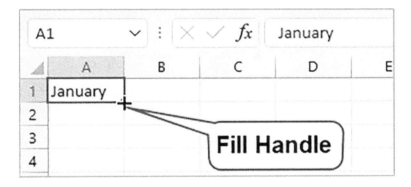

So, you first need to click the cell to select it and then hover over the bottom right corner to display the small plus sign (+).

To AutoFill dates, enter *January* or any other starting month in one cell, then grab the small fill handle and drag it across the other cells.

AutoFill also works with abbreviations, but they must be three letters. For example, if you enter Jan and then drag down, Excel will fill the cells with Feb, Mar, Apr, May, etc.

Let's say you want to enter the seven days of the week as your row headings. In the first cell of your range, enter *Monday* or *Mon*. Then drag the autofill handle down over the remaining six cells. Excel will AutoFill the remaining cells with Tuesday to Sunday.

Excel keeps the filled days selected, giving you a chance to drag the handle back if you went too far or to drag it further if you didn't go far enough.

You can also use the **AutoFill Options** drop-down menu to refine your fill options further. To access the AutoFill options, you will see a drop-down button that appears on the last cell with the cells still selected. When you click it, Excel displays a list of options that enable you to choose whether you want to copy the data across the cells, fill the series, copy formatting only, ignore the formatting, flash fill, etc.

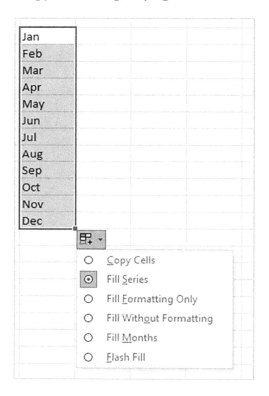

Note If you don't see a button that enables you to access the AutoFill Options drop-down menu (shown in the image above) after an autofill, it is most likely because the option hasn't been enabled in Excel Options.

To enable AutoFill Options, do the following:

1. On the Ribbon, click **File** > **Options** > **Advanced**.

2. Under the **Cut, copy, and paste** section, select the checkbox for **Show Paste Options button when content is pasted**.

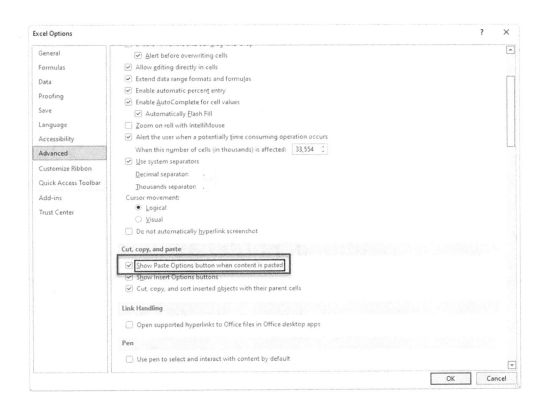

AutoFill Incremental Values

To AutoFill other incremental values, you need to first let Excel know the difference. Thus, you would need to enter values in at least two cells before dragging the fill handle across the other cells.

For example, let's say you want to enter dates that increment by seven days, i.e., a weekly interval. You would need to enter two dates (for example, 01/10/22 and 01/17/22). Then you select <u>both</u> cells and drag across the empty cells to autofill the other cells with dates having an interval of seven days.

You can do the same with other numbers. If you enter number 1 and drag down the fill handle, the number 1 will just be copied to the other cells. However, if you enter numbers 1 and 2 in two cells and then select both cells and drag the fill handle down (or to the right), you will get 3, 4, 5, 6, etc.

AutoFill Formulas

To AutoFill a formula across several cells, enter the formula in the first cell and drag the fill handle over the other cells in the range. If the cell references are relative, then the references will also change to match the position of the active cell.

For example, if the first cell of your formula is $= A1 + B1$, when you drag this formula down to the other cells, the formula in the other cells will be, $=A2+B2$, $=A3+B3$, $=A4+B4$, and so on.

Another way to use AutoFill is to click the **Fill** button in the **Editing** group on the **Home** tab.

📝**Note** If the cell references in your formula are absolute, then the cell references will not change when you use AutoFill to copy it to other cells. See the difference between relative and absolute cell references in chapter 6 in this book.

AutoFill the Same Values

To AutoFill the same value across a series of cells, enter the value in the first cell, then hold down the **Ctrl** key while dragging the fill handle across the other cells.

For example, if you want to fill a range of cells with January:

1. Enter **January** in the first cell.

2. Hold down the **Ctrl** key.

3. Hover over the fill handle (small square in the lower-right of the cell pointer), click and then drag it across the other cells.

   Excel will enter January in all the selected cells.

Using Flash Fill

Flash Fill is a feature introduced in Excel 2013 that enables you to split and rearrange data automatically. In the past, you would need to combine several Excel text functions like LEFT and MID to get the same results that you can now get with the Flash Fill command.

Example 1

In this example, we have a name field (made up of the first name and last name) that we want to sort by **Last Name**. To sort by Last Name, we need to re-enter the names in another column with the last name first. This change is required because Excel starts sorting with the field's first character, then the next, etc.

With Flash Fill, you can insert a new column next to the name column and enter the first value starting with the last name. When you enter the second value, Excel will figure out what you're trying to do and automatically Flash Fill the other cells in the format it predicts you want to enter the data. This automation will save you a lot of time as you only need to enter two cells to have the rest automatically completed for you.

B3			fx	West, Peter	
	A	B	C	D	
1	Employee		Month1	Month2	
2	Jane Smith	Smith, Jane	$1,453.00	$1,946.00	
3	Peter West	West, Peter	$1,713.00	$1,251.00	
4	Derek Brown	Brown, Derek	$1,467.00	$1,582.00	
5	Jason Fields	Fields, Jason	$1,356.00	$1,097.00	
6	Mark Powell	Powell, Mark	$1,919.00	$1,118.00	
7	Julie Rush	Rush, Julie	$1,282.00	$1,437.00	
8					
9					

Steps in Flash Fill:

1. Enter the value in the first cell in the new format.

2. Start entering the second value in the next cell.

3. You'll see a preview of the rest of the column displaying the suggested entries.

4. Press **Enter** to accept the suggestions.

Excel populates the other cells in the column with the data in the new format.

Another way to use Flash Fill is to use the **Flash Fill** command button in the **Data Tools** group on the **Data** tab.

To use the Flash Fill command button for the same example above, do the following:

1. Enter the value the way you want it in an adjacent cell and press enter.

2. On the **Data** tab, in the **Data Tools** group, click the **Flash Fill** button.

Excel automatically enters the rest of the values in the same format as the first cell.

Example 2

To quickly split a full name field up into first name and last name fields, do the following:

1. Assuming the full name is in column A2, enter the first name in B2 and press enter.

2. On the **Data** tab, in the **Data Tools** group, click **Flash Fill**.

    Excel populates the other rows in column B with the first name from column A.

3. Enter the last name from A2 in C2 and apply the Flash Fill command.

    Excel populates the other rows with the last name from column A.

C2		⌄	⋮	✕ ✓	fx	Smith	

◢	A	B	C	D
1	**Name**	**First name**	**Last name**	
2	Jane Smith	Jane	Smith	
3	Peter West	Peter	West	
4	Derek Brown	Derek	Brown	
5	Jason Fields	Jason	Fields	
6	Mark Powell	Mark	Powell	
7	Julie Rush	Julie	Rush	
8				

Chapter 3

Design and Organize Workbooks

This chapter will cover various tasks to do with organizing your workbook.

In this chapter, we will cover:

- Adding and removing worksheets.
- Moving, copying, hiding, and deleting worksheets.
- Freezing rows and columns.
- Applying themes to your worksheets.

Adding New Worksheets

We covered creating a new workbook in Chapter 1. When you first create a workbook, you'll have one worksheet named **Sheet1**.

To add a new sheet to your workbook, click the plus sign (+) at the bottom of the worksheet area, to the right of Sheet1, and it will create a new worksheet named Sheet2. You can add more worksheets to your workbook this way.

The number of worksheets you can have in a workbook is unlimited. You're only limited by your computer resources like RAM and hard disk space. However, try not to have too many sheets in one workbook as the file can become very large, and taking longer to open.

Naming a Worksheet

To name your worksheet, double-click the name tab at the bottom of the screen, and the name will become editable. For example, if you double-click *Sheet1*, the name will be selected with the cursor blinking, allowing you to type in the new name.

Moving and Copying Worksheets

You can move and reorder your worksheets by clicking the name and dragging it to the left or right. You can also move a sheet by right-clicking the name and selecting **Move or Copy** from the pop-up menu.

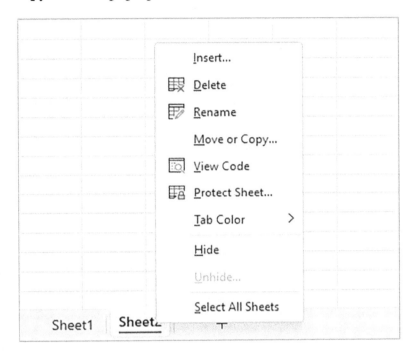

On the **Move or Copy** screen, select a name from the list and click OK. The selected worksheet will be moved to the front of the sheet selected.

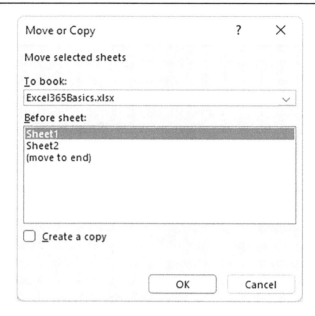

If you want the worksheet copied instead of moved, select the **Create a copy** checkbox before clicking OK. A copy will be placed in front of the selected sheet.

Removing a Worksheet

On the Sheet tab, right-click the sheet you want to remove and click **Delete**.

If the sheet is empty, it will be deleted right away. If the sheet has data, Excel will prompt you with a message asking you to confirm the deletion. Click **Delete** to confirm the deletion.

Hiding and Unhiding Worksheets

To **hide** a worksheet, right-click the name tab of the sheet you want to hide and select **Hide** on the pop-up menu.

To **unhide** a worksheet, right-click any of the sheet name tabs. The **Unhide** option will be enabled on the pop-up menu if a sheet is hidden. Select **Unhide** to display a window listing the hidden sheets. You can select any sheet on the list and click **OK** to show it again.

Freezing Rows and Columns

When you have a large worksheet with lots of data, you may want your data headers (row and/or column) to remain visible as you scroll down or to the right of the page.

To make your column headings always visible, you can freeze them on the page so that scrolling down does not take them out of view.

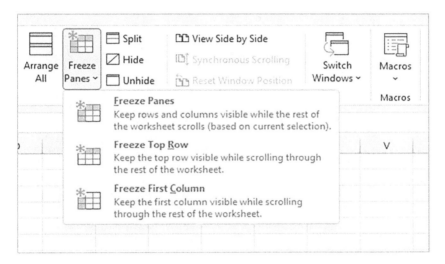

To quickly freeze the top row of your worksheet:

1. Click the **View** tab on the Ribbon.

2. In the Window group, click **Freeze Panes** and select **Freeze Top Row.**

When you now scroll down the page, the top row will always remain visible.

To quickly freeze the first column of your worksheet:

1. Click the **View** tab on the Ribbon.

2. In the Window group, click **Freeze Panes** and select **Freeze First Column.**

When you now scroll to the right of the page, the first column will always remain visible.

Excel 2022 Basics

On some occasions, you may want to freeze rows and columns other than the first ones.

To freeze any row of your choosing:

1. Place the cell pointer directly under the row you want to freeze to make it the active cell.

2. Click the **View** tab.

3. In the Window group, click **Freeze Panes** and select **Freeze Panes** from the pop-up list.

To freeze any column of your choosing:

1. Select a cell on the first row of the column that's to the right of the one you want to freeze. For example, if you want to freeze *column B,* then you would select cell *C1*.

2. Click the **View** tab.

3. In the Window group, click **Freeze Panes** and select **Freeze Panes** from the pop-up list.

Other examples:

- If you want to freeze the first row and first column of your worksheet, select cell **B2** and then select **View** > **Freeze Panes** > **Freeze Panes**.

- If you want to freeze only rows 1 and 2, select cell **A3** and select **View** > **Freeze Panes** > **Freeze Panes**.

- If you want to freeze only columns A and B, click cell **C1** and select **View** > **Freeze Panes** > **Freeze Panes**.

Unfreeze panes:

To unfreeze any frozen row or columns, click **View** > **Freeze Panes** and select **Unfreeze Panes** from the pop-up menu.

52

Applying Themes to Your Worksheet

A theme is a predefined formatting package that you can apply to your worksheet that may include colors for headers, text fonts, the size of cells, etc.

There are several themes in Excel that you can apply to your whole worksheet.

To change the look and feel of your worksheet with themes, do the following:

1. Click the **Page Layout** tab on the Ribbon.

2. In the Themes group, click the **Themes** button to display a drop-down list with many themes you can apply to your worksheet.

3. You can hover over a theme on the list to get an instant preview of how your worksheet would look with that theme without selecting it.

4. When you find a theme you want, click it to apply it to your worksheet.

Removing a Theme

If you apply a theme, you don't like, simply click the **Undo** button on the **Home** tab to undo the changes and return your worksheet to its previous state.

Chapter 4

Organizing Your Data

I n this chapter, we will cover some essential tasks to do with organizing your data in Excel.

This chapter covers:

- Copying and pasting data.
- Moving data.
- Inserting/deleting rows and columns.
- Finding and replacing data.
- Sorting data.
- Filtering data.

Copying, Moving, and Deleting Data

Selecting a Group of Cells

Method 1

1. Click the first cell of the area.

2. Ensure your mouse pointer is a white plus sign.

3. Click and drag over the other cells in the range you want to include in the selection.

Method 2

1. Click the top-left cell in the range, for example, A2.

2. Hold down the Shift key and click the bottom-right cell in the range, for example, D10.

Excel selects range A1:D10.

Deselecting Cells

Sometimes, you might accidentally select more cells than you intended when selecting several cells or ranges. With the deselect feature, you can deselect any extra cells within the selected range.

To deselect cells within a selection, hold down the **Ctrl** key, then click (or click and drag) to deselect any cells or ranges within the selection.

If you need to reselect any cells, hold down the **Ctrl** key and click the cells to select them again.

Copying and Pasting Data

Quick Copy and Paste

To quickly copy and paste values in a range, do the following:

1. Select the range that you want to copy.

2. On the **Home** tab, in the **Clipboard** group, click **Copy**.

    You will see a dotted rectangle around the area, which is called a bounding outline.

3. Click the first cell of the area where you want to paste the contents.

4. Click **Paste**.

    The bounding outline remains active to let you know that you can carry on pasting the copied content if you wish to paste it in multiple areas. To get rid of the bounding outline, hit the **ESC** key.

Using the Shortcut Menu

Another way to copy or move data is to use commands on the shortcut menu:

1. Select the source range.

2. Right-click the source range and select Copy (or Cut) from the shortcut menu.

3. Right-click the first cell of the destination range and select the Paste icon (the first icon under Paste Options) on the shortcut menu.

Other Pasting Options

To access other pasting options, after copying data, click the drop-down arrow on the **Paste** command button to display a drop-down menu with several paste options.

You can hover over each icon on the menu for a tip on what each one does. You'll also see a preview of the paste action on your worksheet.

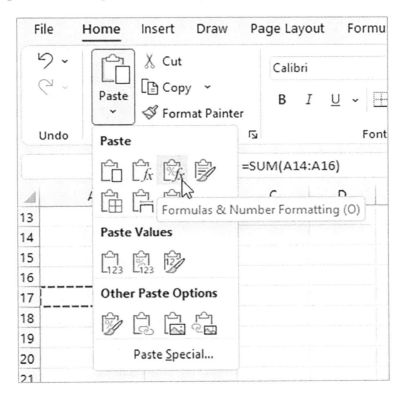

Hover over an icon for a description of what it does

For example, to copy and paste a range while maintaining the column widths, do the following:

1. Select and copy the source range.

2. In the destination worksheet, click the down-arrow on the **Paste** button and select the option that says **Keep Source Column Widths (W)**. This icon is on the second row of the menu.

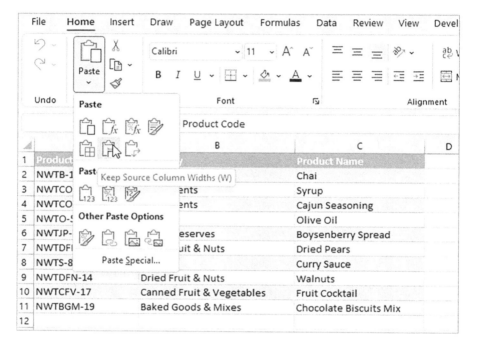

3. Select that option to paste the data and the cell formatting and column width.

4. Once done, remove the bounding outline around the source range by hitting the ESC key. Pressing ESC tells Excel you've completed the copying action.

Using Paste Special

Another way to copy and paste values is to use the **Paste Special** command. Paste Special provides more paste options, including basic calculations like addition, subtraction, and multiplication with the paste operation.

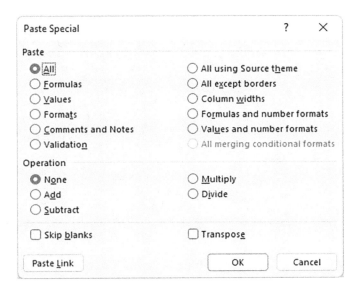

In the following example, we want to convert a list of negative values to positive values. We can use the **Multiply** operation in the Paste Special dialog box to help us perform this action.

To convert a range of negative numbers to positive values, do the following:

1. In any cell in your worksheet, enter **-1**.

2. Copy the value to the clipboard.

3. Select the range of cells with the negative numbers you want to convert.

4. On the Home tab, in the Clipboard group, select **Paste** > **Paste Special**.

   Excel displays the Paste Special dialog box.

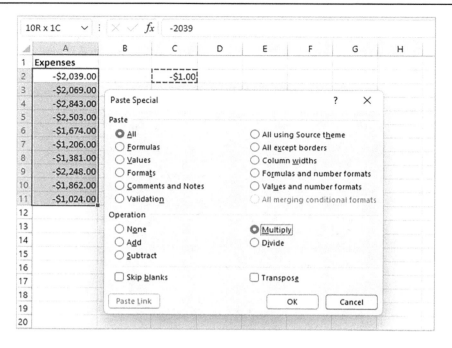

5. In the Paste Special dialog box, select **All** and **Multiply**.

6. Click **OK**.

Excel converts the values in the range to positive numbers by multiplying them by -1 during the paste action.

Moving Data

To move content, you follow a similar set of actions as we did with copying, but you would **Cut** the data instead of **Copy** it.

To move content, do the following:

1. Select the range you want to move.

2. On the Home tab, click the **Cut** button (this is the command with the scissors icon). A bounding outline will appear around the area you've chosen to cut.

3. Click the first cell of the destination range. You only need to select one cell.

4. On the Home tab, click **Paste**. Excel will move the content from its current location to the destination range.

The copy & paste action automatically copies the format of the cells across, but not the width. So, you need to adjust the width of the cells if necessary.

Insert or Delete Rows and Columns

To insert a column, do the following:

1. Click the column letter immediately to the right of the column where you want to insert the new column. For example, select column B if you want to insert a column between columns A and B.

2. On the **Home** tab, in the **Cells** group, click the **Insert** button.

Excel will insert a new column to the left of the column you selected, and the new column will now be B.

Inserting a new column by using the pop-up menu:

1. Click the column letter to the right of the insertion point to select the whole column.

2. Right-click and select **Insert** from the pop-up menu to insert the new column.

Inserting a new row by using the pop-up menu:

1. Click the row number directly below the insertion point to select the whole row.

2. Right-click and select **Insert** from the pop-up menu to insert a new row directly above the selected row.

You could also insert new rows and columns with the **Insert** command button on the **Home** tab.

Inserting multiple rows or columns:

1. Hold down the Ctrl key.

2. One by one, select the rows up to the number you want to insert. For example, if you want to insert four rows, select four rows directly under the insertion point.

3. Click **Home** > **Insert** (or right-click and select **Insert**).

Excel will insert four new rows above the insertion point.

Finding and Replacing Data

A worksheet can have over a million rows of data, so it may be difficult to locate specific information in a large worksheet. Excel provides a Find and Replace feature to quickly find and replace data in your worksheet if required. If you have used the Find function in other Microsoft 365 applications, you should be familiar with this feature.

To find text or numbers in your worksheet, do the following:

1. On the **Home** tab, in the **Editing** group, click **Find & Select > Find**. Alternatively, press **Ctrl+F**.

    Excel displays the Find tab of the **Find and Replace** dialog box.

    Note By default, Excel displays a dialog box with Options hidden (if it wasn't expended when previously used). Click the **Options >>** button to expand the dialog box, as shown below.

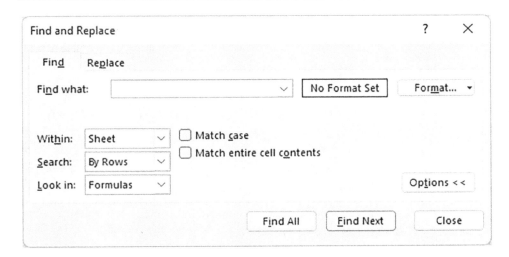

2. In the **Find what** box, enter the text or number you want to find.

    You can also click the down-arrow on the **Find what** box and select a recent item you've searched for.

    Click **Find All** (to find all instances of your criteria) or **Find Next** (to find them one by one).

> **📝Note** When you click **Find All**, Excel lists every instance of your criteria. Click a column heading to sort the results by that column. Click an item on the list to select its cell in the worksheet.

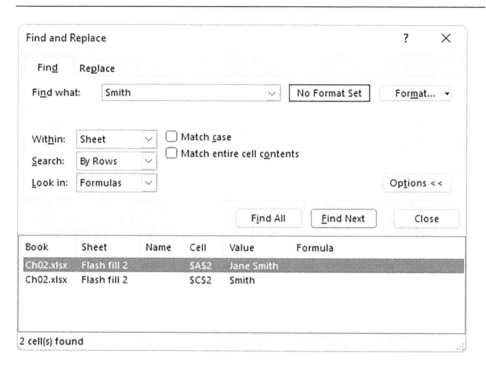

3. The expanded dialog box (when you click **Options >>**) gives you the following additional search options:

    -   **Format:** This option allows you to select the data format you're searching for.

    -   **Within:** Allows you to search the current worksheet or the whole workbook.

    -   **Search:** Allows you to search by rows (default) or columns.

    -   **Look in:** Enables you to search for Formulas, Values, Notes, or Comments. The default is Formulas.

        Select **Values** here if the search area has formulas, but you want to find the values derived from those formulas. Otherwise, leave this setting as the default.

    -   **Match case:** This option enables you to only find values that match the case of the entry in the **Find what** box.

- **Match entire cell contents:** Select this option to only find values that match the exact value in the **Find what** box.

- **Options**: The **Options >>** button expands the dialog box with more options to refine your search.

Replacing Data

To replace text or number in your worksheet, go to **Home** > **Editing** > **Find & Select** > **Replace**. Alternatively, press **Ctrl+H**.

If the Find dialog box is already open, click the **Replace** tab.

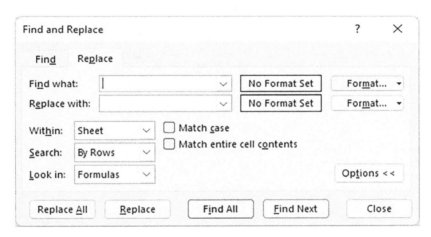

In addition to the options on the Find tab (described above), the Replace tab has the following options:

- **Replace with**: Use this box to specify an alternative value to replace any values found in your worksheet that match the criteria specified in **Find what**.

- **Replace All**: Automatically replaces all instances found with the value in **Replace with**.

- **Replace**: Replaces only the next one found.

All the other options on the dialog box remain the same on this tab as described for Find.

-☀-**Tip** If you use **Replace**/**Replace All** to change data by mistake, use the **Undo** button on the Home tab to reverse your changes.

Sorting Data

Excel offers various methods to sort your data, from a quick and basic sort to more complex sorts using your own custom list. We will be covering the popular methods in this section.

Quick Sort

To quickly sort data in Excel, do the following:

1. Select any single cell in the column you want to sort.

2. Right-click the cell. From the pop-up menu, select **Sort A to Z** (for ascending) or **Sort Z to A** (for descending).

   If your column is a number field, you'll have **Sort Smallest to Largest** (for ascending) and **Sort Largest to Smallest** (for descending).

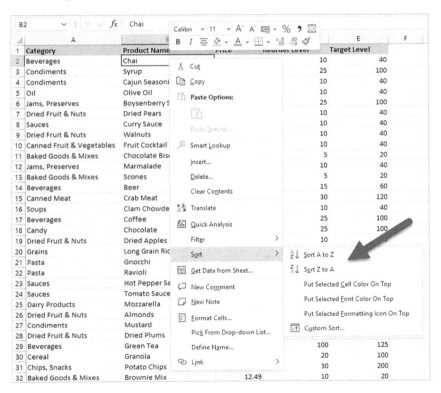

The Sort action does not change your data in any way. It simply reorders your rows according to your chosen sort order and column.

Custom Sort

In the example above, we sorted using just one column. However, you can sort using multiple columns. For example, in the data shown below, we may want to sort by *Category* and *Product Name*. We would use the Custom Sort command on the Ribbon in this case.

	A	B	C
1	Category	Product Name	Price
2	Beverages	Chai	18.00
3	Condiments	Syrup	10.00
4	Condiments	Cajun Seasoning	22.00
5	Cereal	Granola	4.00
6	Chips, Snacks	Potato Chips	1.80
7	Baked Goods & Mixes	Brownie Mix	12.49
8	Baked Goods & Mixes	Cake Mix	15.99
9	Beverages	Tea	4.00
10	Canned Fruit & Vegetables	Pears	1.30
11	Canned Fruit & Vegetables	Peaches	1.50
12	Canned Fruit & Vegetables	Pineapple	1.80
13	Canned Fruit & Vegetables	Cherry Pie Filling	2.00
14	Canned Fruit & Vegetables	Green Beans	1.20
15	Canned Fruit & Vegetables	Corn	1.20
16	Canned Fruit & Vegetables	Peas	1.50
17	Canned Meat	Tuna Fish	2.00
18	Canned Meat	Smoked Salmon	4.00
19	Cereal	Hot Cereal	5.00
20	Soups	Vegetable Soup	1.89
21	Soups	Chicken Soup	1.95
22			

To apply a Custom Sort, do the following:

1. Select a single cell anywhere in the data.

2. On the **Home** tab, in the **Editing** group, click **Sort & Filter**, then select **Custom Sort** from the pop-up menu.

    Excel displays the **Sort** dialog box.

3. In the **Sort by** list, select the first column you want to sort.

4. In the **Sort On** box, you can select Cell Values, Cell Color, Font Color, or Conditional Formatting Icon. If you're sorting by value, select **Cell Value**.

5. In the **Order** list, select the order for the sort. For a text column, you can choose **A to Z** (ascending order) or **Z to A** (descending order).

    For a number column, you can choose **Smallest to Largest** or **Largest to Smallest**.

6. Click **OK** when you're done.

Your data will now be sorted according to the criteria you've entered.

Sorting with a Custom List

In the Sort dialog box, the **Order** drop-down list has an option named **Custom List**, which enables you to sort data by days of the week or months.

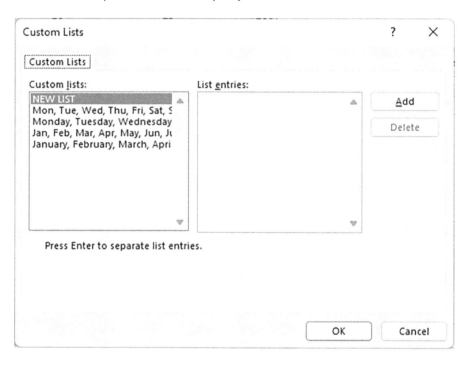

You can add a custom list if none of the pre-defined custom lists meet your needs. Creating your custom list is useful for sorting with an order different from the standard ascending or descending.

For example, if we wanted to sort our data by *employee grade*, we could enter the grades in our list in the order we want the data sorted.

To add a new custom list, do the following:

1. Select NEW LIST in the **Custom lists** box.

2. In the **List entries** box (on the right), enter your list items, one item per line. Press Enter to go to the next line.

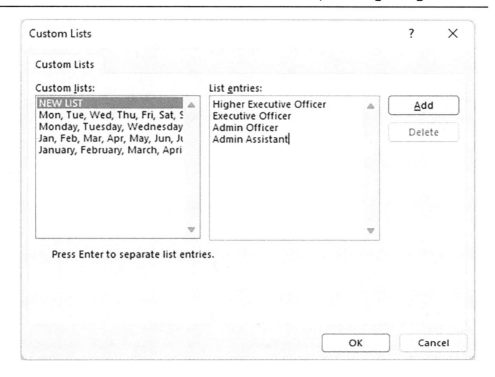

3. When you're done, click the **Add** button to add the list.

4. You can now select the list under **Custom lists** and click **OK** to use it for your sort.

Your custom list will now be available to all Excel workbooks on the PC.

Filtering Data

Excel worksheets can hold a lot of data, and you might not want to work with all the data at the same time. For example, you might want to only display a category of products or products within a certain price range.

Excel provides several ways to filter your data so that you can view only the data you want to see. Filters provide a quick way to work with a subset of data in a range or table. When you apply a filter, you temporarily hide some of the data so that you can focus on the data you need to work with.

Excel tables have column headings by default, but if your data is just a range, ensure you have column headings like Category, Product Name, Price, etc. Column headings makes filtering and sorting much easier.

Category	Product Name	Price	Reorder Level	Target Level
Beverages	Chai	18.00	10	40
Condiments	Syrup	10.00	25	100
Condiments	Cajun Seasoning	22.00	10	40
Oil	Olive Oil	21.35	10	40
Jams, Preserves	Boysenberry Spread	25.00	25	100
Dried Fruit & Nuts	Dried Pears	30.00	10	40
Sauces	Curry Sauce	40.00	10	40

Column headings

You can add column headings to your data by inserting a new row at the top of your worksheet and entering the headings. Column headings are important because Excel will use the first row for the filter arrows.

Quick Filter

To filter data, do the following:

1. Select any cell within the data that you want to filter.

2. Select **Home** > **Editing** > **Sort & Filter** > **Filter**.

   Alternatively, select **Data** > **Sort & Filter** > **Filter**.

   You will get a **filter arrow** at the top of each column, also called an **AutoFilter**. Note that in Excel tables, filter arrows are turned on by default.

3. Click the AutoFilter of the column you want to filter. For example, Price.

4. Uncheck **Select All** and check the values you want to use for the filter.

5. Click **OK**.

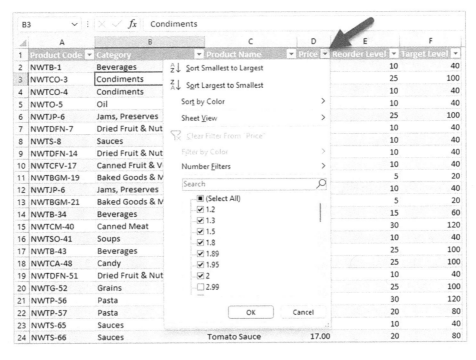

The AutoFilter changes to a funnel icon to show that the column is filtered. If you look at the row heading numbers, you'll see that they're now blue, indicating which rows are included in the filtered data.

Custom Filter

You can create a custom filter if the default options do not meet your needs. To access the **Custom Filter** command, click the **AutoFilter** of the column you want to use to filter the data.

You'll get the following options depending on the data type of the selected column:

- **Text Filters**: Available when the column is a text field or has a mixture of text and numbers. The filter options available include, Equals, Does Not Equal, Begins With, Ends With, or Contains.

- **Number Filters**: This option is available when the column contains only numbers. The filter options available include, Equals, Does Not Equal, Greater Than, Less Than, or Between.

- **Date Filters**: This option is available when the column contains only dates. The filter options available include, Last Week, Next Month, This Month, and Last Month.

- **Clear Filter from [Column name]:** This option is only available if the column already has a filter. Select this option to clear the filter.

When you select an option related to any of the three options above, Excel displays the **Custom AutoFilter** dialog box, where you can specify your custom filter criteria.

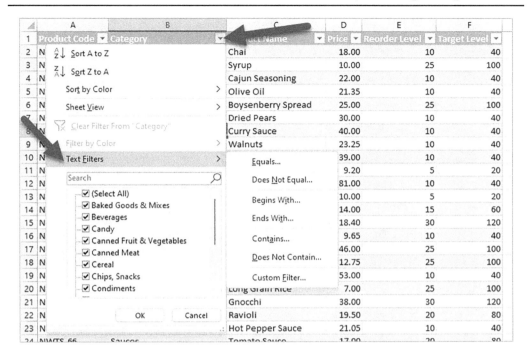

Example

Let's say we wanted to display only data with a price range between $2 and $10.

Follow the steps below to filter the data for the chosen criteria:

1. Click the AutoFilter on the **Price** column, and on the dropdown menu, select **Number Filters** > **Between**.

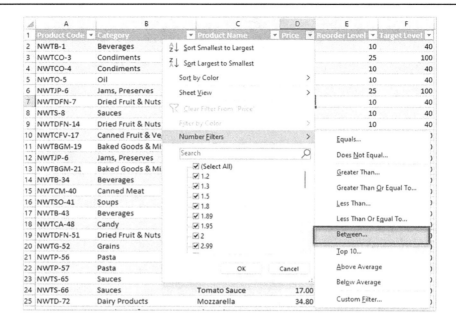

The **Custom AutoFilter** dialog box allows you to enter the criteria and specify the condition.

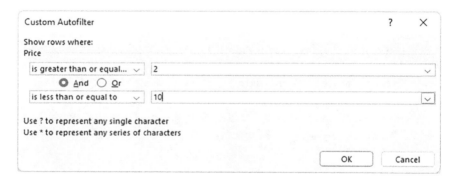

2. Enter the values you want to use for the filter. In our example, the values would be 2 and 10.

3. Select the logical operator. In this case, we will need **And**, as both conditions must be true.

Price >= 2 And <= 10.

If only one of the conditions needs to be true, select **Or**.

4. Click **OK** when done.

Excel filters the data to only show records where the Price is between $2 and $10.

Changing the Sort Order of a Filtered List

To change the sort order of the filtered results, click the **AutoFilter** icon on the column used for the filter.

Select either **Sort Smallest to Largest** or **Sort Largest to Smallest**. For a text column, it would be **Sort A to Z** or **Sort Z to A.**

Removing a Filter

To remove a filter, do the following:

1. Select any cell in the range or table.

2. On the **Data** tab, in the **Sort & Filter** group, click **Clear**.

Excel removes the filter and displays all the data.

Another way to remove a filter is to click the AutoFilter of the filtered column and select **Clear Filter From "[Column name]"** to display all the data.

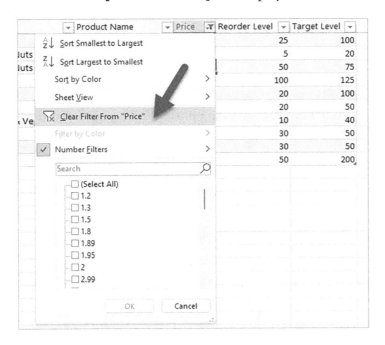

Chapter 5

Formatting Cells

In this chapter, we will cover various methods to format and resize cells in your worksheet to present your data in your desired format.

This chapter covers:

- Resizing cells, rows, and columns.
- Hiding and unhide rows and columns.
- Merging cells and aligning data.
- Hiding and unhiding worksheets.
- Applying predefined cell styles.
- Applying different types of number formats to cells.
- Creating and applying custom cell formats.
- Applying conditional formatting to add visual representations to your data.

Arrange Cells, Rows, and Columns

Resizing Rows and Columns

You can resize rows and columns with your mouse or use the **Format** command on the toolbar.

To resize a **column**, do the following:

1. Click any cell in the column.

2. Click the right edge of the column letter and drag it to the right to widen the column.

To resize a **row**, do the following:

1. Click any cell in the row.

2. Click the bottom edge of the row number, then drag it down to increase the row's height.

Resizing Cells with the Cells Format Command

You can increase the column width and row height of a range of cells simultaneously by using the **Format** command on the **Home** tab of the Ribbon.

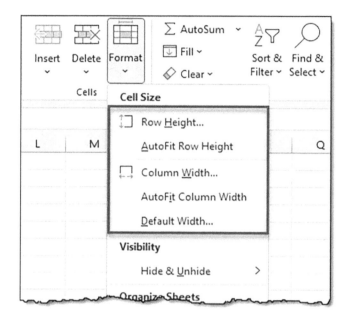

For example, to increase the widths of columns A to E, do the following:

1. Hover over the header for column A until you see a downward pointing arrow.

2. Click **A** to select the column and drag to column **E** to select columns A to E.

> -💡-**Tip** Another way to select a range of columns is to select the first column, hold down the **Shift** key, and select the last column.

3. Click **Home > Format > Column Width**.

4. Enter the **Column width** in the box.

5. Click **OK**.

To increase the height of rows 1 to 14, do the following:

1. Hover over the header of row 1 until you get an arrow pointing right.
2. Click to select the whole row.
3. Hold down the Shift key and click the header of row 14.
4. Go to **Home** > **Cells** > **Format** > **Row Height...**
5. The default row height is 15. Thus, you can enter any number higher than 15 to increase the height of the selected rows.
6. Click **OK**.

Automatically adjust columns to fit your data using AutoFit:

1. Select the columns you want to adjust.
2. On the **Home** tab, in the **Cells** group, select **Format** > **AutoFit Column Width**.

Excel adjusts each column to fit the length of all entries.

Automatically adjust row heights to fit your data using AutoFit:

1. Select the rows to which you want to apply AutoFit.
2. On the **Home** tab, in the **Cells** group, select **Format** > **AutoFit Row Height**.

Excel adjusts each column to fit the height of all entries. This setting is particularly useful if you have **Wrap Text** enabled, and some cells have more than one line of text.

Set the default column width for the whole workbook:

1. On the **Home** tab, in the **Cells** group, select **Format** > **Default Width**.
2. Enter the new default value in the **Standard column width** box.

Hide Rows and Columns

Sometimes, with very large worksheets, you may want to hide some rows or columns to make it easier to access the data with which you want to work.

To hide rows:

1. Select the rows you want to hide.

2. Go to **Home** > **Cells** > **Format**.

3. On the pop-up menu, under **Visibility**, select **Hide & Unhide**, and then click **Hide Rows**.

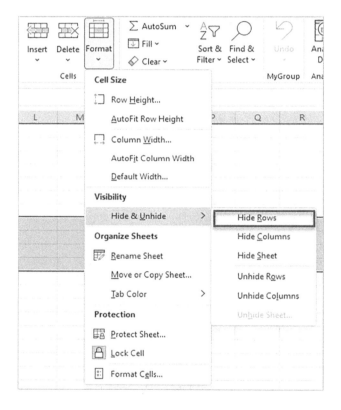

To hide columns:

1. Select the target columns

2. Go to **Home** > **Cells** > **Format**.

3. On the pop-up menu, under **Visibility**, select **Hide & Unhide** and then click **Hide Columns**.

To unhide rows and columns:

Go to **Home** > **Cells** > **Format** > **Hide & Unhide** and then select **Unhide Columns** to display hidden columns (or **Unhide Rows** to display hidden rows).

Hide and Unhide a Worksheet

You can use two methods to Hide a worksheet:

- **Method 1:** Right-click the worksheet's name tab and select **Hide** from the pop-up menu.

- **Method 2:** Ensure the worksheet you want to hide is the active one, then on the Ribbon, select **Home > Cells > Format > Hide & Unhide > Hide Sheet**.

To hide multiple worksheets simultaneously, do the following:

1. Select the first worksheet's name tab.

2. Hold down the **Ctrl** key and click any additional worksheet tabs you want to hide.

3. Right-click any of the worksheet tabs and select **Hide** on the shortcut menu.

There are two ways to Unhide a worksheet:

- **Method 1:**
  1. Right-click any of the tabs at the bottom of the workbook and select **Unhide** on the shortcut menu.
  2. Select the worksheet name in the **Unhide** dialog box and click **OK**.

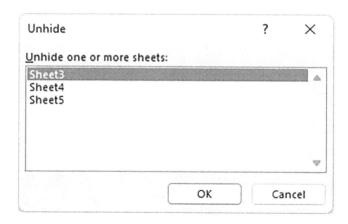

- **Method 2**:

    1. On the Ribbon, go to **Home** > **Cells** > **Format** > **Hide & Unhide** > **Unhide Sheet**.

    2. Select the worksheet name in the **Unhide** dialog box and click **OK**.

Note To unhide more than one worksheet, hold down the **Ctrl** key and select any additional worksheets you want to unhide in the Unhide dialog box.

Applying Cell Styles

You can select a predefined color format for your cells from a wide selection of styles from the **Styles** group on the **Home** tab.

To format a cell or range with a different style:

1. Select the cell or range that you want to format.

2. On the **Home** tab, in the **Styles** group, click the **More** dropdown arrow to expand the style gallery.

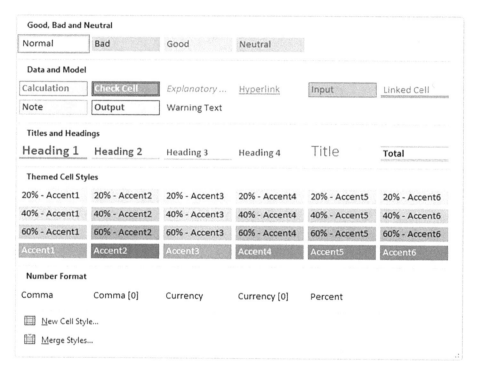

You can hover over the different styles for a preview on your worksheet before selecting one.

3. Select a style on the gallery to apply it to your worksheet.

Merging Cells and Aligning Data

To **merge** cells on your worksheet, select the cells you want to merge. On the **Home** tab, click **Merge & Center**. Alternatively, you can click the drop-down button for Merge & Center and choose other merge options from the drop-down menu.

To **unmerge** cells, select the merged cells, then on the **Home** tab, click the drop-down button for **Merge & Center**. Select **Unmerge Cells** from the drop-down menu.

Text Alignment and Wrapping

To align text in a cell, select the cell and click one of the alignment options in the **Alignment** group on the **Home** tab. You can also wrap text and merge cells from the command options available.

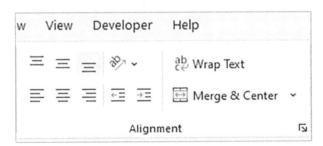

Shrink to Fit and Text Direction

The **Format Cells** dialog box provides additional formatting options like **Shrink to fit** and **Text direction**. To open the dialog box, click the dialog box launcher on the bottom-right of the **Alignment** group.

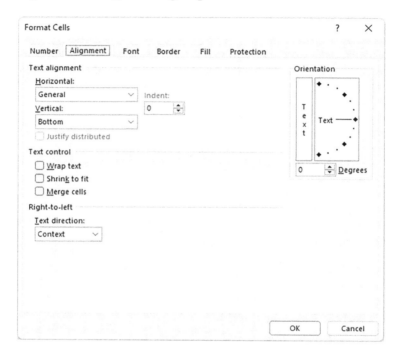

On the Alignment tab, you can:

- Align text in your cells vertically and horizontally.

- Wrap text to go to a new line in a cell instead of continuing into other cells to the right.

- Shrink text to fit one cell.

- Merge cells.

Applying Number Formats

To quickly set the format for a range of cells:

1. Select the range of cells that you want to format.

2. On the **Home** tab, in the **Number** group, click the dropdown arrow on the **Number Format** box.

3. Select the format you want from the dropdown menu.

The selected cell/range will now be formatted in the format you selected.

Number Format dropdown menu.

Accessing More Formats

To access formats not available on the **Number Format** dropdown menu, open the **Format Cells** dialog box.

For example, if you're in the US and you want to change currency formats in your worksheet to UK pounds, do the following:

1. Select the range of cells that you want to format.

2. On the **Home** tab, in the **Number** group, click the dropdown arrow on the **Number Format** box, and select **More Number Formats**.

    Excel displays the **Number** tab of the **Format Cells** dialog box.

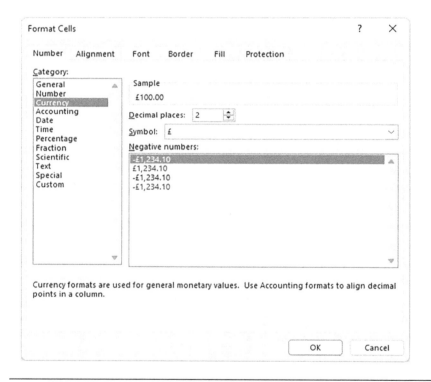

🔅**Tip** Another way to display the Format Cells dialog box is to click the dialog box launcher in the **Number** group on the **Home** tab.

---

3. On the left side of the dialog box, under **Category**, select **Currency**.

4. Click the **Symbol** field to display a dropdown list. Select the British pound

sign (£) from the list.

You can also set the number of decimal places and the format you want for negative numbers on this tab. The **Sample** box displays how the selected format will look on your worksheet.

5. Click **OK** to confirm your changes when done.

Creating Custom Numeric Formats

Excel has many predefined number formats you can select and then amend to create your own custom format if none of the predefined formats meets your needs.

For example, imagine that you have a column in your worksheet that you use to record a set of numbers. It could be product serial numbers, unique product IDs, or even telephone numbers. You may want the numbers to appear in a certain format regardless of how they've been entered.

In some applications like Microsoft Access, this would be called a *format mask*.

In Excel, you can create a custom format for a group of cells so that every entry is automatically formatted with your default format.

To create a custom format, follow the steps below:

1. Select the range of cells to be formatted.

2. Right-click any area in your selection and select **Format Cells** from the pop-up menu.

    Alternatively, on the **Home** tab, in the **Number** group, click the dialog box launcher to open the **Format Cells** dialog box.

3. Under **Category,** select **Custom**.

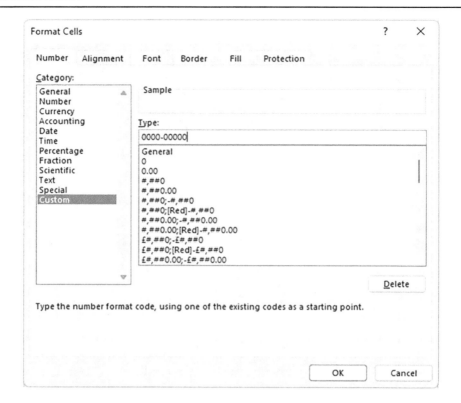

4. In the **Type** box, select an existing format close to the one you would like to create.

> **Note** If you find a format on the list that meets your needs, you can select that one and click OK.

5. In the **Type** box, enter the format you want to create. For example, *0000-00000*.

6. Click **OK**.

◢	A	B	C
1	Serial Number		
2	234401107	2344-01107	
3	234434589	2344-34589	
4	234466123	2344-66123	
5	234455692	2344-55692	
6	234234500	2342-34500	
7	234410976	2344-10976	
8	232310978	2323-10978	
9	234093419	2340-93419	
10	230923100	2309-23100	
11	234109035	2341-09035	
12	234102345	2341-02345	
13	234109093	2341-09093	
14			

In the image above, column A has a set of numbers. Column B shows the same numbers with a custom format (*0000-00000*) now applied to them.

Copy Cell Formatting

A quick way to format a cell or group of cells based on another cell in your worksheet is to use the **Format Painter** in the **Clipboard** group on the **Home** tab. The Format Painter can be a time saver as you only create the format once and copy it to other cells in your worksheet.

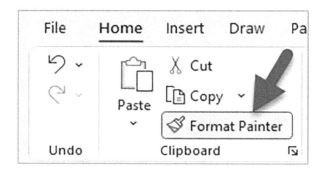

To copy cell formatting with the **Format Painter**, do the following:

1. Select the cell with the format you want to copy.

2. On the **Home** tab, in the **Clipboard** group, click **Format Painter**. The mouse pointer will turn into a plus sign (+) and a brush icon.

3. Click and drag over the cells to which you're applying the format.

The destination cells will now have the same format as the source cell.

Tip When clicked once, the **Format Painter** is enabled for only one use and then turned off. If you want to apply the same format to multiple ranges, double-click the Format Painter to turn it on for multiple uses. It remains enabled until you click it again to turn it off.

Example:

In the following example, we want to copy the **Currency** format in cell **A2** and apply it to range **A3:A14**.

Follow the steps below to copy the format using the Format Painter:

1. Click cell *A2* to select it.

2. Select **Home** > **Clipboard** > **Format Painter**.

3. In the worksheet area, click *A3* and drag to *A14*.

Excel applies the currency format in *A2* to the range A3:A14.

Clearing the Cell Format

To remove formatting from a cell or range, do the following:

1. Select the cells you want to clear.

2. Select **Home** > **Editing** > **Clear**.

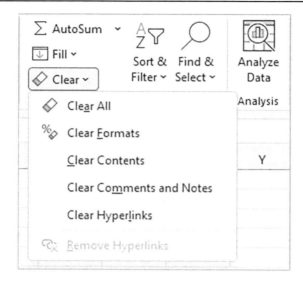

3. Excel displays a dropdown menu with several options - Clear All, Clear Formats, Clear Contents, Clear Comments and Notes, and Clear Hyperlinks.

4. To clear just the format and not the values, click **Clear Formats**.

Excel returns the format of the selected cells to **General,** which is the default.

Conditional Formatting

You can format your data based on certain criteria to display a visual representation that helps to spot critical issues and identify patterns and trends. For example, you can use visual representations to clearly show the highs and lows in your data and the trend. This type of formatting is called conditional formatting in Excel.

In the example below, we can quickly see the trend in sales and how they compare to each other.

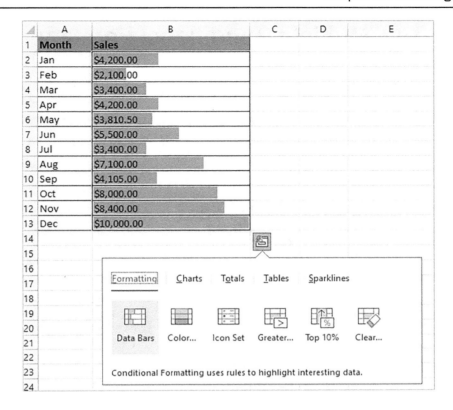

To quickly apply a conditional format:

1. Select the range of cells you want to format. The quick analysis button will be displayed at the bottom-right of the selection.

2. Click the Quick Analysis button, and use the default **Formatting** tab.

3. Hover over the formatting options on the Formatting tab to see a live preview of what your data will look like when applied.

4. Click **Data Bars** to apply the formatting to your data.

You now have a visual representation of the data that's easier to analyze.

Use Multiple Conditional Formats

You can apply more than one conditional format to the same group of cells. Select the cells, click the Quick Analysis button, and click another format option, for example, **Icon Set**. The arrows illustrate the upper, middle, and lower values in the set of data.

Formatting Text Fields

You can apply conditional formatting to text, but the formatting options for text are different from that of numbers.

For example, to highlight all the rows with "Sauce" in the name, do the following:

1. Select the range.

2. Click the Quick Analysis button.

3. Select **Text** on the Formatting tab.

4. In the **Text That Contains** dialog box, enter "Sauce" in the first box and select the type of formatting from the drop-down list.

	J	K	L	M	N	O	P
	Product Code	Product Name					
	6866	Chai					
	1801	Syrup					
	8374	Cajun Seasoning					
	8725	Olive Oil					
	8223	Boysenberry Spread					
	8181	Dried Pears					
	7837	Curry Sauce					
	5963	Salad Sauce					
	4840	Fruit Cocktail					
	4443	Chocolate Biscuits Mix					
	6416	Marmalade					
	2409	Pepper Sauce					

Text That Contains   ?   ✕

Format cells that contain the text:

Sauce   ⬆   with   Light Red Fill with Dark Red Text ⌄

OK   Cancel

You can explore the formatting options for different data types by selecting the data to be formatted and clicking the Quick Analysis button.

Conditionally Formatting Time

Let's say we had a list of projects, and we wanted to see which projects are overdue, that is, the ones with a due date before today.

To highlight the overdue projects, do the following:

1. Select the cells in the *Due date* column.

2. Click the Quick Analysis button, and then click Less Than.

3. Type in **=TODAY()**

    You could type in today's date, but that would mean updating the conditional formatting daily, which would get tedious fast and even introduce errors! The TODAY function will always return today's date.

4. Select the formatting you'll like to use from the drop-down list.

5.   Click **OK**.

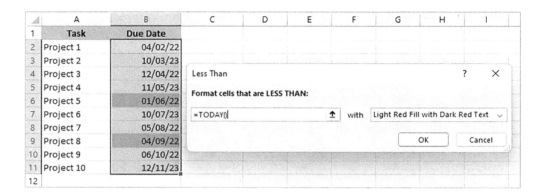

The overdue projects now stand out on the list and are easy to identify immediately. The date format used here is **mm/dd/yy**.

Note   You can also sort the data in this example to figure out the overdue projects, but depending on your data, sorting is not always an available option.

Creating Conditional Formatting Rules

An alternative way to create conditional formatting is by creating **Rules** in Excel.

To launch the **New Formatting Rule** dialog box:

1. Select the range to which you want to apply the conditional formatting.

2. On the Ribbon, go to **Home** > **Styles** > **Conditional Formatting** > **New Rule**.

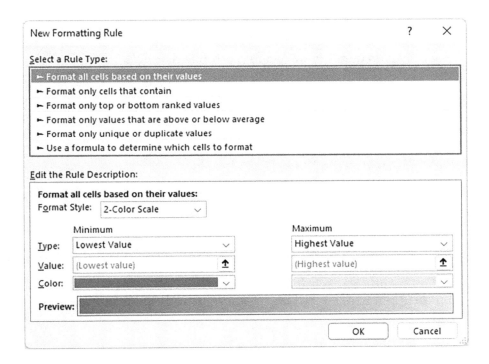

You can use the New Formatting Rule dialog box to create more complex rules using a series of conditions and criteria.

You can select a rule type from the following options:

- Format all cells based on their values.

- Format only cells that contain.

- Format only top or bottom ranked values.

- Format only values that are above or below average.

- Format only unique or duplicate values.

- Use a formula to determine which cells to format.

The bottom section of the dialog box, labeled **Edit the Rule Description**, gives you different fields to define your rule for each rule type.

Example:

Let's say you had a list of products, and you want to format the whole row grey if one of the fields, the product Stock, fell below 10.

Follow the steps below to create a conditional formatting rule for the above scenario:

1. Select the range you want to conditionally format, that is, A2:C18. Note that A2 is the active cell.

2. On the Ribbon, select **Home** > **Styles** >**Conditional Formatting** > **New Rule**.

3. In the **New Formatting Rule** dialog, select **Use a formula to determine which cells to format**.

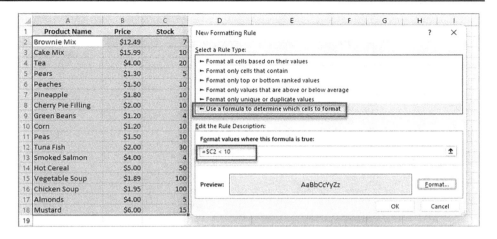

	A	B	C	D	E	F	G	H	I
1	Product Name	Price	Stock						
2	Brownie Mix	$12.49	7						
3	Cake Mix	$15.99	10						
4	Tea	$4.00	20						
5	Pears	$1.30	5						
6	Peaches	$1.50	10						
7	Pineapple	$1.80	10						
8	Cherry Pie Filling	$2.00	10						
9	Green Beans	$1.20	4						
10	Corn	$1.20	10						
11	Peas	$1.50	10						
12	Tuna Fish	$2.00	30						
13	Smoked Salmon	$4.00	4						
14	Hot Cereal	$5.00	50						
15	Vegetable Soup	$1.89	100						
16	Chicken Soup	$1.95	100						
17	Almonds	$4.00	5						
18	Mustard	$6.00	15						
19									

New Formatting Rule ? ×

Select a Rule Type:
- Format all cells based on their values
- Format only cells that contain
- Format only top or bottom ranked values
- Format only values that are above or below average
- Format only unique or duplicate values
- Use a formula to determine which cells to format

Edit the Rule Description:

Format values where this formula is true:

=$C2 < 10

Preview: AaBbCcYyZz Format...

OK Cancel

Since A2 is the active cell, you need to enter a formula that is valid for row 2 and will apply to all the other rows.

4. Type in the formula *=$C2 < 10*.

The dollar sign before the C means it is an **absolute reference** for column C ($C). The value in column C for each row is evaluated and used to determine if the format should be applied.

Note The difference between an absolute reference and a relative reference is covered in chapter 6.

5. For the fill color, click the **Format** button, select the fill color you want, and click **OK**, and **OK** again to apply the rule.

The rows with Stock below 10 will now be filled with grey.

	A	B	C
1	**Product Name**	**Price**	**Stock**
2	Brownie Mix	$12.49	7
3	Cake Mix	$15.99	10
4	Tea	$4.00	20
5	Pears	$1.30	5
6	Peaches	$1.50	10
7	Pineapple	$1.80	10
8	Cherry Pie Filling	$2.00	10
9	Green Beans	$1.20	4
10	Corn	$1.20	10
11	Peas	$1.50	10
12	Tuna Fish	$2.00	30
13	Smoked Salmon	$4.00	4
14	Hot Cereal	$5.00	50
15	Vegetable Soup	$1.89	100
16	Chicken Soup	$1.95	100
17	Almonds	$4.00	5
18	Mustard	$6.00	15
19			

Chapter 6

Carrying out Calculations with Formulas

Excel provides tools and features that enable you to perform different types of calculations, from basic arithmetic to complex engineering calculations using formulas.

This chapter covers:

- Operator precedence in Excel and its effect on calculations.
- How to enter formulas in Excel.
- How to calculate percentages, dates, and time.
- How to use the AutoSum feature for automated calculations.
- The difference between relative and absolute cell references.
- How to access data in other worksheets in your formulas.

Operators in Excel

Arithmetic Operators

The following arithmetic operators are used to perform basic mathematical operations such as addition, subtraction, multiplication, or division.

Arithmetic operator	Meaning	Example
+ (plus sign)	Addition	=4+4
– (minus sign)	Subtraction	=4–4
		=-4
	Negation	
* (asterisk)	Multiplication	=4*4
/ (forward slash)	Division	=4/4
% (percent sign)	Percent	40%
^ (caret)	Exponentiation	=4^4

Comparison Operators

Comparison operators allow you to compare two values and produce a logical result, that is, TRUE or FALSE.

Comparison operator	Meaning	Example
=	Equal to	=A1=B1
>	Greater than	=A1>B1
<	Less than	=A1<B1
>=	Greater than or equal to	=A1>=B1
<=	Less than or equal to	=A1<=B1
<>	Not equal to	=A1<>B1

Operator Precedence

If you combine several operators in a single formula, Excel performs the operations in the following order.

Operator	Description
: (colon) (single space) ,(comma)	Reference operators
–	Negation (as in –1)
%	Percent
^	Exponentiation
* and /	Multiplication and division
+ and –	Addition and subtraction
&	Connects two strings of text (concatenation)
= <> <= >= <>	Comparison

At a basic level, you just need to remember that Excel performs multiplication and division before addition and subtraction. If a formula contains operators with the same precedence, for instance, multiplication and division, Excel will evaluate the operators from left to right.

Parentheses and Operator Precedence

You can change the order of evaluation by enclosing parts of your formula in parentheses (). The part of the formula in parentheses will be calculated first.

For example, the following formula produces 75 because Excel calculates multiplication before addition. So, Excel multiplies 7 by 10 first before adding 5 to the result.

=5+7*10

Answer = 75

In contrast, if we enclose 5+7 in parentheses, Excel will calculate 5 + 7 first before multiplying the result by 7 to produce 120.

=(5+7)*10

Answer = 120

In another example, we want to add 20% to 300. The parentheses around the second part of the formula ensure Excel calculates the addition first before the multiplication to produce 360.

=300 * (1 + 0.2)

Answer = 360

Entering a Formula

To enter a formula in a cell, always start your entry with an equal sign (=) in the formula bar. The equal sign tells Excel that your entry is a formula, not a static value.

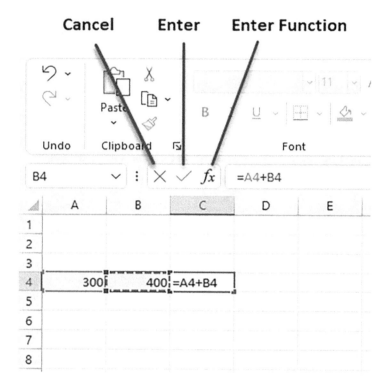

Next to the formula bar, you have the **Enter** command (checkmark) that you use to confirm your formula. You enter your formula in the formula bar and click **Enter** to confirm the entry. If you wish to cancel your entry, click **Cancel** to discard it.

For example, if you wanted to add two numbers, 300 + 400, you would do the following:

1. Enter 300 in cell **A4**.

2. Enter 400 in cell **B4**.

3. In cell C4, enter **= A4 + B4**.

4. Click **Enter**.

5. C4 will now have the sum of the two figures, 700.

Tip To minimize errors, avoid typing cell references directly into the formula bar as much as possible. After you type in the leading equal sign (=) in the formula bar, you can add cell references to your formula by selecting them on the worksheet with your mouse. Select the cell on the worksheet with your mouse to automatically enter its reference in the formula bar whenever you want to reference a cell.

Thus, for the basic calculation we performed above, the way you would enter it in the formula bar is as follows:

1. Enter 300 in cell **A4**, and 400 in cell **B4**.

2. Select **C4**.

3. Type "=" in the formula bar.

4. Select **A4**.

5. Type "+" in the formula bar.

6. Select **B4**.

7. Click **Enter**.

Excel displays the sum of the two cells, 700, in cell C4.

Calculating Percentages

In this example, we want to calculate 20% of a value and then add it to the total, the way sales tax is calculated in invoices.

The product price is $2,900, and the sales tax is 20%.

Note 100 percent is 1 in Excel. Anything less than 100 percent will be less than 1. Hence, 20 percent will be 0.2. Always enter a percent as a decimal place number unless it is 100% or greater.

For the **Sales tax,** we then enter 0.2 in cell B3.

We can format the cell as a **Percentage** data type (although this is not compulsory when calculating percentages in Excel). On the **Home** tab, in the **Numbers** group, click the % sign. Excel changes the 0.2 you entered in the cell to 20%.

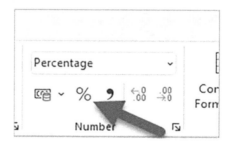

For the **Price**, enter $2,900.

For the Sales Tax formula, enter =*A6*B3* to calculate 20% of $2,900, which is $580.00.

For the **Total**, you can use the AutoSum tool to generate the sum, or you can enter the formula directly =*SUM(A6:B6)* to produce the total figure of $3,480.00.

B6	▾	⋮	✕	✓	*fx*	=A6*B3

◢	A	B	C	D
1	Calculating percentages			
2				
3	Sales tax rate:	20%		
4				
5	Price	Sales Tax	Total	
6	$2,900.00	$580.00	$3,480.00	
7				

You can use the same method above to subtract percentages. For example, to subtract the Sales Tax from the Price, enter =A6-B6 in cell c6.

Using AutoSum

The AutoSum tool can be found on the **Home** tab, in the **Editing** group. It is the Greek Sigma symbol. AutoSum allows you to insert functions in your worksheet. The tool automatically selects the range to be used as your argument. You can use AutoSum with the SUM, AVERAGE, COUNT, MAX, and MIN functions.

AutoSum will default to the SUM function when clicked, but you can use a different function with AutoSum. Click the AutoSum drop-down button to display a pop-up menu of the other functions you can use. Select another function on the menu, for example, **Average**, to insert it as the function used with AutoSum.

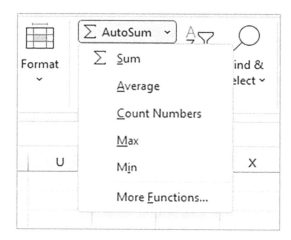

A *range* in Excel is a collection of two or more cells that contain the data with which you're working. See chapter 8 for more on ranges.

A function *argument* is a piece of data that a function needs to run. The SUM function, for example, can have one or more arguments for the input ranges to be summed.

=SUM(A2:A10)

=SUM(A2:A10, C2:C10)

The great thing about AutoSum is that it selects the most likely range of cells in the current column or row that you want to use. It then automatically enters them in the function's argument.

For the most part, it selects the correct range of cells and marks the selection with a moving dotted line called a bounding outline. For non-continuous data, AutoSum may not automatically select everything. In those cases, you can manually correct the range by dragging the selection (bounding outline) over the other cells you want in the formula.

Example

In the following example, we have figures in B2 to B14 that we want to sum up, and we can do this quickly with the AutoSum command.

Follow the steps below to apply AutoSum to a range of continuous data:

1. Click the cell where you want the total displayed. For this example, this would be **B14**.

2. Click the **AutoSum** command button (**Home** > **Editing** > **AutoSum**).

3. AutoSum will automatically select the range of cells with continuous data (above or to the side of the cell with the formula). In this case, it selects B2 to B13.

4. Click **Enter** (the checkmark button next to the formula bar) or hit the **Enter** key.

Cell B14 will now show the sum of the numbers.

| SUM | ⌄ | ⋮ | ✕ ✓ f_x | =SUM(B2:B13) |

◢	A	B	C	D
1	**Month**	**Expenses**		
2	Jan	$950.00		
3	Feb	$716.00		
4	Mar	$981.00		
5	Apr	$903.00		
6	May	$625.00		
7	Jun	$825.00		
8	Jul	$930.00		
9	Aug	$983.00		
10	Sep	$745.00		
11	Oct	$768.00		
12	Nov	$950.00		
13	Dec	$824.00		
14	**Sum**	=SUM(B2:B13)		
15		SUM(**number1**, [number2], ...)		
16				

Using AutoSum with Non-contiguous Data

A non-contiguous range has blank rows or columns in the data. AutoSum will only select the contiguous range next to the cell with the formula. So, you must manually drag the selection over the rest of the data.

To use AutoSum with non-contiguous data, do the following:

1. Click the cell where you want the total to be displayed.

2. Click the **AutoSum** command button.

3. AutoSum will automatically select the range of cells next to the cell with the formula.

4. Hover your mouse pointer over the right edge of the selection until it turns into a double-headed arrow. Then drag over the rest of the cells in your range.

5. Click the **Enter** button or hit the **Enter** key on your keyboard.

The formula cell will now show the sum of the numbers.

	A	B	C	D
	B17	⌄ ⋮ ✕ ✓ fx	=SUM(B2:B16)	
1	Month	Expenses		
2	Jan	$950.00	Drag up	
3	Feb	$716.00		
4	Mar	$981.00		
5				
6	Apr	$903.00		
7	May	$625.00		
8	Jun	$825.00		
9				
10	Jul	$930.00		
11	Aug	$983.00		
12	Sep	$745.00		
13				
14	Oct	$768.00		
15	Nov	$950.00		
16	Dec	$824.00		
17	Sum	=SUM(B2:B16)		
18		SUM(number1, [number2], ...)		

Using AutoSum with Different Ranges

Sometimes the data you want to calculate may be in different parts of your worksheet or even on different sheets in the workbook. With AutoSum, you can have arguments for individual values, cell references, ranges, or a mix of all three. To calculate different ranges, you add different ranges to the AutoSum calculation.

To sum values in different ranges, do the following:

1. Click the cell where you want the formula, and then click **AutoSum**.

2. If AutoSum does not select the first range for you, then select it by clicking the first cell and dragging to the last cell of the range.

3. Hold down the **Ctrl** key and select any additional ranges you want to add to the calculation.

4. Click **Enter**.

B4	⌄ ⋮ ✕ ✓ *fx*	=SUM(D4:D13,B4:B13)			
	A	B	C	D	E
1					
2					
3		Month 1		Month 2	
4	Hugo	$1,848.00		$1,190.00	
5	Felipe	$1,897.00		$1,642.00	
6	Wayne	$1,267.00		$1,639.00	
7	Mae	$1,149.00		$1,421.00	
8	Lee	$1,571.00		$1,061.00	
9	Oscar	$1,659.00		$1,791.00	
10	Fannie	$1,509.00		$1,043.00	
11	Terrance	$1,307.00		$1,680.00	
12	Sylvester	$1,589.00		$1,884.00	
13	Elijah	$1,426.00		$1,768.00	
14					
15	Total (all months)			=SUM(D4:D13,B4:B13)	
16				SUM(number1, [number2], ...)	
17					

The sum of both ranges will now be entered. You can include up to 255 ranges as arguments in the SUM function.

Using AutoSum for Other Aggregate Functions

Despite its name, you can also use the AutoSum feature to calculate the **Average**, **Count**, **Max**, and **Min**. To select these other functions, click the drop-down arrow on the AutoSum command button and select an option on the menu.

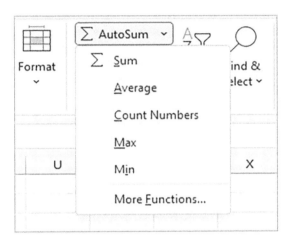

For example, to calculate the average of a row of numbers in cells B4 to G4, you would do the following:

1. Place the cell pointer in the cell where you want to display the average, which is H4 for this example (see image below).

2. On the **Home** tab, click **AutoSum** > **Average**.

    AutoSum will automatically select the cells with numbers next to the formula cell. In this example, AutoSum selects the range B4:G4.

3. Click **Enter** (or press the **Enter** key) to accept the selection.

    Excel calculates the average of the selection using the AVERAGE function in cell H4.

	YEAR	⌄	⋮	✕ ✓	fx	=AVERAGE(B4:G4)				
◢	A	B	C	D	E	F	G	H	I	J
1	**Exam Marks**									
2										
3	Students	Math	English	Physics	Chemistry	Biology	Computer Sci	Average		
4	Barbara	44	69	25	83	78	35	=AVERAGE(B4:G4)		
5	Michelle	69	85	57	28	26	56	AVERAGE(**number1**, [number2], ...)		
6	Pamela	79	57	73	34	74	48			
7	Mildred	88	71	90	73	97	88			
8	Kathy	66	94	85	61	81	92			
9	Bruce	41	25	76	42	87	25			
10	Kathleen	90	77	31	43	61	63			
11	Joshua	92	84	64	78	82	56			
12	Andrew	91	73	42	87	90	88			
13	Todd	33	56	79	76	40	85			
14	Kathryn	55	33	30	33	69	43			
15	Irene	38	72	59	32	87	32			
16										
17										

Quick Sum with the Status Bar

If you want to quickly see the sum of a range of cells, select the range and view the information on the Status Bar.

To select a range of cells, click the first cell in the range, hold down the **Shift** key, and click the last cell in the range.

Once you have selected the range, look at the lower right-hand side of the Excel **Status Bar**. You'll see the **Average**, **Count**, and **Sum** for the selected cells.

	Month 1	Month 2
Hugo	$1,848.00	$1,190.00
Felipe	$1,897.00	$1,642.00
Wayne	$1,267.00	$1,639.00
Mae	$1,149.00	$1,421.00
Lee	$1,571.00	$1,061.00
Oscar	$1,659.00	$1,791.00
Fannie	$1,509.00	$1,043.00
Terrance	$1,307.00	$1,680.00
Sylvester	$1,589.00	$1,884.00
Elijah	$1,426.00	$1,768.00

Average: $1,517.05   Count: 20   Sum: $30,341.00

This feature provides a way of quickly viewing aggregate data for a range of values in a worksheet without entering a formula.

Calculating Date and Time

Native support for date and time calculations has vastly improved in Excel over previous editions. You can now perform many date and time calculations in the worksheet area using arithmetic operators where functions were previously needed. The trick is to apply the right data format to the cells to get the right results. This section will cover some of the common date and time calculations.

Adding Time

When you enter two numbers separated by a colon, for example, 8:45, Excel recognizes the value as time and will treat it as such when you perform calculations based on that cell.

In the following example, we calculate how many hours and minutes it took to complete two trips. The first trip took 8 hours and 45 minutes, and the second one took 6 hours and 30 minutes.

B4					fx	=SUM(B2:B3)

◢	A	B	C	D
1	**Trip**	**Time**		
2	Trip 1	08:45		
3	Trip 2	06:30		
4	Total	15:15		
5				

We enter **08:45** in B2 and **06:30** in B3.

The values are added in cell B4 with the formula **=SUM(B2:B3)**, and it returns an answer of **15:15** (15 hours and 15 minutes).

As you can see from the example above, when we sum the two values, Excel uses hours and minutes to perform the calculation rather than hundreds.

Note that Excel only recognizes time up to 24 hours by default. If you want to calculate time greater than 24 hours, you'll need to format the cell to accept time over 24 hours.

To format a cell to display values over 24 hours, do the following:

1. Click the dialog box launcher in the **Number** group on the Home tab.

2. In the **Format Cells** dialog box, click **Custom**.

3. In the **Type** box, enter **[h]:mm**. This custom format tells Excel to display values beyond 24 hours.

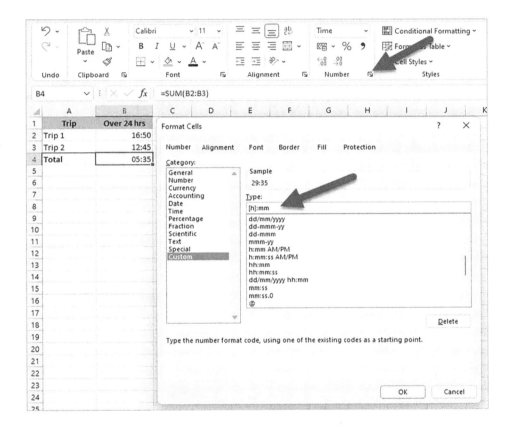

After this change to the cell format, when you add 16:50 + 12:45, you now get **29:35** instead of 05:35.

C4		⌄ ⋮ ✕ ✓ *fx*	=SUM(C2:C3)	
◢	A	B	C	D
1		**Less than 24 hrs**	**Over 24 hrs**	
2	Trip 1	08:45	16:50	
3	Trip 2	06:30	12:45	
4	Total time	15:15	29:35	
5				

Subtracting Time

You can calculate the number of hours between two times by subtracting one from another, like in a work timesheet.

E4		⌄ ⋮ ✕ ✓ *fx*	=(D4-B4)-C4		
◢	A	B	C	D	E	F

	A	B	C	D	E	F
1	**Timesheet**					
2						
3		**Start time**	**Break (hrs:min)**	**End time**	**Total (hrs:min)**	
4	Mon	9:30 AM	1:00	7:30 PM	9:00	
5	Tue	9:00 AM	0:40	5:00 PM	7:20	
6	Wed	8:10 AM	0:50	4:30 PM	7:30	
7	Thu	7:50 AM	1:30	4:30 PM	7:10	
8	Fri	8:00 AM	0:30	4:30 PM	8:00	
9						

If you enter the time with a colon between the hours and minutes, a simple subtraction can be used to calculate the difference between two times.

In the example above, the simple formula we need to calculate the total time worked per day is:

=(D4-B4)-C4

This formula first subtracts the **Start time** (B4) from the **End time** (D4), then subtracts the **Break** (C4) from the difference to create the total time worked for the day.

Just a few years back, you would need a series of nested IF functions to create the same solution we have achieved above. You would have to perform all the calculations in hundredths and then use logical tests to derive the minutes. So, Excel (and spreadsheet technology in general) has come a long way since then!

Note To ensure the elapsed time is displayed correctly, format the cells showing hours and minutes rather than AM/PM (in this case, C4:C8 and E4:E8) with a custom time format **[h]:mm**. On the other hand, the cells showing AM/PM time (in this case, B4:B8 and D4:D8) have been given the custom format **h:mm AM/PM**.

Calculating Time Across Days

You can use the same method above to calculate the time elapsed across days.

In the following example, we have two times:

Time1: *11/24/22 12:30*

Time2: *11/25/22 14:40*

If **Time1** is in cell **A2** and **Time2** is in cell **B2**, the formula **=B2-A2** will produce the result **26:10** (26 hours and 10 minutes).

Note that the cell containing the result has to be formatted as **[h]:mm** to display the result accurately.

C2	fx	=B2-A2	
	A	B	C	D
1	Time1	Time2	Result	
2	11/24/2022 12:30	11/25/2022 14:40	26:10	
3				
4				
5				
6				

Using the TIME Function

You can use the TIME function to properly convert values to hours, minutes, and seconds if directly entered in the formula bar.

Syntax:

=TIME(hour, minute, second)

The following example subtracts 1 hour 40 minutes from 8:20 AM. We want to subtract the value in the formula bar rather than enter it in a cell. If the time is in cell A4, we could use the following formula to subtract 1 hour 40 minutes from it:

=A4 - TIME(1,40,0)

B4	⌄ ⋮ ✕ ✓ *fx*	=A4-TIME(1,40,0)		
	A	B	C	D	E
1	Subtract 1 hour 40 minutes				
2					
3	Source	Result			
4	8:20 AM	6:40 AM			
5					
6					

For more on date functions, see chapter 9 - Working with Functions.

Adding and Subtracting Dates

Excel now has improved native functionality for handling dates. For example, in the past, if you wanted to add several days to a date, you would need to use a specific function to make the calculation. You can now just use basic addition and subtraction, and Excel handles all the complexity behind the scenes.

Example 1

Add 40 days to 12/17/2023

1. Enter *12/17/2023* in cell A2 and *40* in cell B2.
2. Enter the formula *=A2+B2* in cell C2
3. Click Enter.

The result will be *01/26/2024*.

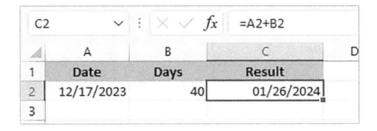

Example 2

Subtract 30 days from 12/14/2022

1. Enter *12/14/2022* in cell A2 and *30* in cell B2.
2. Enter the formula *=A2-B2* in cell C2
3. Click Enter.

The result will be *11/14/2022*.

C2		⌄	⋮	× ✓	*fx*	=A2-B2

◢	A	B	C	
1	**Date**	**Days**	**Result**	
2	12/14/2022	30	11/14/2022	
3				

For more on calculating dates, see chapter 9 - **Working with Functions**.

Relative and Absolute Cell Reference

Relative Cell Reference

By default, a cell reference in Excel is relative. When you refer to cell **B2** from cell **E3**, you are pointing to a cell that is three columns to the left (E minus B) and one row above (3-2). A formula with a relative cell reference changes as you copy it from one cell to another.

For example, if you copy the formula **=C2+D2** from cell E2 to E3, the formula changes to **=C3+D3**. The relative positions of the cells in the formula remain on the same columns but are one row down. When copying a formula with relative cell references, you need to be aware that the formula will change.

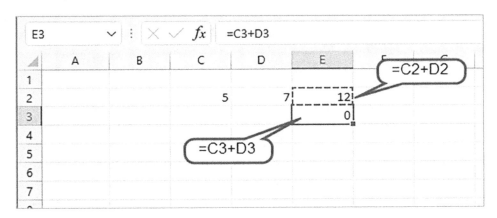

Examples of relative references:

=D2+E2

=A3*B3

Absolute Cell Reference

Suppose you want to maintain the original cell reference when copying a formula. In that case, you need to make the cell reference *absolute* by inserting a dollar sign ($) before the column letter and row number, for example, **=$C$2 + $D$2**. The dollar sign before the column and row tells Excel that the cell reference does not change when the formula is copied to other cells. When you copy the formula **=$C$2 + $D$2** from E2 to E3, the formula stays the same.

To convert a cell reference to an absolute reference, select the reference in the formula bar (or place the cursor between the column letter and row number) and press the **F4** key.

For example, if you have =C2 + D2 in the formula bar and want to make C2 an absolute reference, select C2 in the formula bar and press F4. Excel converts it to **$C$2**.

If you keep pressing F4, Excel cycles through the different types of cell references available as listed below:

- **Relative reference** (default): Relative columns and rows. For example, **A2**.

- **Absolute reference**: Absolute columns and rows. For example, **$A$2**.

- **Mixed reference**: Relative columns and absolute rows. For example, **A$2**.

- **Mixed reference**: Absolute columns and relative rows. For example, **$A2**.

Example

In the example below, we calculate the Sales Tax on various items. The Tax Rate of **20%** has been entered in cell B3. The cell format of B3 is **Percentage**.

The formula in cell C6 is **=B6*$B$3**.

As you can see, cell B3 in the formula has been set to an absolute reference. Thus, when we copy the formula (using autofill) to the rest of the cells under Tax (column C), the reference to cell B3 remains the same.

If the Tax Rate were to change in the future, we would only change the value in cell B3. The Tax for all the items will automatically be updated.

| C6 | | fx | =B6*$B$3 |

▲	A	B	C
1	Sales Tax Calculation		
2			
3	Tax Rate:	20%	
4			
5	Product	Price (excl. tax)	Tax
6	Item 1	$40.00	$8.00
7	Item 2	$58.00	$11.60
8	Item 3	$85.00	$17.00
9	Item 4	$47.00	$9.40
10	Item 5	$56.00	$11.20
11	Item 6	$28.00	$5.60
12	Item 7	$31.00	$6.20
13	Item 8	$65.00	$13.00
14	Item 9	$25.90	$5.18
15	Item 10	$78.30	$15.66
16	Item 11	$69.30	$13.86
17	Item 12	$56.80	$11.36
18			

Mixed Cell Reference

In some cases, you may want to use a "mixed" cell reference. You prefix either the column letter or row number with a dollar sign to lock it as an absolute reference, but allow the other to be a relative reference.

For example, **=$B2 + $C2**

This formula says the columns in cell references (B and C) are locked down as absolute, but row (2) is left free to be relative.

When this formula is copied from E4 to F5 (one column to the right and one row down), it will change to **=$B3 + $C3**. The columns remain the same, but the row changed because the formula moved down one row. You can also lock down the row and leave the column as relative, for example, **=B$2**.

Examples of mixed references:

=$D2+$E2

=A$3*$B3

Using Data from Other Worksheets

On some occasions, you may be working on one worksheet, and you want to access data on another worksheet in your formula. Or perhaps you may decide to separate your summary reports from your data using different worksheets. For example, you may want to have the raw data on **Sheet2** and the summary calculations on **Sheet1**.

Example 1

The following example has a formula in cell **A6** on **Sheet1** and grabs a value from cell **A1** on **Sheet2**.

1. Place the cell pointer in A6 on Sheet1.

2. Enter *=Sheet2!A1* in the formula bar.

3. Click **Enter**.

Excel will now reference cell A1 from Sheet2 as part of your formula in A6 on Sheet1.

Another way to reference a cell on another sheet in your formula is to select it with your mouse. Follow the steps below to reference a cell on another sheet:

1. Select **A6** on **Sheet1**.

2. Type the equal sign (**=**) in the formula bar.

3. Click the **Sheet2** tab (at the bottom of the window).

4. Select cell **A1** on **Sheet2**.

5. Click **Enter**.

Excel enters the reference **Sheet2!A1** automatically in cell A6 in Sheet1.

The same method applies when your reference is a range. Sometimes you may want your data on one sheet, and your summary calculations on another sheet.

If you want to reference more than one cell, like a range, click Sheet2 and select the range of cells. For example, A1:A10. The reference **Sheet2!A1:A10** will now be added to the formula bar in Sheet1. If you have a named range, you can use the range's name in place of the cell reference, for example, **Sheet2!MyRange**.

Example 2

In the following example, we have our raw data on Sheet2, and we're calculating the totals for each Quarter on Sheet1.

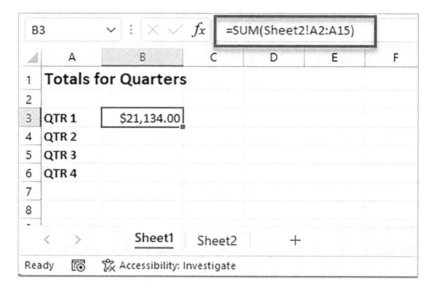

1. On **Sheet1**, select B3, and in the formula bar, enter *=SUM(*.

2. Click the **Sheet2** tab at the bottom of the window.

3. On Sheet 2, select cells **A2:A15** by selecting A2 and dragging down to A15.

   Excel adds **Sheet2!A2:A15** in the formula bar. Your syntax should now look like this =SUM(Sheet2!A2:A15.

4. Click in the formula bar and enter the closing bracket. Your formula should now look like this **=SUM(Sheet2!A2:A15)**.

5. Click **Enter** to confirm the entry.

The sum of the figures from A2 to B15 on Sheet2 will now be shown in sheet1.

Chapter 7

Drop-down Lists and Validation Rules

A drop-down list enables you to restrict the values users can enter in a cell to a subset of predefined values. Having a predefined list of values can help streamline workflow and minimize errors. A validation rule allows you to restrict the type of data, or the range of values users can enter into a cell. You can insert validation rules in cells to ensure the entered data meets a certain set of criteria.

In this chapter, we will cover:

- Entering data with a drop-down list.
- Creating data validation rules for cells.

Entering Data with a Drop-down List

There are occasions when you can make your worksheet more efficient by using drop-down lists in cells. Drop-down lists enable users to select an item from a list you create instead of entering their own values. On occasions where you have a defined set of values from a lookup list or column, being able to select the value directly from the source data saves time and reduces errors.

You can use a comma-delimited list or a range in your worksheet for the data source of your drop-down list.

Using a Comma-Delimited List as the Source

In the following example, we'll use a comma-delimited list for a drop-down list used to populate the grades for students. The grades we'll use as our source are - Merit, Credit, Pass, and Fail.

	A	B
1	**Student**	**Grade**
2	Judith	
3	Paul	
4	David	
5	Randy	
6	Mary	
7	Dorothy	
8	Kimberly	
9	Raymond	
10	Shirley	

Follow the steps below to create a drop-down list with comma-delimited values:

1. Select all the cells for which you want to add a drop-down list. For our example, we'll select B2:B10.

2. On the Ribbon, click the **Data** tab. Then click the **Data Validation** command.

3. In the Data Validation dialog box, set **Allow** to **List**.

4. Click in the **Source** box and enter your values separated by commas.

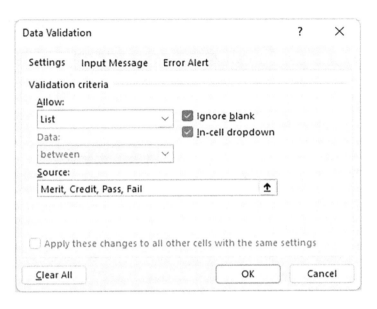

5. Click **OK**.

The selected cells now have a drop-down list.

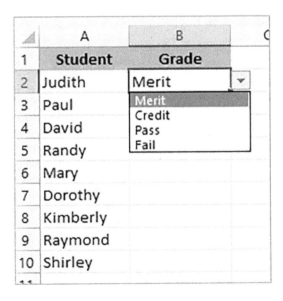

Using a Range as the Source

In the following example, the source for our drop-down list will be from a worksheet named **SalesData** in a different worksheet in the same workbook. Our drop-down list will be pulling data from the Product column (C4:C51).

	A	B	C
1	Sales		
2			
3	Date	Salesperson	Product
4	4/25/2022	Anne Hellung-Larsen	Cora Fabric Chair
5	4/26/2022	Jan Kotas	Lukah Leather Chair
6	4/27/2022	Mariya Sergienko	Habitat Oken Console Table
7	4/28/2022	Michael Neipper	Hygena Fabric Chair
8	4/29/2022	Anne Hellung-Larsen	Harley Fabric Cuddle Chair
9	4/30/2022	Jan Kotas	Windsor 2 Seater Cuddle Chair
10	5/1/2022	Mariya Sergienko	Fabric Tub Chair
11	5/2/2022	Laura Giussani	Verona 1 Shelf Telephone Table
12	5/3/2022	Anne Hellung-Larsen	Floral Fabric Tub Chair
13	5/4/2022	Jan Kotas	Fabric Chair in a Box
14	5/5/2022	Mariya Sergienko	Slimline Console Table
15	5/6/2022	Nancy Freehafer	Martha Fabric Wingback Chair
16	5/7/2022	Nancy Freehafer	Slimline Console Table
17	5/8/2022	Nancy Freehafer	Fabric Wingback Chair
18	5/9/2022	Nancy Freehafer	Fabric Chair in a Box

< >   Standard FILTER | SalesData | +

Follow the steps below to create the drop-down list:

1. On a blank worksheet, select the cell where you want to create the drop-down list. For example, cell B3 in a blank worksheet.

2. On the **Data** tab, in the **Data Tools** group, click the **Data Validation** command. Excel opens the **Data Validation** dialog box.

3. On the **Settings** tab, in the **Allow** box, select **List**.

4. Click in the **Source** box, then select the data range you want to display in your list.

   For our example, we're selecting range C4:C51 on the SalesData worksheet. Excel will automatically enter the selected range in the Source box.

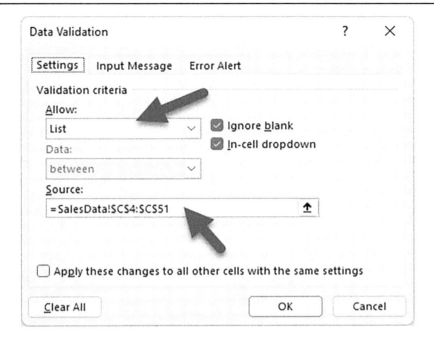

5. Click **OK** to finish creating the drop-down list.

When done, the drop-down list will display a list of values from the selected source when you click the drop-down arrow.

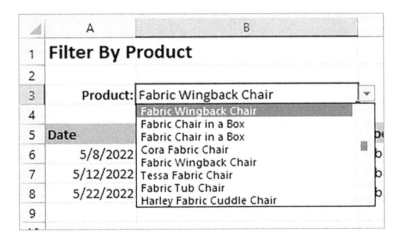

Creating Data Validation Rules

In the following example, let's say we have a product list that is updated by different staff members, and we want to ensure data entry is consistent. The list has the following columns: **Product Code**, **Product Name**, and **Price**. We want to insert a validation rule to ensure that the **Product Code** (column A) can only be between 5 and 10 characters.

Below is an example of the list.

	A	B	C
1	**Product Code**	**Product Name**	**Price**
2	NWTB-1	Chai	18
3	NWTCO-3	Syrup	10
4	NWTCO-4	Cajun Seasoning	22
5	NWTO-5	Olive Oil	21.35
6	NWTJP-6	Boysenberry Spread	25
7	NWTDFN-7	Dried Pears	30
8	NWTS-8	Curry Sauce	40
9	NWTDFN-14	Walnuts	23.25
10	NWTCFV-17	Fruit Cocktail	39
11	NWTBGM-19	Chocolate Biscuits Mix	9.2
12	NWTJP-6	Marmalade	81
13	NWTBGM-21	Scones	10

To add a validation rule for the Product Code, do the following:

1. Select the cells for which you want to apply the rule. For our example, we select column A.

2. On the **Data** tab, in the **Data Tools** group, click the **Data Validation** command.

    Excel opens the Data Validation dialog box.

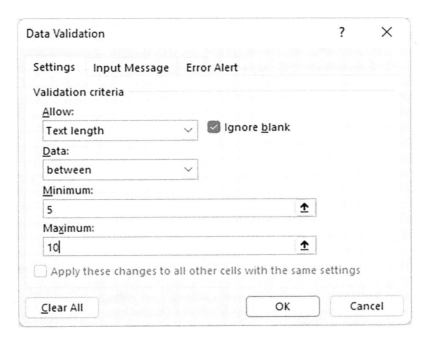

3. On the **Settings** tab, enter the following settings:
    *   **Allow:** Text length
    *   **Data:** between
    *   **Minimum:** 5
    *   **Maximum:** 10

4. On the **Input Message** tab, add a **Title** and the **Input message**.

    Excel displays this message as a small pop-up when the user clicks on a cell with the validation rule.

    For this example, we can add a message like:

"The Product Code can be alphanumeric, and it should be between 5 and 10 characters."

5. On the **Error Alert** tab, we define the message to display when an entry fails the validation rule.

    - Set **Style** to **Stop**.

      The Stop icon is ideal for this scenario because a value that does not meet the validation rule cannot be entered.

    - In the **Title** box, enter: *"Invalid Entry."*

    - In the **Error Message** box, enter: *"Invalid entry. Please enter a value between 5 and 10 characters in length."*

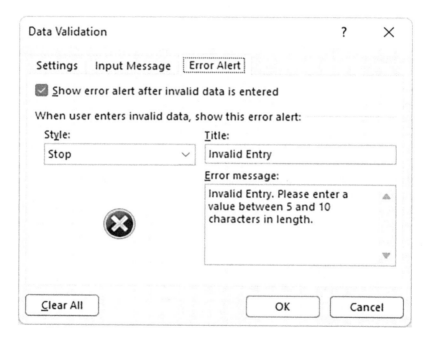

6. Once you have completed all the tabs, click **OK.**

Data validation will now be applied to the selected cells.

Editing or Removing Data Validation Rules

Occasionally you may want to change or remove data validation. To remove data validation, do the following:

1. Select the cells where data validation has been applied.

2. On the **Data** tab, in the **Data Tools** group, click the **Data Validation** command to open the Data Validation dialog box.

3. To change the validation rule, simply edit the various entries and click OK when done.

4. To remove the validation rule, click **Clear All**.

5. Click **OK**.

Chapter 8

Named Ranges

When working with a lot of data, it is sometimes useful to identify your data as a group with one name to make it easier to reference in your formulas. A named range is a group of cells in Excel selected and given one name. After you specify a name for the selection, the range can now be referenced as one unit using that name in Excel formulas and functions. A named range is similar to a table with a name but different from Excel tables.

This chapter will cover:

- Defining a named range.
- Editing and renaming a named range.
- Removing a named range.
- How to use named ranges in your formulas.

Creating a Named Range

In the following example, we have a list of contacts we would like to use in formulas. We could either use A1:G17 to identify the range of data, or we could name the range "Contacts" and then use that name to reference the data throughout our worksheet.

One of the benefits of using a named range is that Excel makes it an absolute reference by default. When you create a formula with that name, you can copy and paste the formula anywhere in your workbook, including different worksheets in the workbook, and the name will always point to the same group of cells.

There are two ways you can create a named range:

Method 1

1. Select the cells you want to include in the named range.

2. Click in the **Name** box (the box on the left side of the window, just above the worksheet area) and enter the name for your named range.

3. Press **Enter** on your keyboard to save the name.

The example below has A1:G17 defined as a named range called "Contacts" in the Name box. You can now use Contacts in place of A1:G17 in all formulas and functions in the workbook. When you create a named range using this method, the name will be available across all worksheets in your workbook.

	A	B	C	D	E	F	G
							Contacts ⌄ fx Company
1	Company	Last Name	First Name	Job Title	Address	City	State/Province
2	Company A	Bedecs	Anna	Owner	123 1st Street	Seattle	WA
3	Company B	Gratacos Solsona	Antonio	Owner	123 2nd Street	Boston	MA
4	Company C	Axen	Thomas	Purchasing Representative	123 3rd Street	Los Angelas	CA
5	Company D	Lee	Christina	Purchasing Manager	123 4th Street	New York	NY
6	Company E	O'Donnell	Martin	Owner	123 5th Street	Minneapolis	MN
7	Company F	Pérez-Olaeta	Francisco	Purchasing Manager	123 6th Street	Milwaukee	WI
8	Company G	Xie	Ming-Yang	Owner	123 7th Street	Boise	ID
9	Company H	Andersen	Elizabeth	Purchasing Representative	123 8th Street	Portland	OR
10	Company I	Mortensen	Sven	Purchasing Manager	123 9th Street	Salt Lake City	UT
11	Company J	Wacker	Roland	Purchasing Manager	123 10th Street	Chicago	IL
12	Company K	Krschne	Peter	Purchasing Manager	123 11th Street	Miami	FL
13	Company L	Edwards	John	Purchasing Manager	123 12th Street	Las Vegas	NV
14	Company M	Ludick	Andre	Purchasing Representative	456 13th Street	Memphis	TN
15	Company N	Grilo	Carlos	Purchasing Representative	456 14th Street	Denver	CO
16	Company O	Kupkova	Helena	Purchasing Manager	456 15th Street	Honolulu	HI
17	Company P	Goldschmidt	Daniel	Purchasing Representative	456 16th Street	San Francisco	CA

Method 2

This method enables you to specify more settings as you create the named range:

1. Select the cells you want to include in the named range.

2. On the Ribbon, click the **Formulas** tab, and in the **Defined Names** group, click **Define Name**.

    Excel displays the **New Name** dialog box.

3. In the **New Name** dialog box, specify the following settings:

    - In the **Name** box, enter the name of your range.

    - Leave the **Scope** box as **Workbook** (the default) unless you want to restrict the name to the current worksheet.

    - In the **Refers to** box, check the reference that it matches your selection. You can use the up-arrow on the box to reselect the range if necessary.

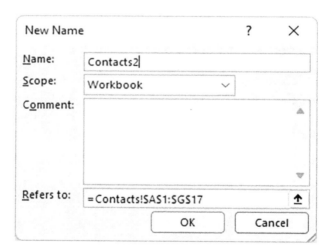

4. Click **OK** when done.

Note If you set the scope of a named range to **Workbook**, the name will be available in all worksheets in the workbook. You can't create another named range using the same name in that workbook. If the scope is set to a particular sheet, then the name can be used within the sheet only. Also, you'll be able to use that name for named ranges within the scope of other sheets.

Note Excel creates a named range that is an absolute reference by default. If you want a relative named range, remove the $ sign from the reference in the **Refers to** box. See chapter 6 for more on relative and absolute references.

Editing a Named Range

Follow the steps below to edit a named range:

1. On the **Formulas** tab, in the **Defined Names** group, click **Name Manager**.

   Excel displays the Name Manager dialog box with a list of all the named ranges and tables in the workbook.

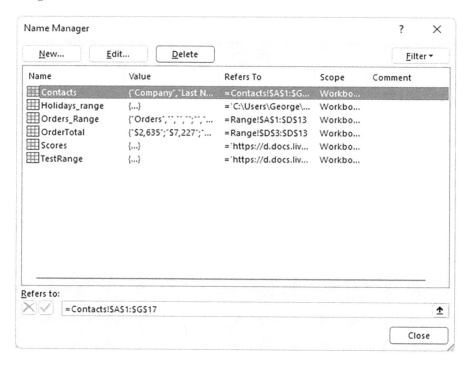

2. In the Name Manager dialog box, select the name you want to edit and click the **Edit** button.

3. In the Edit Name dialog box, enter the name in the **Name** box.

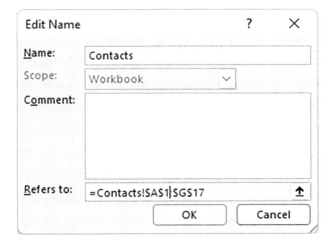

4. To change the reference, click in the **Refers to** box.

   Excel selects the current range on the worksheet, allowing you to resize it if necessary. You can adjust the current selection by holding down the **Shift** key and resizing it with your mouse.

5. Click **OK** on the Edit Name box.

6. Click **Close**.

Using a Named Range

To select a named range, click the drop-down arrow on the Name box and select the name from the drop-down list. Excel will display the worksheet with the range (if you're on a different worksheet) and select all the rows and columns in the range.

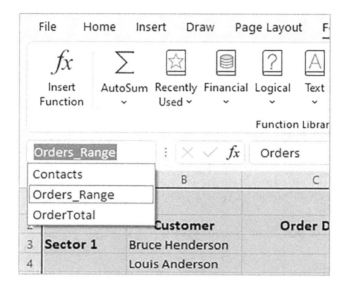

Example

The following example shows the use of two named ranges, *Orders_Range and OrderTotal,* in place of the cell references, A1:D13 and D3:D13. The formulas below use the named ranges as arguments in place of cell references.

=COUNT(Orders_Range)

=COUNTBLANK(Orders_Range)

=SUM(OrderTotal)

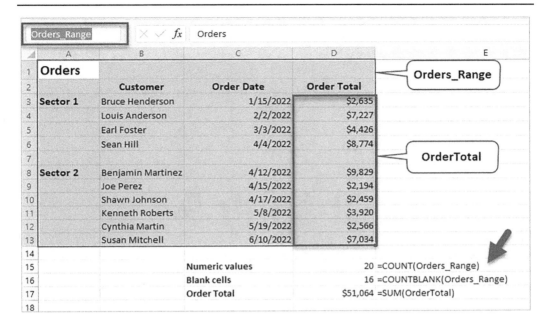

Orders_Range		f_x	Orders	
	A	B	C	D	E

	A	B	C	D
1	**Orders**			
2		**Customer**	**Order Date**	**Order Total**
3	**Sector 1**	Bruce Henderson	1/15/2022	$2,635
4		Louis Anderson	2/2/2022	$7,227
5		Earl Foster	3/3/2022	$4,426
6		Sean Hill	4/4/2022	$8,774
7				
8	**Sector 2**	Benjamin Martinez	4/12/2022	$9,829
9		Joe Perez	4/15/2022	$2,194
10		Shawn Johnson	4/17/2022	$2,459
11		Kenneth Roberts	5/8/2022	$3,920
12		Cynthia Martin	5/19/2022	$2,566
13		Susan Mitchell	6/10/2022	$7,034
14				
15			Numeric values	20 =COUNT(Orders_Range)
16			Blank cells	16 =COUNTBLANK(Orders_Range)
17			Order Total	$51,064 =SUM(OrderTotal)
18				

Orders_Range

OrderTotal

Deleting a Named Range

You may need to delete names as you tidy up your workbook on some occasions. Also, a name can only be used once in a workbook, so deleting a name frees that name for reuse. Deleting a name does not delete the data. It simply removes that name as a reference from the worksheet.

Follow the steps below to delete a named range:

1. On the **Formulas** tab, click **Name Manager**.

2. Select the named range you want to delete from the list.

3. Click the **Delete** button.

4. Click **Close** when done.

Chapter 9

Working with Functions

The Excel function library is vast, ranging from basic aggregate functions to more specialized functions for statisticians, mathematicians, and engineers. This book will cover some of the most useful functions for everyday Excel tasks at home or work.

The more specialized and dedicated functions are outside the scope of this book. However, information is provided at the end of the chapter on how to access other functions in Excel.

This chapter will cover:

- Carrying out calculations with aggregate functions like SUM, AVERAGE, MIN, MAX, and COUNT.
- Creating conditional formulas with the IF function.
- Finding and returning information from a range using XLOOKUP and VLOOKUP.
- Performing date calculations using various date functions.
- Manipulating and rearranging strings with text functions.

How to Enter a Function

You enter a function in the same way you enter a formula. All functions have an opening and closing bracket, and most functions have arguments enclosed in the brackets.

A **function argument** is a piece of data that a function needs to run. Most functions need at least one argument, but a select few, like the TODAY and NOW functions, do not have arguments.

To insert a function:

1. Click in the cell where you want to display the result.

2. Click in the formula bar.

3. Enter an equal sign (=) and start typing the function name. At this point, you'll get a drop-down list with all the Excel functions related to your entry.

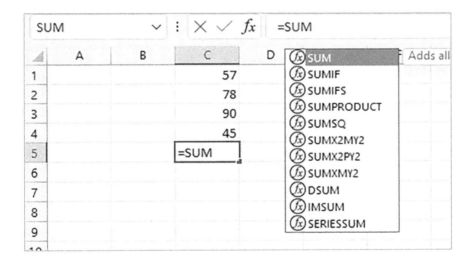

4. Use your up/down arrow keys to highlight the function you want on the list, and press the **Tab** key once to select it. Excel enters the function and the opening bracket in the formula bar, enabling you to enter the argument(s).

5. Enter the argument(s) and the closing bracket, for example, =SUM(C1:C4).

	B	C	D	E
		57		
		78		
		90		
		45		
		270		

Formula bar: fx =SUM(C1:C4)

6. Click **Enter** or press the **Enter** key to confirm your entry.

-̣Q̣-Tip   As much as possible, avoid typing cell references directly into the formula bar as it could introduce errors. Instead, enter the name of the formula and the open bracket. For example, enter **=SUM(**. Then select the cells you want for your argument in the worksheet before entering the closing bracket.

Using the Insert Function Dialog Box

A second way you can enter a function is by using the **Insert Function** dialog box:

1. Click in the formula bar and click the **Insert Function** command on the **Formulas** tab or the Insert Function button next to the formula bar.

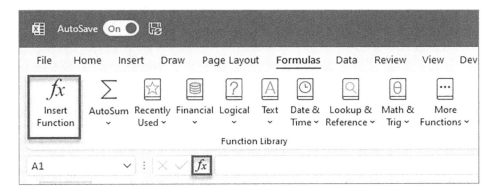

   Excel displays the **Insert Function** dialog box. This dialog box provides the option to search for the function or select it from a category.

2. To search for the function, enter the function's name in the **Search for a function** box.

   For example, if you're searching for the IF function, enter IF in the search box and click **Go**. The **Select a function** list will display all functions related to your search term.

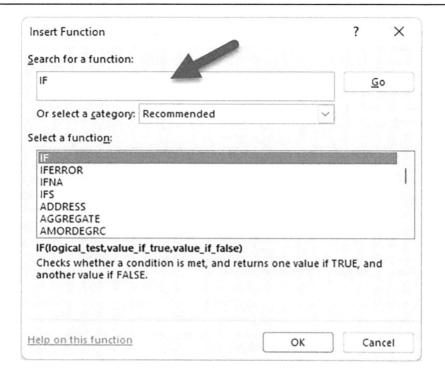

You can also use the **category** drop-down list to narrow down the functions in the list below when looking for a function in a specific category. For example, you can find the IF function in the **Logical** category.

If you have used a function recently, it'll be listed in the **Most Recently Used** category.

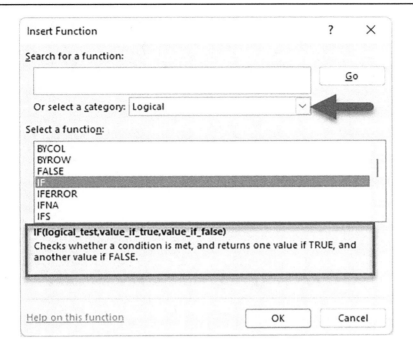

3. Select a function on the list to see the syntax and description of the function in the box below.

4. Click OK.

   Excel opens the **Function Arguments** dialog box.

5. Enter your arguments in the Function Arguments dialog box.

   The Function Arguments dialog box is particularly useful if you are unfamiliar with a particular function. It describes each argument, the results of any logical tests, and the result returned by the function.

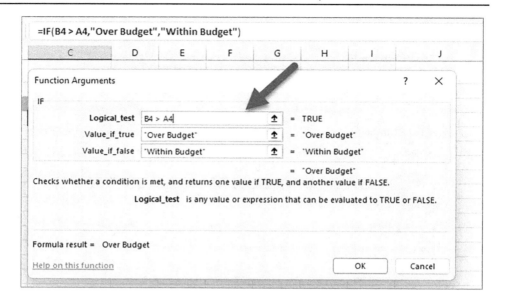

6. Click **OK** after entering the arguments.

Excel inserts the formula in the formula bar.

Perform Aggregate Calculations with Functions

An aggregate function is a function that groups values from multiple rows into a single value. A summary can add meaning to the data depending on what you're analyzing. Aggregate functions include SUM, AVERAGE, MIN, MAX, etc.

SUM Function

The SUM function enables you to sum values in your spreadsheet. You can add individual values, cell references, ranges, or a mix of all three. You can sum up adjacent cells or non-adjacent cells.

Syntax

=SUM(number1,[number2],...)

Arguments

Argument	Description
Number1	Required. The first cell reference, range, or number for which you want to calculate the sum. The argument can be a number like 4, a cell reference like A10, or a range like A2:A10.
Number2, ...	Optional. Additional cell references, ranges, or numbers for which you want to calculate the sum, up to a maximum of 255.

Example 1 - Summing contiguous data:

This example has values in cells B2 to B13 that we want to sum up. We could either use the AutoSum command on the Ribbon or enter the formula in the formula bar:

=SUM(B2:B13)

Entering the formula manually:

1. Select the cell you want to use for the sum. In this case, it is B14.

2. Click in the formula bar and enter **=SUM(**.

3. Select B2 and drag down to B13.

4. Type **)** in the formula bar to close the function.

   The contents of the formula bar should now look like this **=SUM(B2:B13)**.

5. Click the **Enter** button or press **Enter** on your keyboard.

B2		✓ ⋮ ✕ ✓ *fx*	=SUM(B2:B13)
	A	B	C	SUM(**number1**, [number2], …)

	A	B	C
1	Month	**Expenses**	
2	Jan	$547.00	
3	Feb	$880.00	
4	Mar	$717.00	
5	Apr	$540.00	
6	May	$620.00	
7	Jun	$423.00	
8	Jul	$937.00	
9	Aug	$683.00	
10	Sep	$633.00	
11	Oct	$551.00	
12	Nov	$680.00	
13	Dec	$766.00	
14	Total	=SUM(B2:B1	
15			

Example 2: Summing non-contiguous data:

To sum up data in different ranges, i.e., non-contiguous data, you can enter the ranges as different arguments in the SUM function.

For example:

=SUM(B2:B13,D2:D13,F2:F13,H2:H13)

Entering the formula:

1. Select the cell where you want to place the formula.

2. Click in the formula bar and type the function name with the opening bracket. For example *=SUM(*.

3. Select the first range.

4. Type in a comma i.e. *=SUM(B2:B13,*.

5. Select the next range and type in a comma.

6. Select any additional ranges, making sure you type a comma after each range.

7. Enter the closing bracket. You should now have something like this,

   =SUM(B2:B13,D2:D13,F2:F13,H2:H13).

8. Click **Enter** to confirm your entry.

SUM	▾	⋮	✕	✓	*fx*	=SUM(B2:B13,D2:D13,F2:F13,H2:H13)

SUM(number1, [number2], **[number3]**, [number4

◢	A	B	C	D	E	F	G	H	
1		**Store1**		**Store2**		**Store3**		**Store4**	
2	Jan	$547.00		$934.00		$412.00		$447.00	
3	Feb	$880.00		$590.00		$961.00		$605.00	
4	Mar	$717.00		$961.00		$460.00		$652.00	
5	Apr	$540.00		$542.00		$574.00		$754.00	
6	May	$620.00		$497.00		$531.00		$462.00	
7	Jun	$423.00		$874.00		$799.00		$699.00	
8	Jul	$937.00		$755.00		$877.00		$446.00	
9	Aug	$683.00		$715.00		$792.00		$742.00	
10	Sep	$633.00		$421.00		$877.00		$576.00	
11	Oct	$551.00		$941.00		$675.00		$598.00	
12	Nov	$680.00		$520.00		$867.00		$916.00	
13	Dec	$766.00		$524.00		$401.00		$707.00	
14									
15	**Total**					F2:F13,H2:			
16									

AVERAGE Function

The AVERAGE function is one of the widely used aggregate functions in Excel. It returns the average of the arguments. The average is the arithmetic mean of a series of numbers and is calculated by adding up the numbers and then dividing by the count of those numbers.

Syntax

=AVERAGE(number1, [number2], ...)

Arguments

Argument	Description
Number1	Required. The first cell reference, range, or number for which you want to calculate an average.
Number2, ...	Optional. Additional cell references, ranges, or numbers for which you want to calculate an average, up to a maximum of 255.

Notes

- Arguments can be numbers, named ranges, or cell references that contain numbers.

- AVERAGE returns an error if any of the cells referenced in the arguments contain an error value.

- Text, logical values, and empty cells are ignored, but cells with the value zero (0) are included.

Example

In the example below, we use the AVERAGE function to calculate the average of the scores in the range B2:C16.

Formula: =AVERAGE(B2:C16)

F1				▾ ⋮ ✕ ✓ *fx*		=AVERAGE(B2:C16)	

◢	A	B	C	D	E	F	
1	Student	Subject 1	Subject 2		Average score	53.3	
2	Bruce	0	55				
3	Louis	57	61				
4	Earl	51	47				
5	Sean	74	74				
6	Benjamin	50	50				
7	Joe	30	52				
8	Shawn	95	N/A				
9	Kenneth	8	70				
10	Cynthia	30	45				
11	Susan	57	40				
12	John	67	76				
13	Bruce	81	60				
14	Louis	50	61				
15	Earl	30	47				
16	Kenneth	79	50				
17							

Notice that one of the cells has N/A. That cell will be ignored and not counted as part of the average.

MAX, MIN, MEDIAN Functions

The MAX, MIN, and MEDIAN functions are some of the most used functions in Excel and are very similar in their arguments and how they're used. MAX returns the largest number in a specified set of values. MIN returns the smallest number in a set of values. MEDIAN returns the median, which is the number in the middle of a set of numbers.

Syntax

=MAX(number1, [number2], ...)

=MIN(number1, [number2], ...)

=MEDIAN(number1, [number2], ...)

Arguments (similar for all three functions)

Argument	Description
Number1	Required. The first argument is required and can be a number, range, array, or reference that contains numbers.
number2, ...	Optional. You can have additional numbers, cell references, or ranges up to a maximum of 255 arguments that you want to evaluate.

Remarks

- If the arguments contain no numbers, these functions return 0 (zero).

- If an argument is a reference or an array, only numbers in that reference or array are used. Logical values, text values, and empty cells in the reference or array are ignored.

- If arguments contain error values or text that cannot be translated into numbers, the functions will return an error.

- Text representations of numbers and logical values that you directly type into the arguments list are counted.

- The MEDIAN function will calculate the average of the two middle numbers if there is an even number of numeric arguments.

Example

In the example below, we want to show the maximum, minimum, and median values for the Sales column (D2:D12) in our table.

The following formulas return the desired results:

- =MAX(D2:D12)

- =MIN(D2:D12)

- =MEDIAN(D2:D12)

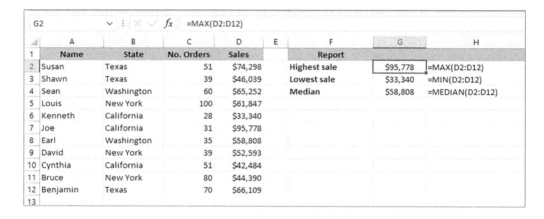

To add more cell references or ranges to the list of arguments, separate them with a comma, for example, MAX(C1:C5, G1:G5).

COUNT Function

The COUNT function will count the number of cells that contain numbers in a range or a list of numbers provided as arguments. The COUNT function only counts populated cells. For example, if you have a range with 20 cells, and only 5 of the cells have numbers, the count function will return 5.

Syntax

=COUNT(value1, [value2], ...)

Arguments

Argument	Description
Value1	Required. The first range in which you want to count numbers.
Value2	Optional. Additional cell references or ranges in which you want to count numbers. You can have a maximum of 255 arguments for this function.

Remarks

- Each argument could be a number, a cell reference, or a range.

- The COUNT function counts numbers, dates, or text representations of numbers (i.e., a number enclosed in quotation marks, like "1").

- Cells with error values or text that can't be translated into numbers are not counted.

- Use the COUNTIF or COUNTIFS function when only counting numbers that meet a certain condition.

Example

In this example, we use the COUNT function to count the values in two ranges.

The formula is:

=COUNT(A3:D20,F3:I20)

Here, we have a simple formula with two arguments to represent the two ranges we want to count: A3:D20 and F3:I20. Note that the blank cells are not counted.

L2				f_x	=COUNT(A3:D20,F3:I20)						
	A	B	C	D	E	F	G	H	I	J	K	L
1			2021					2022				
2	QTR1	QTR2	QTR3	QTR4		QTR1	QTR2	QTR3	QTR4		Count	131
3	70	83	16	37		26	56	47	17			
4	73	71	88	52		87	57	36	87			
5	38	65		19		38	50	51	68			
6	87	56	91	55		62	40	26	77			
7	18	97	39	82			98	98	25			
8	86	15		85		47	59	60	61			
9	28		98	86		41	19	10	11			
10	45	80	43	73			92	95	59			
11	60	92	98	34		51	38	13	91			
12	51	64	25	50		81	84		60			
13	79	29	69	27		62	69	17	65			
14	65	54	95	22		73	53	40	67			
15	91		10	91		66		83	74			
16	88	97	91	89		48	58	78	25			
17	40	88		15		66	12	55	85			
18	12	54	22	87		59	10	66	20			
19	42	17	51	33			67		26			
20	78			32		52	32	62	61			
21												

Creating Conditional Formulas

A conditional function requires a test before carrying out one of two calculations. If the test evaluates to TRUE, it executes one statement, and if the test is FALSE, it executes a different statement. The statements can be calculations, text, or even other functions.

A conditional formula requires:

- The logical test to carry out.

- What to return if the test evaluates to TRUE.

- What to return if the test evaluates to FALSE.

Conditional functions can also be nested if we have more than one test to perform.

IF Function

The IF function is the most popular conditional function in Excel. The IF function allows you to perform a logical test with an expression using comparison operators. The function returns one value if the expression is TRUE and another if FALSE.

Syntax:

=IF(logical_test, value_if_true, [value_if_false])

Arguments

Argument	Description
logical_test	Required. A value or expression that can be TRUE or FALSE.
value_if_true	Required. The value returned if the logical test is true.
value_if_false	Optional. The value returned if the logical test is false. If the logical test is FALSE and this argument is omitted, nothing happens.

In its simplest form, this is what the function says:

IF (something is TRUE, then do A, otherwise do B)

Therefore, the IF function will return a different result for TRUE and FALSE.

Entering IF with Insert Function

If you're new to the IF function, you could use the **Insert Function** dialog box to enter the function. This process provides a wizard that guides you through entering the function arguments, enabling you to see if your logical test produces the expected result.

The **Function Arguments** dialog box lets you debug your logical tests and fix errors before inserting the function.

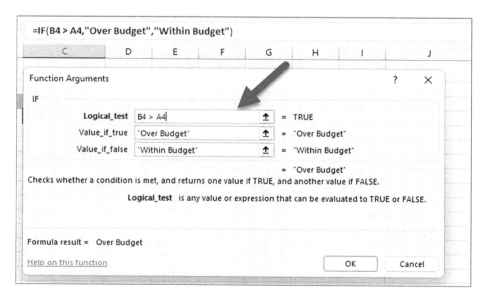

See the section, **How to Enter a Function** earlier in this chapter for how to use the Insert Function feature.

Example 1

A common way the IF function is used is to determine if a calculated cell has any value or not. If the result is false, then it returns a blank cell.

In the example below, the formula for the total for **Jan** was entered in cell **I2**. We then autofill the formula for the other cells in the column covering Feb to Dec. Without the IF function, Excel would display $0 for the unpopulated months. We want the totals for the unpopulated months to be blank instead of $0, even with the formula in place.

SUM					f_x	=IF(SUM(B2:H2) >0,SUM(B2:H2) ,"")					
	A	B	C	D	E	F	G	H	I	J	K	L
1	Month	Store 1		Store 2		Store 3		Store 4	Total			
2	Jan	$633		$569		$472		$587	B2:H2) ,"")			
3	Feb	$734		$442		$561		$440				
4	Mar	$612		$563		$790		$791				
5	Apr	$575		$588		$488		$551				
6	May	$494		$527		$431		$724				
7	Jun											
8	Jul											
9	Aug											
10	Sep											
11	Oct											
12	Nov											
13	Dec											

Function Arguments   ?   ✕

IF

Logical_test   SUM(B2:H2) >0   ⬆ = TRUE
Value_if_true   SUM(B2:H2)   ⬆ = 2261
Value_if_false ""   ⬆ = ""

                                                    = 2261

Checks whether a condition is met, and returns one value if TRUE, and another value if FALSE.

              Logical_test is any value or expression that can be evaluated to TRUE or FALSE.

Formula result = 2261

Help on this function   OK   Cancel

Thus, the formula for Jan in cell **I2** is:

=IF(SUM(B2:H2) >0,SUM(B2:H2) ,"")

The IF function in this example checks to see if the sum of Jan is greater than zero. If true, it returns the sum. If it is false, then it returns a blank string.

When we populate the other fields with the formula, we get the following.

| I2 | | | | | f_x | =IF(SUM(B2:H2) >0,SUM(B2:H2),"") | | | |

▲	A	B	C	D	E	F	G	H	I	J
1	Month	Store 1		Store 2		Store 3		Store 4	Total	
2	Jan	$633		$569		$472		$587	$2,261	
3	Feb	$734		$442		$561		$440	$2,177	
4	Mar	$612		$563		$790		$791	$2,756	
5	Apr	$575		$588		$488		$551	$2,202	
6	May	$494		$527		$431		$724	$2,176	
7	Jun									
8	Jul									
9	Aug									
10	Sep									
11	Oct									
12	Nov									
13	Dec									
14										
15										
16										

Example 2

In another example, we could use the results of an evaluation to return different values in our worksheet. The following budget report has a **Status** column that reports whether a project is within or over budget.

We can use an IF statement to test whether the actual figure is greater than the budgeted figure. If **Actual** is greater than **Budgeted**, the formula returns **Over Budget**. Otherwise, it returns **Within Budget**.

C4				fx	=IF(B4 > A4,"Over Budget","Within Budget")		
⊿	A	B		C	D	E	F
1	**Expenses**						
2							
3	**Budgeted**	**Actual**		**Status**			
4	$138,000	$140,050		Over Budget			
5	$132,000	$132,000		Within Budget			
6	$157,000	$160,040		Over Budget			
7	$193,000	$193,574		Over Budget			
8	$360,000	$360,854		Over Budget			
9	$332,000	$332,717		Over Budget			
10	$229,000	$229,010		Over Budget			
11	$230,000	$220,244		Within Budget			
12	$263,000	$253,409		Within Budget			
13	$215,000	$245,183		Over Budget			
14	$373,000	$343,749		Within Budget			
15	$173,000	$183,769		Over Budget			
16	$361,000	$311,880		Within Budget			
17							

=IF(B2 > A2,"Over Budget", "Within Budget")

The IF function checks whether the value in B2 is greater than the value in A2. If true, the formula returns **Over Budget.** Otherwise, the formula returns **Within Budget**.

Example 3

In another example, we have products for sale, and when **ten or more** of a product is purchased, we apply a **10%** promotional discount.

The logical test checks if C4 is greater than or equal to 10.

If true, the formula returns the subtotal minus 10%.

If false, the formula returns the subtotal.

=IF(C4>=10,D4 - (D4 * 0.1),D4)

When we populate the other cells with the AutoFill handle (a + sign that appears when you place the mouse pointer on the lower-right corner of the active cell), we get the following result (shown in the image below).

E4			fx	=IF(C4>=10,D4 - (D4 * 0.1),D4)	
	A	B	C	D	E	F

	Product	Cost	Qty	Sub total	Total (with discount)	Formulatext
1	**Sales**					
2						
3	**Product**	**Cost**	**Qty**	**Sub total**	**Total (with discount)**	**Formulatext**
4	Beer	$1.50	15	$22.50	$20.25	=IF(C4>=10,D4 - (D4 * 0.1),D4)
5	Brownie Mix	$4.20	10	$42.00	$37.80	=IF(C5>=10,D5 - (D5 * 0.1),D5)
6	Cake Mix	$4.80	10	$48.00	$43.20	=IF(C6>=10,D6 - (D6 * 0.1),D6)
7	Chai	$1.80	10	$18.00	$16.20	=IF(C7>=10,D7 - (D7 * 0.1),D7)
8	Chocolate Biscuits Mix	$5.20	5	$26.00	$26.00	=IF(C8>=10,D8 - (D8 * 0.1),D8)
9	Coffee	$2.00	25	$50.00	$45.00	=IF(C9>=10,D9 - (D9 * 0.1),D9)
10	Green Tea	$2.00	50	$100.00	$90.00	=IF(C10>=10,D10 - (D10 * 0.1),D10)
11	Scones	$4.90	5	$24.50	$24.50	=IF(C11>=10,D11 - (D11 * 0.1),D11)
12	Tea	$1.30	20	$26.00	$23.40	=IF(C12>=10,D12 - (D12 * 0.1),D12)
13						
14						
15	*Apply a 10% discount if the quantity sold per item is 10 or more.					
16						

Nested IF Functions

You can use an IF function as an argument inside another IF function. This kind of formula is called a nested IF statement.

If you need to carry out more than one logical test in your function, you might require a nested IF statement. In the example below, we use a nested IF statement to test for three possible values and return a different result for each one.

Let's say we have a spreadsheet to record the score of exams, and we want to mark everything under 40 as FAIL, between 40 and 69 as CREDIT, and 70 or more as MERIT.

The formula would look like this:

=IF(B2 < 40, "FAIL",IF(B2 < 70,"CREDIT","MERIT"))

C2		fx	=IF(B2 < 40, "FAIL",IF(B2 < 70,"CREDIT","MERIT"))				
	A	B	C	D	E	F	G
1	Student	Mark	Grade				
2	Judith	67	CREDIT				
3	Paul	57	CREDIT				
4	David	51	CREDIT				
5	Randy	74	MERIT				
6	Mary	50	CREDIT				
7	Dorothy	30	FAIL				
8	Kimberly	95	MERIT				
9	Raymond	8	FAIL				
10	Shirley	30	FAIL				
11	Gary	57	CREDIT				
12	Lori	67	CREDIT				
13	Fred	81	MERIT				
14	Virginia	50	CREDIT				
15	Cheryl	30	FAIL				
16	Ruth	79	MERIT				

Formula explanation:

The first IF function checks if B2 is less than 40. If it is true, it returns FAIL. If it is false, it executes the second IF function.

The second IF function checks if B2 is less than 70. If true, it returns CREDIT, and if false, it returns MERIT.

Advanced IF Functions

Excel also includes several other conditional functions you could use in place of the standard IF function. These functions are a combination of a logical function and an aggregate function. These are known as advanced IF functions, hence outside the scope of this book regarding in-depth coverage.

To learn more about advanced If functions, enter the function name in the Search box on Excel's title bar, and select *Get Help on [function name]* from the pop-up menu.

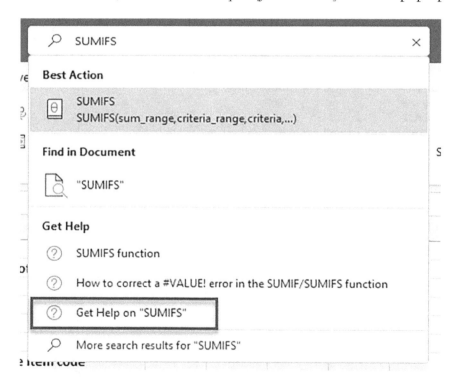

AVERAGEIF

Syntax:

=AVERAGEIF(range, criteria, [average_range])

This function returns the average (arithmetic mean) of data that meets the value you've entered as your criteria. The optional *average_range* argument allows you to specify another range for the values if it is separate from the one with the criteria.

Example:

=AVERAGEIF(A2:A20,"<2000")

This formula returns the average of all the values in cells A2 to A20 over 2000.

AVERAGEIFS

Syntax:

=AVERAGEIFS(average_range, criteria_range1, criteria1, [criteria_range2, criteria2], ...)

This function is similar to AVERAGEIF, but it allows you to specify multiple ranges and multiple criteria in the arguments. You can specify up to 127 ranges and criteria.

COUNTIF

This function returns the count of the values in a range that meets the specified criteria.

Syntax:

=COUNTIF(range, criteria)

In its simplest form, this function says:

=COUNTIF(Where do you want to look?, What do you want to look for?)

Example:

=COUNTIF(A2:A10, "New York")

This formula will return the count of the number of cells in A2:A10 with the value "New York."

COUNTIFS

COUNTIFS(criteria_range1, criteria1, [criteria_range2, criteria2]…)

This function is like the COUNTIF function in that it returns a count based on a condition you specify. However, you can specify multiple ranges and criteria. You can specify up to 127 range/criteria pairs.

SUMIF

This function returns the sum of values in a range based on the specified criteria.

Example:

=SUMIF(A2:A10, ">10")

This formula returns the sum of all the values in cells A2 to A10 greater than 10.

SUMIFS

Syntax:

SUMIFS(sum_range, criteria_range1, criteria1, [criteria_range2, criteria2], …)

This function returns the sum of values that meet multiple criteria. You can specify up to 127 range/criteria pairs.

Calculate Dates with Functions

Date functions enable you to calculate and manipulate dates and times. In this section, we will be covering the most common date functions for general use.

Note that you can now perform some date calculations in Excel without using functions. Some date calculations that previously required a function can now be done in Excel using arithmetic operators. See chapter 6 on Calculating Date and Time for more. The date convention used in the following examples is **m/d/yyyy**.

Note Excel sometimes automatically detects a date entry and formats the cell accordingly. However, if you copied and pasted a date from another source, you may need to manually set the cell to a date format to display the date properly.

Add and Subtract Dates Using the DATE Function

The DATE function enables you to combine different values into a single date.

Syntax

=DATE (year, month, day)

Arguments

Argument	Description
Year	Required. This argument can have one to four digits. Excel uses the Date & time settings on your computer to interpret the year argument.
Month	Required. The month argument should be a positive or negative integer between 1 to 12, representing January to December.
Day	Required. This argument can be a positive or negative integer from 1 to 31, representing the day of the month.

Notes:

- If the month argument is a negative number (*-n*), the function returns a date that is *n* months back from the last month of the previous year. For example, =DATE(2024,-4,2) will return the serial number representing August 2, 2023.

- If the month argument is greater than 12, the function adds that number of months to the last month of the specified year. If Day is greater than the number of days in the specified month, the function adds that number of days to the first day of the next month of the specified date.

-Tip To prevent unwanted results, always use four digits for the year argument. For example, "04" could mean "1904" or "2004." Using four-digit years prevents any confusion.

Example 1

In this example, we want to combine values from different cells for the month, day, and year into a date value recognized in Excel.

- Month: 4
- Day: 14
- Year: 1980

When we use the DATE function to combine the values into a single date, we get the following:

=DATE(C2,A2,B2)

D2			fx	=DATE(C2,A2,B2)	
	A	B	C	D	E
1	**Month**	**Day**	**Year**	**Date**	
2	4	14	1980	4/14/1980	
3					
4					

Example 2

The following example calculates contract dates for different durations. We can combine the YEAR, MONTH, and DAY functions
with the DATE function to perform these calculations.

Function	Description
YEAR(serial_number)	Returns the year corresponding to a date entered as its argument.
MONTH (serial_number)	Returns the month corresponding to a date entered as its argument.
DAY (serial_number)	Returns the day corresponding to a date entered as its argument.

When we combine these functions with the DATE function, we can perform the following date calculations:

- Add 5 years to 12/15/2022.

- Add 15 months to 12/15/2022.

- Add 60 days to 12/15/2022.

The image below shows the formulas used to perform these calculations.

	A	B	C	D	E
1	**Contracts**				
2					
3	**Start Date**	**Years**	**End Date**	**Formula Text**	
4	12/15/2022	5	12/15/2027	=DATE(YEAR(A4)+B4,MONTH(A4),DAY(A4))	
5					
6	**Start Date**	**Months**	**End Date**		
7	12/15/2022	15	3/15/2024	=DATE(YEAR(A7),MONTH(A7)+B7,DAY(A7))	
8					
9	**Start Date**	**Days**	**End Date**		
10	12/15/2022	60	2/13/2023	=DATE(YEAR(A10),MONTH(A10),DAY(A10)+B10)	
11					
12					

Formula Explanation

Add 5 years to 12/15/2022

=DATE(YEAR(A4)+B4,MONTH(A4),DAY(A4))

The **year** argument of the DATE function has **YEAR(A4)+B4** (i.e., 2022 + 5, which returns 2027). The other nested functions return the month and day respectively in the **month** and **day** arguments. To subtract years, use the minus sign (−) in place of the plus sign (+) in the formula.

Add 15 Months to 12/15/2022

=DATE(YEAR(A7),MONTH(A7)+B7,DAY(A7))

In this formula, **MONTH(A7)+B7** adds 15 months to the start date. The other nested functions return the year and day respectively in the year and day arguments of the DATE function. To subtract months, use the − sign in place of the + sign in the formula.

Add 60 days to 12/15/2022

=DATE(YEAR(A10),MONTH(A10),DAY(A10)+B10)

In this formula, **DAY(A10)+B10** adds 60 days to the start date. The other nested functions return the year and month respectively in the year and month arguments of the DATE function. To subtract days, use the − sign in place of the + sign in the formula.

Calculate the Difference Between Two Dates Using DATEDIF

The DATEDIF function calculates the difference between two dates. This function provides one of the easiest ways in Excel to calculate the difference between two dates. It can return the number of days, months, or years between two dates.

DATEDIF is a "hidden" function in Excel because you'll not find it on the list of date functions or when you search for it using the Insert Function dialog box. You must enter it manually any time you want to use it. It is a legacy function from Lotus 1-2-3 but operational on all versions of Excel.

Syntax

=DATEDIF(start_date, end_date, unit)

Arguments

Argument	Description
start_date	Required. This argument represents the start date of the period.
end_date	Required. This argument represents the end date of the period.
unit	Required. This argument represents the unit of measurement you want to return - days, months, or years. It should be entered as a string.
	It can be one of Y, M, D, YM, or YD.
	"Y" = Calculates the number of years in the period.
	"M" = Calculates the number of months in the period.
	"D" = Calculates the number of days in the period.
	"YM" = Calculates the difference between the months in start_date and end_date. The days and years of the dates are ignored.
	"YD"= Calculates the difference between the days of start_date and end_date. The years of the dates are ignored.

Note An "MD" argument also calculates the number of days while ignoring the month and years. However, Microsoft no longer recommends using the MD argument in this function because, under some conditions, it could return a negative number.

Example 1

In the example below, we want to calculate the age of someone born on December 26, 1980. Combining the DATEDIF function with the TODAY function gets the desired result.

Formula:

=DATEDIF(A2,TODAY(),"Y")

B2					fx	=DATEDIF(A2,TODAY(),"Y")		
	A		B			C	D	E
1	Date of Birth		Years					
2	12/26/1980		41					
3								
4								

The TODAY function returns today's date, so this formula will always use the current date to calculate the age. Using "Y" for the unit argument returns the difference in years.

Example 2

To calculate the number of months between two dates, enter "M" in the unit argument of the function.

=DATEDIF(A2,B2,"M")

| C2 | | ⌄ | ⋮ | ✕ ✓ | *fx* | =DATEDIF(A2,B2,"M") |

◢	A	B	C	D	E
1	**Start Date**	**End Date**	**Months**		
2	12/6/2010	12/6/2024	168		
3					
4					

Calculate the Days Between Two Dates Using the DAYS Function

The DAYS function returns the number of days between two dates.

Syntax

=DAYS (end_date, start_date)

Arguments

Argument	Description
start_date	Required. This argument represents the start date of the period.
end_date	Required. This argument represents the end date of the period.

Example

In this example, we want to calculate the number of days between two dates, December 6, 2023, and December 5, 2024.

Formula:

=DAYS(B2, A2)

C2				fx	=DAYS(B2, A2)	
	A	B	C	D	E
1	**Start Date**	**End Date**	**Days**		
2	12/6/2023	12/5/2024	365		
3					
4					
5					

If you're entering the dates directly into the formula bar, you must enclose them in quotation marks.

For example:

=DAYS("11/30/2024","12/01/2023") will return 365 days.

Lookup and Reference Functions

Find Data with XLOOKUP

XLOOKUP is a fairly new function introduced as a replacement for the VLOOKUP function. Like its predecessor, XLOOKUP searches a range or an array and returns a value corresponding to the first match it finds on the same row in another range.

For instance, you can look up the **Price** of a product in a data list using the **Product ID** or **Name**. Similarly, you can return an employee's name using their employee ID. If XLOOKUP does not find a match, you can tell it to return the closest (approximate) match.

Unlike VLOOKUP, which only allows you to return values from a column to the right of the lookup range, XLOOKUP can return values from columns to the left or the right of the lookup range. XLOOKUP also returns exact matches by default, making it easier and more convenient than its predecessor.

Note The XLOOKUP function was introduced in 2020 and is available in Excel for Microsoft 365 and Excel 2021. If you're using an older perpetual license version of Excel, XLOOKUP will not be available.

Syntax:

=XLOOKUP(lookup_value, lookup_array, return_array, [if_not_found], [match_mode], [search_mode])

Arguments and Descriptions

Argument	Description
lookup_value	Required. What value are you searching for? Excel will look for a match for this value in the *lookup_array*. You can provide a value here or a cell reference containing the value you want to find.
lookup_array	Required. Where do you want to search? This value is the lookup range containing the columns you want to include in your search, for example, A2:D10.
return_array	Required. Which range contains the values you want to return? This value is the return range. The return range can have one or more columns as XLOOKUP is about to return more than one value.
[if_not_found]	Optional. This optional argument enables you to enter a piece of text to return if a valid match is not found. If this argument is omitted and a valid match is not found, XLOOKUP will return the #N/A error.
[match_mode]	Optional. This optional argument enables you to specify a match mode from four options: 0 (or omitted) = Exact match. If no match is found, Excel returns an error (#N/A), the default if you omit this argument. -1 - Exact match or the next smallest item if an exact match is not found. 1 - Exact match or the next largest item if an exact match is not found. 2 - Performs a wildcard match where you can use the characters *, ?, and ~ for wildcard searches.
[search_mode]	Optional. This optional argument enables you to specify the order in which you want to perform the search: 1 (or omitted) - Search first to last. This setting is the default if this argument is omitted.

-1 - Perform the search in reverse order - last to first.

2 - Perform a binary search for data sorted in ascending order. If lookup_array is not sorted in ascending order, invalid results will be returned.

-2 - Perform a binary search for data sorted in descending order. If lookup_array is not sorted in descending order, invalid results will be returned.

-Tip Regarding the **search_mode** argument, in earlier versions of Excel, performing binary searches on sorted lists produced quicker results, but in Microsoft 365, non-binary searches are equally fast. Hence, it is no longer beneficial to use binary search options for sorted lists. Using 1 or -1 for the search_mode argument is easier because you don't require a sorted table.

Vertical Lookup

In this example, we are using XLOOKUP to return the Reorder Level of the product entered in cell F1. The formula is in cell F2.

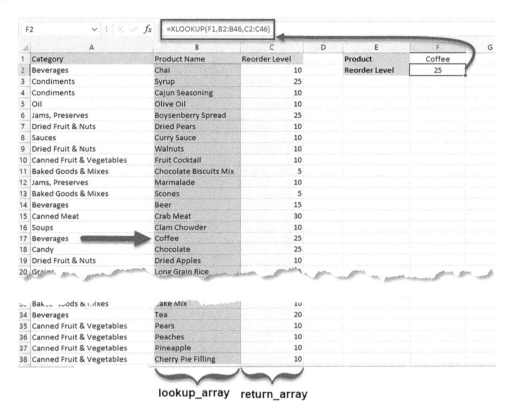

lookup_array   return_array

Formula explanation:

=XLOOKUP(F1,B2:B46,C2:C46)

The formula says, in range B2:B46, find the value in cell F1 (which in this case is "Coffee") and return the value on the same row in range C2:C46.

The *if_not_found* argument has not been provided here, so if a match is not found, it will return an error which is the default behavior.

The VLOOKUP equivalent of this formula would look like this:

=VLOOKUP(F1,B2:C46,2,0)

One benefit of using the XLOOKUP equivalent over this formula is that if we decide at some point to insert a column between columns B and C, it will not break the formula.

The lookup_array does not need to be sorted because XLOOKUP will return an exact match by default.

Horizontal Lookup

XLOOKUP can perform both vertical and horizontal lookups. So, you can also use it in place of the HLOOKUP function.

In the example below, we can retrieve the value associated with a month using the month.

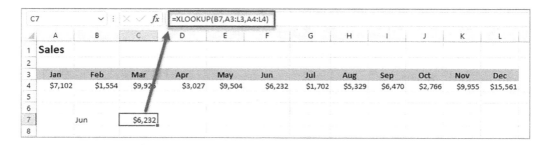

=XLOOKUP(B7,A3:L3,A4:L4)

The formula uses only the first three arguments of the XLOOKUP function. B7 is the lookup_value, A3:L3 is the lookup_array, and A4:L4 is the return_array.

Note that a horizontal lookup_array must contain the same number of columns as the return_array.

Simultaneous Vertical and Horizontal Lookup

This example will use two XLOOKUP functions to perform both a vertical and horizontal match. Here, the formula will first look for a "Mark" in range A4:A15, then look for "Q3" in the top row of the table (range B3:E3) and return the value at the intersection of the two. Previously, you would need to use the INDEX/MATCH/MATCH combination to achieve the same result.

	A	B	C	D	E	F	G	H	I	J
I4					f_x	=XLOOKUP(G4,A4:A15,XLOOKUP(H4,B3:E3,B4:E15))				
1	**Sales data**									
2										
3	**Salesperson**	**Q1**	**Q2**	**Q3**	**Q4**					
4	Penny	17,526	23,972	61,066	22,596		Mark	Q3	19,062	
5	Leslie	49,405	36,646	21,899	62,629					
6	Sally	78,658	16,529	14,976	68,184					
7	Shaun	80,176	84,918	66,561	65,326					
8	Julie	86,988	29,692	30,197	80,960					
9	Velma	94,514	13,333	78,000	59,718					
10	Ian	23,183	21,547	40,408	57,767					
11	Cassandra	70,597	19,615	54,664	68,175					
12	Mark	16,832	91,907	19,062	22,267					
13	Kathy	45,446	14,638	52,312	92,069					
14	Renee	34,583	78,213	21,295	26,964					
15	Judith	18,689	91,081	66,795	96,860					

Formula explanation:

=XLOOKUP(G4,A4:A15,XLOOKUP(H4,B3:E3,B4:E15))

The first XLOOKUP function has the following arguments:

- lookup_value = G4
- lookup_array = A4:A15
- return_array = XLOOKUP(H4,B3:E3,B4:E15)

The second XLOOKUP, executed first, performs a horizontal search on B3:E3, using the value in cell H4 ("Q3") as the lookup_value, then returns the range **D4:D15**. Notice that the second XLOOKUP returns a range rather than a value. This range is used as the return_array argument for the first XLOOKUP.

So, after the second XLOOKUP has been executed, the first XLOOKUP will look like this:

=XLOOKUP(G4,A4:A15,D4:D15)

Examining the Formula with the Evaluate Formula Command

To examine how the formula performs the task, you can use the **Evaluate Formula** command to see how each formula part is evaluated.

Follow the steps below to open the Evaluate Formula dialog box:

1. Select the cell with the formula you want to evaluate. In this case, it is cell **I4**.

2. On the Formulas tab, in the **Formula Auditing** group, click the **Evaluate Formula** command button.

3. In the Evaluate Formula dialog box, click the **Evaluate** button until the nested XLOOKUP function has been evaluated and its result displayed in the formula.

   For this example, we need to click the Evaluate button three times.

You will notice that the second XLOOKUP performs a search using the lookup_value, "Q3", and then returns the range **D4:D15** (displayed as an absolute reference **$D$4:D15**). We can use XLOOKUP here as the *return_array* argument of the first XLOOKUP function because XLOOKUP can return a range and value.

Next, the main XLOOKUP performs a lookup using the value in cell G4, "Mark" as the lookup_value, cells A4:A15 as the lookup_array, and cells D4:D15 as the return_array to return the final result.

Return Multiple Values with Horizontal Spill

In this example, we want to be able to enter the name of a sales rep and return the number of orders and sales associated with them. Hence, the function will return more than one value. XLOOKUP is also an array function in that it can return an array of values from the return_array.

In the formula below, the lookup_value is in cell G2, the *lookup_array* argument is range A2:A12, and the *return_array* argument is range C2:D12.

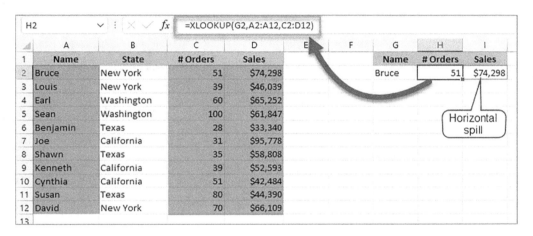

Formula explanation:

=XLOOKUP(G2,A2:A12,C2:D12)

As you can see from the formula, the return_array contains columns C and D. When we enter the name "Bruce" in cell G2, XLOOKUP returns the values in columns C and D from the same row. As the function returns more than one value, the result spills into cell I2.

The range containing the spilled result has a blue border around it, which is how you can tell that the result has spilled into other cells.

Return Multiple Values with Vertical Spill

To get the formula to spill vertically, we can use another example where we need to return the sales for more than one person on our list.

In this example, we first use the FILTER function to generate a filtered list of names based in **New York**. The function returns an array of names that spill vertically in the range G2:G4.

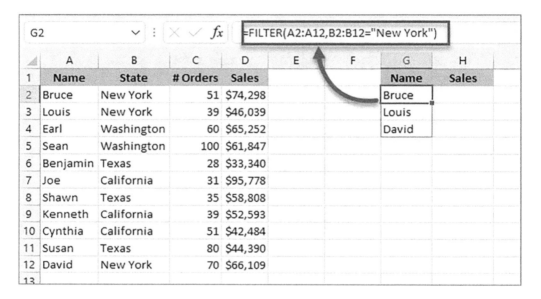

Next, we want to get the **Sales** associated with the names on our filtered list and insert them in column H. To do this, we use XLOOKUP in cell H2 and select cells G2:G4 for our lookup_value argument.

When you select the *lookup_value* (G2:G4), XLOOKUP will recognize the range as a dynamic array and denote that with a hash (#) in the formula.

	A	B	C	D	E	F	G	H
	H2			fx	=XLOOKUP(G2#,A2:A12,D2:D12)			
1	Name	State	# Orders	Sales			Name	Sales
2	Bruce	New York	51	$74,298			Bruce	$74,298
3	Louis	New York	39	$46,039			Louis	$46,039
4	Earl	Washington	60	$65,252			David	$66,109
5	Sean	Washington	100	$61,847				
6	Benjamin	Texas	28	$33,340				
7	Joe	California	31	$95,778				
8	Shawn	Texas	35	$58,808				
9	Kenneth	California	39	$52,593				
10	Cynthia	California	51	$42,484				
11	Susan	Texas	80	$44,390				
12	David	New York	70	$66,109				
13								
14								
15								

Formula explanation:

=XLOOKUP(G2#,A2:A12,D2:D12)

The lookup_value argument in the formula is G2#.

G2# (note the hash) designates the entire range of the spill data. It tells us that G2 is the starting point of the array of values returned from a dynamic array formula.

The lookup_array is the Name column (A2:A12), and the return_array is the Sales column (D2:D12).

When you type in the formula in cell H2 and press Enter, XLOOKUP will return all the sales related to the names in the dynamic array in column G. As we have more than one value, it will spill down vertically in column H2.

One benefit of using XLOOKUP is that the formula will adjust to the dynamic array in column G. If we change the filter and add more names to column G, the formula in cell H2 would still work in finding the values corresponding to the new names. We don't have to worry about copying the formula down to additional cells.

Common XLOOKUP Errors and Solutions

#N/A error

If an exact match is not found, and the **if_not_found** and **match_mode** arguments are omitted, XLOOKUP will return an #N/A error.

There may be scenarios where you will not know if your formula will generate this error, for example, when a formula is copied to multiple cells in a column. If you want to catch and replace this error with a meaningful message, specify it in the **if_not_found** argument.

For example:
=XLOOKUP(F2,B2:B12,D2:D12,"Item not found")

#VALUE! error

This error is often generated because the lookup and return arrays are not the same length. When you get this error, check that these ranges are the same length. If you are carrying out a vertical lookup, they should have the same number of rows. If the lookup is horizontal, they should have the same number of columns.

#NAME? in cell

This error usually means that there is an issue with a cell reference. A typo in the cell reference or omitting the colon can generate this error. When you get this error, check your cell references. To help avoid errors and typos in cell references, select them on the worksheet with your mouse rather than typing them in the formula.

#REF! error

If XLOOKUP is referencing another workbook that is closed, you will get a #REF! error. Ensure all workbooks referenced in your formula are open to avoid this error.

#SPILL! Error

When returning multiple values, if there is already data in the spill range, Excel returns the #SPILL! error. To avoid this error, ensure there is no data in the range that will contain the returned results.

Find Data with VLOOKUP

VLOOKUP is still one of the most popular lookup functions in Excel despite the introduction of XLOOKUP. If you intend to share your workbook with people using older versions of Excel without XLOOKUP, you might want to use VLOOKUP for looking up data. VLOOKUP enables you to find one piece of information in a workbook based on another piece of information. For example, if you have a product list, you can find and return a **Product Code** by providing the corresponding **Product Name** to the VLOOKUP function.

Syntax

=VLOOKUP (lookup_value, table_array, col_index_num, [range_lookup])

Arguments

Argument	Description
lookup_value	Required. What value are you searching for? This argument is the lookup value. Excel will look for a match for this value in the leftmost column of your chosen range. You can provide a value here or a cell reference.
table_array	Required. What columns do you want to search? This argument is the range you want to include in your search, e.g., A2:D10.
col_index_num	Required. Which column contains the search result? Count from the first column to determine what this number should be, starting from 1.
range_lookup	Optional. For an exact match, enter FALSE/0. For an approximate match, enter TRUE/1. For TRUE, ensure the leftmost column is sorted in ascending order for correct results. This argument defaults to TRUE if omitted.

Example

In the example below, we use VLOOKUP to find the *Price* and Reorder Level of a product by entering the **Product Name** in cell G2. The formula is in cell G3, and as you can see from the image below, it searches the table for **Pears** and returns the price from the next column.

Formula Explanation

To look up the **Price** for **Pears**, the formula is:

=VLOOKUP(G2, B2:D46, 2, FALSE)

The function uses a lookup_value from cell **G2** to search a table_array which is **B2:D46**.

The col_index_num is **2,** so it returns a value from the second column in the search range (table_array), the **Price** column.

The range_lookup is **FALSE**, meaning we want an exact match.

To look up the **Reorder Level** for Pears, we use the same formula and just change the column containing the search result (col_index_num) to 3 to return a value from the third row of the table array.

=VLOOKUP(G2, B2:D46, **3**, FALSE)

In this case, the VLOOKUP search for Pears returns a Reorder Level of **10**.

Best Practices for VLOOKUP

- **Use absolute references for the table array**.

  Using absolute references allows you to fill down a formula without changing the cell references. An absolute reference ensures VLOOKUP always looks at the same table array when the formula is copied to other cells.

- **Do not store a number or date as a text value.**

  When searching for numbers or dates, ensure the data in the first column of the table array is not stored as text. Otherwise, the formula might return an incorrect or unexpected value. Number and date values are right-aligned, while text values are left-aligned by default. Therefore, if your numbers or dates are left-aligned in the cell, you must check that they are using the right cell format.

- **Sort the first column.**

  If you want VLOOKUP to find the next best match when the **range_lookup** argument is TRUE, make sure the first column in **table_array** is sorted.

- **Use wildcard characters.**

  You can use a wildcard in **lookup_value** if **range_lookup** is FALSE and lookup_value is text. A question mark (?) matches any single character, and an asterisk (*) matches any sequence of characters. If you want to find an actual question mark or asterisk as part of the search criteria, type a tilde (~) in front of the character.

  For example, =VLOOKUP("Dried*",B2:D46,2,FALSE) will find the first item starting with "Dried" in the first column of table_array.

- **Make sure your data does not contain erroneous characters.**

  If you are searching for text values in the first column of the table array, ensure the data in the first column does not have leading or trailing spaces, non-printable characters, and inconsistent use of straight and curly quotation marks. In cases like these, the formula might return an unexpected value.

  To clean up your data, you can use the TRIM function to remove any extra spaces or use the CLEAN function to remove all nonprintable characters.

Common VLOOKUP Errors and Solutions

- **Wrong value returned**

  If you omit the **range_lookup** argument or set it to TRUE (for an approximate match), you need to sort the first column of **table_array** in alphanumeric order. If the first column is not sorted, Excel may return an unexpected value. Use FALSE for an exact match or sort the first column of the table array for an approximate match.

- **#N/A error in cell**

  If the range_lookup argument is FALSE, and an exact match is not found, you will get an #N/A error. You will also get an #N/A error if **range_lookup** is TRUE and the **lookup_value** is smaller than the smallest value in the first column of **table_array**.

- **#REF! in cell**

  You will get the #REF error if the col_index_num argument is greater than the number of columns in the table array.

- **#VALUE! in cell**

  You will encounter a #VALUE! error if the **lookup_value** argument is over 255 characters. Use wildcards for partial matches if the values in the lookup range are over 255 characters.

  Excel will also generate the #VALUE! error if the **col_index_num** argument contains text or is less than 1. Ensure **col_index_num** is not less than 1.

- **#NAME? in cell**

  This error usually means that the formula is missing quotes. If you enter a text value directly in your formula (instead of a cell reference), ensure you enclose the value in quotes. For example, =VLOOKUP("Dried Pears", B2:D46, 2, FALSE). You will also get this error if you make a mistake when typing in the cell reference. Select cell references on the worksheet with your mouse rather than typing them in the formula to avoid cell reference typos.

Manipulating Text with Functions

If you work with Excel extensively, there will be occasions when you would need to use functions to manipulate text, especially when you work with data imported from other programs. For example, you may want to strip off part of a text value or rearrange text.

☼-Tip The **Flash Fill** command on the **Home** tab enables you to perform many text manipulation tasks for which you would previously use functions. For example, the quickest way to split text into several columns is to use Flash Fill as described in Chapter 2.

Extracting Text Portions with LEN and MID

The LEN function returns the number of characters in a text string. This function is mostly used with other Excel functions like MID, where you use LEN to return the length of a string for one of the arguments in MID.

The MID function lets you extract a portion of a text string based on the starting position you specify and the number of characters you want to extract.

Syntax

=LEN(text)

Argument	Description
Text	Required. This argument is a text string or a cell reference containing the text for which you want to find the length. Spaces are counted as characters.

=MID(text, start_num, num_chars)

Argument	Description
text	Required. A text string or a cell reference containing the characters you want to extract.
start_num	Required. The position of the first character you want to extract in *text*. The first character position in *text* 1, the second is 2, and so on.
num_chars	Required. This argument is a number that specifies the number of characters you want to extract from *text*.

Remarks:

- If the start_num argument is larger than the length of the string in our text argument, MID will return an empty text ("").

- MID will return the #VALUE! error if start_num is less than 1.

- MID returns the #VALUE! error if num_chars is a negative value.

Example 1

In the following example, we use the LEN function to count the number of characters in an item code. The example also demonstrates how the LEN function can be combined with the MID function to return part of a string.

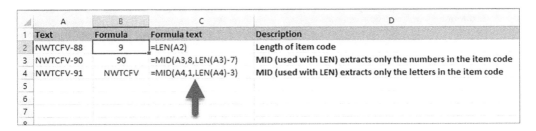

	A	B	C	D
1	Text	Formula	Formula text	Description
2	NWTCFV-88	9	=LEN(A2)	Length of item code
3	NWTCFV-90	90	=MID(A3,8,LEN(A3)-7)	MID (used with LEN) extracts only the numbers in the item code
4	NWTCFV-91	NWTCFV	=MID(A4,1,LEN(A4)-3)	MID (used with LEN) extracts only the letters in the item code
5				
6				
7				

Column C shows the formulas in column B

=LEN(A2)

This formula simply returns the length of a text value in its argument.

=MID(A3,8,LEN(A3)-7)

LEN returns the length of the string, and we subtract 7 character from it for the num_chars argument of MID. MID is used here with LEN to extract only the numbers in the item code.

=MID(A4,1,LEN(A4)-3)

MID is used here with LEN to extract a portion of the string minus the last 3 characters.

Example 2

The examples below use the MID function to extract characters from several text values.

B2		fx	=MID(A2,4,3)	
	A	B	C	D
1	**Product Number**	**Extracted**	**Formula Text**	
2	01-345-4000	345	=MID(A2,4,3)	**Extract the 3 characters in the middle of the serial number**
3	01-378-7890	378	=MID(A3,4,3)	
4	01-375-7891	375	=MID(A4,4,3)	
5	01-376-7892	376	=MID(A5,4,3)	
6				
7	NWTCFV-88	88	=MID(A7,8,2)	**Extract only the number portion of the item code**
8	NWTCFV-89	89	=MID(A8,8,2)	
9	NWTCFV-90	90	=MID(A9,8,2)	
10	NWTCFV-91	91	=MID(A10,8,2)	

Column C shows the formulas in column B

Formula description

=MID(A2,4,3)

For this formula, A2 is the cell containing the string from which we want to extract text - "01-345-4000". The first character we want to extract is 3, which starts at position four, so we have 4 as our **start_num** argument. We want to return three characters, so we have 3 as the **num_chars** argument.

=MID(A7,8,2)

This formula has A7 as the **text** argument and 8 as **start_num** because we want to start with the 8th character in the string. The **num_chars** argument is 2 as this is the number of characters we want to return.

The benefit of using formulas like these is that you create them once and use the fill handle of the first cell to copy the formula to the other cells.

Joining Text Values with TEXTJOIN

The TEXTJOIN function lets you combine text values from multiple text strings into one string. The difference between the TEXTJOIN and the CONCAT function is that TEXTJOIN has extra arguments that allow you to specify a delimiter as a separator. It also has an argument you can set to ignore empty cells. If you enter an empty text string in the delimiter, this function will concatenate the values.

Syntax

=TEXTJOIN(delimiter, ignore_empty, text1, [text2], ...)

Arguments

Argument	Description
delimiter	Required. This argument is the delimiter you want to use as a separator for text items in your string. The delimiter can be a string, one or more characters enclosed in double quotes, or a cell reference containing a text string. If this argument is a number, it will be treated as text.
ignore_empty	Required. This argument should be either TRUE or FALSE. If TRUE, it ignores empty cells.
text1	Required. This argument is the first text item to be joined. It can be a string, a cell reference, or a range with several cells.
[text2, ...]	Optional. Additional optional text items to be joined. You can have up to 252 arguments for the text items, including text1. Each can be a string, a cell reference, or a range with several cells.

TEXTJOIN will return the #VALUE! error if the resulting string exceeds 32767 characters, which is the cell limit.

Example

In the following example, we use TEXTJOIN in column C to combine the First name and Last name values from A2:A7 and B2:B7. The flexibility of TEXTJOIN enables us to swap the order of the names in some of the formulas.

C2			f_x	=TEXTJOIN(", ", TRUE,B2,A2)	
	A	B	C		D
1	First name	Last name	Combined		Formula
2	Bruce	Henderson	Henderson, Bruce		=TEXTJOIN(", ", TRUE,B2,A2)
3	Louis	Anderson	Anderson, Louis		=TEXTJOIN(", ", TRUE,B3,A3)
4	Earl	Foster	Foster, Earl		=TEXTJOIN(", ", TRUE,B4,A4)
5	Sean	Hill	Sean Hill		=TEXTJOIN(" ", TRUE,A5,B5)
6	Benjamin	Martinez	Benjamin Martinez		=TEXTJOIN(" ", TRUE,A6,B6)
7	Joe	Perez	Joe Perez		=TEXTJOIN(" ", TRUE,A7,B7)
8					
9	Name				
10	Bruce Henderson				
11	Louis Anderson				
12	Earl Foster				
13	Sean Hill				
14					
15	Combined				
16	Bruce Henderson, Louis Anderson, Earl Foster, Sean Hill				=TEXTJOIN(", ",TRUE,A10:A13)
17					

Explanation of formula

=TEXTJOIN(", ", TRUE,B2,A2)

The **delimiter** argument in the formula above is a comma enclosed in quotes. The **ignore_empty** argument is set to TRUE to ignore empty cells. The **text1** and **text2** arguments are the cell references for the text values we want to combine.

=TEXTJOIN(" ", TRUE,A5,B5)

The delimiter in the formula above is a blank space in quotes to separate the first name and the last name.

=TEXTJOIN(", ",TRUE,A10:A13)

The above formula uses the TEXTJOIN function to concatenate names in a range of cells (A10:A13) into a single string with a comma used as a separator.

Accessing More Functions in Excel

To access the full function library in Excel, click the **Formulas** tab on the Ribbon. You will see a list of command buttons for several categories of functions.

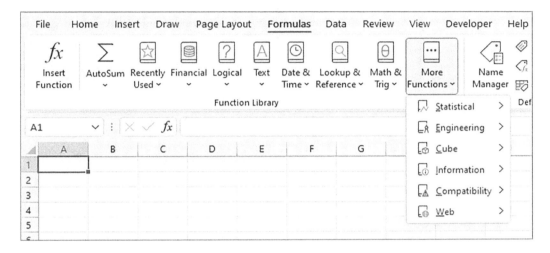

The functions are grouped under the following categories:

- Recently Used
- Financial
- Logical
- Text
- Date & Time
- Lookup & Reference
- Math & Trig
- Statistical
- Engineering
- Cube
- Information
- Compatibility
- Web

You can explore the various functions by clicking on the drop-down button for each one of the command buttons, and you'll get a dropdown list of the functions related to each button.

Many of these functions are for specialist tasks and professions, so don't let them overwhelm you, as you'll never get to use most of them. For example, the **Financial** functions will mostly be used by accountants, and engineers mostly use the **Engineering** functions, etc.

The most used functions will be listed under the **Recently Used** list for easy access.

To get more details about each function, hover over a function name on the list, and a small pop-up message will appear, giving you more details of the function and what arguments it takes. For example, if you hover over the **IF** function, you will see the function description and the arguments it takes.

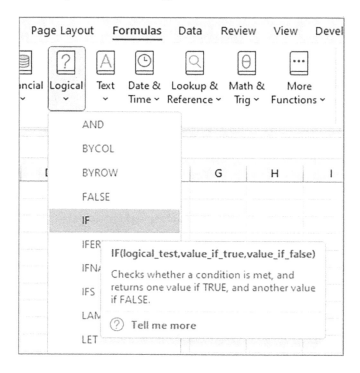

Getting More Help with Functions

To get more information on using any function in Excel, press **F1** to display the Help panel. Then type "Excel functions" in the search bar. Excel will give you a list of all the functions in Excel by category. You can locate the one you want and click it to see more details on its use.

Chapter 10

Working with Tables

You can turn your Excel data into a table. Creating a table in Excel makes managing and analyzing your data easier. You also get built-in sorting, filtering, Banded Rows, and you can add a Total Row.

In this chapter, we will cover how to:

- Convert a range to an Excel table.
- Apply different styles to a table.
- Sort and filter data in a table.
- Add a totals row to a table.
- Remove table attributes (if you want to convert your list back to a range).
- Use a table name in a formula.

Preparing Your Data

Before creating a table, ensure there are no empty columns or rows in the data.

In the next example, we will convert the following range of data into a table.

	A	B	C	D	E
1	Last Name	First Name	Company	Job Title	Address
2	Bedecs	Anna	Company A	Owner	123 1st Street
3	Gratacos Solsona	Antonio	Company B	Owner	123 2nd Street
4	Axen	Thomas	Company C	Purchasing Represen	123 3rd Street
5	Lee	Christina	Company D	Purchasing Manager	123 4th Street
6	O'Donnell	Martin	Company E	Owner	123 5th Street
7	Pérez-Olaeta	Francisco	Company F	Purchasing Manager	123 6th Street
8	Xie	Ming-Yang	Company G	Owner	123 7th Street
9	Andersen	Elizabeth	Company H	Purchasing Represen	123 8th Street
10	Mortensen	Sven	Company I	Purchasing Manager	123 9th Street
11	Wacker	Roland	Company J	Purchasing Manager	123 10th Street
12	Krschne	Peter	Company K	Purchasing Manager	123 11th Street
13	Edwards	John	Company L	Purchasing Manager	123 12th Street
14	Ludick	Andre	Company M	Purchasing Represen	456 13th Street
15	Grilo	Carlos	Company N	Purchasing Represen	456 14th Street
16	Kupkova	Helena	Company O	Purchasing Manager	456 15th Street

First, check that there are no empty columns or rows in your data:

1. Select any cell within the data and press **Ctrl + A**.

2. Then press **Ctrl + .** (period) a few times to move around the data.

Note **Ctrl + A** selects the data range in question. **Ctrl + .** moves around the four edges of the data so you can see where the data starts and ends.

Create an Excel Table

To convert a range to a table, do the following:

1. Select any cell within the data.

2. Click the **Insert** tab, and in the **Tables** group, click **Table**.

3. Excel displays a dialog box showing you the range for the table. You can adjust the range here if necessary.

4. Select **My table has headers** to ensure that the first row of your table is used as the header.

-☀️-**Tip** If your table has no column headers, create a new row on top and add column headers. Row headers make it easier to work with tables in Excel.

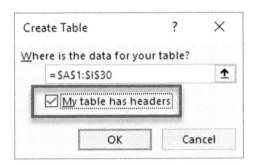

5. Click **OK**.

Excel creates the table with the first row used as column headers.

	A	B	C	D	E
1	**Last Name** ▼	**First Name** ▼	**Company** ▼	**Job Title** ▼	**Address** ▼
2	Bedecs	Anna	Company A	Owner	123 1st Street
3	Gratacos Solsona	Antonio	Company B	Owner	123 2nd Street
4	Axen	Thomas	Company C	Purchasing Represen	123 3rd Street
5	Lee	Christina	Company D	Purchasing Manager	123 4th Street
6	O'Donnell	Martin	Company E	Owner	123 5th Street
7	Pérez-Olaeta	Francisco	Company F	Purchasing Manager	123 6th Street
8	Xie	Ming-Yang	Company G	Owner	123 7th Street
9	Andersen	Elizabeth	Company H	Purchasing Represen	123 8th Street
10	Mortensen	Sven	Company I	Purchasing Manager	123 9th Street
11	Wacker	Roland	Company J	Purchasing Manager	123 10th Street
12	Krschne	Peter	Company K	Purchasing Manager	123 11th Street
13	Edwards	John	Company L	Purchasing Manager	123 12th Street
14	Ludick	Andre	Company M	Purchasing Represen	456 13th Street
15	Grilo	Carlos	Company N	Purchasing Represen	456 14th Street
16	Kupkova	Helena	Company O	Purchasing Manager	456 15th Street

Tip Other ways to quickly create a table:

Select the cells in the range, and on the Ribbon, click **Home** > **Format as Table.**

Choosing a Table Style

When you convert a range to a table, Excel applies a style with alternating row colors to the table. You can change this style by selecting a new style from many options provided by Excel if you want.

When you select any cell in the table, Excel displays the **Table Design** contextual tab on the Ribbon. This tab includes the groups, **Table Style Options**, and **Table Styles**. Table Styles provides several predefined styles you can apply to your table, while Table Style Options provides further options to style your table.

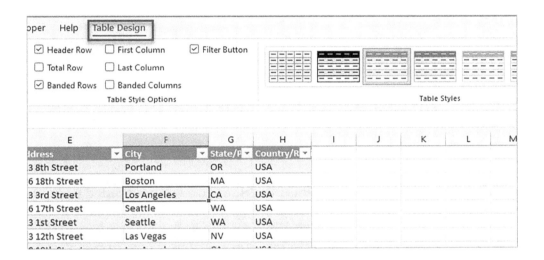

Applying a Table Style

To apply a predefined style to your table, do the following:

1. Select a cell within the table.

2. On the **Table Design** tab, locate the **Table Styles** group and click the drop-down button for the styles. A drop-down menu will show you more styles.

3. Hover over each style to preview how applying it would look on your worksheet.

4. When you find a style you want, click it to apply it to your table.

Applying Table Style Options

Here you have several options for configuring the style of your table.

For example, you can change your table from **Banded Rows** to **Banded Columns**. Banded rows are the alternating colors applied to your table rows. The Banded Rows setting is the default, but if you want banded columns instead, uncheck **Banded Rows** and check **Banded Columns** to have your columns alternate in color instead of your rows.

Note that if a new column or row is added to the table, it will inherit the current table style automatically. When you add a new row, any formulas applied to your table will also be copied to the new row.

Sorting Data in a Table

Before sorting data, ensure there are no blank rows and blank columns. Also, ensure your table header is a single row. If the header is more than one row, change it to a single row to make things easier.

Tip To check for blank rows or columns, select a cell within the data and press **Ctrl + A**. Then press **Ctrl + .** (period) a few times. This keystroke moves the cell pointer around the four corners of the range so that you can see the whole area.

Sort by One Column

To quickly sort your table using one column, do the following:

1. Select a cell in the column you want to use for the sorting. For example, **Last Name**.

2. On the **Data** tab, in the **Sort & Filter** group, click **AZ** (to sort the table in ascending order) or **ZA** (to sort the table in descending order).

That's it. Excel sorts your table in the order you've chosen.

Sort by Multiple Columns

There are often occasions when you want to sort a table using more than one column. A **Custom Sort** is required to sort a table by multiple columns.

To sort your data using several columns, follow these steps:

1. Select any cell within the data.

2. On the **Home** tab, in the **Editing** group, click **Sort & Filter**.

3. Select **Custom Sort** from the drop-down menu.

    Excel displays the **Sort** dialog box.

    Tip: Another way to open the Custom Sort dialog box is to click **Data** > **Sort** (in the **Sort & Filter** group).

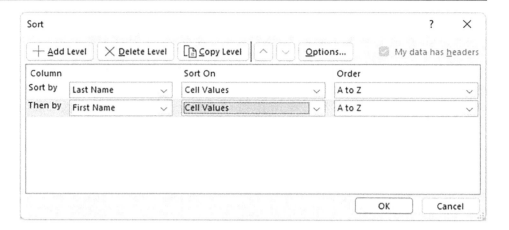

4. Click **Add Level**.

5. Under **Column**, select the column you want to **Sort by** from the drop-down list. Select the second column you want to include in the sort in the **Then by** field. For example, Sort by Last Name and First Name.

6. Under **Sort On**, select **Cell Values**.

7. Under **Order**, select the order you want to sort on, **A to Z** for ascending order, and **Z to A** for descending order.

8. Click **OK**.

You can add additional columns to your sort. Excel allows you to have up to 64 sort levels. For each additional column you want to sort by, repeat steps 4-7 above.

Filtering Table Data

Excel provides an array of options to filter your data so that you can view only the data you want to see. Filters provide a quick way to work with a subset of data in a range or table. When you apply the filter, you temporarily hide some of the data so that you can focus on the data you need to view.

Follow the steps below to filter data in an Excel table:

1. Select any cell in the table that you want to filter.

2. Click **Home** > **Sort & Filter** > **Filter** (or click **Data** > **Filter**).

3. You will get filter arrows at the top of each column.

4. Click the arrow in the column header. For example, **Price**. This arrow is also known as the AutoFilter.

5. Uncheck **Select All** and check the values you want to use for the filter.

6. Click **OK**.

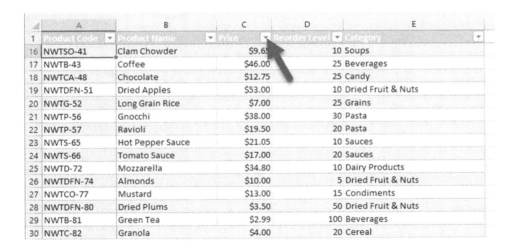

The AutoFilter changes to a funnel icon to indicate that the column is filtered. If you look at the row heading numbers, you'll see that they're now blue, indicating which rows are included in the filtered data.

To remove the filter, on the **Data** tab, in the **Sort & Filter** group, click **Clear**. The filter will be removed, and all data will be displayed.

Applying a Custom Filter

A custom filter allows you to manually define your criteria for filtering the data.

To apply a custom filter to an Excel table, do the following:

1. Click the arrow (AutoFilter) on the column you want to filter.

2. Depending on the format of the column being filtered, you'll get one of the following options:

   - **Text Filters:** Available when the column has text values or has a mixture of text and numbers.

   - **Number Filters:** Available when the column contains only numbers

   - **Date Filters:** Available when the column contains only dates.

   - **Clear Filter from [Column name]:** Available when a filter has already been applied to the column. Select this option to clear the filter.

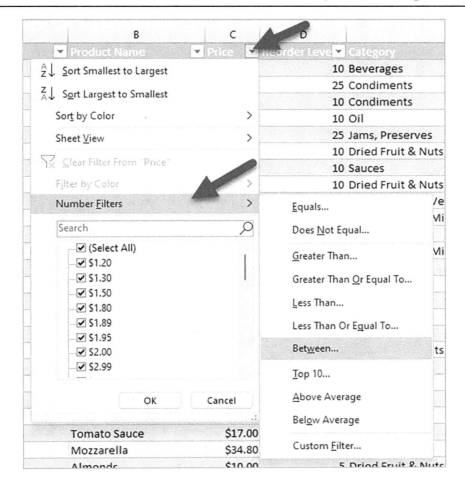

3. Select one of the first three options (Text Filters, Number Filters, or Date Filters) and then select a comparison. For this example, we've selected **Between**.

Excel opens the **Custom AutoFilter** dialog box.

4. Enter the filter criteria.

For the logical operator, select **And** if both conditions must be true, or select **Or** if only one of the conditions needs to be true.

Our example filters the **Price** column so that only rows between $2 and $10 are displayed in the table.

5. Click **OK**.

The AutoFilter changes to a Filter icon. You can click this icon to change or clear the filter.

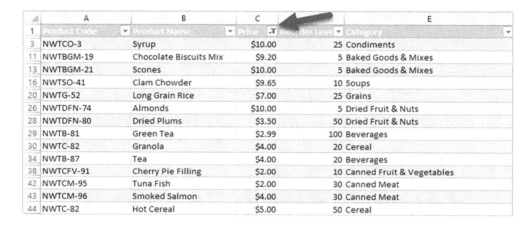

⊿	A	B	C		E	
1	Product Code ▼	Product Name ▼	Price ▼	Reorder Leve ▼	Category	▼
3	NWTCO-3	Syrup	$10.00	25	Condiments	
11	NWTBGM-19	Chocolate Biscuits Mix	$9.20	5	Baked Goods & Mixes	
13	NWTBGM-21	Scones	$10.00	5	Baked Goods & Mixes	
16	NWTSO-41	Clam Chowder	$9.65	10	Soups	
20	NWTG-52	Long Grain Rice	$7.00	25	Grains	
26	NWTDFN-74	Almonds	$10.00	5	Dried Fruit & Nuts	
28	NWTDFN-80	Dried Plums	$3.50	50	Dried Fruit & Nuts	
29	NWTB-81	Green Tea	$2.99	100	Beverages	
30	NWTC-82	Granola	$4.00	20	Cereal	
34	NWTB-87	Tea	$4.00	20	Beverages	
38	NWTCFV-91	Cherry Pie Filling	$2.00	10	Canned Fruit & Vegetables	
42	NWTCM-95	Tuna Fish	$2.00	30	Canned Meat	
43	NWTCM-96	Smoked Salmon	$4.00	30	Canned Meat	
44	NWTC-82	Hot Cereal	$5.00	50	Cereal	

Filtered results

-🔆-**Tip** To change the order of the filtered results, click the filter icon and then select either **Sort Largest to Smallest** or **Sort Smallest to Largest**. For a text column, it would be **Sort A to Z** or **Sort Z to A.**

Adding a Totals Row to Your Table

You can add totals to a table by selecting the **Total Row** check box on the **Design** tab. Once added to your worksheet, the Total Row drop-down button allows you to add a function from a list of options.

To add totals to your table:

1. Select a cell in a table.

2. Select **Table Design** > **Total Row**. Excel adds a new row to the bottom of the table called the **Total Row**.

3. On the Total Row drop-down list, you have an array of functions you can select like **Average**, **Count**, **Count Numbers**, **Max**, **Min**, **Sum**, **StdDev**, **Var**, and more.

NWTS-65	Hot Pepper Sauce	$21.05	10 Sauces
NWTS-66	Tomato Sauce	$17.00	20 Sauces
NWTS-8	Curry Sauce	$40.00	10 Sauces
NWTSO-41	Clam Chowder	$9.65	10 Soups
NWTSO-98	Vegetable Soup	$1.89	100 Soups
NWTSO-99	Chicken Soup	$1.95	100 Soups
Total		$713.06 ▾	

None
Average
Count
Count Numbers
Max
Min
Sum
StdDev
Var
More Functions...

Tip If you need to add a new row of data to your table at any point, deselect **Total Row** on the **Table Design** tab, add the new row, and then reselect **Total Row**.

Giving Your Table a Custom Name

After creation, Excel gives your table a default name like Table1, Table2, etc. However, you can give your table a custom name, especially if you want to use that name to reference data in the table in formulas.

Follow the steps below to give your table a custom name:

1. On the Ribbon, click the **Table Design** tab.

2. In the **Properties** group, type in your table name in the **Table Name** field (overwriting the default name).

3. Press **Enter**.

   You can now use to table name in formulas to reference data in the table.

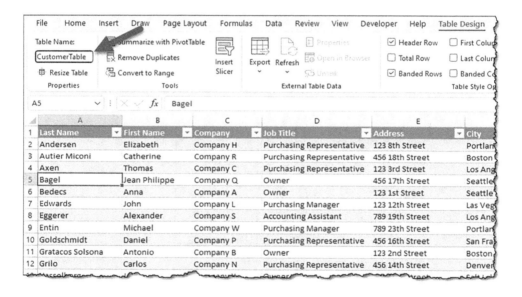

Using Table Names in Formulas

In the following example, instead of using the range **B2:B11**, the formulas use **Sales[Sales Amount]** to refer to that range. The table name is **Sales**, and the column name is **Sales Amount**.

This reference uses the combination of the table and column names to refer to the data range in the table. This type of reference is called a structured reference.

=SUM(Sales[Sales Amount])

=MAX(Sales[Sales Amount])

=AVERAGE(Sales[Sales Amount])

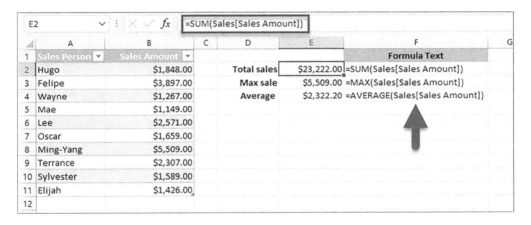

Structured references provide certain benefits, including the following:

- The name is an absolute reference, so you can copy the formula to any part of your workbook without the reference changing.

- You don't need to adjust the reference in your formulas when you add or remove rows from the table.

- You could find it easier to refer to ranges in your formulas. For example, it may be easier to enter the table and column name in your formula in a large workbook instead of identifying explicit cell references.

Removing Table Attributes

On some occasions, you may want to switch a table back to a normal range. Maybe you want to perform tasks where a table is unnecessary or transform the data before converting it to a table again.

You can convert an Excel table back to a range using one of the following methods.

Method 1

1. Click anywhere in the table so that the cell pointer is inside the table.

2. Click the **Table Design** tab, and in the Tools group, click **Convert to Range**.

3. Click **Yes** to confirm the action.

   The table will now be converted to a normal range of cells without Excel's table features.

Method 2

1. Right-click anywhere in the table.

2. On the pop-up menu, select **Table** > **Convert to Range**.

3. Click **Yes** at the confirmation prompt.

   Excel removes all table attributes and returns the data to a range.

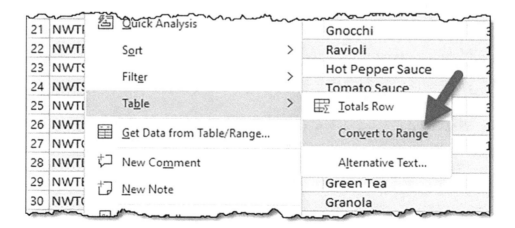

After converting a table back to a range, the range will still retain the style and formatting that was applied to the table, like banded rows, for example. However, the formatting does not affect the behavior of the range.

To clear all formatting, do the following:

1. Select the range.

2. Click the **Home** tab.

3. In the **Editing** group, click **Clear** > **Clear Formats**.

Chapter 11

Introduction to Pivot Tables

An Excel PivotTable is a powerful tool that dynamically calculates, summarizes, and analyzes data from different views. You can change the grouped columns or change the arrangement of the summarized data by switching between row and column headings. An Excel PivotTable allows you to group your data into summary information from different views without affecting the original data.

This chapter covers:

- How to create a pivot table manually.
- Formatting your pivot table.
- Filtering and sorting data in a pivot table.

Preparing Your Data

Some preparation is required to get a dataset ready for a PivotTable. The source data used for a PivotTable needs to be organized as a list or converted to an Excel table (recommended although not compulsory).

A few steps to prepare the source data for a PivotTable:

1. The data should have column headings in a single row on top.

2. Remove any temporary totals or summaries.

3. The data cannot have empty rows, so delete any empty rows.

4. Ensure you do not have any extraneous data surrounding the list.

5. Ideally, you may want to create an Excel table with the data (although it is not a pre-requisite).

Once the data has been prepared, we can now create a PivotTable.

Creating a Pivot Table

To create a PivotTable:

1. Click any cell in your range or table.

2. On the Insert tab, click the PivotTable button.

   The **Create PivotTable** dialog will be displayed.

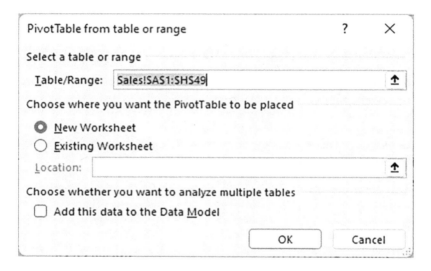

Excel will figure out the table or range you intend to use for your PivotTable and select it in the **Table/Range** field. If this is not accurate, you can manually select the range by clicking the up arrow (Expand Dialog) on the field.

The next option on the screen is where you want to place the PivotTable. The default location is a new worksheet. It is best to have your PivotTable on its own worksheet, separate from your source data, so you want to leave the default selected here.

3. Click **OK**.

A new worksheet will now be created with a PivotTable placeholder, and on the right side, you'll see a dialog box - **PivotTable Fields**.

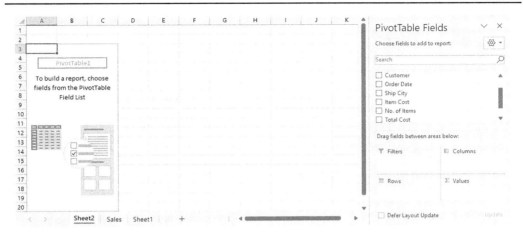

The bottom half of the PivotTable Fields pane has four areas where you can place fields:

Rows, Columns, Values, and **Filters.**

To add a field to your PivotTable, select the checkbox next to the field name in the PivotTables Fields pane. When you select fields, they are added to their default areas. Non-numeric fields are added to the **Rows** box. Date and time fields are added to the **Columns** box. Numeric fields are added to the **Values** box.

You can also drag fields from the list to one of the four areas you want to place it. To move one field to another, you can drag it there.

To remove a field from a box, click it and click **Remove Field** from the pop-up menu. You can also just uncheck it in the fields list or drag it away from the box and drop it back on the fields list.

Example

In this example, let's say we want a summary of our data that shows the total spent by each customer.

1. Select the **Customer** field on the list to add it to the Rows box.

    Excel updates the PivotTable with the list of customers as row headings.

2. Next, select the **Total Cost** field to add it to the **Values** box.

The PivotTable will now be updated with the **Sum of Total Cost** for each Customer.

3	Row Labels	Sum of Total Cost
4	Acme LTD	13226
5	Acorn USA	13292
6	Apex Homes	33082
7	B&B Seaside	48997
8	Elgin Homes	54504
9	Empire Homes	9355
10	Express Builders	11004
11	Home Designers	52322
12	Impressive Homes	14775
13	Infinity Homes	85612
14	Mecury Builders	17760
15	Northern Contractors	2001
16	Orion Spaces	4806
17	Grand Total	360736

We have been able to get a quick summary of our data, grouped by Customer, with just a few clicks. If you had hundreds of thousands of records, this task could have taken many hours to accomplish if done manually.

We can add more values to the table by dragging them to the Values box from the list.

For example, if we wanted to add the total number of items per customer, we'll select **No. of Items** on the list or drag it to the **Values** box.

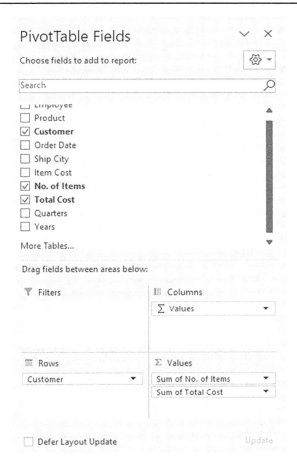

Excel adds the **Sum of No. of Items** for each customer to the PivotTable, as shown below.

Row Labels	Sum of No. of Items	Sum of Total Cost
Acme LTD	43	13226
Acorn USA	53	13292
Apex Homes	73	33082
B&B Seaside	88	48997
Elgin Homes	123	54504
Empire Homes	40	9355
Express Builders	14	11004
Home Designers	94	52322
Impressive Homes	31	14775
Infinity Homes	143	85612
Mecury Builders	52	17760
Northern Contractors	7	2001
Orion Spaces	33	4806
Grand Total	794	360736

To view the summary from the perspective of **Products**, that is, the total number of items sold and the total cost for each product, we would put the **Product** field in the Rows box and both **Total Cost** and **No. of Items** in the Values box.

To view the summary from the perspective of the **Employees** column, we would place the **Employee** field in the Rows box and **No. of Items** and **Total Cost** in the Values box.

Here we see the data summarized by Employee, i.e., how many items each employee sold, and the revenue generated.

Row Labels	Sum of No. of Items	Sum of Total Cost
Andrew Cencini	40	21418
Anne Hellung-Larsen	149	53969
Jan Kotas	110	70865
Laura Giussani	26	18690
Mariya Sergienko	176	78334
Michael Neipper	105	40203
Nancy Freehafer	181	75256
Robert Zare	7	2001
Grand Total	794	360736

If we wanted to see the number of items sold per city, we would place **Ship City** in the Rows box and **No. of Items** in the Values box.

3	Row Labels ▾	Sum of No. of Items
4	Boise	40
5	Chicago	106
6	Denver	45
7	Las Vegas	95
8	Los Angelas	43
9	Memphis	53
10	Miami	44
11	Milwaukee	94
12	New York	93
13	Portland	143
14	Salt Lake City	7
15	Seattle	31
16	**Grand Total**	**794**

Summarizing Data by Date

To display the columns split into years, drag a date field into the Columns box, for example, Order Date. The PivotTable tool will automatically generate PivotTable fields for Quarters and Years. Once these fields have been generated, you should remove the Order Date field from the Columns box and place it in the Quarter or Year field, depending on which one you want to use for your summary.

To display the row headings by date, place **Order Date** (or your date field) in the Rows box.

This combination will produce the following results.

Sum of Total Cost	Column Labels		
Row Labels	2016	2017	Grand Total
Jan	39569	7772	47341
Feb		22819	22819
Mar	5502	1854	7356
Apr	22724	57618	80342
May	3105	14510	17615
Jun	24021	596	24617
Jul	16060		16060
Aug	316	12141	12457
Sep	42763	9615	52378
Oct	16752		16752
Nov	34347	9756	44103
Dec	18896		18896
Grand Total	224055	136681	360736

Applying Formatting

As you can see, we can dynamically change how we want to view our data with just a few clicks. When you're happy with your summary, you can apply formatting to the appropriate columns. For example, you could format any currency field as **Currency** before any formal presentation of the data.

The good thing about Excel PivotTables is that you can explore different types of summaries with the pivot table without changing the source data. If you make a mistake that you can't figure out how to undo, you can simply delete the PivotTable worksheet and recreate the PivotTable in a new worksheet.

Filter and Sort a Pivot Table

On some occasions, you may want to limit what is displayed in the PivotTable. You can sort and filter a PivotTable just like you can do to a range of data or an Excel table.

To filter a PivotTable:

1. Click the AutoFilter (down arrow) on the Row Labels cell.

   The pop-up menu provides a list of the row headings in your PivotTable. You can select/deselect items on this list to limit the data displayed in the PivotTable.

2. Uncheck **Select All.**

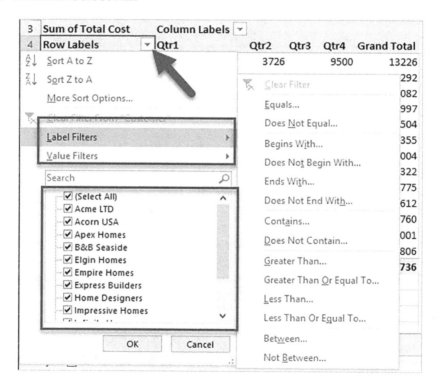

3. Scroll through the list and manually select the items you want to display.

4. Click **OK**.

   The PivotTable will now show only the selected columns.

Applying a Custom Filter

You can also use the **Label Filters** and **Value Filters** menu commands to apply a custom filter to your PivotTable the same way you would for a range or table. Please see **Filtering Data** in chapter 4 for detailed steps on how to apply a custom filter.

Sorting PivotTable Data

To arrange the order of your data in a PivotTable, you use the same sorting methods you would use for a range or table.

- Click the **AutoFilter** button on the column named **Row Labels**.

- Click **Sort A to Z** (to sort in ascending order) or **Sort Z to A** (in descending order). If your column headings are dates, you'll get **Sort Oldest to Newest** (for ascending) and **Sort Newest to Oldest** (for descending).

Chapter 12

Creating Charts

Excel charts provide a way to analyze and present your data visually. As the saying goes, *a picture is worth a thousand words*. Some of us don't absorb numbers as easily as others because we're more visual, and this is where charts come in. A visual representation may sometimes create more of an impact on your audience.

This chapter covers:

- Creating a quick chart with the Quick Analysis tool.
- Manually creating a chart.
- Editing and customizing your chart with different styles and formats.
- Creating a sparkline chart.

Preparing Your Data

To prepare your data for charting, you'll need to organize it in a list with only the items you want to report on. Leave out any extraneous data and grand totals you don't want on the chart. Ideally, you should have column headings. The example below has **Product Name** and **Total Sales** as column headings. Excel's charting tools will use the column headings when labeling your chart.

	A	B
1	**Product Name**	**Total Sales**
2	Chai	$1,800.00
3	Beer	$3,400.00
4	Coffee	$4,600.00
5	Green Tea	$200.00
6	Tea	$1,400.00
7	Chocolate Biscuits Mix	$900.20
8	Scones	$1,000.00
9	Brownie Mix	$1,200.49
10	Cake Mix	$1,500.99
11	Granola	$400.00
12	Hot Cereal	$500.00
13	Chocolate	$1,200.75
14	Fruit Cocktail	$3,900.00
15	Pears	$100.30
16	Peaches	$1,000.50

Creating a Chart with the Quick Analysis Tool

The Quick Analysis tool appears as a button on the bottom-right of your selection when selecting a range of data in Excel. The Quick Analysis button offers a host of features for quickly adding conditional formatting, totals, tables, charts, and Sparklines to your worksheet.

To generate a chart using the Quick Analysis tool:

1. Select the range you want to use for your chart. The Quick Analysis button is displayed at the bottom-right of the selection.

2. Click the Quick Analysis button and then click **Charts**. You'll get a list of recommended charts.

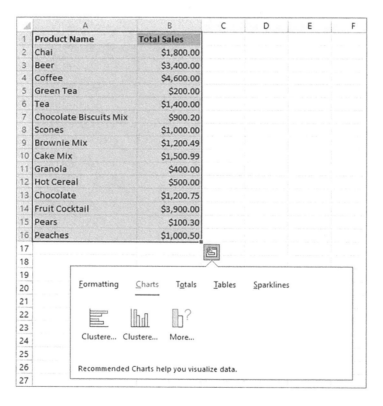

3. Click the second option to generate a column chart.

A floating chart will be created in the same worksheet as your data. You can click and drag this chart to another part of the worksheet if necessary.

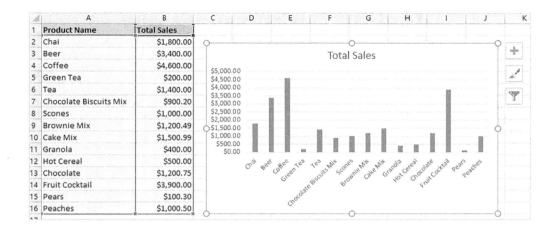

	A	B
1	**Product Name**	**Total Sales**
2	Chai	$1,800.00
3	Beer	$3,400.00
4	Coffee	$4,600.00
5	Green Tea	$200.00
6	Tea	$1,400.00
7	Chocolate Biscuits Mix	$900.20
8	Scones	$1,000.00
9	Brownie Mix	$1,200.49
10	Cake Mix	$1,500.99
11	Granola	$400.00
12	Hot Cereal	$500.00
13	Chocolate	$1,200.75
14	Fruit Cocktail	$3,900.00
15	Pears	$100.30
16	Peaches	$1,000.50

To create another type of chart, for example, a pie chart, you can click the **More** option on the Quick Analysis menu to show a list of all chart types.

-☽-Tip Another way to create a quick chart is to select the data and press the **F11** key to generate a chart of the default type on a new chart sheet. The default chart created would be the column chart unless you've changed the default chart. To create an embedded chart using this method (in the same worksheet as the data), press the **Alt** + **F1** keys together.

Creating a Chart Manually

The **Charts** group in the **Insert** tab has several commands to create different types of charts. You can click a chart type, for example, the pie chart icon, to display a list of chart options available for that chart type.

Alternatively, you can open the **Insert Chart** dialog box that shows a list of all the chart types you can create in Excel.

To create a chart from the Insert Chart dialog, do the following:

1. Select the range of data for your chart.
2. On the Ribbon, click **Insert** > **Recommended Charts** > **All Charts**.
    Excel displays the **Insert Chart** dialog box.
3. Select the type of chart you want to create from the list of charts on the left.
4. Click **OK**.

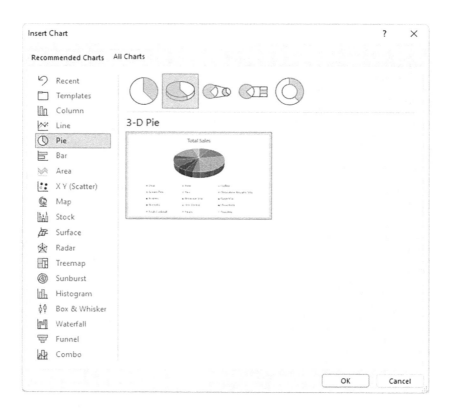

Excel creates a floating chart in the same worksheet as your data. You can click and drag this chart to another part of the screen if necessary.

To delete a chart, simply select the chart and press the **Delete** key.

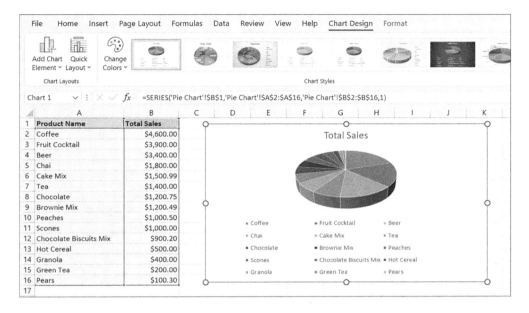

When you select a chart by clicking it, Excel displays the **Chart Design** tab on the Ribbon. This tab provides many options for editing and styling your chart. The next section will cover editing the chart axis labels and style.

Customizing Charts

After creating a chart, Excel provides several commands for customizing the chart to your liking. For example, you can swap the axis, change/adjust the data source, update the chart title, adjust the layout, apply a chart style, and apply a theme color to your chart.

To demonstrate some of these options, let's say we need to create a chart with four quarters of sales, as shown in the image below.

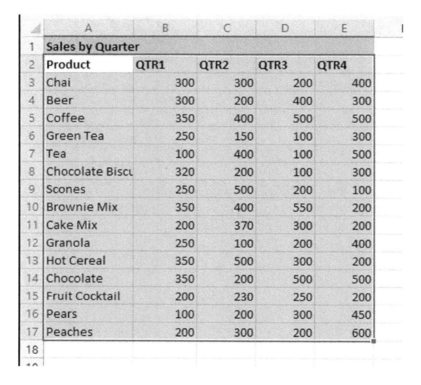

	A	B	C	D	E
1	Sales by Quarter				
2	Product	QTR1	QTR2	QTR3	QTR4
3	Chai	300	300	200	400
4	Beer	300	200	400	300
5	Coffee	350	400	500	500
6	Green Tea	250	150	100	300
7	Tea	100	400	100	500
8	Chocolate Biscu	320	200	100	300
9	Scones	250	500	200	100
10	Brownie Mix	350	400	550	200
11	Cake Mix	200	370	300	200
12	Granola	250	100	200	400
13	Hot Cereal	350	500	300	200
14	Chocolate	350	200	500	500
15	Fruit Cocktail	200	230	250	200
16	Pears	100	200	300	450
17	Peaches	200	300	200	600
18					

To create the chart:

1. Select the range with the data, including the column headers and row headers.

2. Select **Insert** > **Charts** > **Recommended Charts**.

   Excel displays the **Insert Chart** dialog with several chart recommendations for your data.

3. Select the **Clustered Column** option.

4. Click **OK**.

A chart will be created and added to your worksheet.

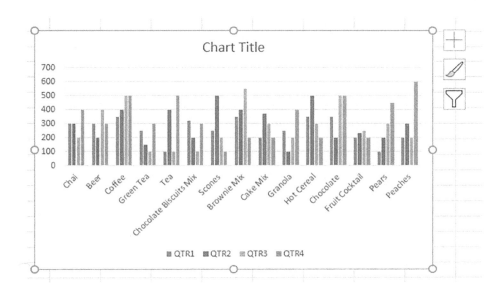

Switching the X and Y Axes

You can switch the values Excel applies to the vertical axis (also called the y-axis) and horizontal axis (also called the x-axis).

To switch the values applied to the axes:

1. Select the chart.
2. Click **Chart Design** > **Switch Row/Column**.

Excel swaps the values applied to the vertical and horizontal axes.

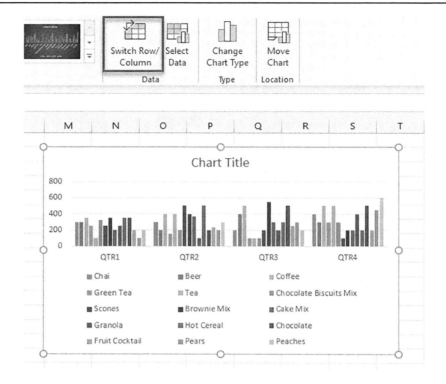

To swap the values back, simply click the **Switch Row/Column** button again.

Change the Data Source

To change the data used as the source of the chart, do the following:

1. Click the Chart to activate the **Chart Design** tab.

2. In the **Data** group, click **Select Data**.

    Excel displays the **Select Data Source** dialog.

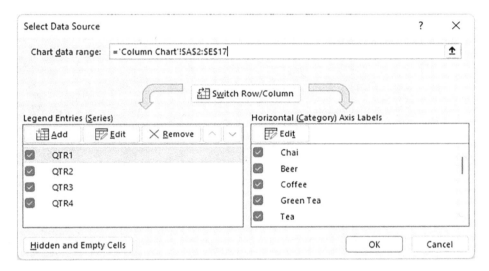

3. Click the Expand Dialog button (up-arrow) on the **Chart data range** field.

4. Select the cells you want in the worksheet area and click the Collapse Dialog button (down-pointing arrow) to return to the **Select Data Source** dialog box.

5. Click **OK** to confirm the change.

    The new data source will now be used for the chart.

Adding Axis Titles

When you create a new chart, you'll see "Chart Title" as a placeholder that needs to be edited with the chart's title. There are also no labels at the axis, and we may want to add them to the chart.

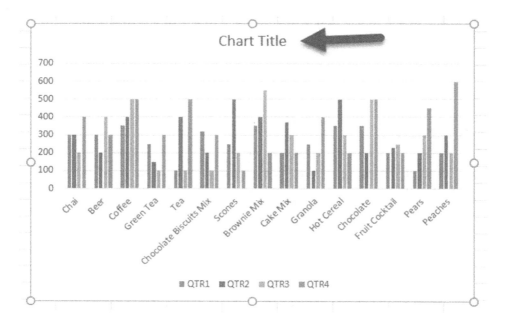

To change the **Chart Title**, you can simply click it and type in the title. Alternatively, you can select the name from a field on your worksheet. For example, to change the chart title to *Sales by quarter,* a value in cell **A1** of the worksheet, click the **Chart Title** label and enter "=A1" in the formula bar. Excel will use the value in cell A1 for our chart title.

We can also add titles down the left-hand side and at the bottom of the chart. These are called axis titles. The left side is the *y*-axis, while the bottom is the *x*-axis.

To change the layout of your chart, click **Chart Design** > **Quick Layout**.

You'll get a pop-up with several chart layouts. With the chart selected, you can hover over each layout to view more details and get a preview of how your chart will look with that layout. A few of the options provide axis titles and move the legend to the right of the chart. If you want a layout with both axis titles, then **Layout 9** is a good option.

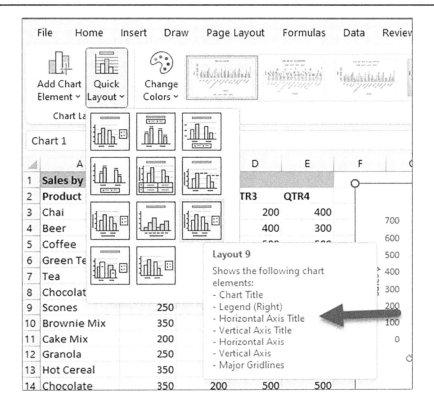

If we select **Layout 9**, we get a chart with labels that we can edit to add titles to the x-axis and y-axis.

You can edit the axis labels as described above. You can click the labels and type in the text directly or pull the text from your worksheet area by typing in a cell reference, for example, **=A1**, assuming cell A1 as the text you want for that label.

Chart Styles

The **Chart Design** tab shows up on the Ribbon when you click a chart. On this tab, you have various **Chart Styles** you can choose from to change your chart's overall look and color.

To change your Chart Style, do the following:

1. Click the chart to select it.

2. On the **Chart Design** tab, in the **Chart Styles** group, click the down arrow to expand the list of predefined styles.

3. You can hover over each style to preview how your graph will look with that style.

4. When you find the one you want to use, click it to apply it to your graph.

To change the color of the plot area:

1. Click the plot area to select it (this is the center of the chart).

2. On the Ribbon, click the **Format** tab, and in the **Shape Styles** group, click the drop-down button to expand the list of Theme Styles.

3. Hover over each style to see a preview of what your chart would look like if selected.

4. When you find the style you like, click it to apply it to your graph.

To change the colors of the bars on the graph, do the following:

1. Click the chart to select it.

2. On the **Chart Design** tab, in the **Chart Styles** group, click **Change Colors**.

3. Hover over the color combinations to see how your graph will look with an option. When you see the one you like, select it to apply it to your graph.

Creating Sparkline Charts

Sparklines are mini charts you can place in single cells to show the visual trend of your data. Excel allows you to quickly add Sparkline charts to your worksheet in a few steps. Sparklines are an excellent visual representation that can be viewed alongside the data. The following example uses the Quick Analysis tool to add sparklines to a dataset.

Adding a Sparkline:

1. Select the data you want to create a Sparkline chart for. You'll see the **Quick Analysis** tool on the lower-right edge of the selection.

2. Click the Quick Analysis tool to open a pop-up menu of Quick Analysis options - **Formatting**, **Charts**, **Totals**, **Tables**, and **Sparklines**.

3. Click **Sparklines** and select one option from **Line**, **Column**, or **Win/Loss**.

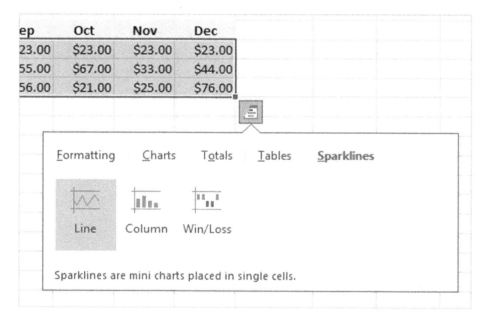

This example uses the **Line** option. The sparklines will be created in the cells immediately to the right of the selected values.

Notice how it's easier to see the data trend with the sparkline than with the figures.

Formatting a Sparkline Chart

Select the chart to display the **Sparkline** contextual tab on the Ribbon. The Sparkline tab provides various options to edit, format, and style your sparkline chart.

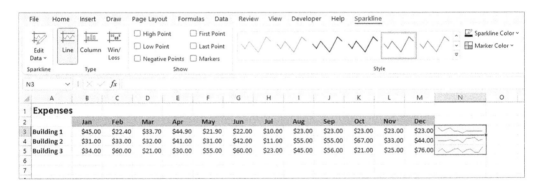

You can use the following options on the Sparkline tab to format and design your sparkline:

- In the **Type** group, you can use the **Line**, **Column**, or **Win/Loss** buttons to change the chart type.

- The **Show** group provides options to add Markers that highlight specific values in the Sparkline chart.

- You can select a different **Style** for the Sparkline.

- You can change the **Sparkline Color** and the **Marker Color**.

- Click **Sparkline Color > Weight** to change the width of the Sparkline.

- Click **Marker Color** to change the color of the markers.

- Click **Axis** to show the axis if the data has positive and negative values.

Chapter 13

Printing Your Worksheet

Even though we live in an increasingly digital world, on some occasions, you may need to print your worksheet on paper as part of a report or present it to others. Excel provides several features that allow you to print your data.

This chapter covers:

- Configuring your print settings in Page Setup.
- Setting the Print Area.
- Previewing and printing your document.

Page Setup

Before you print your document, you may need to change some settings to get the page layout the way you want it. The Page Setup dialog lets you configure several page layout settings in one area.

To open the Page Setup dialog box, click the **Page Layout** tab, and in the **Page Setup** group, click the dialog box launcher.

Excel displays the Page Setup dialog.

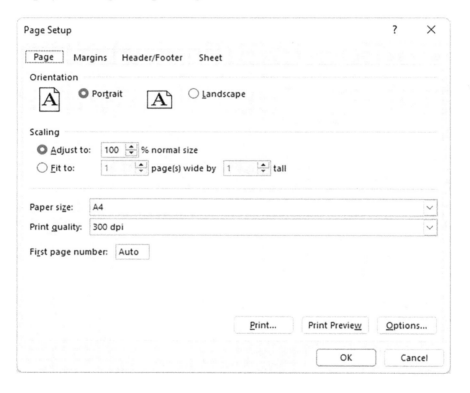

There are several settings on this page that you can configure to get the layout exactly how you want it for your printed document.

❏ Orientation

On the **Page** tab, set the orientation to **Landscape**. Landscape is usually the best layout for printing worksheets unless you have specific reasons to use Portrait.

❏ Scaling

Under scaling, you have two options:

- **Adjust to:** This option enables you to scale the font size of your document up or down. 100% means it will print in normal size. For example, if the normal size of your content is larger than one page, but you would like it to print as one page, you would reduce the percentage to less than 100%.

- **Fit to:** This option lets you choose the document's width (number of pages across) and how tall (number of pages down). For example, you may choose to fit the width on one page and make it more than one page tall.

❏ Paper Size

The default paper size is A4. However, if you are printing to another paper size, you can change it here.

❏ Margins

On the Margins tab, you can change the size of the Top, Bottom, Left, and Right margins, including the size of the Header and Footer.

❏ Header/Footer

You can insert a header or footer on this tab. For example, you can insert a document header that'll appear on all pages and a page number in the footer. You can either select an option from the dropdown list or enter a custom header/footer by clicking the **Custom Header** or **Custom Footer** buttons.

Click **OK** to save your changes and close the Page Setup window when you're done.

Setting the Print Area

You need to set the Print Area so that unpopulated parts of the worksheet are not included in your print, as this could lead to blank pages. You can set the print area in the Page Setup dialog, but it is easier to use the **Print Area** command on the Ribbon.

To set the print area:

1. Select the area in the worksheet that contains the data you want to print.
2. On the **Page Layout** tab, click the **Print Area** button.
3. Select **Set Print Area**.

Note To clear the print area at any point, click the Print Area button and select **Clear Print Area**.

Preview and Print Your Worksheet

Click **File** to display the Backstage view, then click **Print** from the menu on the left.

Excel displays the Print page. You can adjust several settings here to change the page layout, many of which are also available in the Page Setup dialog.

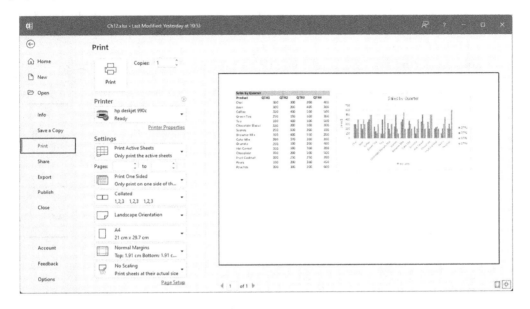

The options on this screen are self-explanatory and similar across Microsoft 365 applications. However, we'll touch on the ones you'll most likely need to set.

Printer

This option allows you to choose the printer to which you want to print. If your printer has been configured on the computer, it will be available for selection here. You also can print to an electronic document like PDF, OneNote, Microsoft XPS Document Writer, etc.

Settings

Print Active Sheets is the default. Leave this option selected if you want to print only the active worksheet. If your workbook has more than one worksheet and you want to print the entire workbook, then click the drop-down list and select **Print Entire Workbook** from the list. If you have selected a range and want to print only those cells, use the **Print Selection** option.

The last option on this page is **scaling**. If you have not set the scale in the Page Setup dialog box, there are four predefined scaling options to choose from here:

- **No Scaling**: The document will be printed as it is, with no scaling.
- **Fit Sheet on One Page**: All columns and rows in the print area will be scaled into one page.
- **Fit All Columns on One Page**: All the columns in the print area will be scaled down to fit one page, but the rows can carry on to other pages.

-💡-**Tip** This is the recommended option if you have many rows of data but a few columns. Always try to scale the columns into one page, if possible, so that you can see a full record on one page.

- **Fit All Rows into One Page**: All rows in the print area will be scaled to fit one page, but the columns can carry on to other pages.

Previewing Your Document

The right side of the screen shows a preview of how your printed document would look. If you have more than one page, use the navigation buttons at the bottom of the screen to view the other pages.

📝**Note** Always preview your document before printing to ensure you're happy with the layout. You'll save yourself a ton of ink and paper!

The other settings on the Print page are self-explanatory.

When you're happy with your settings and the preview, click the **Print** button to print your document.

Chapter 14

Securing Your Workbook

Excel enables you to protect your workbook with a password to prevent others from editing your data, deleting worksheets, or renaming worksheets in the workbook.

⚠️ **Important** Before you protect your workbook with a password, ensure you have the password written down and stored in a safe place where it can be retrieved if necessary. Without an advanced password cracking tool, it is impossible to gain access to an Excel file that has been password-protected if the password has been forgotten.

How to set a password for your Excel workbook:

To set a password on your Excel workbook:

1. Click **File** > **Info** > **Protect Document** > **Encrypt with Password**.

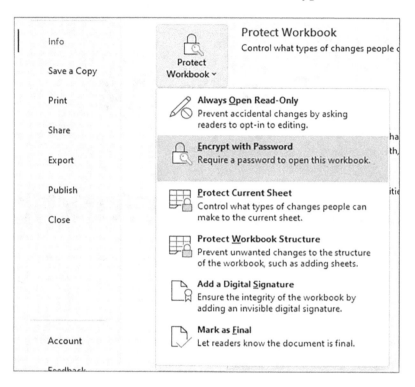

2. At the prompt, enter your password, then confirm it.

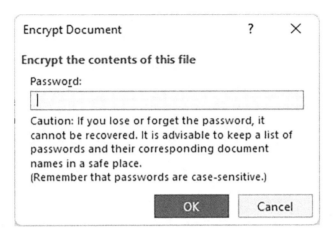

3. Click **OK** after confirming the password.

4. Save and close the workbook.

5. When you reopen the workbook, Excel will prompt you for the password.

Removing a Password from an Excel Workbook

On some occasions, you may want to remove a password from an Excel workbook. The process of setting a password encrypts the workbook, so you'll need to remove the encryption. Carry out the following steps to remove the password.

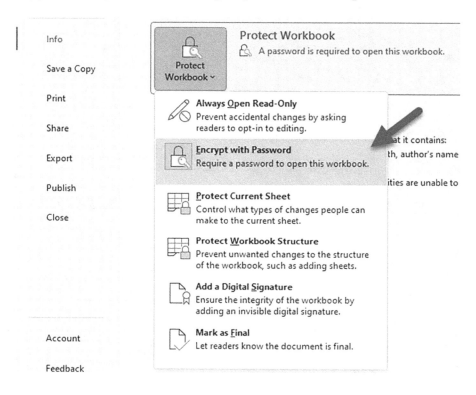

1. Open the workbook and enter the password in the **Password** box.

2. Click **File** > **Info** > **Protect Workbook** > **Encrypt with Password**. Excel displays the Encrypt Document dialog box.

3. Delete the contents of the **Password** box.

4. Click **OK**.

5. Save the workbook and close it.

When you reopen the workbook, Excel will not challenge you for a password.

Appendix A: More Help with Excel

For more help with Excel, you can visit Excel's official online help site.

https://support.office.com/en-gb/excel

This website is a comprehensive help center for Excel. Although not an organized tutorial like this book, it is useful when you're looking for help on a specific topic. You'll also find resources like Excel templates that you can download and use as the starting basis for your worksheets.

You can also visit our website for many free Excel tips and techniques.

https://www.excelbytes.com

Appendix B: Keyboard Shortcuts (Excel for Windows)

The Excel Ribbon comes with new shortcuts called Key Tips. Press the **Alt** key when Excel is the active window to see Key Tips.

The following table lists the most frequently used shortcuts in Excel.

Keystroke	Action
F1	Opens Excel's Help window
Ctrl+O	Open a workbook
Ctrl+W	Close a workbook
Ctrl+C	Copy
Ctrl+V	Paste
Ctrl+X	Cut
Ctrl+Z	Undo
Ctrl+B	Bold
Ctrl+S	Save a workbook

Ctrl+F1	Displays or hides the Ribbon
Delete key	Remove cell contents
Alt+H	Go to the Home tab
Alt+H, H	Choose a fill color
Alt+N	Go to the Insert tab
Alt+A	Go to the Data tab
Alt+P	Go to the Page Layout tab
Alt+H, A, then C	Center align cell contents
Alt+W	Go to the View tab
Shift+F10, or Context key	Open context menu
Alt+H, B	Add borders
Alt+H,D, then C	Delete column
Alt+M	Go to the Formula tab
Ctrl+9	Hide the selected rows
Ctrl+0	Hide the selected columns

Access Keys for Ribbon Tabs

To go directly to a tab on the Excel Ribbon, press one of the following access keys.

Action	Keystroke
Activate the Search box.	Alt+Q
Open the File page, i.e., the Backstage view.	Alt+F
Open the Home tab.	Alt+H
Open the Insert tab.	Alt+N
Open the Page Layout tab.	Alt+P
Open the Formulas tab.	Alt+M
Open the Data.	Alt+A
Open the Review.	Alt+R
Open the View.	Alt+W

To get a more comprehensive list of Excel for Windows shortcuts, press **F1** to open Excel Help and type in "Keyboard shortcuts" in the search bar.

Glossary

Absolute reference

A cell reference that doesn't change when you copy a formula containing the reference to another cell. For example, $A$3 means the row and column have been set to absolute.

Active cell

The cell that's currently selected and open for editing.

Alignment

The way a cell's contents are arranged within that cell, which could be left, centered, or right.

Argument

The input values a function requires to carry out a calculation.

AutoCalculate

An Excel feature that automatically calculates and displays the summary of a selected range of figures on the status bar.

AutoComplete

Completes data entry for a range of cells based on values in other cells in the same column or row.

Backstage view

The screen you see when you click the **File** button on the Ribbon. It has several menu options for managing your workbook and configuring global settings in Excel.

Cell reference

The letter and number combination representing the intersection of a column and row. For example, B10 means column B, row 10.

Conditional format

A format that's only applied when certain conditions are met by the cell content.

Conditional formula

A conditional formula calculates a value from one of two expressions based on whether a third expression evaluates to true or false.

Dialog box launcher

You'll see a diagonal down-pointing arrow in the lower-right corner of some groups on the Excel Ribbon. When you click the arrow, it opens a dialog box containing several additional options for that group.

Excel table

A cell range that has been defined as a table in Excel. Excel adds certain attributes to the range to make it easier to manipulate the data as a table.

Fill handle

The Fill handle is a small square on the lower right of the cell pointer. You can drag this handle to AutoFill values for other cells.

Fill Series

A feature that allows you to create a series of values based on a starting value and any rules or intervals included.

Formula

An expression used to calculate a value.

Formula bar

The area just above the worksheet grid that displays the value or formula in the active cell. You can enter a formula directly in the formula bar.

Function

A function is a predefined formula in Excel that just requires input values (arguments) to calculate and return a value.

Named range

A group of cells in your worksheet given a name that is then used to collectively refer to that range of cells.

OneDrive

A cloud storage service provided by Microsoft which automatically syncs your files to a cloud drive, hence providing instant backups. You get OneDrive automatically with a Microsoft 365 subscription.

PivotTable

An Excel summary table that lets you dynamically summarize data from different perspectives. PivotTables are highly flexible, and you can quickly adjust them depending on how you need to display your results.

Quick Access Toolbar

A customizable toolbar with a set of commands independent of the tab and Ribbon commands currently on display.

Relative reference

Excel cell references are relative references by default. When you copy a formula to another cell, the references will change based on the relative position of columns and rows.

Ribbon

The top part of the Excel window containing the tabs and commands.

Sort

A sort means to reorder the data in a worksheet in ascending or descending order by one or more columns.

Sparkline

A small chart that visually represents data in a single worksheet cell.

Validation rule

A test that data must pass to be a valid entry in a cell.

Workbook

The Excel document itself, which can contain one or more worksheets.

Worksheet

A worksheet is like a page in an Excel workbook.

x-axis

The horizontal axis of a chart where you could have time intervals etc.

y-axis

The vertical axis of a chart, which usually depicts value data.

Index

About the Author

Nathan George is a computer science graduate with several years' experience in the IT services industry in different roles which included Access programming, Excel/VBA programming, end-user support of Excel power users, and Excel training. One of his main interests is using computers to automate tasks and increase productivity. As an author, he has written several technical and non-technical books.

Other Books by Author

Excel 2019 Functions

70 Top Excel Functions Made Easy

Leverage the full power of Excel functions in your formulas!

Excel 2019 Functions is a practical guide covering 70 of the most useful and relevant Excel functions from different categories, including logical, reference, statistical, financial, math, and text. Excel functions are predefined formulas that make creating answers to your questions easier and faster.

This guide comes with Excel sample files for all examples in the book available online. You can copy and use the formulas in your worksheets. *Excel 2019 Functions* will be a great resource for you whether you're a beginner or experienced with Excel.

For more, go to:
https://www.excelbytes.com/excel-books

Excel 2019 Macros and VBA

An Introduction to Excel Programming

Take your Excel skills to the next level with macros and Visual Basic for Applications (VBA)!

Create solutions that would have otherwise been too cumbersome or impossible to create with standard Excel commands and functions. Automate Excel for repetitive tasks and save yourself time and tedium.

With *Excel 2019 Macros and VBA,* you'll learn how to automate Excel using quick macros as well as writing VBA code. You'll learn all the VBA fundamentals to enable you to start creating your own code from scratch.

For more information, visit:
https://www.excelbytes.com/excel-books

Mastering Access 365

An Easy Guide to Building Efficient Databases for Managing Your Data

Has your data become too large and complex for Excel? If so, then Access may just be the tool you need. Whether you're new to Access or looking to refresh your skills on this popular database application, you'll find everything you need to create efficient and robust database solutions for your data in this book.

Mastering Access 365 offers straightforward step-by-step explanations with practical examples for hands-on learning. This book covers Access for Microsoft 365 and Access 2021.

Visit our website for more info:

https://www.excelbytes.com/access-book

Support and Feedback

Thank you for buying this book. The topics have been kept at the beginner to intermediate level to ensure you're not overwhelmed if you're new to Excel. If you have any questions or comments, please feel free to contact me at **support@excelbytes.com**.

For additional book support and information, please visit:

https://www.excelbytes.com/contact

Errata

Every effort was made to ensure the accuracy of this book and the supplementary content. But if you discover an error, please submit it to us using the link below.

https://www.excelbytes.com/submit-errata

All reported issues will be investigated, and any necessary changes will be incorporated in future editions of this book.

www.ingramcontent.com/pod-product-compliance
Lightning Source LLC
LaVergne TN
LVHW082035050326
832904LV00005B/184